RUSSIAN WRITERS AND THE FIN DE SIÈCLE

Russian literature has a reputation for gloomy texts, especially during the late nineteenth century. This volume argues that a "fin-de-siècle" mood informed Russian literature long before the chronological end of the nineteenth century, in ways that had significant impact on the development of Russian realism. Some chapters consider ideas more readily associated with fin-de-siècle Europe, such as degeneration theory, biodeterminism, Freudian psychoanalysis, or apocalypticism alongside earlier Russian realist texts by writers such as Turgenev, Dostoevsky, or Tolstoy. Other chapters explore the changes that realism underwent as modernism emerged, examining later nineteenth-century or early twentieth-century texts in the context of the earlier realist tradition or their own cultural moment. Overall, a team of emerging and established scholars of Russian literature and culture present a wide range of creative and insightful readings that shed new light on later realism in all its manifestations.

KATHERINE BOWERS is a research associate in the Department of Slavonic Studies at the University of Cambridge and holds a research fellowship at Darwin College, Cambridge.

ANI KOKOBOBO is an assistant professor in the Slavic Department at the University of Kansas where she received a Hall Center for the Humanities fellowship.

RUSSIAN WRITERS AND THE FIN DE SIÈCLE

The Twilight of Realism

EDITED BY

KATHERINE BOWERS AND ANI KOKOBOBO

CAMBRIDGE
UNIVERSITY PRESS

To Luke

Contents

Illustrations

Contributors

KATHERINE BOWERS, University of Cambridge

ALEXANDER BURRY, The Ohio State University

EDITH W. CLOWES, University of Virginia

YURI CORRIGAN, Boston University

JANE COSTLOW, Bates College

CONNOR DOAK, University of Bristol

CARYL EMERSON, Princeton University

KATE HOLLAND, University of Toronto

JENNY KAMINER, University of California – Davis

ANI KOKOBOBO, University of Kansas

EMMA LIEBER, Rutgers University

MUIREANN MAGUIRE, University of Exeter

ROBIN FEUER MILLER, Brandeis University

THOMAS NEWLIN, Oberlin College

S. CEILIDH ORR, The Ohio State University

ILYA VINITSKY, University of Pennsylvania

Acknowledgments

The publication of this volume, from our initial vision to the final product, has been a lengthy process assisted by numerous colleagues. We wish to thank Richard Ratzlaff for initial suggestions on our book proposal, Ilya Vinitsky for his encouragement and for helping with our title, and Caryl Emerson for her afterword and editorial assistance along the way. We are grateful for Amanda Allan's careful copyediting and formatting of the original manuscript. The idea behind this book arose from discussions about the decline of the Russian novel at annual conferences, and we would like to acknowledge fellow panelists and eventual volume authors Edith Clowes, Jane Costlow, Jenny Kaminer, and Tom Newlin, who participated in these discussions. We extend our thanks to the rest of our contributors, whose hard work and grace under pressure have made this book possible. We also owe gratitude to the Hall Center for the Humanities at the University of Kansas, whose generous fellowship during Fall 2014 allowed Ani Kokobobo to work on this volume. Lastly, we would like to extend our thanks to the editorial team at Cambridge University Press, and particularly Linda Bree for believing in this project.

Beyond these debts of gratitude accrued in the development of the book as a whole, the editors and authors of the volume would also like to thank the following people for their support during the writing of the individual chapters: Mike Basker, Robert L. Belknap, Sara Dickinson, Julie Fedor, Tatiana Filimonova, Simon Franklin, Katharine Hodgson, Robert Louis Jackson, Liza Knapp, Colleen McQuillen, Susan McReynolds, Diane Thompson, Derek Offord, and Cathy Popkin.

Introduction
The fin-de-siècle mood in Russian literature
Ani Kokobobo and Katherine Bowers

> Russian writers, especially the most notable, did not believe in the
> stability of civilization, in the stability of those principles upon which
> the world rests . . . ; they are full of terrible forebodings of impending
> disaster.
>
>   – Nikolai Berdiaev[1]

Often used to describe the period between 1880 and 1900, the expression
"fin de siècle," French for "end of century," encompasses a meaning considerably broader than its literal definition. In a conversation toward the end
of Oscar Wilde's novel *The Picture of Dorian Gray* (1890), two characters,
Lord Henry and Lady Narborough, relate the fin de siècle to the end of the
world, or *fin du globe*. "I wish it were *fin du globe*," weighs in the perpetually
bored Dorian Gray, "Life is a great disappointment."[2] The conflation of
fin de siècle with *fin du globe*, Dorian's boredom, his despair at reality's
failure to evoke any hope or inspiration, and the tension between life and
a longing for the end of the world come together in this scene to illustrate
the fin de siècle's distinctly broader associations.

 The concept of the fin de siècle runs over its chronology, embodying
an overarching mood that affects both individuals and society as a whole.
Contemporary scholar Elaine Showalter argues that we tend to experience
the end of a century intensely and emotionally, and ascribe to it "metaphors
of death and rebirth."[3] In *Degeneration* (1892), Max Nordau defines this
emotional state in terms of illness, impotence, and exhaustion, but also an
unfulfilled yearning for life and vitality:

> [The fin-de-siècle mood] is the impotent despair of a sick man, who feels
> himself dying by inches in the midst of an eternally living nature blooming
> insolently for ever. It is the envy of a rich, hoary voluptuary, who sees a pair
> of young lovers making for a sequestered forest nook; it is the mortification
> of the exhausted and impotent refugee from a Florentine plague, seeking in
> an enchanted garden the experiences of a Decamerone, but striving in vain
> to snatch one more pleasure of sense from the uncertain hour.[4]

In Nordau's description, the fin-de-siècle mood is located in the tension between the feeling of death and the desire for life, in the figure of the frustrated sensualist unable to reach satisfaction, the despairing quest for vitality met with indifference and the inevitability of one's own decay. For Nordau, the mood is symptomatic of the "Dusk of Nations," a time when "mankind with all its institutions and creations is perishing in the midst of a dying world," characterized by a broad and overwhelming pessimism.[5] Nordau and Showalter's perception of the fin de siècle as a mentality and "mood" rather than a simple chronological marker fits with its original parameters in France[6] as well as with the broad outlines in which we construe the term. Similarly, Kermode observes that fin-de-siècle anxieties were not unique to the end of the nineteenth century: "The anxiety reflected by the fin de siècle is perpetual, and people don't wait for centuries to end before they express it."[7]

Our volume examines the fin-de-siècle mood in Russian realism, from inception to twilight. Realism existed before, but also concurrently with, and following literary and cultural movements more commonly associated with the chronological fin de siècle such as symbolism and decadence. As such, we do not treat the fin de siècle merely as a transition that fills a gap between realism and modernism, nor as an illustration of Russia's transition from a traditional to a more modern society. Rather, in our definition, the fin de siècle in Russian literature and culture constitutes a fluid mentality outside temporal framing, characterized by a fascination with themes of foreboding, decline, degeneration, decay, and ending.

Compared to the fin de siècle and its corresponding zeitgeist in Europe, the Russian "fin-de-siècle mood" was gloomier, as scholars note.[8] Eugène-Melchior de Vogüé, writing about the nineteenth-century Russian novel in 1886, found Russia to be a "nation prematurely rotten" with a spirit anchored in the "stormy sea of nihilism and pessimism."[9] Moreover, as Mark Steinberg points out, fin-de-siècle attitudes in Russia in the latter half of the nineteenth century were substantially more intense than in the rest of Europe; for Russians, the fin de siècle became a modern "time of troubles" depicted through a public "vocabulary of sickness and crisis."[10] Steinberg identifies "modern melancholy" – hopelessness and despondent despair with no particular cause – as the dominant emotion in the fin-de-siècle Russian psyche.[11]

Just as the fin-de-siècle mood was more intense in Russia, so too was it more protracted. It has deep roots in Russian realism where it can be traced long before 1880. Similarly, it persisted in Russian culture, drawn out well into the twentieth century. In part, this persistence could be due to the atmosphere of crisis and ending in the early decades of twentieth-century Russia, which saw widespread unrest. Considering the 1905 Revolution, the February and October 1917 Revolutions, and the Civil War (1917–1922), the period is marked by multiple social and political endings, the most notable being the end of the tsarist epoch. These manifold grand historical finales have led some historians to situate the end of the Russian fin de siècle as late as 1914, with the start of World War I, or even the February 1917 Revolution.[12]

In removing the temporal boundaries from the fin de siècle, the recurrent crises, denouements, and moments of possibility that punctuated nineteenth-century Russian history become strikingly apparent. Broadly speaking, Alexander I's victory over Napoleon led to new ties with the West, and the emergence of new philosophical ideas, but democratic idealism was crushed with the Decembrists' execution and exile in 1825. The myth of Russian military dominance was exploded by a humiliating defeat at the hands of Great Britain and France in the Crimean War (1853–1856), which exposed the backwardness of the Empire's infrastructure and the stagnation of Nicholas I's repressive reign. The obvious need for change inspired Alexander II to undertake a series of wide-reaching political reforms throughout the 1860s and 1870s. The first, most significant of these Great Reforms was the Emancipation of the Serfs, which disrupted the traditional estate (*soslovie*) order – made up of nobility, clergy, merchants, and peasants – and, in so doing, upset all areas of Russian society and life. In addition to these social changes, late nineteenth-century Russia saw the introduction of state-led capitalism in its economy without a corresponding political system, the sharp rise of industry and consequent modernization, and, as a result, significant disruption of traditional life and structures.

The appearance of the fin-de-siècle mood could also be called a symptom of the negotiation of modernity, characterized simultaneously by extremes of optimism and pessimism.[13] Anxiety and foreboding about the end of the world fostered a culture of viewing present-day life as contemptible, and, instead, privileging the individual's utopian search for meaning through both physical and metaphysical means. Certainly, the symbolist and decadent movements commonly associated with the chronological fin de siècle suggest such a reading in their different approaches to the binary of crisis and possibility. Decadents believed they were living in an age of decline; Viacheslav Ivanov described decadence as "the sense both oppressive and exalted of being the last of a series."[14] Symbolists, too, believed the end of the world was nigh, searching for truth and meaning in a space out of time.

The crisis of ending in symbolist philosophy, however, was accompanied by transcendent rebirth into a new world.[15] Both decadence and symbolism were marked by the pessimism of the present, but the sense of vitality and possibility that runs through modernity persisted as well. Apocalyptic imagery in Russian symbolism displays dark overtones, reflected through images of burning cities and Satanism in Konstantin Balmont's poetry, Schopenhauerian pessimism in the poetry of Andrei Bely and others, as well as general melancholy in the works of Fyodor Sologub and others or exhaustion in Alexander Blok's later poetry, whereas symbolist philosopher Vladimir Solovev saw the apocalypse in a positive, productive light.

Although the fin-de-siècle mood appears readily in Russian symbolism and decadence, these strands emerged after Nordau diagnosed the Russians with the fin-de-siècle malaise in 1892. Nordau's diagnosis hinges on earlier realist writers he singles out as key representatives of the mood. He mentions Tolstoy's Schopenhauerian despair, fears of death, and general mystical irrationalism as a prime example of the fin-de-siècle mindset. Though he dwells on later, post-conversion works from the 1880s, Nordau also cites Tolstoy's earlier fiction from the 1850s as an example of this unfulfilled utopianism and messianic drive.[16] In this vein, Nordau also describes Turgenev's novella *A Nest of the Gentry* (1859) as a pessimistic narrative reflecting the fin-de-siècle mood, reading the character Lavretsky at the novella's end as an embodiment of the fin-de-siècle man, broken down, depressed, and having lost his love.[17] Contemporary scholars such as Laura Engelstein and Olga Matich similarly suggest ties between the fin de siècle and earlier Russian literary works, particularly Nikolai Chernyshevsky's utopian novel *What is to Be Done?* (1863).[18] Tolstoy, Turgenev, and Chernyshevsky are an odd grouping as the three display opposing artistic, religious, political, even cultural tendencies. However, interestingly, all three are considered progenitors of the fin-de-siècle mood. It is the presence of this mood throughout Russian realism that may be said to provide one of the more distinctive features of this canon.

European literary realism is conventionally understood as a movement primarily concerned with the illusion of verisimilitude or the impression of reproducing all details of life. Ian Watt describes the realist novel as "a full and authentic report of human experiences ... under an obligation to satisfy its reader with such details ... as the individuality of the actors concerned, the particulars of the times and places of their actions, details which are presented through a more largely referential use of language than is common in other literary forms."[19] Peter Brooks takes the notion of referentiality further, describing realism as not only verisimilitude, but suggests that referential details conjure visuality in the realist text. "[R]ealism is by definition highly visual," writes Brooks, "Thus any honest accounting for the real, in the sense of the appearances of the world, . . . needs to give a sense of the thereness of the physical world, as in a still-life painting."[20] This sense of being present is often seen as a key feature in the European realist novel. Indeed, as D. A. Miller's Foucaultian study posits, the realist novel not only recreates but also reinforces the present. In their representations of reality, realist novels insidiously reinvent the policing power of the law "in the very practice of novelistic representation," thus inhibiting actions that could disrupt social stability.[21]

Yet in this scheme Russian realism emerges as quite another tradition. Unlike European realisms, Russian novelistic prose was hardly grounded on the middle class. As William Mills Todd, III has argued, terms such as "middle class" or "bourgeois" cannot be comfortably translated to a Russian context.[22] Todd continues, "Russian novels do not celebrate capitalism, secular society, or the modern state – none of which were well or long developed in the Russia of their time."[23] Given this, it is unsurprising that rather than celebrating the status quo or reveling in the stability of bourgeois existence, Russian realism was riddled with instability and reeling in untimely fin-de-siècle anxiety. A canon notable for – to use Henry James's playful terminology – "loose and baggy monsters," the Russian realist tradition lacked a sense of literary ending and "poetic closure" (in the phrasing of literary scholar Barbara Herrnstein Smith),[24] but reflected timely social concerns and ideological questions. Thus themes of crisis, pessimism, decay, degeneration, and apocalypse permeated even novels deemed affirmational. With its accursed questions, purported sincerity, and general rebellion against empirical rationalism, mid-century Russian realism set the stage for fin-de-siècle despair and yearning.

In *The Origin of Russian Communism* (1937), Berdiaev reflects that Russian realists:

> Did not believe in the stability of civilization, in the stability of those principles upon which the world rests, what was called the bourgeois world of their time; they are full of terrible forebodings of impending disaster. European literature does not know that sort of religious and social unrest, for it belongs to a civilization which is more fixed and crystallized, more formed, more self-contented and calm, more differentiated and distributed into categories.[25]

He goes on to suggest that there was inherently more to Russian realism than mere representations of reality: "It [nineteenth-century Russian realism] was realist, but certainly not realist in the scholastic sense of the word. It was realist in an almost religious sense and in its highest form purely religious."[26] There was a divergent, prophetic quality – exceptional and, in Berdiaev's view, spiritual – in Russian literature that yielded a great deal more than rudimentary documentation. Berdiaev describes this other quality with language that evokes the fin-de-siècle malaise with its "terrible forebodings of impending disaster." Of course, Berdiaev's reading of the nineteenth-century canon enjoys the benefits of hindsight: his work on Russian Communism appears after he has already endured the tumult of revolution, the terror of interrogation, the displacement of exile, and the ending of a way of life.

If the twentieth century was a fulfillment of the prophecies laid out in the gloom and despair of nineteenth-century Russian realist novels, it also saw the rise of a realism shaped by engagement with the fin de siècle. As decadence and symbolism flourished, new strands of realism simultaneously emerged such as neorealism. In the twentieth century's early decades, Russian literary critics observed a "return to reality," a "new expanded realism that had not only been enriched by impressionistic and symbolic devices, but was characterized by a sense of the artist's function which differed from that of traditional nineteenth-century critical realism."[27] This perceptible shift in Russian realism, as this volume maintains, can be understood as yet another manifestation of the fin-de-siècle mood that runs through Russian realism. Perhaps ironically, the "sense of an ending" that characterizes it served also as a catalyst for realism's never-ending artistic creativity and literary experimentation, both before and after the chronological fin de siècle.

This volume investigates the fin-de-siècle mood's pervasiveness and resonance across Russian realism. Its chapters explore the Russian literary experience of the fin de siècle from an array of perspectives with two main directions in mind: a consideration of ways in which the fin-de-siècle mood predated the turn of the century in Russian literature; and the effects of this mood's intensification during the chronological fin-de-siècle period on later Russian realism. We divide the volume into four sections – "Anxieties of Disintegration," "Destabilizing Gender and Sexuality," "Generic Experimentation and Hybridity," and "Facing Death and Decay" – each featuring a cluster of linked chapters addressing various manifestations of the fin-de-siècle mood. Parts I and II focus on avant la lettre studies, while Parts III and IV emphasize realism at the turn of the century and beyond, showing the fin-de-siècle mood's far-reaching effects.

Part I analyzes narratives of disintegration in the context of emerging scientific, philosophical, and political ideas, as well as generic experimentation. In these chapters' examination of various modes of disintegration – familial, internal, generic, and societal – anxiety comes to the fore, exposing the "terrible forebodings of impending disaster" Berdiaev observes in Russian realism. Kate Holland's chapter examines the relationship between Zola's *Les Rougon-Macquart* novel cycle (1871–1893) and Saltykov-Shchedrin's satiric family novel *The Golovlev Family* (1875–1880) through the prism of degeneration theory, which gained rapid popularity in France and was just entering Russian intellectual discourse in the 1870s. Holland uses Saltykov-Shchedrin's novel about family decline to study Zola's rise and fall in popularity, as well as the concurrent debates about degeneration in the Russian journalistic press. Turning from the family to the individual, Yuri Corrigan's chapter examines the crisis of the self as the basis for societal decline in Dostoevsky's *The Adolescent* (1875). Corrigan considers Dostoevsky's hero, Arkady, within the context of the desperate fin-de-siècle search for a stable concept of the personality, reading the novel as an early philosophical attempt to solve the crisis. Through Arkady's attempts to conceive of a personal identity, which he imagines to reside in a variety of locations, Dostoevsky diagnoses Russia's growing social disintegration as emanating from a deeper insecurity and sense of emptiness within the self.

Robin Feuer Miller's chapter examines the darker side of childhood in Dostoevsky's "A Boy at Christ's Christmas Party" (1876), identifying a source for the story in two related genres: the fairy tale and the Christmas story. The chapter investigates how Dostoevsky subverts generic convention to undermine reader expectations, while crafting a powerful portrait of childhood in the face of social ills such as poverty and neglect. Dostoevsky's fin-de-siècle foray ends in pessimism in Corrigan's analysis, but Miller exposes the writer's affirmational side despite his gloomy subject matter. Rounding out the section, Alexander Burry and S. Ceilidh Orr take Tolstoy's *Anna Karenina* (1877) as their focus, considering the novel's apocalyptic imagery and its relationship to political philosophy and industrial progress. In their reading, the collision of apocalyptic and utopian elements in the novel, intriguingly focused around the character of Stiva, is a manifestation of the anxiety and pessimism surrounding the development of Slavophilism in the 1870s. The sense of terror and disintegration promoted by these elements serves as an indicator of the fin-de-siècle mood avant la lettre.

Part II revisits the theme of disintegration, but focuses on anxieties surrounding gender roles and sexual politics in the second half of the nineteenth century. Emma Lieber's chapter dwells on the relationship between repression, decay, and degeneration, exposing Turgenev's "uncivilized" fin-de-siècle turn, a surprising one for an author widely known for his works' civilizational effect. Using Freud's theories in her reading of *First Love* (1860) and "A Living Relic" (1874), Lieber reveals the way images of degeneration in Turgenev's works illustrate the pathological effects of civilization's repression of sexuality and other primal urges. While Lieber focuses on sexuality, Connor Doak's chapter concentrates on gender as he explores anxieties related to masculine degeneration in Dostoevsky's novel *Demons* (1872). Doak identifies two kinds of degenerate masculinity in the novel: the effeminate, ineffectual 1840s men whose failures pave the way for the brutally violent 1860s men. While Dostoevsky condemns both forms of masculinity, he struggles to locate a favorable alternative, and ultimately it is the masochistic and effete Stepan Trofimovich whom he chooses to undergo Christian conversion. *Demons* thus resists simplistic calls for the remasculinization of society of the kind found in the work of Nordau and other fin-de-siècle reactionaries. The anxieties surrounding masculinity resurface in Jenny Kaminer's chapter on the contrast between female heroism and masculine superfluity in Chekhov's plays *Ivanov* (1887) and *The Seagull* (1896). The chapter examines Chekhov's heroines in the context of the paradigm of female heroism suggested more than thirty years earlier in Dobroliubov's 1860 essay praising the purposeful female protagonist of Ostrovsky's play *The Storm* (1859). In Kaminer's analysis, Dobroliubov's vision of Ostrovsky's heroine as a "ray of light in the kingdom of darkness," standing against the status quo propagated by the play's superfluous man-hero, establishes a paradigm of female heroism that Chekhov revisits in his fin-de-siècle negotiation of gender roles.

In Part III, the chapter cluster centers around the generic experimentation and productive hybridity that proved critical in late realism's development. While Miller's earlier chapter introduces the notion of genre as a realist tool, the four chapters in this section explore fin-de-siècle motifs through the prism of genre, emphasizing crises of family, sexuality, individuality, and, ultimately, of realist vision itself. Katherine Bowers's chapter traces the gothic "fall of the house" plot in three works spread across realism: Aksakov's *The Family Chronicle* (1856), Saltykov-Shchedrin's *The Golovlev Family*, and Bunin's *Dry Valley* (1911). In Bowers's analysis, the gothic mode and its gloomy generic conventions offered Russian realists a means to capture fears about family decline as well as widespread social anxiety, both before and during the chronological fin de siècle. Ani Kokobobo's chapter provides a study of the grotesque in Tolstoy's later theological and philosophical works and his novel *Resurrection* (1899), as well as Artsybashev's novel *Sanin* (1907). As Kokobobo argues, the novels by Tolstoy and Artsybashev reflect a "grotesque realism" that enables ideologically opposed writers to showcase differing moral positions, condemning and praising sexuality, respectively. In its hybridity and estrangement, the grotesque appears as a manifestation of the zeitgeist in a society with unmistakable loss of spirituality, collapsing under the weight of pessimism and despair. In her examination of Russian fantastic realism, Muireann Maguire argues that symbolism altered the genre's course, developing a darker, self-destructive variation on the natural school's original archetypal hero, the put-upon clerk or "little man." Maguire's chapter compares the liberating vengeance achieved by Gogol's protagonist in "The Overcoat" (1842) with the frustration suffered by his twentieth-century descendants in Sologub's "The Little Man" (1907) and Krzhizhanovsky's "Quadraturin" (1926).

While the examples of the gothic, grotesque, and fantastic emphasize anxiety in the face of social breakdown, these dark meditations are offset by Vladimir Korolenko's late-century sketches (*ocherki*) in Jane Costlow's chapter, which concludes this section. Korolenko's sketches of rural life present a fluid and nuanced picture, their very genre emphasizing realism's inherent visual quality. In Costlow's reading, Korolenko's fresh realism is a product of late-century Russia that emphasizes the importance of observation and experience. If the predominant fin-de-siècle mood emphasizes the anxiety caused by the "sense of an ending," Korolenko's sketches provide a counter-weight, in that they resist closure. Although themes of apocalypse and religious mysticism surface as part of Korolenko's larger mosaic of Russian life, the meaning behind these phenomena is always ultimately left to the reader.

The final section considers notions of decay, both corporeal and environmental, across late realism, underscoring the anxiety inherent in facing one's end, whether metaphorically, through abjection, or experientially. Thomas Newlin's chapter explores the "decadent ecosystems" of Chekhov's naturalist drama *Uncle Vanya* (1897), mapping the play's preoccupation with fragmentation and decline in five main areas: the play itself, the "gentry nest" more broadly, its surrounding district, the global ecosystem, and, finally, Chekhov's own body as his tuberculosis symptoms intensified. Newlin's telescopic analysis of Chekhov's play allows for a new understanding of Russian culture at the chronological fin de siècle that emphasizes predominant anxieties about degeneration, as well as burgeoning ecological awareness and the existential experience of human mortality. Edith Clowes's chapter on Andreev's neorealism similarly emphasizes corporeality that appeals to what some might call the "lower senses." Clowes's reading of three stories – "The Abyss" (1902), "The Red Laugh" (1904), and "Seven People Hanged" (1907) – highlights what she terms "abject realism"; Andreev's fin-de-siècle art does not celebrate sensory experience's fullness, but instead exhibits a strongly ascetic disgust of the body. His realist focus on the distorted and dismembered body, in Clowes's reading, denies human endurance and, ultimately, human goodness.

In Newlin and Clowes's chapters, decay abounds, and Ilya Vinitsky's chapter closes the volume with this theme, reflecting on its transposition between realism and symbolism. Vinitsky studies the Balzacian thinking oyster – an image representing a cognizant being trapped in its own lifeless, useless husk of a body – in Turgenev's later works, and the way this image changes when taken up by symbolist Konstantin Annensky following the realist's death. The painful physical decay of Turgenev's cancerous body and his existential torments – a palpable experience of ending – effects a shift in his realist vision, argues Vinitsky, a shift that resonates with fin-de-siècle philosophies as Annensky incorporates the thinking oyster into his own artistic vision.

While the chapter clusters outlined above provide one way of thematically linking elements of the fin-de-siècle mood we identify in Russian realism, organic links between individual chapters open myriad productive avenues for consideration of this volume's subject. Debates about psychology, degeneration theory, and sexuality underlie the chapters by Holland, Lieber, and Doak. Similarly, an emphasis on disease and the body's mortality link Lieber, Newlin, and Vinitsky. Transgression and perversions of childhood feature in chapters by Corrigan, Miller, Lieber, and Doak, while an emphasis on family decline connects Holland, Bowers, and Newlin. The visuality of realism plays a crucial role in Korolenko's open-ended *ocherki* in Costlow's chapter, but also in Andreev's abject realism and in Tolstoy and Artsybashev's grotesque strands as discussed by Clowes and Kokobobo, respectively. This visuality necessitates an emphasis on exterior life, a perfect balance for Corrigan's exploration of the crisis of interiority. Apocalypticism, broadly conceived, unites the chapters by Burry and Orr, Bowers, and Maguire, but appears tempered in Korolenko's *ocherki* and Annensky's symbolism in Costlow and Vinitsky's chapters, respectively. Despite this tendency toward darkness and gloom, the fin-de-siècle mood provides some glimpses of light. Kaminer's analysis of female heroism – a "ray of light" in the words of Dobroliubov – provides one point, as do

Miller's investigation of childhood in Dostoevsky's Christmas story, Artsybashev's celebration of sexuality in Kokobobo's chapter, and Costlow's study of phenomenological realism.

The chapters in this collection demonstrate the fin-de-siècle mood's presence throughout the nineteenth and early twentieth centuries, as well as its impact on later realism. While realism remains a "loose and baggy monster" in its own right, as this volume's breadth and scope demonstrate, the fin-de-siècle mood we identify is a strand that persists throughout the movement. Although often gloomy and pessimistic, the fin-de-siècle mood and the effect it had on the Russian realist canon proved fruitful, giving rise to a long-lasting period of intellectual and artistic energy. While the fin de siècle is by definition preoccupied with a sense of ending, we hope that the connections and relationships forged through the studies showcased here will serve instead as a beginning, a starting point for future research working to untangle the knotty problem of Russian realism.

Note on the text

This volume uses modified Library of Congress for the transliteration of Russian words and names from Cyrillic. However, in the text body and notes, we use more familiar English spellings for certain common names. Thus, for example, Dostoevsky appears in the text, but the bibliography cites Dostoevskii.

NOTES

1 Nikolai Berdiaev, *The Origin of Russian Communism*, translated by R. M. French (Ann Arbor: University of Michigan Press, 1960), 77.
2 Oscar Wilde, *The Major Works* (Oxford University Press, 1989), 151.
3 Elaine Showalter, *Sexual Anarchy: Gender and Culture at the Fin de Siècle* (New York: Viking, 1990), 2.
4 Max Nordau, *Degeneration* (Lincoln: University of Nebraska Press, 1993), 3. This edition's text is reprinted from an English translation (New York: D. Appleton & Company, 1895); neither version specifies the translator.
5 Ibid., 2.
6 Eugen Weber, *France: Fin de Siècle* (Cambridge, MA: Harvard University Press, 1986), 1.
7 Frank Kermode, *The Sense of an Ending: Studies in the Theory of Fiction with a New Epilogue* (Oxford University Press, 2000), 98.
8 Mark Steinberg, *Petersburg Fin de Siècle* (New Haven, CT: Yale University Press, 2011), 1; Walter Laqueur, *Fin de Siècle and Other Essays on America and Europe* (New Brunswick, NJ: Transaction Publishers, 1997), 10.

9   Eugène-Melchior de Vogüé, *The Russian Novel* (New York: Knopf, 1916), 17–18.
10 Steinberg, *Petersburg Fin de Siècle*, 1.
11 Ibid., 235.
12 Steinberg's study of fin-de-siècle Petersburg focuses on the years 1890–1917.
    Laura Engelstein links the Russian fin de siècle to the 1905 Revolution, and
    considers the period from the Great Reforms of the 1860s to the eve of World
    War I in 1914. See *The Keys to Happiness: Sex and the Search for Modernity in
    Fin-de-Siècle Russia* (Ithaca, NY: Cornell University Press, 1992), 10–11.
13 Steinberg, *Petersburg Fin de Siècle*, 3.
14 Olga Matich, *Erotic Utopia: The Decadent Imagination in Russia's Fin de Siècle*
    (Madison: University of Wisconsin Press, 2005), 3.
15 Avril Pyman, *A History of Russian Symbolism* (Cambridge University Press,
    1994), 226–242.
16 Nordau, *Degeneration*, 144–171.
17 Ibid., 3.
18 Matich, *Erotic Utopia*, 165; Engelstein, *The Keys to Happiness*, 380–383.
19 Ian Watt, *The Rise of the Novel: Studies in Defoe, Richardson, and Fielding*
    (Berkeley: University of California Press, 2001), 32.
20 Peter Brooks, *Realist Vision* (New Haven, CT: Yale University Press, 2005), 16.
21 D. A. Miller, *The Novel and the Police* (Berkeley: University of California Press,
    1988), 20.
22 William Mills Todd, III, "The Ruse of the Russian Novel," in *The Novel*,
    vol. 1: *History, Geography, and Culture*, edited by Franco Moretti (Princeton
    University Press, 2006), 404.
23 Ibid., 402.
24 See Barbara Herrnstein Smith, *Poetic Closure: A Study of How Poems End*
    (University of Chicago Press, 2007).
25 Berdiaev, *The Origin of Russian Communism*, 77.
26 Ibid.
27 Alex M. Shane, "Remizov's *Prud*: From Symbolism to Neo-Realism," *California
    Slavic Studies* 6 (1971): 71.

PART I

Anxieties of disintegration

CHAPTER I

The Russian Rougon-Macquart
Degeneration and biological determinism in
The Golovlev Family

Kate Holland

In an article entitled "The Role of Psychological Heredity" published in
the left-wing Russian journal *Deed (Delo)* in 1878, P. N. Tkachev argued
that the question of heredity opened up by Darwin's theory of evolution
was a burning issue, a popular theme not just for psychologists, physiol-
ogists, criminologists, and psychiatrists, but also for artists and writers.[1]
For Tkachev, a leftist revolutionary preoccupied by questions of social and
economic inequality, the idea of heredity, or the transmission of inherited traits, was central in determining the speed and possibility of social
and economic change. In considering the problem of heredity, the Russian thinker was participating in a European-wide conversation about the
nature of human motivation and behavior. Throughout much of Europe
this conversation took the form of fears over the proliferation of disorders such as alcoholism and suicidal thoughts, which had formerly been
ascribed social causes, but which were now associated with heredity, and
believed to pose a major threat to the idea of progress.[2] In *Degeneration*,
Max Nordau identified the problem of heredity as lying at the very root of
the European fin-de-siècle malaise.[3] Nordau believed European culture to
be under threat, its traditional respect for reason and morality disintegrating into mysticism and decadence. The decline of culture, he argued, was
a sign of the sickness of European society, plagued by the twin scourges
of degeneration and hysteria. The idea of degeneration has its origins in
the eighteenth century but took on a new relevance and authority, especially in France, following the international success of Darwin's *Origin of
Species* and its revelations about the importance of heredity in the process
of evolution.[4] The French psychiatrist Bénédict Augustin Morel argued
that most mental illness was inherited and traced the breakdown of families over several generations as each successive generation bore the marks
(or stigmata) of hereditary degeneracy.[5] The degeneration of such families ended in infertility and the family line's extinction. Later writers and
social theorists, such as Nordau, saw the phenomenon of degeneration as

threatening the idea of progress itself. The inherited traits identified by Morel were seen as marks of atavism, signs that humans had stopped evolving and begun devolving to a more primitive state.

Scholars have examined the influence of degeneration theory in Russia following *Degeneration*'s publication in the 1890s, but the earlier diffusion of degeneration ideas in the 1870s has remained largely unexamined.[6] As Emma Lieber and Connor Doak show in their contributions to the present volume, the degeneration theme proliferates in Russian literature of the 1870s, well before the publication of Nordau's treatise, and indeed it was the novel, rather than scientific tracts, which brought degeneration discourse to Russia in this period. French naturalist writer Émile Zola's works served as a central source of early degeneration discourse. The first volumes of Zola's novel cycle, *Les Rougon-Macquart*, enjoyed enormous popularity among the Russian reading public when first published in Russia in 1872. Their portrait of a family's decline as a result of hereditary degeneracy over several generations gave new direction to discussions of the disintegration of the family already occurring in Russian thick journals during the early 1870s.

This chapter examines debates around degeneration discourse in Russian literary, critical, and journalistic circles in the 1870s and their reverberations in the Russian realist novel. It analyzes how Zola's novels, and French naturalism more broadly, served as the conduit through which degeneration discourse entered the Russian literary scene and considers how the Russian response to degeneration's biological determinism developed against the backdrop of the rise and fall of Zola's popularity in Russia. Mikhail Saltykov-Shchedrin's *The Golovlev Family* (*Gospoda Golovlevy*) serves as a case study in this investigation. Heavily involved in the world of journalism and editor from 1877 of the radical journal *Fatherland Notes* (*Otechestvennye zapiski*), Saltykov-Shchedrin was well positioned to engage in discussions of Zola's ideas. As a satirist and social critic, he was also aware of the threat posed by ideas of heredity and biological determinism for the social and moral worldview of the Russian realist novel, a tradition fascinated with the complexity of human motivation and supportive of human moral potentiality. In its experimentation with ideas of biological determinism and its ultimate rejection of the empiricism and scientific objectivity of French naturalism, *The Golovlev Family* reflects the broader concerns of the Russian literary and journalistic worlds over the assumptions and worldview of French naturalist literature. The work's structural transformation over time, from a series of satirical sketches into a novel, becomes the formal embodiment of a movement away from an exclusive narrative of biological determinism and toward a plurality of moral and social explanations for the Golovlevs' decline.

Les Rougon-Macquart in Russia

Zola's twenty-novel cycle, *Les Rougon-Macquart*, is a social and biological drama which follows the Rougon-Macquart family's lives and fates over more than four generations, from their origins in the Provençal town of Plassans to their diffusion throughout all levels of French society. The family's progenitor, Adélaïde Fouque, suffers from a mild mental illness, and Zola demonstrates how that original defect recurs in subsequent generations to devastating effect. Adélaïde's three children from her husband Rougon and her lover Macquart, the legitimate Pierre and the illegitimate Antoine and Ursule, each represent a different branch of a family with a distinct path through French society. Adélaïde's original mental disorder recurs in a different form in each branch, testifying to Zola's claim that "Heredity, like gravity, has its laws."[7] The mark of hereditary degeneracy is weakest in Pierre and his descendants, who achieve great success in high society, politics, finance, and medicine, though it does manifest itself in their ruthless ambition and hunger for power, as well as in the inherited hemophilia that afflicts the fourth generation. The tainted blood of Adélaïde manifests itself in the Mourets, the priests, farmers, and revolutionaries who are the descendants of Ursule, in nervous disorders, religious hysteria, and neuroses. The hereditary curse makes its most serious mark on the descendants of Antoine; the children of Antoine's daughter, Gervaise, herself the alcoholic protagonist of *L'Assommoir*, are depicted as criminal, sexually degenerate, suicidal, and homicidal.

Adélaïde's mental disorder manifests differently in each individual family member, sometimes exacerbated or inflamed by environmental factors such as poverty or the influence of social immorality, sometimes held in check by good fortune, healthy living conditions, or good relationships. Zola himself inherited from Morel and Lamarck the idea that environmental circumstances could give rise to changes in the organism and then become inherited traits.[8] The poverty and squalor characterizing one generation's living conditions could become fused with inherited defects to produce a potent mix of tainted blood inherited by the next generation. Zola's aim was to examine the complex relationship between biological and social causation through the Rougon-Macquarts' lives. As he wrote in the preface to *La Fortune des Rougon*, "By resolving the duplex question of temperament and environment, I shall endeavour to discover and follow the thread of connection which leads mathematically from one man to another."[9] He continued, "[p]hysiologically the Rougon-Macquarts represent the slow succession of accidents pertaining to the nerves or the blood, which befall a race after the first organic lesion, and, according to environment, determine

in each individual member of the race those feelings, desires and passions –
briefly, all the natural and instinctive manifestations peculiar to humanity –
whose outcome assumes the conventional name of virtue or vice."[10]

The ideas of biological determinism so integral to *Les Rougon-Macquart*
had little immediate effect on Russian literature; indeed, it was the Russian
novel's rejection of the scientific objectivism so beloved of French naturalism which led to Eugène-Melchior de Vogüé's embrace of the tradition in
Le Roman russe (1886), a work that caused a national backlash in France
against naturalism in favor of Russian novelists such as Tolstoy and Dostoevsky.[11] These two giants of Russian literature both famously expressed
deep skepticism toward Zola's novels and his representation of biological
determinism. Yet notwithstanding this later contempt for Zola's artistic
principles in Russia and France, the *Rougon-Macquart* cycle's earliest works
were enormously popular with the Russian reading public in the 1870s
when they were first translated and serialized in thick journals and daily
newspapers. It was precisely in the politically engaged world of *publitsistika*, rather than in higher literary circles, that Zola's ideas had the greatest
impact. In 1872 *La Fortune des Rougon* and *La Curée*, the cycle's first two
volumes, were introduced to the Russian public in abridged translations on
the pages of the liberal journal *The European Messenger*, while subsequent
volumes were quickly picked up by other journals.[12] In 1874 Turgenev, who
was living in Paris and knew Zola well, wrote telling him that "in Russia
they read only you."[13]

Zola's cultivation of his Russian readership began in 1872, when journalistic opportunities in his native France dried up. In 1874, following the
enormous success of the cycle's first four volumes, Turgenev persuaded
Stasiulevich, the editor of *The European Messenger*, to take on Zola as the
paper's Paris correspondent.[14] Between 1875 and 1880, Zola wrote a series
of articles on literary, cultural, and social topics called *Parizhskie pis'ma*
(*Letters from Paris*). The journal also published a Russian translation of *La
Faute de l'Abbé Mouret*, the cycle's fifth volume, before it even came out in
France.[15] By 1876 Zola was being courted by newspapers and journals on
both ends of the political spectrum. By the end of 1880 all political camps
had united around condemnation of the naturalistic description of *Nana*
and Zola's collaboration with *The European Messenger* had come to an end.

The cycle's publication mode helps explain the peculiar circumstances
of Zola's reception in Russia. Journal subscribers read a vastly excerpted
version, often little more than a plot outline, frequently framed by commentary on the novel written by the translator or a prominent critic. The
first few commentaries to the excerpted translations from 1872 provided

the pattern for Zola's subsequent reception. In his introduction of the first two Rougon-Macquart works, Vladimir Chiuko emphasized Zola's ability to combine a broad perspective on history and society with the intimacy of the family novel yet failed to recognize the family's radically new importance in a scheme of biological determinism.[16] Later critics also commented on the family's centrality as a structuring unit in the Rougon-Macquart cycle, reading it in familiar social terms rather than in the new biological vein suggested by Zola in the preface to *La Fortune des Rougon*. They saw the Rougon-Macquarts not as the biological breeding ground for social ills mapped out in ever greater scale and detail, but rather as the symbol of a sick society.

Degeneration discourse and biological determinism in *The Golovlev Family*

A few writers did respond to the profound implications of Zola's ideas about heredity for the novel as a genre. Mikhail Saltykov-Shchedrin was one of the first Russians to adopt degeneration discourse and use it to structure a work of fiction.[17] In his 1875–1880 novel-chronicle, *The Golovlev Family*, he represented a family afflicted by hereditary degeneracy, in which the older generation's defects were reproduced in the younger, as each subsequent generation exhibited more telltale "stigmata of degeneracy" such as alcoholism, suicide, and prostitution. Upon first serialization *The Golovlev Family* was immediately recognized by critics as a "Russian Rougon-Macquart," a work heavily influenced by Zola's depictions of hereditary degeneracy.[18] Yet though degeneration discourse shapes the overall conception of *The Golovlev Family*, it is tempered by a strong ideological and moral narrative voice, which insists on the continuing possibility of human moral potentiality and individual agency. This narrative perspective, coupled with the novel's parodic recreation of earlier models of the Russian noble family novel, reveals a distinctly Russian degeneration discourse, in which biological factors compete with social and historical circumstances as explanations for human behavior. In this regard, *The Golovlev Family* reflects an increasingly self-confident Russian critical discourse that defends the national realist tradition against the predations of French naturalism.

The Golovlev Family's serialization in the radical journal *Fatherland Notes* from 1875 to 1880 coincided with the rise and fall of Zola's reputation in Russia. While working on *The Golovlev Family*, Saltykov-Shchedrin himself became caught up in Zola mania. He was sent to Paris in 1875–1876 by *Fatherland Notes* to attempt to persuade Zola to contribute to the journal.[19]

By 1880 his initial enthusiasm toward Zola and his works had turned into disapproval of the French writer's naturalist excesses, particularly his candid representation of what many perceived as degenerate female sexuality in *Nana*, the 1880 *Rougon-Macquart* cycle installment.[20] The ambiguities of Saltykov-Shchedrin's own response to Zola reflect in microcosm the French writer's Russian reception, which in turn shapes the history and reception of *The Golovlev Family*.

As Katherine Bowers points out in her contribution to the present volume, *The Golovlev Family*'s plot follows the traditional, gothic-inspired "fall of the house" model and is structured vertically around a single family, the Golovlevs, tracing their decline from the heyday of the matriarch Arina Petrovna to the disgrace and death of her grandchildren. Two sons, Stepan and Pavel, die of alcoholism, while the third, the "bloodsucker" or "little Judas," Porfiry, succeeds his mother as head of the family, impregnates his housekeeper, sends his illegitimate child to a Moscow orphanage, and experiences incestuous desire for his niece. Two of Arina Petrovna's grandchildren commit suicide, one dies soon after being exiled to Siberia for stealing government money, and two pursue their dream of becoming actresses, soon falling into drunkenness and prostitution. The novel ends with the actual and anticipated deaths of all "direct-line" Golovlevs and a concluding narrative focus on Nadia Galkina, representative of an illegitimate line.

The Golovlevs' degeneration begins with Stepan's decline and death in "Family Tribunal." The narrator foregrounds both environmental and hereditary factors as critical in Stepan's character's formation. On the one hand he is "a gifted boy who absorbed quickly and readily the impressions of his environment," on the other he "inherited from his father his inexhaustible naughtiness, and from his mother the capacity for quickly discerning people's weak points."[21] Stepan's alcoholism, inherited from his father, reflects the contemporary view, which originated in Morel's reading of Lamarck, that such disorders could have environmental causes in one generation – the suggestion here is that Arina Petrovna drove her husband to drink – but could subsequently transform into hereditary ailments. Alcoholism was identified by Morel as one of the most significant "stigmata" of degeneration in his 1857 *Traité des dégénérescences physiques, intellectuelles et morales de l'espèce humaine*. Such "stigmata" were unmistakable signs of the degenerate's "morbid deviation from a normal type of humanity."[22] Morel believed that alcoholism could cause neurosis, idiocy, and even infertility, a perspective that is reflected in *The Golovlev Family* as Vladimir Mikhailovich's drinking makes itself felt in the early deaths of each subsequent generation and the Golovlevs' eventual extinction.[23]

Despite the importance of Vladimir Mikhailovich's original alcoholism that destroys the family, Saltykov-Shchedrin chooses to focus on the son rather than the father. Stepan is an exemplary model of the corrupting forces of environment and heredity. An atmosphere of constant humiliation as well as inherited degenerate traits shape Stepan's life trajectory, which follows the same downward spiral as that of the family itself. When he gambles away his property, he is forced to return to Golovlevo, which feels like a coffin to him.[24] This return represents both his descent into the grave and his regression into the womb. Arriving at his mother's estate, he is unrecognizable: "Life had played such havoc with him that there was no trace of a gentleman born left in him, nor the slightest indication of his having once been to a university and enjoyed the benefits of a liberal education."[25] The description of his physical appearance reflects not only the stigmata of alcoholism but also the fear of atavism or reverse evolution, human regression back to an ape-like state: "Disproportionately tall, with long ape-like arms and narrow chest, he was thin from underfeeding, dirty and unkempt. His face was bloated, his grayish hair and beard disheveled, his protruding eyes were inflamed by drink and rough weather."[26] His regression continues as his mind is gradually clouded by alcohol, and he loses control over his senses. As an early commentator on the novel astutely pointed out, the alcoholism afflicting Stepan, as well as the manner of its description, recalls the hereditary curse of Zola's Macquarts, especially the alcoholic regression of Gervaise, the heroine of the 1877 novel *L'Assommoir.*[27]

Saltykov-Shchedrin describes at length Stepan's long, slow fall first into delirium tremens, and then into a kind of alcoholic dementia. At the end, he completely loses the capacity for thought: "His brain was working at something, but that something had no relation either to the present or to the future."[28] Stepan's demise sets the pattern for the decline and death of the rest of the Golovlev clan; Ehre astutely observes that the novel is organized around the idea of dying.[29] Pavel undergoes a similar alcoholic decline and deathbed regression to an animalistic state – his dying groans sound like a dog's bark – but he also experiences paranoid fantasies of victory over his brother Porfiry, which are fueled by the fevered imagination of his final days.[30] As the narrator later observes, "Uncontrolled imagination creates an illusory reality which, owing to perpetual mental excitement, becomes concrete, almost tangible."[31] The retreat into a fantasy world prefigures Porfiry's later fall into mysticism and recalls the moral stigmata of degeneration that Nordau would later develop in *Degeneration.* The dying Stepan's vacant mind and the dying Pavel's flights of fancy mark the two poles of the Golovlev condition; each subsequent character falls into one of these two mental conditions at the point of death.

Porfiry's last disease is likened by the narrator to his brothers' alcoholism: "his was a different kind of drunkenness, a mental intoxication."[32] This final madness consists of immersing himself increasingly in fantastic schemes of acquisition and vengeance until he becomes the absolute ruler of his own all-encompassing universe. The physical effects of this enslavement to fantasy recall drunkenness: "his eyes glittered, his trembling lips were covered with foam, his face turned pale and looked menacing."[33] This physiological description of imagination's power is an exemplary model of degeneration discourse: "Men cease to be human, their faces are distorted, their eyes glitter, their tongues babble incoherently, their bodies make involuntary movements."[34] Here the curse of inherited degeneracy deprives the sufferer of his individual subjectivity as he becomes nothing more than the sum of diseased body parts. Anninka undergoes a similar physical transformation on her final return to Golovlevo: at first unrecognizable to Porfiry, "she was a feeble broken creature, with a flat chest, sunken cheeks, a hectic color, and languid movements; she seemed round-shouldered, almost stooping."[35] The physical stigmata of degeneration recur in each generation along with moral stigmata like the incestuous desire that Porfiry experiences for Anninka, a reflection of the incest represented in the second volume of *Les Rougon-Macquart, La Curée*.

Saltykov-Shchedrin's Russian hybridic model of degeneration discourse

The Golovlev Family emerged out of a regular series of satirical sketches of provincial life in *Fatherland Notes* called *Well-Intentioned Speeches* (*Blagonamerennye rechi*). "Family Tribunal" (*Semeinyi sud*), "Good Relatives" (*Po-rodstvennomu*), and "The Casting Up" (*Semeinye itogi*) were published as loosely connected sketches attacking the Russian nobility. In the spring of 1876, in response to suggestions by Turgenev and Stasiulevich, Saltykov-Shchedrin began to conceive of the sketches as an entire self-contained work, a "chronicle," subtitled "Episodes from the History of a Family" (*Epizody iz istorii odnogo semeistva*). This new design allowed him to develop the degeneration theme from a longer-term perspective. He explained the changes in a May 1876 letter written to his editor Nekrasov from Paris.[36] Already in the fourth section, "The Niece" (*Plemiannushka*), serialized that same month, he had broadened and deepened the Golovlev degeneration. The death of Petia, Porfiry's last remaining son, shortly after the demise of Arina Petrovna, demonstrates both the diminishing life spans of each succeeding generation and the repetition of the same flaws, or, in degenerationist terms, the appearance of the same stigmata, in each new generation. The consignment of Porfiry's illegitimate child by his housekeeper Evpraksiia to the Moscow Foundling Home only a few days after birth signals the end of the Golovlev line. The sixth installment, "The Derelict" (*Vymorochnyi*), published in August 1876, again invokes the pattern of regression. As Evpraksiia begins to rebel against his rule, Porfiry regresses into a kind of infancy, locking himself up in his room and retreating into hallucinatory fantasies, as if taking on the identity of the child he has sent away. This regression recalls that of Stepan, and the family chronicle seems to come full circle. The transformation of the sketches into the novel also broadens and deepens the representation of Golovlev degeneration, suggesting moral explanations that break down the biologically deterministic narrative.

Working against the structures of degeneration and impulse of biological determinism throughout the novel is the voice of the narrator, who upholds the values of morality and irony and who reveals the novel's characters' culpability in their own fates, thus avoiding the tragic conclusions implicit in pure biological determinism. The narrator reveals the irony between the words and actions of characters in Arina Petrovna's fondness for the word "family" despite the fact that she "had completely lost the habit of family life," and the gap between Porfiry's moralizing words and lascivious deeds.[37] This dichotomy of words and deeds suggests a more multilayered conception of human motivation and moral choice than the narrative of degeneration might imply.

The novel's pattern of biological determinism is robustly questioned in "The Niece," which focuses on Anninka's visit to Golovlevo following the death of her grandmother. This chapter fits uneasily into the work's overall structure, having been substantially rewritten in 1880 in preparation for publication as a stand-alone work. Though it begins directly after the previous chapter, following Arina Petrovna's curse on Porfiry, it leaps forward in time, representing the deaths of Petia and Arina Petrovna and their aftermath. The fifth chapter, "Illicit Family Joys" (*Nedeozvolennennye semeinye radosti*), moves back to the period before Arina Petrovna's death to chronicle her response to Evpraksiia's pregnancy. The central significance of "The Niece," however, lies not so much in the way it flouts the work's overall chronology, but rather in its staging of a brief moment of reprieve from the otherwise merciless fatalism of the novel's trajectory. It is a key moment in the work's transformation both from sketches to novel and from biological explanations of degeneration to moral explanations. The chapter begins by chronicling Arina Petrovna's death, a seminal moment in the family's decline. From this point, Porfiry becomes increasingly isolated – he is the last to know about his son Petia's death.

Porfiry's isolation is interrupted only by the niece Anninka's brief home-coming. The presence of his attractive relative reawakens Porfiry to the pleasures of life, while return to Golovlevo triggers in Anninka a real-ization of her own decline since she lived at Dubrovino with her grand-mother. She suddenly sees the gap between her vague dreams of indepen-dence and the sordid reality of life as a provincial actress. The narrator explains:

> There are moments when a person who has so far merely *existed* suddenly begins to understand that he really *lives* and there is some canker in his life . . . Such a sudden revelation is equally painful to everyone, but its sub-sequent effects vary according to the person's temperament. It regenerates some people, inspiring them with the resolution to begin a new life, on a new basis: in others it merely causes temporary distress, leading to no change for the better but making them more miserable for the moment than those whose awakened conscience looks forward to a brighter future as a result of their new resolutions.[38]

Anninka, the narrator goes on to convey, belongs to the second category; her temperament prevents her from changing, yet she experiences a period of introspection that reveals her as an exception in the parade of passive and insensible victims of Golovlev degeneration. She becomes aware that men see her body as public property and her "art" has been debased, but is unable to act on this revelation and instead passively submits to the order of things. She continues on her fatalistic trajectory, but the narrator's perspective allows the reader to perceive that she had a choice, but her moral weakness led her to reject the only viable escape – a life of hard work. The narrative of determinism is displaced onto Anninka's perspective, revealing her as both victim and agent of Golovlev degeneration. This distances the reader from the force of determinism and demonstrates that escape from a downward trajectory remains possible. In fact, Anninka bequeaths her vision of an alternative life to another character, Evpraksiia, making her aware of Porfiry's tendency to talk aimlessly and incessantly. Evpraksiia realizes the truth of this alternative, which liberates her from Porfiry's power and enables her to punish him for depriving her of their child.[39]

The last chapter, "The Reckoning" (*Raschet*), published in 1880, stages a conflict between the two explanatory narratives of Golovlev decline:

biological determinism and the gentry class's vulnerability to social and historical change. Its final third is focused entirely on establishing causality for the chain of events that have destroyed the Golovlevs. Anninka places responsibility for her fate within the space of Golovlevo: "Golovlevo – that was death itself, cruel greedy death that is forever stalking a fresh victim."[40] This reading forms part of Saltykov-Shchedrin's parodic attack on the family chronicle genre in general and on Aksakov's *Family Chronicle* in particular which Todd, Kramer, and Bowers have examined; the gentry estate is transformed from a space of sanctuary to the graveyard of a dynasty.[41] The cause of the Golovlevs' decline is transformed from a biologically deterministic drama of tainted blood to necessary historical extinction in a world that no longer needs the gentry class. Anninka's attempt to escape her gentry roots by remaking herself in the provincial theater has been defeated by her social birthright; she is doomed to die in the same grave that swallowed up her uncle Stepan.

The narrator provides his own explanation of the Golovlevs' decline. Observing that a kind of predestination appears to hang over some families, he ascribes this determinism to social factors and historical change: "One notices it particularly among the class of small landowners scattered all over Russia, who, having no work, no connection with public life, and no political importance, were at one time sheltered by serfdom, but now, with nothing to shelter them, are spending the remainder of their lives in their tumble-down country houses."[42] Such families, he continues, are subject to contingency; they lack control over their own lives. Sometimes they experience periods of good fortune, when, thanks to various social successes such as good marriages, they are able to improve their lot. One generation gives birth to another, and the family seemingly flourishes until family members begin to regard happiness as their birthright and are unable to keep up their temporary success. Over time, these failures are passed from generation to generation as chance circumstances turn hereditary and contingency becomes biological determinism. Saltykov-Shchedrin brings social, historical, and biological determinism together with chance in a hybridic model of causality that is profoundly novelistic. Degeneration discourse is fused with commentary on historical and social change as Saltykov-Shchedrin explains that, while formerly the domain of the affluent was walled off, that wall has recently been breached. Thanks to a demand for "new men," and "the degeneration of the 'stale ones,'"[43] families perceived as affluent have increased in numbers. In the Golovlev family, fin-de-siècle biological determinism battles with a quintessentially mid-century account of social advancement.

This is, however, immediately followed by an explanation that falls squarely within the realm of degeneration discourse:

> Side by side with successful families, however, there exist a great number of others upon whom their household gods seem to shower nothing but ill-luck . . . It was precisely this kind of doom which hung over the Golovlev family. Three characteristics had marked its history in the course of several generations: love of idleness, incapacity for any kind of work, and passion for drink. The first two characteristics resulted in moral shallowness, empty talk, and idle fancies; the third was as it were the inevitable conclusion of their failure in life.[44]

These paragraphs provide a degenerationist commentary on the novel as a whole, allowing readers to understand the Golovlevs' fate in a new biological context. The family becomes not merely the symbol of a broader social sickness but its very source. As if to confirm this account, Porfiry and Anninka soon fall prey to the same alcoholic degeneration afflicting so many other Golovlevs, living out their final days reproaching one another for the family's destruction.

The novel ends with an ethical jolt, a final resistance to the lengthy determinist explanations given by the narrator. Toward the end of Holy Week, Porfiry has a sudden revelation about the extent of his own guilt: "suddenly the awful truth dawned upon his conscience – dawned too late, for there was no revoking or remedying the past."[45] He regrets having taken Evpraksiia's son and atones for the lies and materialism that have dominated his life. His urgent need for forgiveness is rendered doubly ironic through the fact that there is no one left to forgive him. That Porfiry's moral awakening takes place in complete isolation gives the novel its final satirical thrust, a move that would be impossible within the limits of a purely biological determinist vision. His final revelation fails to create any change, as Anninka's earlier moment of truth also failed to do. Saltykov-Shchedrin is no Dostoevsky, and may even be parodying the resurrection narrative of *Crime and Punishment*, as Todd points out. Yet Porfiry's revelation nonetheless serves to distance the novel's narrative perspective from the kind of scientific objectivism favored by Zola and the naturalists.[46] The novels of *Les Rougon-Macquart* contain no moralizing authorial asides to resist the cycle's biological determinism; the reader is expected to make his or her ethical conclusions based on the "human documents" presented. In *The Golovlev Family* by contrast, Saltykov-Shchedrin creates a peculiarly Russian hybridic model of degeneration discourse, which is assimilated into an account of social and historical decline grafted onto a parody of the dying genre of the aristocratic family chronicle. The novel's final ambiguities are refocused on the shadowy figure of Nadia Galkina, the cousin who will inherit the estate after the Golovlevs are gone. Will she continue the decline, or does she represent an agent of change? Saltykov-Shchedrin offers no answer.

The Russian rejection of naturalism

Saltykov-Shchedrin's ambivalent perspective on degeneration discourse and biological determinism, as well as his rejection of the scientific objectivism of naturalist narration, can be seen as part of a growing skepticism on the part of Russian authors, critics, and readers toward naturalism and its claims to scientific objectivity during the second half of the 1870s.[47] As early as 1873, one conservative critic argued that Zola's biological determinism contradicted one of the main premises of literary realism, the idea of individual freedom:

> The charlatanism of the author [Zola] could only deceive our homebred Darwinists, who perceive in his works a new application of "sexual selection" and the "struggle for existence." [They] have not reflected that Zola's program of scientific fiction contradicts the very nature of literary art, which is nourished by the free variety of types and for which the freely acting individual is as necessary material as social environment.[48]

Increasing suspicion of naturalism and its goals emerged in discussions in the literary reception of Zola's monthly series for *The European Messenger*, *Letters from Paris*.[49] In this series, Zola propagandized his newly formulated theory of naturalism in literature through extracts from his own works and championed like-minded authors such as the Goncourt brothers. In their engagement with these columns, Russian critics were bemused by the naturalist emphasis on biological determinism:

> The Goncourts are convinced that human feelings and events are guided exclusively by physiological processes. A man carries in his blood particular appetites which look for satisfaction, and lead him to take some actions rather than others . . . Thus, for example, even religious exaltation is nothing but the disguised result of an incorrect physiological process.[50]

Conservative critics such as this reviewer saw biological determinism as "an undoubted negation of every ideal, and every moral sense of life." Yet the implications of this critic's question – "If the reason of all reasons lies in physiological processes and animal appetites, if man exists solely in the flesh, then what can society or civilization strive for?" – were equally problematic for those on the left, as became clear after the publication of Zola's naturalist manifesto, "The Experimental Novel."[51]

The publication of "The Experimental Novel" marked the nadir of Zola's Russian reception.[52] Critical responses to the essay largely reflected two main concerns about Zola's naturalist theory. The first was discomfort with the idea of a novelist adopting scientific objectivity when approaching his or her material and the threat it posed to the novel's status as a moral or ideological force. The second was a sense that the photographic accuracy of naturalism sacrificed the whole for the sake of the parts, effectively dismembering the novelistic subject while anatomizing its constituent parts. Konstantin Arsenev, writing in *The European Messenger* in 1880, summed up the stark message that many liberals and radicals took from Zola's theory: "The unconditional triumph of the experimental novel, as Zola understands it, would be the death sentence of the tendentious novel, that is, of one of the most powerful weapons of progress."[53] Zola's vision for the novel, he argued, would exclude satire of the kind practiced by Juvenal, Barbier, Thackeray, and Saltykov-Shchedrin. Blagosvetlov, writing in *Delo*, had sympathy for Zola's materialism: "I completely agree with Zola that it's much better and richer to use a surgeon's scalpel if not in the heart of a man, then at least in his kidneys, than to send one's imagination off into the stratosphere, where there's nothing real, which is full of ghosts and old wives' tales."[54] The "surgeon's scalpel" he invokes is Zola's own trope, the tool of the physiologist whose experimental techniques he recommends in "The Experimental Novel." Blagosvetlov argued that this act of aesthetic dissection should not be seen as an end in itself. "It's only the first step of that long staircase which the authentic realist artist must make. However rich the material gathered by the artist, if the material stays cold and dead, does not live in the spirit, then it will be that empty mass upon which the anatomist works, or the prosecutor, pronouncing judgment in the case of murder . . . Realism without an end goal is empty."[55] Here we see Zola's own analogy being used against him to reveal the violence of his dismembering gaze in opposition to the implied vitality of the Russian realist imagination. Saltykov-Shchedrin himself later made this opposition even clearer:

> The extent of our realism is different from that of the modern school of French realists. We include under this heading the whole man, in all the variety of his definitions and actuality; the French for the most part interest themselves in the torso, and of the whole variety of his definitions dwell with greater enjoyment in his physical abilities and amorous feats.[56]

He certainly means here to draw attention to the frank depictions of sexuality in works such as *Nana*, but the contrast he draws between Russian realism's holistic vision and French naturalism's fragmenting one cuts to the heart of what many Russian critics and novelists found most threatening about this foreign literary movement and its relationship to the Russian realist tradition. In Zola's mind, the scalpel evokes the new scientific principles upon which the new naturalist novel is constructed; it is able to reveal the complex mechanisms operating beneath the skin of the social body. Seen through Russian eyes, this same scalpel becomes a tool for the dismemberment of the living body of the Russian realist novel.

Against this background, *The Golovlev Family*'s formal transformation from sketch series into novel can be seen as part of a rejection of naturalism's fragmenting vision. Just as Saltykov-Shchedrin rejects Zola's scalpel, so he rejects the sketch form's narrowly analytical lens and embraces the novelistic form's impulse toward complexity and ambiguity, providing a final account of Golovlev decline that privileges moral and social explanations and rejects the closed ending demanded by biological determinism.

Conclusion

Writing in 1881, Saltykov-Shchedrin declared that, "I took on the family, property and the state, and sought to show that they are hollow . . . I wrote the Golovlevs as an attack on the family principle."[57] In *The Golovlev Family* he brought a multi-pronged attack to bear on the idea of the family, establishing the principle of hereditary degeneracy through the regression, decline, and death of each generation. He represented the recurrence of the stigmata of degeneration over three generations, while at the same time stopping short of demonstrating absolutely that the Golovlevs' fates are biologically determined. The family's degenerative decline is tempered by a parallel insistence on a social interpretation of their fate, the suggestion of their class obsolescence, as well as a strong moralizing voice, which insists on the culpability and individual agency of the Golovlevs themselves. His interest in degeneration and its effects does not lead Saltykov-Shchedrin to abandon his role as a social satirist. Indeed, his own subsequent antipathy toward Zola suggests an awareness of the ideological and artistic risks of biological determinism for the politically committed novelist. *The Golovlev Family*'s transformation from a sketch series into a novel shows an increasing insistence on moral explanations for the Golovlev decline. In its final incarnation, *The Golovlev Family* follows the lead of Saltykov-Shchedrin's contemporaries in the world of *publitsistika* in its reaffirmation of the moral

judgment of the satirical tradition and rejection of the scientific objectivity
so central to the French naturalist school.

NOTES

1 P. N. Tkachev, "Rol' psikhicheskoi nasledstvennosti," *Delo* (1878): 11, in *Petr Nikitich Tkachev: Sochineniia v dvukh tomakh* (Moscow: Mysl', 1976), 1:402–433.

2 Daniel Pick, *Faces of Degeneration: A European Disorder, c. 1848–c. 1918* (Cambridge University Press, 1993), 1–33.

3 Nordau, *Degeneration*, 1–44.

4 William Greenslade, *Degeneration, Culture and the Novel, 1880–1940* (Cambridge University Press, 1994), 15–17.

5 B. A. Morel, *Traité des dégénérescences physiques, intellectuelles et morales de l'espèce humaine et des causes qui produisent ces variétés maladives* (Paris: J. B. Baillière, 1857), 5–6.

6 On degeneration discourse in Russia in the 1890s, see Daniel Beer, *Renovating Russia: The Human Sciences and the Fate of Liberal Modernity, 1880–1930* (Ithaca, NY: Cornell University Press, 2008), 27–58, and Riccardo Nicolosi, *Degeneration erzählen. Wissenschaft und Literatur im Russland der 1880er und 1890er Jahre* (Munich: Wilhelm Fink, 2015). For an examination of ideas of degeneration as early as the 1870s, see Nicolosi, "Degeneraty gospoda Golovlevy. Saltykov-ščedrin i diskurs vyroždenija 19-ogo veka," in *Telo, duch i duša v russkoj literature i kul'ture*, edited by J. van Baak and S. Brouwer, *Wiener Slawistischer Almanach* 54 (2004): 337–350.

7 Émile Zola, *Les Rougon-Macquart, Histoire naturelle et sociale d'une famille sous le second Empire* (Paris: Gallimard, 1960–1967), 1:3. The translations from the author's preface of *La Fortune des Rougon* are all from *The Fortune of the Rougons*, translated by Ernest Alfred Vizetelly (New York: Mondial, 2004). All quotations are taken from page 6.

8 Pick, *Faces of Degeneration*, 44–106.

9 Zola, *Les Rougon-Macquart*, 1:3.

10 Ibid.

11 On the influence of *Le Roman russe*, see F. W. J. Hemmings, *The Russian Novel in France* (Oxford University Press, 1950).

12 Vladimir Chiuko, "Vtoraia Imperiia v romane Emilia Zola. Les Rougon Macquart, histoire naturelle et sociale d'une famille sous le second Empire, par Émile Zola. Tome premier: La fortune des Rougon. Paris, 1871. Stat'ia pervaia," *Vestnik Evropy* 7 (1872): 112–168; "Vtoraia Imperiia v romane Emilia Zola. Les Rougon Macquart, histoire naturelle et sociale d'une famille sous le second Empire, par Émile Zola. Tome deuxième. La curée. Paris, 1871. Stat'ia vtoraia," *Vestnik Evropy* 8 (1872): 549–663. *Iskra, Delo, Biblioteka deshevaia i obshchedostupnaia, Pravitel'stvennyi vestnik*, and *Otechestvennye zapiski* all published translations of *Le Ventre de Paris* and *La Conquête de Plassans*.

13 Quoted in E. Paul Gauthier, "Zola's Reputation in Russia prior to 'L'Assommoir,'" *The French Review* 33:1 (1959): 37–44.

14 See M. K. Lemke, ed., *M. M. Stasiulevich i ego sovremenniki v ikh perepiske* (St. Petersburg, 1912), iii:594–630, *passim*; M. K. Kleman, "Iz perepiski E. Zolia s russkimi korrespondentami," *Literaturnoe nasledstvo* 31–32 (1937): 943–980.

15 Émile Zola, "Prostupok abbata Mure," *Vestnik Evropy* (1875) 1:253–329; 2:694–774; 3:271–364.

16 Chiuko, "Vtoraia imperiia v romane Emilia Zolia. Stat'ia pervaia," 112–168.

17 For a previous analysis of degeneration discourse in *The Golovlev Family*, see Riccardo Nicolosi, "Vyrozhdenie sem'i, vyrozhdenie teksta. 'Gospoda Golovlevy': frantsuzskii naturalizm i diskurs degeneratsii xix veka," in *Russkaia literatura i meditsina. Telo, predpisania, sotsialnaia praktika*, edited by K. Bogdanov, J. Murašov, and R. Nicolosi (Moscow: Novoe izdatel'stvo, 2006), 170–193; Nicolosi, "Degeneraty gospoda Golovlevy," 337–350.

18 S. I. Sychevskii, "Zhurnalnye ocherki," *Odesskii vestnik* 3 (1877): 465–466. See also K. K. Arsen'ev, *Saltykov-Shchedrin (Literaturno-obshchestvennaia kharakteristika)* (St. Petersburg: Tipografiia "Obshchestvennaia Pol'za," 1906), 194.

19 A. S. Bushmin, *Khudozhestvennyi mir Saltykova-Shchedrina* (Leningrad: Nauka, 1987), 349–352.

20 Saltykov-Shchedrin wrote scathingly about the obscenity of *Nana* in his travelogue, *Za rubezhom (Abroad)*. See M. E. Saltykov-Shchedrin, *Sobranie sochinenii v dvadtsati tomakh* (Moscow: Khudozhestvennaia literatura, 1965–1976), xiv:154–161, hereafter referred to as *SS*.

21 *SS* viii:11–12. M. E. Saltykov-Shchedrin, *The Golovlyov Family*, translated by Natalie Duddington (New York Review Books, 2001), 8–9. Subsequent citations provide the Russian edition page number first, followed by the English edition.

22 Morel, *Traité*, 5, quoted in Fae Brauer, "The Stigmata of Abjection: Degenerate Limbs, Hysterical Skin and the Tattooed Body," in *A History of Visual Culture: Western Civilization from the 18th to the 21st Century*, edited by Jane Kromm and Susan Benforado Bakewell (Oxford: Berg, 2010), 170.

23 Brauer, "Stigmata," 170.

24 30; 33.

25 22; 22–23.

26 22; 23. On degeneration, see Pick, *Faces of Degeneration*, 109–152.

27 Arsen'ev, *Saltykov-Shchedrin*, 193.

28 *SS* 53; Saltykov-Shchedrin, *The Golovlyov Family*, 63.

29 Milton Ehre, "A Classic of Russian Realism: Form and Meaning in *The Golovlyovs*," *Studies in the Novel* 9:1 (1977): 3–16.

30 66–67, 77; 81–82, 94–95.

31 217; 277.

32 215; 275.

33 217; 277.

34 217; 277.

35 230; 295.

36 *SS* XVIII:2, 287–289.

37 10; 6.

38 153; 196.

39 162; 206.

40 249; 318.

41 William Mills Todd, III, "The Anti-Hero with a Thousand Faces: Saltykov-Shchedrin's Porfirii Golovlev," *Studies in the Literary Imagination* 9:1 (1976): 102–103; Karl Kramer, "Satiric Form in Saltykov's *Gospoda Golovlyovy*," *Slavic and East European Journal* 14:4 (1970): 455; and Katherine Bowers's contribution to the present volume.

42 251; 321.

43 252; 322.

44 253; 322–323.

45 257; 328.

46 Todd, "Anti-Hero," 103–105.

47 For an overview of Russian "Zolaism" and its backlash, see John A. McNair, "Zolaizm in Russia," *Modern Language Review* 95:2 (2000): 450–462.

48 V. W., "Nravy i literatura vo Frantsii," *Russkii vestnik* 11 (1873): 239, quoted in Gauthier, "Zola's Reputation in Russia," 39.

49 On the reception of *Letters from Paris* in Russia, see Philip A. Duncan, "The Fortunes of Zola's *Parizskie pis'ma* in Russia," *Slavic and East European Journal* 3:2 (1959): 107–121.

50 W., "Roman i kritika vo Frantsii," *Russkii mir* 37:9 (Feb. 21, 1877): 37–39.

51 Ibid.

52 See Philip A. Duncan, "Echoes of Zola's Experimental Novel in Russia," *Slavic and East European Journal* 18:1 (1974): 11–19.

53 Written under K. K. Arsen'ev's pseudonym, Z. Z., "Sovremennyi roman i ego predstaviteliakh. 4. Viktor Giugo," *Vestnik Evropy* 1 (1880): 297, quoted from "Teoriia eksperimental'nogo romana," *Kriticheskie etiudy po russkoi literature*, III:348.

54 Grigory E. Blagosvetlov writing as "Kritik bez kriticheskoi merki," *Delo* 2:2 (1878): 327–345.

55 Ibid., 334.

56 In *M. Saltykov-Shchedrin o literature i iskusstve*, edited by L. F. Ershov (Moscow: Iskusstvo, 1953), 396. Quoted in R. Poggioli, "Realism in Russia," *Comparative Literature* 3:3 (1951): 260.

57 *SS* XIX:1, 194.

CHAPTER 2

The hiding places of the self in Dostoevsky's Adolescent

Yuri Corrigan

"Koshchei is difficult to overcome: his death is on the end of a needle, that needle is in an egg, that egg is in a duck, that duck is in a rabbit, that rabbit is in a chest, and the chest stands on a tall oak tree. Koshchei guards that tree like his own eye."

– Afanas'ev, "The Frog-Princess"[1]

Commentators at the fin de siècle differed widely in their attempts to diagnose the sense of personal malaise – the "catastrophe of the self" or "crisis of the soul" – that so pervaded Russian society.[2] On the one hand, many insisted that the educated Russian individual had become too inwardly oriented, too absorbed with the "cult of one's own psychic 'I'" that characterized egoistic and decadent bourgeois culture.[3] Others argued, on the contrary, that it was the *neglect* of the inner life, the obsessive preoccupation with external social phenomena, that was causing disease and imbalance in the soul of the *intelligent*.[4] At the heart of the disagreement lay the problem of what in fact constituted an "inner life" and what "doctrine of the personality" could provide guidance to a populace which, having largely discarded its traditional religious teachings on the nature of the human being, hungered for something definite with which to replace them.[5]

Dostoevsky's *Adolescent*, though written in the 1870s, foreshadows these arguments of the fin-de-siècle period in the novel's creative, if largely overlooked, examination of the crisis of individual identity. *The Adolescent* is by no means alone among Dostoevsky's works in exuding fin-de-siècle angst, as we see clearly in Connor Doak's and Robin Feuer Miller's chapters. Whether in Doak's reading of masculine degeneration in *Demons*, or in Miller's exploration of the darkening of the Christmas tale genre, we feel Dostoevsky's palpable anxiety with regard to societal decline. The initial impetus for *The Adolescent* was to explore this growing sense of "disintegration" and "disorder" in Russian society.[6]

The novel as it materialized, however, came to investigate cultural deterioration through the more specific lens of personhood. Dostoevsky explores his young protagonist's longing for, and attempts to conceive of, a robust concept of the personality in an environment that provides little guidance. In this light, Dostoevsky addresses social disorder as the consequence of a deeper, more ominous, absence of interior infrastructure within the self. Through Arkady Dolgoruky's experiments with three seemingly irreconcilable theories of personality (self as private, concealed depths, self as outward, relational activity, and self as physical incarnation), Dostoevsky explores the extreme difficulties that confront a young hero in the late nineteenth century in his quest to discover an indwelling principle of identity, or soul.[7] Each of Arkady's theories, which I shall examine sequentially, represents an isolated part of a more comprehensive conception of the self, and I trace Arkady's attempts to synthesize these theories through his adventures with a concealed "document," a piece of paper in his possession that acquires vast symbolic potential in the context of his quest.

In reading *The Adolescent* as an exploration of the problem of personhood, I hope to challenge some of the canonical readings of Dostoevsky's concept of the personality – as radically social, dialogical, and relational in nature – by emphasizing Arkady's desperate attempts to conceal and thus to preserve private, inward dimensions of self. I also hope to challenge some of the recurring criticisms of the novel, the most frequent of which identify a lack of coherent connection between its constitutive parts – those parts having been described as:

1. the "psychological mystery novel, in which Arkadii seeks to solve the riddle of [Versilov,] his complex and enigmatic biological father";
2. the "bildungsroman, in which the young man tries out several designs for living, including miserly accumulation of capital, the dissipated gambling life of a young aristocrat, and the holy quest for '*blagoobrazie*' ('blessed form')"; and
3. the "penny-dreadful tale of intrigue" involving the concealed "document" that Arkady wields, and the blackmail plot that it entails.[8]

I shall argue that these seemingly unconnected "plots," from Arkady's "idea," to the "document," to the gambling episodes, to the mysterious all-importance of Versilov, cohere powerfully if we read the novel in the context of Russian society's growing need for a practical theory of the personality as the fin de siècle approached. In accommodating Arkady's experiment with selfhood to the shape of a novelistic plot, Dostoevsky develops a catalogue of images of the self that resonate throughout his work in general and provide us with a point of access to the vast meditation on the structure of the personality that underlies his psychological realism.

First theory: "I am altogether different, higher and deeper"

Arkady's constant preoccupation in the novel's first part is to imagine secure interior locations for the self as a defense against external forces that threaten to destroy it or deny its existence. In this sense, his sacred, much discussed "idea" is not the pursuit of wealth, as phrased initially, nor can it be exhausted by the terms that clothe it throughout: "power," "solitude," "darkness," or "mystery."[9] Rather, Arkady's "idea" is the thesis of a non-material indwelling identity, or a soul. As he lets slip to Kraft, he believes he possesses a secure interior location for the self, a place of refuge from the world of others:

> "Wouldn't it be better to break from them utterly? Eh?"
> "And go where?" asked [Kraft].
> "To yourself [*k sebe*], to yourself alone! That's what my whole idea consists of, Kraft!" I said triumphantly . . .
> "And do you have such a place: 'to yourself'?"
> "I do."[10]

Arkady later admits that he might have exaggerated in his confidence on the matter of "having such a place" as a self: "I told Kraft that I have 'my own place' . . . I said this proudly."[11] Like the folkloric Koshchei the Deathless who hides his "death" on the tip of a needle, which is then placed in a series of objects, swallowed successively by ever larger animals, Arkady seeks out a variety of semi-secure locations – in the realm of thought, in concealed objects, and in memory – in which to house and conceal this most fragile thesis.

Due to the initial form of its expression ("My idea is to become a Rothschild"[12]), the hero's "idea" has often been interpreted as an attraction to Western-style capitalist materialism.[13] As a result, critics have found the "idea," which Dostoevsky intended as the central axis of the novel's construction,[14] to be self-contradictory and confusing, assuming prominence and then disappearing almost entirely.[15] Arkady's "idea" of Rothschild, however, is in fact inherently opposed to any form of materialism. He insists continually that his fantasy is not for any actual material prosperity, but rather for the sensation of being impervious to time and space. He denies any material dimension to his desire for wealth: "was it really money that I needed then? I swear I only needed the idea!"[16] In its Rothschild guise, the idea is presented more as a perversion of European romantic notions of selfhood, something similar to what Marx had in mind in his identification of the "power of money" with the conception of the self in capitalist society.[17]

The emphasis of Arkady's idea is not upon actual wealth but upon money's ability to defer identity; it represents the desire to locate the self *elsewhere*, away from the threatening gaze of others. Inspired by accounts of beggars who sewed thousands of rubles into their clothing, Arkady formulates his dream in imitation. To be a "Rothschild," for Arkady, means to assume the outward guise of a pauper while possessing immense concealed riches: "If I were a multimillionaire, I would find pleasure in walking in the oldest clothing so that they would take me for the most wretched person."[18] These hidden riches, the secret "idea" or the concealed wealth, assume the vocabulary of soul, becoming for Arkady the "only source" of "life," "light," "dignity," and "consolation," a "treasure of power," an oasis within consciousness, a location of inviolability that continues to exist "regardless of how ridiculous and humiliated I seemed."[19] The "idea" also constitutes the location of identity and individuality since, as Arkady explains, "when I express my idea to someone, I'll suddenly have nothing left, will come to resemble everyone else, and maybe even discard my idea; and so I cherished and guarded it and trembled at the thought of blabbing."[20]

Such a distortion of the romantic concept of inner depth is by no means original in the Russian literary tradition. Arkady draws here explicitly on Pushkin's *The Covetous Knight* (1830) in which the Baron's passion for hoarding wealth can readily be interpreted "in the context of the romantic concept of selfhood."[21] We also detect an implicit allusion to Gogol's Poprishchin of "Diary of a Madman" (1834) who defers his own identity into the "king of Spain," in order to escape his humiliating insignificance in the eyes of others.[22] Arkady's Rothschild is an approximate equivalent of Poprishchin's Spanish monarch – an inviolable, distant, transcendental, majestic, interior self, invisible to others. Indeed, Arkady's "idea" first shows up in the notebooks as the "desire to become the king of an island known to no one, at the Pole, or in a lake in Central Africa."[23] Both Pushkin's Baron and Gogol's clerk, moreover, were fodder for Arkady's precursor, Mr. Prokharchin, in Dostoevsky's early story of that name (1846). In "Mr. Prokharchin," the protagonist, a humiliated, pathetic, Gogolian functionary, hides large amounts of wealth in his mattress, and, as he lies silently over his concealed riches, he nurtures an alternate personality – a proud, imperious, "Napoleonic" self that emerges unexpectedly and momentarily.[24]

Dostoevsky took great pains to weave his novel's plot into Arkady's experiment of selfhood. The dream of being located elsewhere becomes distilled in the image of the "document" that Arkady carries with him, the invisible location of all his secret inward power, which is in fact nothing more than a potentially embarrassing letter forged by the heroine attempting to wrest control of her father's wealth.[25] In this sense, the concealed letter is not at all the stale device of a "moth-eaten melodramatic plot," as critics have all but unanimously identified it.[26] For Arkady, the letter takes the place of those dreamed-of riches, and, like his imagined wealth, is both unknown to all and stitched into his clothing: *interior* in the most literal sense. Throughout, the concealment of the document represents the same mechanism as the "idea." It becomes synonymous with Arkady's ability not to be fully understood or finalized, to retain a secret locus of identity that others "would give anything to possess" and which, unbeknownst to all, makes him "the master of their fate."[27]

The weakness of Arkady's conception of self lies in its inability to include or make room for other aspects of his personality. Indeed, as soon as Arkady finds himself in social space, a body confronted by other consciousnesses, his concept of an interior self falls immediately into a state of crisis. After all Arkady's work at deferring his identity into the secret location, it takes Versilov only a moment to violate the carefully guarded space. Nothing, it turns out, has been successfully concealed:

> "All your secrets are written on your honest face. He has 'his idea'..."
>
> "Let's leave my honest face alone," I continued to burst,... "Yes, I do have 'my idea.' That you expressed it thus is of course a coincidence, but I am not afraid to admit: I have an 'idea'... In any case I will never reveal it to you..."
>
> "You don't have to, my friend. I already know the essence of your idea; it's 'I will withdraw into the desert'... to become Rothschild or something of the sort and to withdraw into his greatness."
>
> I trembled within myself... He had guessed everything.[28]

In this scene we see how Arkady's "idea" is undermined both by the presence of others and by the existence of his body. When confronted in such a direct manner by these other bothersome dimensions of selfhood, he instinctively attempts to hide the principle of self in other, deeper locations, and, in these cases, resorts to the realm of memory for greater security.

The notion of self in memory is richly textured in the novel and, as an interior location for the deferral of the self, appears to be the most robust of Arkady's arsenal. Continually, in situations of extreme anxiety, Arkady stabilizes himself by revisiting his cherished memory of meeting his mother as a child. We learn eventually that he developed the mechanism of deferring to memory at a very young age in order to dissociate himself from his beaten and abused physical incarnation:

> I wrapped myself up to the head in my blanket and, from under my pillow, pulled out the little blue kerchief: . . . I instantly pressed it to my face and suddenly began to kiss it. "Mama, mama," I whispered, remembering, and my whole chest constricted like in a vice. I closed my eyes and saw her face . . . at the church . . . [Lambert] runs up to me and begins to pull the blanket from me, but I hold ever so tightly onto the blanket in which I am wrapped up to my head, . . . he beats me, hitting me painfully with his fist in my back.[29]

The image of the boy concealed in his blanket, impervious to abuse due to a sacred, alternate location of identity hidden in memory, constitutes one of the central images of Arkady's approach to selfhood. Later on, armed with his theory of personal depth and mystery, he no longer feels the need to cover himself physically as he did in his blanket as a child. In fact, he is eager to reveal even the most personal details to strangers, introducing himself as "the illegitimate son of my former master," or responding to the mockery of his peers with "calm yourselves, I still haven't ever known a woman."[30] In other words, to risk revealing everything is to insist that there is something deeper that has been left unrevealed, something essential that is utterly remote from the world of appearances. As he says to Vasin, "I'm a trashy little boy and not worthy of you. I confess this precisely because in other minutes I am altogether different, higher and deeper."[31] These alternate locations of identity, "deeper" and "higher," as we have seen, however, are insecure and constantly shifting places of refuge.

Second theory: "The whirlwind anthropology"

Arkady's idea of personal depth or en-souledness appears in the novel always in contest with another conception: that of a relational self anchored in others, evoked by the image of a "whirlwind." Arkady, it turns out, nurtures more than one "idea" while alone under his blankets, attempting to overcome his empirical limitations: "When I'd lie down in my bed and cover myself in the blanket, I'd dream about you, Andrei Petrovich, about you alone."[32] This "dream" of his father develops into an overwhelming sense of identification, as Arkady becomes like the other characters who "hover" about Versilov, "nourishing him with their . . . life juices."[33] By embracing Versilov as the focal point and organizing principle of his own interior life,

Arkady aspires to become an appendage of a larger, relational personality. The novel comes to examine both conceptions side by side, the self as enclosed or inward and the self as utterly unfolded in relational activity. Since the latter, relational view of the self as inherently social and open-ended was dominant in classical Dostoevsky scholarship, I begin by briefly reviewing some of these foundational descriptions of Dostoevsky's relational selfhood, before examining the problematic nature of the relational self as expressed in the novel.

Classical Dostoevsky scholarship emphasized the intersecting personalities of Dostoevsky's novels as key to his experimental poetics and as the very locus of his departure from psychological realism. As Bakhtin influentially observed, with Dostoevsky's characters we consistently find ourselves in the anteroom of consciousness, on the "threshold," without access to those private inner rooms that would provide psychological infrastructure for the personality. For Bakhtin, this thresholdedness is an attribute of an anti-essentialist philosophical worldview, a radical new vision of personality in which the self only emerges – only, in fact, exists – in "dialogue" or "communion" with other consciousnesses.[34] Those interior realms that Arkady attempts to preserve in his search for an inviolate self are, according to the Bakhtinian approach, sites of a ghostly "semi-existence," for one can only enter into being through dialogical activity.[35] Nikolai Berdiaev, likewise responding to the radically social nature of personality in Dostoevsky, describes the author's use of the "Dionysian whirlwind" as an experimental device that pulls the human being into a frantic vortex of intersecting characters. Dostoevsky's "whirlwind anthropology," as Berdiaev calls it, allows us to see a universal human consciousness contending with all the scattered fragments of its vast, mysterious personality, for example, Stavrogin and all the characters who cling to him in *Demons*, Versilov and his extended family in *The Adolescent*.[36] As Konstantin Mochulsky argues, these are not realistic interactions of psychologically plausible characters but a spiritual allegory, representing the possibility of *sobornost'* or organic all-unity.[37]

At first glance *The Adolescent* seems to lend itself readily to being interpreted as an allegorical examination of cosmic all-unity. Versilov, according to Mochulsky, is the "*sobornyi . . . center of life*," the organic unity to which everyone is drawn, and from which Arkady wants to escape.[38] Arkady's experiments with positing a personal essence are, therefore, a denial of *sobornost'*, a diseased form of individualism which opens up "a fetid underground . . . in the soul of the human being."[39] Instead of the "organic collectivity of souls" centered in the figure of Versilov, Mochulsky argues, Arkady seeks "demonic separation and fragmentation" by means of "might" and "power."[40] Such a polarized reading, however, greatly reduces the complexity of Dostoevsky's notion of the individual inner life by simply juxtaposing it with a grand conception of intersubjective harmony. What such readings tend to overlook are the consequences of the "whirlwind," which, as becomes clear from Arkady's experiment, devastates the individual personality that lacks an adequate concept of self.[41]

As we have seen, Arkady resists assimilation by his father's personality by leaning heavily on his "idea," on his memories, on his concealed document, or on any scrap of selfhood that would free him from "hovering" like those others "around" Versilov. His resistance weakens only when Versilov acts nobly by renouncing an inheritance, and thus by exhibiting the qualities that Arkady dreamed of possessing for himself: disregard for material necessity and inaccessible mystery. As he discards his own personality, he clings to Versilov's "star" as his center of orientation among life's chaos: "And so what, if I'm falling, . . . I'll emerge: I have my star!"[42] Here the notion of the "star" or the "ideal" becomes an external substitute for an interior personal identity. Later Arkady gives in to his father's ability to "grasp and conquer [his] soul," allowing him to utterly renounce selfhood: "'Now I have no need to fantasize and dream, now it is enough to have you! I'll follow you!' I said, giving myself over to him with my whole soul."[43] For Arkady, to love his father means to become his father, to merge into the other, behaving as an extension of that personality. Confusing the boundary between them, he resolves to fight a duel on Versilov's behalf, begins to borrow money in Versilov's name, discovers that he loves the same woman passionately, repeats Versilov's thoughts as his own, and longs for his father to "invade his conscience."[44]

Arkady's engagement with Versilov requires him to embrace a very different conception of self. He finds that he must relinquish his "idea" of self as depth, which is incompatible with social reality, as he becomes "drawn into the whirlpool" of other people's lives "like a sliver."[45] Unable "with all [his] strength to pull [himself] away from the 'whirl,'" he is overcome by the ecstasy of communion with others: "A boundless thirst for this life, for *their* life grasped my entire spirit . . . My thoughts were spinning, but I allowed them to spin."[46] The "whirl" as it is characterized throughout denotes the eradication of interior faculties and the loss of personal identity; "I don't have any affairs of my own now," writes Arkady.[47] In the context of his passionate identification with others, Arkady meditates on the uselessness of all those elements of interior life, those "gloominesses" – ideas, dreams, thoughts, memories – that he had zealously protected and then so suddenly discarded:

> And what were all those former gloominesses for, . . . what for all these old
> sickly lacerations, my lonely and sullen childhood, my stupid dreams under
> the blanket, oaths, calculations and even the "idea"? All this I'd imagined
> and thought up, and it turns out it isn't at all like this in the world.[48]

The more Arkady develops a social being, the more his interior space is
described as devoid of any organizing center, his failing reason "a dark
cloud of dry autumn leaves in the wake of a whirlwind"[49] within which
his personality is powerless: "In my soul it was very troubled, and there
was no wholeness . . . Everything somehow flashed without connection and
order, and, I remember, I myself did not want to stop on anything or to
instill order."[50] This resembles the "threshold space" observed by Bakhtin,
in which "all *distance* between people is suspended" and "all things that
were once self-enclosed, disunified, distanced from one another . . . are
drawn into carnivalistic contacts and combinations," and according to
which a person is always "turned outward" and "does not exist . . . outside
of this living addressivity."[51] For Dostoevsky, however, it is impossible to
exist only on the threshold and to remain "unmerged" and "unfinalized,"
for such relational selfhood obliterates the possibility of an individual
identity.

A brief glance at the treatment of the image of the "whirlwind" in *The
Gambler* (1866) can help to shed light on the nature of the relational self
in *The Adolescent*. Here too Dostoevsky invokes the whirlwind (*vikhr',
krugovorot*) to describe the powerlessness of becoming wholly immersed
in the intensity of human relationships at the expense of one's personal
agency:

> Instead of thinking through my next step, I live under the influence
> of . . . this recent whirlwind that pulled me into that whirl and again threw
> me out somewhere. Sometimes it seems to me that I am still turning in that
> same whirlwind and that again this storm will tear through, grab me with
> its wing, and I'll spring out again from order and . . . I'll spin, spin, spin.[52]

Dostoevsky further dramatizes the "whirl" in the image of the roulette
wheel, in terms of its debilitating power over the self. Being bound to
the wheel means to disintegrate as a self, to become invaded by other
personalities, and to lose one's "memories" and "dreams"[53] while always
still hoping to "find the person within, before he is destroyed altogether."[54]
When the Countess loses self-control at the roulette wheel, Dostoevsky
describes her encounter with demons, "little Poles," who begin to climb
over her, and even "through" her, overriding her will as they dispense with
her wealth at random:

[The little Poles] placed bets each from his own side, one... on red, the other on black. It ended with them completely encircling and confusing grandmother, so that she, finally, almost in tears, addressed herself to the old croupier... to drive them away... But by the end of the day... as many as six little Poles stood behind her... Not only did they not listen to her, but they didn't even notice her, climbed directly through her to the table, grabbed the money themselves, dispensed of it, staked it, argued, and cried out.[55]

In the earlier novella, the whirlwind is the site of the destruction of the self or of the entry of others into the self. These "little Poles" are developed into more fully fledged characters – Stebel'kov, Lambert – in *The Adolescent*.

Like the protagonist of *The Gambler*, Arkady hopes that it is possible to preserve both conceptions, of private and relational self, simultaneously: "Is it really impossible," he wonders, "to go to them, find out everything from them and suddenly to leave them forever, going harmlessly past the wonders and the monsters?"[56] He hopes the relational "whirl" will allow him to preserve his indwelling depths: "And the 'idea'? The 'idea' would be later, the 'idea' would wait."[57] More dangerous than Versilov, however, are those who grasp onto Arkady like the demons at the roulette wheel. Here the band of "blackmailers" is a development of the "little Poles," since their purpose is to invade and exploit the private self, or to discover the secrets of those who "thirst for secrecy" and then threaten to reveal them.[58] Arkady believes he can fend off such invasions by invoking his transcendental defenses: "I have an 'idea'," he tells Lambert. "If it doesn't work out... then I'll go away into my idea; but you don't have an idea." Soon, however, he begins to feel "with horror... the absurdity and the loathsomeness of my [confessions] to Lambert, of my agreement with him," and he holds to the thought of his concealed document as a guarantee of inviolability without suspecting that Lambert will take this from him as well: "But thank God, the document still remained with me! Was still sewn into my side pocket; I felt it with my hand – it was there! This meant that I only had to get up and run away."[59]

Like a whirlwind, the relational self, Arkady discovers, consists of an intense flurry of activity around an empty center. Thus, when Versilov proves untrustworthy, Arkady finds that there is no organizing center to social reality, which "turns" endlessly "like chaos": "And, like in a whirlwind, the figures of Liza, Anna Andreevna, Stebel'kov, the prince, Aferdov, of everyone, flashed without trace in my ailing mind... becoming ever more formless and elusive."[60] Through these images of others spinning chaotically around nothing, Dostoevsky phrases his critique of relational

selfhood. Rather than the "free unanimity" of *sobornost'* advanced by Khomiakov or the "interaction of autonomous and internally unfinalized" and
"unmerged" consciousnesses imagined by Bakhtin, the whirl is a deterministic and impersonal system founded upon an expanding absence.[61] As he
moves more deeply into this whirlwind, Arkady inexorably becomes drawn
to the roulette wheel, and, like the Countess in *The Gambler*, stakes his
wealth continually on "zero," an image of the "essential void" at the heart
of all order. Having given himself up to the arbitrary whirl, he is forcibly
searched by the gambling authorities, experiencing, as Dmitry Karamazov
will later in his turn, the utter annihilation of his inviolate selfhood: "they
carried me into the neighboring room, and there, amid the crowd, they
searched me entirely down to the last fold. I cried and tried to tear myself
away."[62] Defiled and uncovered, the hero searches for the shreds of his violated personality, attempting to return to those locations of identity he had
prepared for himself, the "idea" and the "document": "'I have an "idea!"' I
thought suddenly, '. . . but it is really possible now to crawl back into the
former darkness. Ah, my God, I still didn't burn the "document!"'"[63] Both
the idea and the document come to represent the hidden, reflective spaces
of the self that provide some form of defense against the obliteration of the
personality.

Rather than a mere plot device then, the image of the "document"
becomes inseparable from Arkady's competing theories of self. On the one
hand, it is an expression of self as inviolate in that it is the concealed site
of power and identity. On the other hand, the document also expresses
the relational self in that it rightfully belongs to Akhmakova, is in fact
"assumed to be in Versilov's keeping,"[64] and in that its existence ties Arkady
implicitly to every other character in the novel, drawing him further into
the "whirlwind." Thus, the fate of the document in the novel is connected
directly to the survival of the self, as, clutching desperately to it, Arkady
searches for some way to navigate these polarizing practices of identity.

Third theory: The illumined corner and the opened envelope

Having experimented with these two conceptions of self as absence – deferral of self into interior space and deferral of self into other people – Arkady
becomes fascinated by a third conception of self, now as presence. This
new idea, which Arkady gives the term "*blagoobrazie*," roughly translated
as "seemliness" or, more literally, as "blessed form," represents a reversal of
his initial theory of the self in that the emphasis has shifted to an incarnational or revealed, rather than concealed, *self*.[65] If we follow its unsteady

and idiosyncratic usage in the text, "seemliness" comes to refer to the transformation of the body or, more specifically, of the *face* by soul, by "light," or by divine indwelling presence. Behind the idea of "seemliness," which Arkady grasps intuitively but struggles to understand and to implement, lies Dostoevsky's own conviction that "a human being's face is the image of his personality, his spirit, his human worth."[66] In his discussion of this Neoplatonic Russian Orthodox concept of the illumined countenance, Pavel Florensky explains that "high spiritual attainment transforms the face into a lightbearing countenance" as one comes "to incarnate the hidden inheritance of our sacred likeness to the image of God in the flesh of our personality."[67] Thus, according to the spiritual tradition into which Arkady has stumbled, the "substantive kernel," "core," or "essence" of the personality – which he has been so desperate to conceal – becomes inseparable from the revealed presence of the divine likeness within the human body, and particularly within the face as the expression of both the individual personality and the divine life which animates it.[68]

In order to develop this somewhat obscure conception of revealed self, Dostoevsky allows his characters several tangents on the topic of beauty as the illuminated countenance, all of which occur in the latter section of the novel while Arkady is trying to understand his newfound doctrine of "seemliness." Versilov, for example, explains to Arkady that photographs capture only the material features of the subject in a given moment. Since the "main thought of the face" is usually absent, the artist watches for that "extremely rare" moment in which "we resemble ourselves." Versilov's rumination introduces the theme of the transfigurative effect of light on material features, since, in the daguerreotype of Sonya that he shows to Arkady, it is the light of the sun that "captured Sonya in her salient moment – of modest, meek love and her somewhat wild, fearful chastity."[69] In yet another extended examination of the transformative power of light, Dostoevsky depicts a moment of joyful conversion when Arkady's "corner," an image formerly associated with his attempts at self-concealment ("My idea is my corner"[70]), becomes flooded with light. Under Makar's influence, Arkady shifts from being "infuriated to the point of malice" by the ray of the setting sun that lights up his corner to rejoicing at being "pierced" by light: "suddenly in the corner I saw the bright, light spot of the setting sun . . . , and I remember that my entire soul leapt up and it was as if a new light penetrated into my heart."[71] According to Arkady's new phase of theorizing, moreover, transfigurative light becomes synonymous with "mirth" or "cheerfulness" (*veselie*), since laughter is the principle of illumination, as it brings the whole of the person to the surface. Arkady considers it "one of the most serious conclusions of my life" that "character" or "the entire human being" or the "soul" reveals itself in "cheerful" laughter; one can be stumped by the mystery of a personality, and through laughter "you suddenly see everything there is to know."[72]

"Seemliness," however, like those mangled versions of en-souledness and *sobornost'* Arkady had attempted to adopt, proves elusive and even hazardous in its applications. Throughout all of Arkady's attempts to posit an identity, either internally or externally, others continually remind him that all of his deepest thoughts, desires, and emotions are already visible on his "face."[73] Arkady, as we know, fears such spiritual nakedness, and believes that his "ordinary" face represents an obstacle to his dreams of grandeur.[74] Having adopted "seemliness" as his new doctrine, therefore, he becomes fascinated with how to exert control over his self-revelation so as to experience the reduction to incarnation as glory rather than painful crucifixion and powerlessness. Thus, his notion of the bodily revelation of the self takes the highly idiosyncratic form of wanting to find the right way to reveal his concealed "document" without undergoing pain or mockery. He decides, in a moment of spiritual rapture, that he will reveal the document to its author, asking nothing in return, as a noble gesture of self-sacrifice: "I decided, regardless of all temptation, that . . . tomorrow I will lay this letter before her and if necessary instead of gratitude I will take away even a contemptuous smile, but nevertheless I won't say a word, and I'll go away from her forever."[75] Arkady believes that the revelation of the hidden principle, the document, will unite the three visions of selfhood that he has come to embrace, will testify to his infinite mystery, will reveal that mystery in a physical incarnation, and will bind everyone, each through his or her connection to the document, into a harmonious whole: "I wanted," Arkady explains, "to return the document to her, explaining everything once and for all [. . .] I wanted to justify myself once and for all [. . .] I would take them to my place [. . .] reconcile the warring women there, resurrect the prince and . . . and . . . in short, make everyone happy, at least here in this group, today."[76] Arkady's plan, then, is to redeem the world not through his suffering, but through the revelation and sacrifice of his interior identity.

All of Arkady's theories of selfhood, however, disintegrate simultaneously when the "interior principle" is finally revealed. Lambert, it turns out, has stolen the document, and Arkady has been carrying a blank piece of paper stitched into his vest. Arkady's loss of the power of speech, his reduction to a "pale," "powerless," almost "senseless" being, underscores, perhaps even parodies, the utter loss of any form of interior "idea" or indwelling soul:

We took out the letter; the old envelope was the very same, but from it
protruded a blank piece of paper [. . .] But I was already standing there
without language, pale . . . and suddenly in powerlessness I set myself down
on the chair; it's true, I almost lost my senses.[77]

The scene that occurs so quietly in the novel lies at the heart of the novel's
conception of individual identity and of Arkady's adolescent vision of how
it can be protected, guarded, and revealed. Wanting to bring his disparate
ideas of identity together through an act of nobility, Arkady realizes that
he is hardly a master over his own soul. In what was supposed to be the
hour of his glory, the inner principle has all but evaporated, and the body
is revealed to be an empty envelope.

* * *

Dostoevsky returns directly to this image of the discarded placeholder soul
in his next and final novel, where Dmitry Karamazov's principle of self
is deferred not into a "document" but into a secret "amulet" containing
money that is sewn into a small bag inside his clothing, an image even
more in keeping with Arkady's initial "idea" than Akhmakova's letter.[78]
Like Arkady's document, Dmitry's sewn-in secret wealth belongs rightfully
to another person, to whom he is unwillingly bound, and who attempts to
take control of his personality. Dmitry, moreover, thinks of the "amulet"
explicitly as the location of his soul.[79] Only after the placeholder soul
has been discarded, exposed, and even ridiculed, after Dmitry has been
utterly violated and robbed of his mystery, and his naked body has been
exposed, does Dostoevsky begin to depict the opening of a deeper, more
genuine interior space, first in the dream-image of the starving infant,
possibly a form of recollection preserved from Dmitry's infancy, and finally
in Dmitry's obsessive preoccupation with the archetype of an underground
person laboring in the mines, a classical romantic image of the soul.[80] Thus,
his suffering and "torments" at the hands of the investigators constitute
the loss of his own belated adolescence. In *The Adolescent*, Dostoevsky
focuses the novel's entire plot on the problem of positing inner space, and
crafts a vocabulary of images for the dynamics of interior life – concealed
wealth, the hidden document, the whirlwind, the "zero" on the roulette
wheel, transfiguring light, the illumined face – that point to an attempt to
synthesize a more comprehensive concept of selfhood from its seemingly
incompatible, disintegrated parts.

   For those authors searching for a doctrine of the personality at the turn of
the century, *The Adolescent* provides no stable teaching but experimentally
develops three dimensions of the self that must be integrated into a larger

coherent conception. The idea of "seemliness" suggests a possible synthesis of the conceptions of selfhood at war in the novel since the "mirthful" transfigured face becomes illuminated in response to others, and meanwhile is an expression of a deeply indwelling divine principle. In other words, the illuminated body is inherently relational and of infinite depth. As Arkady encounters them, however, the indwelling, social, and embodied dimensions of selfhood are all mutually hostile. Relationships obliterate the possibility of indwelling depth, and the revelation of the body entails humiliation and destruction at the hands of others. In this way, Dostoevsky examines the dangers for the immature personality of embracing any theory of the self. When we finally see the "document" for the first time at the end of the novel, it is lying on Versilov's table, emptied of all value, as the discarded animating principle of Arkady's adolescence: a concise and haunting image of the spiritual emptiness felt with increasing anxiety as the century drew to a close.

NOTES

1 A. N. Afanas'ev, "Tsarevna-liagushka," in *Narodnye russkie skazki A. N. Afanas'eva* (Moscow: Nauka, 1985), II:267.

2 The term "katastrofa lichnosti" is Vasily Rozanov's, quoted in Steinberg, *Petersburg Fin de Siècle*, 151, 156. Steinberg observes that "contemporary journalists spoke readily about the intelligentsia's crisis of the spirit (*krisis dushi*) after 1905" (167).

3 See Steinberg, *Petersburg Fin de Siècle*, 160–165, 168. See also Matich, *Erotic Utopia*, 15.

4 Such was the basic thesis of *Vekhi*, the influential and controversial 1909 collection of essays. As Sergei Bulgakov contends in his essay, "because it lacks a doctrine of the personality [*uchenie o lichnosti*] (or, more precisely, because it has a distorted one), the intelligentsia totally neglects all that concerns the religious cultivation of the personality, that is, its development and discipline." Sergei Bulgakov, "Heroism and Asceticism," in *Vekhi: Landmarks: A Collection of Articles about the Russian Intelligentsia*, translated by Marshall S. Shatz and Judith E. Zimmerman (New York: M. E. Sharpe, 1994), 34, 46.

5 Ibid., 36.

6 F. M. Dostoevskii, *Polnoe sobranie sochinenii i pisem v tridtsati tomakh* (Leningrad: Nauka, 1972–1990), XVI:16–17. All passages are taken from this edition, hereafter referred to as *PSS*; all translations are mine.

7 These three models of selfhood are compatible with Jerold Seigel's description of the "three dimensions" that provide "the basis of selfhood in Western culture": "the bodily or material, the relational, and the reflective dimensions of the self." Jerold Seigel, *The Idea of the Self: Thought and Experience in Western Europe since the Seventeenth Century* (Cambridge University Press, 2005), 5.

8 I quote here from Susanne Fusso's summary of the "many plots" of the "mad-
   deningly chaotic and unreadable novel." See Susanne Fusso, "Dostoevsky's
   Comely Boy: Homoerotic Desire and Aesthetic Strategies in *A Raw Youth*,"
   in *Discovering Sexuality in Dostoevsky* (Evanston, IL: Northwestern University
   Press, 2006), 44, 231.
9 *PSS* XIII:85, XIII:264, and XIII:78, respectively.
10 *PSS* XIII:60.
11 *PSS* XIII:64.
12 *PSS* XIII:66.
13 See, for example, Nicholas Rzhevsky's representative reading in "*The Adolescent*:
   Structure and Ideology," *Slavic and East European Journal* 26:1 (1982): 33.
   Susanne Fusso sees Arkady as having taken on the capitalist idea without
   having understood the "cost in human suffering" associated with material
   acquisition. "The Weight of Human Tears: *The Covetous Knight* and *A Raw
   Youth*," in *Alexander Pushkin's Little Tragedies: The Poetics of Brevity*, edited by
   Svetlana Evdokimova (Madison: University of Wisconsin Press, 2003), 234.
14 See Dostoevsky's notebooks for the novel, especially *PSS* XVI:175.
15 Tatiana Kasatkina emphasizes the "lack of clarity in the 'idea' of the hero
   and . . . the idea's enigmatic evolution." See "Dostoevsky's *Raw Youth*: The
   'Idea' of the Hero and the Idea of the Author," translated by Liv Bliss, *Russian
   Studies in Literature* 40:4 (2004): 41.
16 *PSS* XIII:66.
17 "That which is for me," Marx wrote in 1844, "that for which I can pay
   (i.e., which money can buy) – that am I myself, the possessor of the
   money . . . Money's properties are my – the possessor's – properties and essential powers." Karl Marx, "Economic and Philosophic Manuscripts of 1844,"
   in *Collected Works* (New York: International Publishers, 1975), III:324. In his
   notebook for 1880, Dostoevsky refers to "wealth" as "the intensification of personality," in *Biografiia, pis'ma i zametki iz zapisnoi knizhki F. M. Dostoevskogo*
   (St. Petersburg: Tipografiia A. S. Suvorina, 1883), 356.
18 *PSS* XIII:36.
19 *PSS* XIII:229.
20 *PSS* XIII:48.
21 Svetlana Evdokimova draws on Percy Shelley's observation that "money is the
   visible incarnation" of "the principle of Self" (114) to read the Baron's hoarding
   of money as a twisted spiritual quest. See "The Anatomy of the Modern Self
   in *The Little Tragedies*," in *Alexander Pushkin's Little Tragedies*, 106–143.
22 For a reading of Poprishchin's "displacement" of self, see Robert Maguire,
   "Place Within: 'Diary of a Madman,'" in *Exploring Gogol* (Stanford University
   Press, 1994), 49–66.
23 *PSS* XVI:9.
24 *PSS* I:257.
25 Kasatkina observes the parallel between the "idea" and the "document," though
   for different reasons. "Dostoevsky's *Raw Youth*," 45.

26 Joseph Frank, *Dostoevsky: The Mantle of the Prophet, 1871–1881* (Princeton University Press, 2003), 171. It appears that only Kasatkina has been willing to read the "document" as anything but a defective device. Konstantin Mochulsky claims Dostoevsky "has recourse to a commonplace device . . . for the sake of sustaining 'interest.'" See *Dostoevsky: His Life and Work*, translated by M. A. Minihan (Princeton University Press, 1967), 509. Nathan Rosen comments that "neither the letter nor the crude melodrama is believable," but that both are necessary for the plot to function. "Breaking Out of the Underground: The 'Failure' of 'A Raw Youth,'" *Modern Fiction Studies* 4:3 (1958): 225–239, 234. See also Gary Cox, *Tyrant and Victim in Dostoevsky* (Bloomington, IN: Slavica, 1984), 19.

27 *PSS* XIII:16, 63. Brian Egdorf connects Arkady's insistence on his own "unfinalizability" with Bakhtin's description of self-consciousness. See "Fyodor Dostoevsky's *The Adolescent* and the Architectonics of Author and Hero," *The Dostoevsky Journal: An Independent Review* 12–13 (2011–2012), especially 23–25.

28 *PSS* XIII:89–90.

29 *PSS* XIII:273–274.

30 *PSS* XIII:50.

31 *PSS* XIII:152.

32 *PSS* XIII:98.

33 *PSS* XIII:104.

34 Mikhail Bakhtin, *Problems of Dostoevsky's Poetics*, edited and translated by Caryl Emerson (Minneapolis: University of Minnesota Press, 1984), 252.

35 M. M. Bakhtin, "Author and Hero in Aesthetic Activity," translated by Vadim Liapunov and Kenneth Brostrom, in *Art and Answerability: Early Philosophical Essays by M. M. Bakhtin*, edited by Michael Holquist and Vadim Liapunov (Austin: University of Texas Press Slavic Series, 1990), 101. See Emerson's description of this process in *The First Hundred Years of Mikhail Bakhtin* (Princeton University Press, 2000), 214. In Gerald Pirog's words: "It is in this sense that we can speak of our absolute aesthetic need for the other, who alone can create my completed personality." See "Bakhtin and Freud on the Ego," in *Russian Literature and Psychoanalysis*, edited by Daniel Rancour-Laferriere (Philadelphia: John Benjamins Publishing Company, 1989), 407–408.

36 Nikolai Berdiaev, *Mirosozertsanie Dostoevskogo* (Prague: YMCA Press, 1923), 42.

37 Mochulsky, *Dostoevsky*, 299–300. For the novel as allegory, see also Lina Steiner who interprets Arkady's development as an allegory for Russia's own maturation as a nation. *For Humanity's Sake: The Bildungsroman in Russian Culture* (University of Toronto Press, 2011), 135–173. For a discussion of *sobornost'* more broadly, see Alexander Burry and S. Ceilidh Orr's chapter in the present volume.

38 Mochulsky, *Dostoevsky*, 506.

39 Ibid., 514.

40 Ibid., 511.

41 For an authoritative look at some of the most persuasive challenges mounted against Bakhtin's theory of polyphony and dialogue with regard to Dostoevsky, see Emerson, *The First Hundred Years*, especially 130–149.

42 *PSS* XIII:163.

43 *PSS* XIII:387, 373.

44 *PSS* XIII:373.

45 *PSS* XIII:338.

46 *PSS* XIII:297.

47 *PSS* XIII:242.

48 *PSS* XIII:164.

49 *PSS* XIII:398.

50 *PSS* XIII:140.

51 Bakhtin, *Problems*, 252.

52 *PSS* V:281

53 *PSS* V:314.

54 *PSS* V:311.

55 *PSS* V:283.

56 *PSS* XIII:338.

57 *PSS* XIII:164.

58 *PSS* XIII:323.

59 *PSS* XIII:355–360.

60 *PSS* XIII:263–264.

61 Alexey Khomiakov, "Letter to the Editor of *L'Union Chrétienne*, on the Occasion of a Discourse by Father Gagarin, Jesuit," in *On Spiritual Unity: A Slavophile Reader*, edited by Boris Jakim and Robert Bird (Hudson, NY: Lindisfarne Books, 1998), 139. Bakhtin, *Problems*, 176, 26.

62 *PSS* XIII:267.

63 *PSS* XIII:264.

64 *PSS* XIII:63.

65 For a reading of Makar's teachings that inspire Arkady's concept of "seemliness" as a refutation of Arkady's "idea" in an even more direct sense, see Liza Knapp, *The Annihilation of Inertia: Dostoevsky and Metaphysics* (Evanston, IL: Northwestern University Press, 1996), 159–160.

66 For an in-depth examination of Dostoevsky's "quest to uncover the meaning and the moral profile of a specific human face," see Konstantin Barsht, "Defining the Face: Observations on Dostoevskii's Creative Process," in *Russian Literature, Modernism and the Visual Arts*, edited by Catriona Kelly and Stephen Lovell (Cambridge University Press, 2000), especially 23–37.

67 Pavel Florensky, "Spiritual Sobriety and the Iconic Face," in *Iconostasis*, translated by Donald Sheehan and Olga Andrejev (Crestwood, NY: St. Vladimir's Seminary Press, 1996), 52–56. On the hesychastic belief that the human being becomes divinized by "receiving the radiance of uncreated light," see Georgios Mantzaridis, *The Deification of Man: St. Gregory Palamas and the Orthodox Tradition*, translated by L. Sherrard (Crestwood, NY: St. Vladimir's Seminary

Press, 1984), especially 96–104. See also Knapp's reading of Palamas in terms of the light imagery in *The Adolescent, Annihilation*, 164–165.
68 Florensky, "Spiritual Sobriety," 54–55.
69 *PSS* XIII:370.
70 *PSS* XIII:48.
71 *PSS* XIII:283, 291.
72 *PSS* XIII:285–286, 285.
73 *PSS* XIII:89–90, 91, 111, 367, 371.
74 *PSS* XIII:74.
75 *PSS* XIII:438.
76 *PSS* XIII:428.
77 *PSS* XIII:439.
78 For Arkady as Dmitry Karamazov's prototype, see Rosen, "Breaking Out of the Underground," 238.
79 Dmitry, who has literally ripped his amulet in two halves, describes his "soul" using the same imagery: "Have mercy, gentlemen, I have torn my soul into two halves before you, and you . . . are digging around in the torn place on both sides" (*PSS* XIV:446). Critics have often noted this conflation of amulet and soul, though attributing the symbolism to Dostoevsky the author rather than to Dmitry the character. See, for example, Richard Peace, *Dostoevsky: An Examination of the Major Novels* (Cambridge University Press, 1971), 234.
80 See Theodore Ziolkowski, "The Mine: The Image of the Soul," in *German Romanticism and its Institutions* (Princeton University Press, 1990), 18–63.

CHAPTER 3

A childhood's garden of despair
Dostoevsky and "A Boy at Christ's Christmas Party"

Robin Feuer Miller

And it is but a child of air
That lingers in the garden there.
                    – Robert Louis Stevenson, "To Any Reader"

It is a truism that periods of artistic expression – whether the gothic, fantastic, romanticism, realism, or fin-de-siècle reactions to such movements – bleed into one another. More compelling is the consideration of realist elements within the boundaries of the gothic, or the fantastic components of realism, or aspects of the fairy tale lurking within the sober meditations of a reform-minded *feuilletonist*. This blending of genres is particularly evident in Dostoevsky's works; he created generic hybrids in everything he wrote, regardless of historical period. This chapter considers Dostoevsky's little story, "A Boy at Christ's Christmas Party" (1876), against this fluid backdrop, examining the work in the context of the popular nineteenth-century children's literature genres it mixes: the Christmas story and the fairy tale. "A Boy" occupies an important place in Dostoevsky's canon, in particular in relationship to his first work of published fiction, *Poor People* (1846), and to his last, *Brothers Karamazov* (1880).

Despite these intimate links with forms and work of the past, in its depiction of childhood, "A Boy" exhibits a troubled worldview that seems consonant with what we think of as a chronologically future period, the fin de siècle. The concept of childhood is a relatively recent phenomenon, coming most insistently to the fore during the nineteenth century.[1] We think of childhood as a time of beginnings, unfettered creative impulses, frequent border crossings between reality and imagination. Yet from the 1850s on, the children and adolescents of Russian fiction inhabited a world where the family and the home were imperiled. As social and familial disintegration spread in society, so too did it spread in fiction, as chapters in the present volume by Kate Holland, Emma Lieber, Connor Doak, and Katherine Bowers attest. The troubled fictional youths in works by authors such as Turgenev, Dostoevsky, Tolstoy, and Chekhov display darker characteristics more often associated with fin-de-siècle pessimism than with the rosier Rousseauian, romantic or sentimental, Victorian notions of childhood prevalent in Europe during the nineteenth century.

Ironically, in Europe the "celebratory attitude to childhood came to prominence in the mid-years of the century, the very moment when fin-de-siècle parents were entering the world."[2] Still more ironically, at mid-century many Russian realists and their fictional children already suffered from fin-de-siècle malaises such as cynicism, boredom, and gloom. Indeed, fin-de-siècle characteristics such as unrelieved foreboding, despair, and exhaustion seem to appear earlier in the experiences of these fictional Russian children than in their European counterparts. The narrator of Turgenev's *First Love* (1860), for example, becomes prey to a lifelong gloom stemming from his youthful infatuation and related dangerous rivalry with his father; the incident infects his whole life, as Lieber describes. Tolstoy's fictional children – whether in the early trilogy *Childhood, Boyhood*, and *Youth* (1852, 1854, 1856), or in later works such as *War and Peace* (1869), *Anna Karenina* (1877), or *The Death of Ivan Ilych* (1886) – experience profound moral doubt, dark imaginings, and the feeling of being surrounded by inauthenticity. None of these elements is neatly resolved. Chekhov's early stories reverberate with depictions of children that display an intense fin-de-siècle atmosphere of foreboding avant la lettre. Such stories as "Oysters" (1884), "Vanka" (1886), "Sleepy" (1888), and even "At Home" (1887) portray childhood as being as deeply fraught as adulthood; Chekhov's child characters are burdened with suffering, a capacity for violence, and moral quandary. These children are not Victorian innocents whose angelic minds are tabula rasa to be marked by experience. They exist precariously in the real world, and, like the adults who often mistreat them, are capable of great good and great evil. They are deeply impressionable – as subject to the effects of dreams and stories as to real events. These darker fin-de-siècle elements of childhood come to the fore in "A Boy at Christ's Christmas Party," one of Dostoevsky's briefest stories – little more than a sketch about a destitute, confused child abroad on the city streets.

Dostoevsky's fictions abound with fully formed, remarkable children; the children who populate his works are worthy of interest singly and collectively and have already been the subject of critical attention. Doak and Corrigan's chapters in the present volume discuss the corruption or disintegration of childhood in *Demons* and *The Adolescent*, but even in Dostoevsky's minor works, children's experiences carry important social and psychological markers. "A Boy at Christ's Christmas Party" presents a fascinating study of childhood at the intersection of conflicting genres. On the one hand, the little, ostensibly realist story is striking for the intensity of the darker fin-de-siècle atmosphere it radiates. Yet, like Chekhov's "Vanka," it is also a "Christmas Story," a genre Dickens made popular – typically characterized by its sentimental affirmation of an array of notions that run contrary to fin-de-siècle gloom and pessimism.

It is surprising to find a collision within "A Boy" between the affirmative tradition and structure of the typical Christmas story and its profoundly unsettling atmosphere of malaise and despair that transcends any message of seasonal good cheer. Why is it surprising? Given Dostoevsky's Christian faith and his ability to write sentimental, heartrending prose, one would imagine that the affirmative message offered by Christ taking a dead child to His Christmas party in heaven might outweigh the effect of society's indifference to the child's suffering and poverty. Yet divine justice, in this little sketch, does not negate or counterbalance the fact of suffering on earth. In *Brothers Karamazov*, a miracle occurs because a brotherhood is founded precisely on the edifice of Ilyusha's unjustified suffering: the boys who threw stones at him – the bullies – are forgiven and become the founding members of Alyosha's glorious brotherhood even though they each, individually and collectively, will probably go on to lives of sin and error. The situation in "A Boy" contains no such earthly resolution despite its Christmas setting.

The archetypal Christmas story is Dickens's *A Christmas Carol* (1843). Like other social novelists in Europe and Russia in the early and mid-nineteenth century, Dickens addressed social issues such as poverty, poor working conditions, and moral indifference to the sufferings of others.[3] This work, like some others within the Christmas story's broad tradition, displays some qualities of a fairy tale but is also a conversion narrative whose main character either made an otherworldly journey to his past or may have only dreamed it. Despite numerous dark themes, including the suffering and illness of a poor child, the story has a cheerful conclusion: Scrooge is reformed, rediscovering tenderness of heart and generosity of spirit; the ailing Tiny Tim does not die.[4] This happy ending relieves readers, even though they know that such a resolution would likely not exist in the real world, and becomes a key convention of the Christmas story genre. "A Boy" resonates in counterpoint to this tradition, both partaking of and overturning it.

"A Boy" also draws powerfully on the nineteenth-century genre of the fairy tale, in particular "The Star Coins" and "The Little Match Girl." Although fairy tales may coalesce at times with the Christmas story and possess, as does "The Little Match Girl," certain of its elements, they were far more widespread and connected to oral traditions than the Christmas story. Christmas stories frequently expressed overt social commentary and, most often, their ultimate location was within the real world. Within fairy tales, in contrast, the laws of the marvelous clearly supersede the real; there is none of the generic hesitation or tension characteristic of the fantastic. Fairy tales, especially those of the Grimm brothers, Hans Christian Andersen, and Alexander Afanas'ev, as well as Charles Perrault, Jeanne-Marie Leprince de Beaumont, and Giovanni Francesco Straparola – immensely popular throughout the nineteenth century – suggest, along with earlier folktale versions of them, the evolving constructions of childhood.[5]

What are the resonances between Dostoevsky's story and the overlapping traditions of the Christmas story and fairy tale? Are the ways in which it seems to transcend or critique these established genres important? Does "A Boy" have anything significant to tell us about childhood in Russia toward the end of the century?

"A Boy," though only four pages long, opens and closes with the kind of complex narrative affirmation and disclaimer typical of virtually all Dostoevsky's first-person narratives.

> But I am a novelist and one "story," it seems, I made up myself. Why do I say "it seems" when I know very well that I made it up? Yet I keep imagining that it really happened somewhere, sometime, and happened precisely on Christmas Eve in a *certain* huge city during a terrible cold spell:
>
> I dreamed there was a boy . . . [6]

The narrator, "Dostoevsky," knows he has invented his narrative, but cannot escape his intuition that the events actually happened. At the end, the story revisits this tension between the truth of the event's occurrence and the act of storytelling:

> So why did I make up a story like that, so little in keeping with the usual spirit of a sober-minded diary, and a writer's diary at that? All the more since I promised stories preeminently about actual events! But that's just the point: I keep imagining that all this could really have happened – I mean the things that happened in the cellar and behind the woodpile; as for Christ's Christmas party – well, I really don't know what to say: could that have happened? That's just why I'm a novelist – to invent things. (17; 314)

Like the other fictional narratives in *The Diary of a Writer* (1873–1881), this story explores boundaries and reciprocities between the fantastic and the real, between memory and invention, between unfettered artistic invention and telling a story to illustrate a particular point. Dostoevsky, the diarist, who promises accounts of actual events, is eclipsed, repeatedly and deliberately, by Dostoevsky the novelist, although he claims, as did Tolstoy, a higher truth for these "invented things." The story occurs in spaces familiar to Dostoevsky's readers – the street, the confined interior of the dark cellar, or the crawlspace behind a woodpile – locales all too familiar in Dostoevsky's fiction as places for despair, rebellion, and death.

In addition to this narrative frame, "A Boy" is framed within *The Diary* more broadly. There are three entries for the second January chapter: Parts I ("The Boy with His Hand Out") and III ("A Colony of Young Offenders. Dark Individuals. The Transformation of Blemished Souls into Immaculate Ones. Measures Acknowledged as Most Expedient Thereto. Little and Bold Friends of Mankind") offer contextual, journalistic frames for the story, which appears in Part II. Part I opens with Dostoevsky reporting that he dreams of children, seeing them in his fancies. Significantly, he separates "dream" from "fancy" ("*oni sniatsia i mereshchatsia*," 13; 309), for the former references autobiography and actual dreams, the latter artistic invention. This same tension occurs elsewhere in *The Diary*. Here, it transpires that Dostoevsky had encountered an actual boy whom, he *imagined*, was newly a beggar. Yet this first entry, despite its touching description of the still-innocent child's appeal, allows Dostoevsky, more importantly, an occasion to meditate upon the exploitation and abuse of such children; after having been sent to beg, they return to their cellars: "Vodka, filth and depravity, but vodka above all . . . Sometimes, for the fun of it, they pour half a bottle into his mouth and roar with laughter when, his breath catching, he falls to the floor scarcely conscious" (13–14; 309).

Dostoevsky does not, as Dickens might, sentimentalize the plight of such children. He instead reports, "These children become fully-fledged criminals . . . It is only natural that they become thieves. Thievery becomes a passion even among eight-year-olds" (14; 310). Yet these eight-year-olds are miniature replicas of Dostoevsky's more fully developed heroes who thirst for freedom and are attracted to the notion that "everything is permitted." He writes, "In the end they bear it all – hunger, cold, beatings – only for one thing, for freedom . . . A wild creature such as this sometimes knows nothing at all – neither where he lives, nor what nation he comes from; whether God exists or the tsar" (14; 310). Is it such a child that Christ takes into his arms in the story that follows?

In Part III Dostoevsky visits the children's penal colony in the forest outside St. Petersburg. Troubled that many of the children – not the youngest – are bed-wetters, he muses about where they come from – what situations could exist, in which people would not teach a child how "to behave in such a case." Astounded by such bestial indifference, he imagines what sort of people these children would have encountered: "Please don't laugh at my inflating this nasty little detail to such dimensions... It indicates... that there are individuals so dark and dreadful that every trace of their humanity... has disappeared" (18; 316). He wonders at the "tiny, savage souls" who have been "forsaken by the human community." Struck by the fact that these children like to be read to – that there are some good readers among them – he laments that Russian literature has nothing to offer them.[7] He indirectly questions the Director about the prevalence of masturbation among the children.[8] He closes Part III by reporting an acquaintance's recent remark, "Heroes – that's what you novelists are looking for. And when you can't find any heroes among us Russians, you start to grumble at the whole country. Let me tell you a little story: once upon a time, a good while ago now... " (25; 324). Then follows an account of a government official so horrified by serfdom that he began to save money from his meager salary to purchase "some serf's freedom." During his life, with painstaking sacrifice, the official managed to raise sufficient funds to free four serfs. Dostoevsky thus closes the triptych with a parable about the powerful efficacy of personal charity, even when it seems futile. All these themes resurface in *Brothers Karamazov*.

To return to the story at the triptych's center, "A Boy" reflects the process and result of Dostoevsky's rendering his journalistic musings into fiction. The child wakes up in the kind of cellar described in Part I. But this child becomes an individual character within a single sentence when, freezing and hungry, he sees white vapor emerging from his mouth and tries to amuse himself by watching it billow. His mother lies dead next to him, but he does not know what her cold body signifies; his fear is of the big dog that might be out on the stairwell. These details immediately render him a fully formed character. His journey across the city, despite distress, cold, and exhausting hunger, also brings him to life as a real child. Dostoevsky knew children well and could breathe life into his child characters simply through passing details.

By the third paragraph, the narrative seamlessly switches from the narrator's descriptions into the mind of the boy himself. The third-person "he" is retained, but the sentences acquire the quality of interior monologue. Dostoevsky forges a hybrid narration which, though third person, moves in and out of his character's mind as though it were first person: "Here's another street – look how wide it is! I'll get run over here for sure. See how everyone's shouting and rushing and driving along, and the lights – just look at them!" (15; 311). Thus both narrative and genre in these four pages exist in hybrid form. Just as the boundaries between third and first person merge in the narration, genre remains unclear: is one reading a tale of dark social realism, a Christmas story that verges on parable, or a fairy tale?

The child, recently arrived from the country, sees the city with fresh eyes. Chekhov may well have read this story as aspects of "Oysters," "Sleepy," and "Vanka," two of them also Christmas stories, echo these pages. These include the image of the child about to beg for the first time, the country memories of the child newly arrived in the city, the cruelty of adults whom the child should be able to turn to and still loves, depictions of drunkenness and hunger – "Oh Lord, I'm so hungry, even just a little bite of something" – and above all, the child's active, creative mind that retains, amidst this suffering, the capacity for wonder and ability to appreciate beauty.[9]

In the child's company, the reader seemingly enters the world of the Christmas story: the boy looks through a big window and sees a "Christmas tree, with oh, so many lights on it" (15; 311–312). He gazes upon toys and happy children, even hearing music through the windowpane. When the unbearable cold encroaches he bursts into tears and runs off. He wanders into a café where he is quickly pushed back into the street. He keeps running, his heart aching from fear and loneliness. He joins a crowd gazing through yet a third window and sees three puppets. Upon realizing they are not actually alive, he bursts out laughing. Just then, an older boy strikes him on the head, stealing his cap. The terrified child dashes into a courtyard to crouch behind a woodpile. Cowering there, he hears his mother's voice singing to him. Calmed, he says, "Mamma, I'm going to sleep; oh, how nice it is to sleep here" (16; 313). As he drifts into sleep, a soft voice invites him to a Christmas party. Someone bends over, hugs him in the darkness, and lifts him in an embrace. Like the Ridiculous Man, the boy journeys to another world, although he is not to return. He sees a Christmas tree and a group of radiant children flying around him. He wants to tell them about the puppets. He learns that they are all dead.

At this moment of release for the boy, Dostoevsky, through the mouths of the dead children, imparts his message:

> he learned that all ... were children just like him, but some had frozen to death in the baskets in which they had been abandoned on door-steps; others had perished in the keeping of indifferent nurses in orphans' homes, still others had died at the dried-up breasts of their mothers during the Samara famine, and yet others had suffocated from the fumes in third-class railway carriages. (16; 313)

Christ blesses them and their "sinful mothers . . . stand apart, weeping; each one recognizes her son or daughter." The children fly to these mothers and forgive them. The vignette starkly foreshadows *Brothers Karamazov* in its depiction of a group of children bullying a lone child, mothers who neglect their children, and the suffering child who forgives.

It is no surprise that the moment of warm sleep is the moment of the boy's death. Moreover, it is perhaps a sentimental, expected Christmas trope that Christ would appear to bring him to heaven.[10] What is unusual is the detailed emphasis on the physical embrace of Christ, the parents' guilt and the spontaneity of the children who forgive them. How to find a resolution to this theme of parents' mistreatment and neglect of children always haunted Dostoevsky. "A Boy" offers a forceful rendering of the question forever unresolved in Dostoevsky's mind: the first version reads, "the next morning, the porters found the tiny body of the runaway boy who had frozen to death behind the woodpile; they found his mother as well . . . She had died even before him." The later version adds a sentence at the end of this passage: "they met in God's Heaven" (16; 314).[11] The earlier version leaves this heavenly meeting in doubt, thus carrying a darker message, which Dostoevsky then sought to soften; an anecdote that could have been narrated by Ivan becomes one that Alyosha might tell instead.

Even though Dostoevsky imagined the story's events had really occurred and the boy at its center resembles the beggar-child he encountered, "A Boy" has multiple other sources. The four-page story reaffirms what critics have repeatedly found in Dostoevsky's fiction – multiple sources drawn from newspapers, autobiographical encounters, other works of fiction, and Dostoevsky's own earlier work. G. M. Fridlender, for example, identified one source in German poet and songwriter Friedrich Rückert's ballad "The Homeless Child of the Holy Christ" (1816).[12] The similarities are remarkable: a child runs through the streets on Christmas Eve. He gazes through various windows; through one he sees a Christmas tree. He feels forgotten "in a strange land." He prays to Christ; his hands are frozen; he sees a light; it is another child, dressed in white and holding a candle. "I – am Christ," he tells the freezing child, "and I was once a child, like you." Christ brings the child to heaven to an awaiting Christmas tree and other children. The basic plotlines are nearly identical, but the ballad is pious and sentimental; it has no fin-de-siècle aura of dark doubt, despite its depiction of a suffering child. The child's dire earthly situation is eclipsed by his journey with Christ toward heaven.

"A Boy," however, bears even more striking resemblance to Andersen's popular fairy tale "The Little Match Girl" (1845–1848). Echoing Bruno Bettelheim, Maria Tatar identifies fairy tales "as instruments of socialization and acculturation precisely because they capture and preserve disruptive moments of conflict and chart their resolution."[13] Such tales reflected high mortality rates for children as well as the parental worry that children might die without grace. As late as 1900 when Freud published *The Interpretation of Dreams*, he noted that half of the human race failed to survive the childhood years. Indeed, Tatar maintains that "misery and suffering are nowhere more brilliantly apotheosized than in the tales of Hans Christian Andersen."[14]

"The Little Match Girl" had two primary sources: a popular woodcut depicting a child selling matches that appeared on a calendar by Danish artist Johan Thomas Lundbye, and a well-known fairy tale, really more of a folk tale, "The Star Coins" (sometimes translated as "The Star Money" or "The Star Talers"). Several almanac editors had written Andersen requesting him to write a story based on one of their pictures or calendars; Andersen quickly responded to Lundbye's 1843 woodcut with "The Little Match Girl."[15] "The Star Coins" was transcribed by the Grimm brothers in 1812, even before Rückert's 1816 ballad.[16] This is the story of a poor orphan girl, "forsaken by all the world," who wanders forth trusting in God, like a kind of child *iurodivaia*. She encounters an old man and four poor children, one after another, giving everything away until she wanders naked. "Suddenly some stars from heaven fell down," and she finds her reward. Yet she does not encounter divine justice, or Christ, nor, as in the archetypal Christmas story of the three Magi, does a star lead her to the child Jesus. Hers is an earthly reward: the heavens rain down coins and fine linen, and she becomes "rich all the days of her life."

Andersen adapts this odd tale into a powerful fairy tale that is also a Christmas or New Year's story bearing marked resemblances to Dostoevsky's – resemblances strong enough to allow speculation that Dostoevsky read the story.[17] Such works as those by Rückert, the Grimms, and Andersen were told and read to children throughout the nineteenth century, potent reminders that these stories and tales tended to be transcriptions and adaptations of each other and are close to the folktale tradition, even when published as original works.

Yet "The Little Match Girl" exerts more than a passing claim to our attention when reading Dostoevsky's story. Not only is it a holiday story – a hybrid Christmas story and fairy tale – about a poor child abroad in the city on a cold night, but its narrative structure, emphasis upon the child's gaze, her suffering, and the eventual transcendence of that suffering all foreshadow Dostoevsky's story with almost uncanny force. The fictive worlds of Dostoevsky and Andersen are darker than anything the Grimm brothers render in their tales, however frightening those tales may be. Tatar's appraisal of Andersen holds partly true for Dostoevsky: "While the Grimms may boil stepmothers in oil or send them down hills in barrels studded with nails, they rarely allow children to endure torture. Andersen, by contrast, promotes what many readers might perceive as a cult of suffering, death, and transcendence for children."[18] The crucial difference between Andersen and Dostoevsky, however, is that Dostoevsky does not cap off a child's suffering with easy religious pieties; moreover, despite depictions of the suffering, and even the suicide of children, he strenuously and consistently avoids promoting "a cult of suffering." Suffering is not necessarily purifying; it can degrade human beings as powerfully as it can, on occasion, ennoble them.[19] Those injustices perpetrated on children always remain unresolved, and the horror of such suffering is, as Dostoevsky's entire oeuvre affirms, irrefutable.

"The Little Match Girl" takes place on New Year's Eve. Its heroine is a poor girl who sells matches on the street. She is barefoot, one shoe lost and the other stolen by a taunting bully, another child. Both Dostoevsky and Andersen are keenly aware of the capability of children for cruelty and theft. Like the boy in Dostoevsky's story, the girl, despite her hunger and cold, is distracted by the beautiful lights shining in the windows. Like him, her imagination stirs. She dares not go home for fear of being beaten by her father. She crouches in a confined space for warmth – not behind a woodpile but "over in a little corner between two houses... there she crouched and huddled with her legs tucked under her."[20]

Unlike Dostoevsky's boy, she does not gaze into three windows; her visions – her creative gaze – are purely imaginary, inspired by three matches she strikes in succession, and not, like those of the boy and Dostoevsky's art as well, an amalgam of the real, the remembered, and the imagined. The first match gives a curious light; she "fancied she was sitting in front of an... iron stove... with such a warm friendly fire burning."[21] It is a scene of domestic coziness not unlike what the boy sees when gazing through the first window. Upon striking the second match, the girl could see a "table... laid with a glittering white cloth... and there, steaming deliciously, was the roast goose stuffed with prunes and apples. Then, what was even finer, the goose jumped off the dish and waddled along the floor with the carving knife and fork in its back." Like Dostoevsky's boy gazing at the café, Andersen's girl has a warm, friendly vision of food in this second imagining. Chekhov's "Oysters" also comes to mind: true hunger – starvation – means being willing to eat a living oyster reproaching you with its froglike eyes or even a waddling goose with a knife and fork in its back. The third match reveals a Christmas tree, burning with hundreds of candles, which becomes a ladder to the stars – "the Christmas candles rose higher and higher, until now she could see they were shining stars. One of them rushed down the sky with a long fiery streak. 'That's somebody dying,' said the girl, for her dead Grannie, who was the only one who had been kind to her, had told her that a falling star shows that a soul is going up to God."[22]

Thus she passes from life into death as seamlessly and as unaware as Dostoevsky's boy. It is not Christ but her dear Grannie who, becoming tall and beautiful, "took the little girl into her arms, and together they flew in joy and splendour, up, up, to where there was no cold, no hunger, nor fear. They were with God."[23] As with the boy nestled in Christ's arms, Grannie's loving, physical embrace of the child during the flight to heaven offers intense comfort at the moment of death.

After gazing through the three windows, Dostoevsky's boy freezes behind the woodpile and is carried, in the loving arms of Christ, to heaven with its waiting Christmas tree. The little match girl, instead, meets her dear old grandmother. She begs to be reunited with her: "Oh Grannie . . . do take me with you! I know you'll disappear as soon as the match goes out – just as the warm stove did, and the lovely roast goose, and the wonderful great Christmas tree." She then lights all her matches at once, and Grannie, as we have seen, takes the child into her arms for their flight heavenward. Both stories then lurch back to earth. Like Dostoevsky's boy, the match girl's frozen body is found. "'She was trying to get warm,' people said."[24] In each tale, the living carry on, unaware of and largely indifferent to the intimate, religious vision experienced by the dying child. The boundary between life and death in these final moments is unclear.

Despite the strong resonance between "A Boy" and "The Little Match Girl," the two works exist in separate contexts. Parents still read Andersen's tale to their children at holiday time. Tatar reports that "[h]ardly a year goes by without a new American edition, in large format, with lavish illustrations, clearly intended to appeal to children and often issued in the holiday season."[25] Dostoevsky's story, on the other hand, despite its strong connections to the inter-related genres of the Christmas story and the fairy tale, remains firmly rooted within the tradition of the socially minded feuilleton. Dostoevsky injects sharp social criticism at the end, whereas Andersen's narrator calmly observes, "Nobody knew what lovely things she had seen and in what glory she had gone with her old Grannie to the happiness of the New Year."[26] Andersen, like Dickens, lets his readers off the hook. Dostoevsky's short story, like all his other fiction, cuts both ways; those left on earth experience no comfortable reprieve.

One final source for "A Boy" is Dostoevsky's first novel, *Poor People*, which Dostoevsky was perhaps also revisiting while writing this story in the last years of his life. In *The Diary* Dostoevsky recounts the well-known anecdote of his literary discovery by Nekrasov and Belinsky; like Yeats in "The Circus Animals' Desertion," he uses *The Diary* to revisit many of his old themes.[27] Toward the end of *Poor People*, in a letter to Varvara, Devushkin describes an encounter with a child that offers a haunting prequel to "A Boy." Devushkin turns onto busy Gorokhovaia Street on a "sad, dark evening" and is affected by familiar elements – the noise, the glittering shops, the bakeries, "the windows that are as glossy as mirrors." He imagines catching a glimpse through a window of a newly rich, plump, and rosy-cheeked Varvara.

Devushkin describes stopping to look at a hurdy-gurdy man. Among the other spectators (cabbies, a prostitute, a grimy little girl), he sees a street urchin, "dressed in a shirt and not much else, and he stood there practically barefoot, listening to the music open-mouthed – like the child he was!"[28] Like our boy, this child stares in wonderment at the dancing puppets, although "his own arms and legs were stiff with cold." He approaches the destitute Devushkin to beg: "his little hands trembling . . . his little voice quavering."[29] Devushkin pities the child, but does not give him anything: "what did I have to give?" But as in Dostoevsky's story thirty years later, Devushkin turns his anger upon the mothers: "What's bad is that these scurvy mothers don't look after their children and go sending them out . . . in cold weather like this."[30] Moreover, the experience of such begging, as in *The Diary*, is not sentimentalized; it is corrupting:

> What does the poor boy learn? . . . His heart merely grows hardened . . . His child's heart grows hardened, and the poor frightened boy shivers . . . like a little bird that has fallen out of a broken nest. His arms and legs are frozen; he gasps for breath . . . it is not long before illness, like some unclean reptile, creeps into his breast, and when you look again, death is already standing over him in some stinking corner somewhere, and there is no way out, no help at hand.[31]

He recounts to Varvara the agony of hearing words like "For the love of Christ" and merely replying "God will provide" as he "walk[s] on."[32] "A Boy" lurks here in embryo to be recalled three decades later, when, as Dostoevsky affirms in his meditation upon memory and invention in "The Peasant Marei," the time for such a memory is ripe.[33] But Devushkin, with

an irresistible, unavoidable "sideward glance" at himself as writer, as one
interested, like Dostoevsky, in the process of spinning a narrative from
experience, confesses to Varvara, "To tell you the truth, my dear, I began
describing all this to you partly in order to unburden my heart, but more
particularly in order to provide you with an example of the good style of
my literary compositions."[34]

In attempting to understand and gauge the fin-de-siècle quality of Dostoevsky's depictions of children, one inevitably follows threads into the
past, whether of the Bible, folk and fairy tales, other literary works, or
of Dostoevsky's own past life and work. Even a short story like "A Boy
at Christ's Christmas Party" brims with such fragments. They aid in the
depiction of the gloom of real life that troubled Dostoevsky in "A Boy,"
simultaneously evoking and predicting a malaise more typical of the end
of the nineteenth century. His family having disintegrated into dust, Dostoevsky's destitute child runs about the streets. He is without home or
education, and the larger human family does not help him; he is "forsaken
by the human community." Had he lived, he would have been too young
to retain memories of family or home life, or any knowledge of his heritage.
Yet the human spark – the capacity for wonder, for imagination – remained
with him until the end.

"A Boy" exudes a terrible anxiety and dejection closely bound to the
approaching fin-de-siècle spirit. Yet the 1876 sketch also demonstrates how
the fin de siècle was an organic product of the *début de siècle*; the end of
the century reflects its beginning just as Dostoevsky's late works shimmer
with reverberations from his earliest ones. But however keenly Dostoevsky
personally felt the anxiety and despair so typical of the fin de siècle, we
see throughout his fiction and particularly lucidly, perhaps, within the
brief sketch "A Boy," how he was able to depict equally powerfully the
ramifications of his fervent belief in transcendence and the multitudinous
capacities of the human spirit.

NOTES

1 Holly Furneaux, "Childhood," in *Dickens in Context*, edited by Sally Ledger
and Holly Furneaux (Cambridge University Press, 2011), 187, who cites Philippe
Ariès, *Centuries of Childhood*, published in English translation in 1962.
2 Kimberley Reynolds, *Children's Literature in the 1890s and the 1990s* (Plymouth,
Eng.: Northcote House, 1994), 2–3.
3 See Furneaux, "Childhood." Dickens's "happiest children usually reside at the
heart of determinedly defamiliarised domestic units" (191). Such may be true
of Dostoevsky's children, though it is difficult to locate a single happy one. He

came to emphasize the negative and the occasional positive role of a variety of "accidental families," as opposed to biological ones. See also Jennifer Sattaur, *Perceptions of Childhood in the Victorian Fin de Siècle* (Cambridge Scholars Publishing, 2011).

4 Dostoevsky's "Dream of a Ridiculous Man" embodies qualities of the Dickens story. See "Unsealing the Generic Envelope and Deciphering 'The Dream of a Ridiculous Man,'" in Robin Feuer Miller, *Dostoevsky's Unfinished Journey* (New Haven, CT: Yale University Press, 2007), 105–128.

5 On fairy tales and evolving notions of childhood see Maria Tatar, *The Classic Fairy Tales* (New York: W. W. Norton, 1999), hereafter abbreviated *CFT*. Tatar includes a selection of tales as well as critical essays.

6 F. M. Dostoevskii, *Polnoe sobranie sochinenii i pisem v tridtsati tomakh* (Leningrad: Nauka, 1972–1990), XXII:14, hereafter referred to as *PSS*; Fyodor Dostoevsky, *A Writer's Diary*, translated by Kenneth Lantz (Evanston, IL: Northwestern University Press, 2009), 1:310. Subsequent references appear in parentheses in the text with Russian preceding English.

7 These passing observations on the inadequacy of Russian literature to offer anything to such children perhaps show a change in his views on literacy and reading from the articles he wrote on this subject in the 1860s.

8 Masturbation surfaces elsewhere in Dostoevsky's fiction, particularly in *Demons* (see Doak's chapter in the present volume) and in his account of the Kroneberg (Dostoevsky's spelling for Kronenberg) trial, one of the most complex, important parts of *The Diary*. For outstanding work on this subject see Susanne Fusso, "The 'Secret Vice' of Mariia Kroneberg," in *Discovering Sexuality in Dostoevsky*, 80–101; Gary Rosenshield's *Western Law, Russian Justice: Dostoevsky, the Jury Trial and the Law* (Madison: University of Wisconsin Press, 2005); Harriet Murav, *Russia's Legal Fictions* (Ann Arbor: University of Michigan Press, 1998). Although "A Boy" does not figure in these analyses, the broader implications of themes raised in the three parts for this January entry contribute to our understanding of the Kroneberg case in Chapter 2 of the February 1876 issue of *The Diary*.

9 Robert Louis Jackson offers a finely observed reading of the story in *The Art of Dostoevsky: Deliriums and Nocturnes* (Princeton University Press, 1981), 260–272. Jackson's readings of the stories in *The Diary* remain unsurpassed, in part because although these stories are generally linked to the more journalistic entries that precede and follow them, Jackson consistently chooses also to read them as finely wrought artistic creations, although they masquerade as having been casually tossed into the mix by the author who pretends to be illustrating this or that point. "A Boy" is a "moving Christmas story, as ecstatic in its religious idealism as it is brutal in its social realism . . . [i]t constitutes a kind of statement on the nature of reality and the scope of realism" (261). By creating a story before the reader's eyes, Dostoevsky "awakens [her] to the purely conventional nature . . . of such designations as 'fiction' and 'reality,' 'realistic' and 'fantastic'" (261). Morson, following Jackson, theorizes this process, labeling *The Diary* a boundary genre and finding this story to be a "threshold story"

within it. See Gary Saul Morson, *The Boundaries of Genre: Dostoevsky's Diary of a Writer and the Traditions of Literary Utopia* (Evanston, IL: Northwestern University Press, 1981). For Jackson the story comprises a rendering of what Dostoevsky meant when claiming that "what the majority calls almost fantastic... is sometimes the very essence of the real." Jackson writes, quoting Dostoevsky's 1869 letter to Nikolai Strakhov about "fantastic realism" (264). "To the child, the world revealed in the three windows is incredible... yet it is real. To the ordinary passerby, that same fantastic world holds nothing astonishing" (266). Dostoevsky "defamiliarizes... almost demonizes, the reader's reality: what had always seemed right and good now seems evil because of its exclusiveness and moral indifference" (266). For Dostoevsky's understanding of how memory blends with fancy to make art, see Miller, *Dostoevsky's Unfinished Journey*, 13–21, 75–78.

10 This description of Christ actually taking the child in his arms – touching him, hugging him – is significant. Boris Tikhomirov, following D. S. Likhachev's characterization of *The Diary* as a unique "generic ensemble," scrutinizes Dostoevsky's notes about Christ's encounters with children and how Dostoevsky adapts his reading of the New Testament to his artistic needs, both in *The Diary* and elsewhere, most notably *Crime and Punishment*. He focuses on *The Diary* for 1877, the year after "A Boy." Tikhomirov emphasizes Dostoevsky's observation in *The Diary*'s notebooks that Christ actually embraced children – that he actually hugged them. Tikhomirov searches for possible sources, ultimately turning to two passages from Mark: "And they brought young children to him... 'Verily I say unto you. Whoever shall not receive the kingdom of God as a little child, he shall not enter therein. And he took them up in his arms, put his hands upon them, and blessed them'" (Mark 10:13–16), and "He took a child, and set him in the midst of them: and when He had taken him in His arms, He said unto them, Whosoever shall receive one of such children in my name, receiveth me: and whosoever shall receive me, receiveth not me, but him that sent me" (Mark 9:36–37). This detail of Christ embracing the children was, Tikhomirov argues, important to Dostoevsky. He adds, "This point in Mark's Gospel is probably even more favourable as a commentary for Dostoevsky's note, which reads: 'Christ, embracing children, defined how we must look at them'" (200); for the original quote see *PSS* XIV:137. Although Tikhomirov does not mention "A Boy," the matter of Christ's actual embrace is central – it is so powerful and intimate that at first the boy, in the darkness, thinks it is his mother. Tolstoy in his late writings also longed to be held in an embrace both motherly and divine. Tikhomirov, "Dostoevsky on Children in the New Testament," in *Dostoevsky on the Threshold of Other Worlds: Essays in Honour of Malcolm V. Jones*, edited by Sarah Young and Leslie Milne (Ilkeston, Eng.: Bramcote Press, 2006), 189–206.

11 "In the original version of *Diary*... Dostoevsky resisted the obvious urge to soften his stark realism." He added the happy meeting of mother and son in heaven only in the second 1879 edition (Jackson, *The Art of Dostoevsky*, 270). Jackson cites Fridlender's essay comparing the story to Rückert's

ballad. G. M. Fridlender, *Realizm Dostoevskogo* (Moscow and Leningrad, 1964), 307.

12 In addition to the article Jackson cites, see "Sviatochnyi rasskaz Dostoevskogo i ballada Riukerta," *Mezhdunarodnye sviazi russkoi literatury*, 370–390, cited by Kenneth Lantz in his notes for his translation of *The Diary* (771). In *PSS*, volume XXII, the editors also cite this reference, offering a translation of Rückert's ballad into Russian (322–323).

13 Maria Tatar, *Off With Their Heads! Fairy Tales and the Culture of Childhood* (Princeton University Press, 1992), xxvii.

14 Ibid., 43.

15 Hans Christian Andersen, *The Stories of Hans Christian Andersen: A New Translation from the Danish*, translated by Diana Crone Frank and Jeffrey Frank (Durham, NC: Duke University Press, 2005), 215.

16 Tatar, "The Pedagogy of Fear in Fairy Tales," in *Off with Their Heads!*, 44–45.

17 In the notes to *PSS*, volume XXII, the editors do not assert that Dostoevsky definitely read Andersen's tale, although they reference both it and Dickens's stories as well-known examples of children's stories (XXII:322). In addition to Dickens's stories for children is another little-known work, *The Life of Our Lord: As Written for His Children during the Years 1846–1849* (New York: Simon & Schuster, 1934). Dickens worked on this while writing *David Copperfield*, a novel both Tolstoy and Dostoevsky loved. Neither would have read it, as it was published posthumously, in 1934. Its sixth chapter tells how Jesus stood before Peter, James, and John, and "His Face began to shine . . . and the robes He wore . . . glistened and shone like sparkling silver, and He stood before them like an Angel" (57). "Jesus called a little child to Him, and took him in His arms," saying that those who are as humble as little children shall enter heaven, and he concludes, moreover, that "[t]he Angels are all children" (59). Important – essential – to both Dickens and Dostoevsky is the image of Jesus embracing, holding, and carrying the child to heaven. This is the image, Tikhomirov emphasized, that appears only in the Gospel of Mark.

18 "Introduction: Hans Christian Andersen," *CFT*, 212.

19 This point has been forcefully elaborated by Robert L. Belknap, "The Didactic Plot: The Lesson about Suffering in *Poor Folk*," in *Actualité de Dostoevskij*, edited by Nina Kauchtschischwili (Genoa: La Quercia Edizioni, 1982), 67–69.

20 "Little Match Girl," in Andersen, *Stories*, 233.

21 Ibid.

22 Ibid., 234.

23 Ibid.

24 Ibid.

25 *CFT*, 212.

26 "Little Match Girl," 234.

27 See my chapter, "Dostoevsky's *Poor People*: Reading 'as if for Life,'" in *Reading in Russia: Literary Communication and Practices of Reading, 1760–1930*, edited by Raffaella Vassena and Damiano Rebecchini (University of Milan Press, 2014). Yeats's poem, "The Circus Animals' Desertion," resonates with Dostoevsky

and his art: "What can I but enumerate old themes?" "Those masterful images because complete/Grew in pure mind, but out of what began?/A mound of refuse or the sweepings of a street . . . Now that my ladder's gone,/I must lie down where all the ladders start,/In the foul rag-and-bone shop of the heart."

28 *PSS* 1:86 and Dostoevsky, *Poor Folk and Other Stories*, translated by David McDuff (London: Penguin Books, 1988), 100.

29 87; 101.

30 Ibid.

31 Ibid.

32 Ibid.

33 In "The Peasant Marei," Dostoevsky celebrates how memories arise at the needed time. In "A Boy" one cannot discern whether Dostoevsky consciously or unconsciously recalled his own prequel to this story in *Poor People*.

34 88; 102.

CHAPTER 4

The railway and the elemental force
Slavophilism, Pan-Slavism, and apocalyptic anxieties in
Anna Karenina

Alexander Burry and S. Ceilidh Orr

Stiva Oblonsky, first introduced as a genial adulterer, acts as a peacemaker for much of Tolstoy's *Anna Karenina* (1877), attempting to resolve his sister's marital problems and providing the setting for Levin's second, successful proposal to Kitty. By the end of the novel, however, his role as a mediator has grown progressively less effective. His indefatigable charm, formerly so effective as a social lubricant, is particularly irrelevant in the face of the Turkish conflict and Anna's death. When we last see him, he is awkwardly interrupting a conversation between Koznyshev and an unnamed Princess over Anna's suicide and Vronsky's decision to volunteer. After Stiva leaves, the Princess worries about the effect of his blithe demeanor on the grieving Vronsky, but softens her criticism by praising his "fully Russian, Slavic nature."[1] Although this appears to be an offhand comment occasioned by Stiva's spontaneous donation of five rubles to the volunteer cause, the Princess's readiness to apply these terms to him, and Koznyshev's tacit agreement, is striking. One wonders what exactly makes Stiva "fully Russian," and how this appellation reflects Tolstoy's thinking about the national character, his views on the Russo-Turkish conflict, and his vision of Russia's future. The Princess's description of Stiva first as "Russian" and then as "Slavic," in particular, unwittingly raises the question of how much overlap there is between Russian and greater Slavic values and political concerns.

Tolstoy's commentary on Russian politics in *Anna Karenina* is most explicit and concentrated in Part VIII, which integrates the Russo-Turkish War and its messianic ideological underpinnings into the family plot-lines that dominate the rest of the novel. However, this section is also the culmination of a more thoroughgoing and anxiety-ridden considera-tion of Russia's political direction. Tolstoy's forebodings over national and societal degradation more than two decades before the century's end reveal an underlying fin-de-siècle mentality avant la lettre. Readers of Tolstoy's time tended to interpret the novel as lacking in contemporary political significance,[2] and in many cases were puzzled by what seemed to be a disjointed (if not self-indulgent) conclusion highlighting Levin's antiwar attitude. Closer examination of *Anna Karenina*, however, reveals that the political concerns Tolstoy expresses in Part VIII are organically linked to the preceding seven parts of the novel.[3] These concerns – felt throughout the novel – are well characterized by Nikolai Berdiaev, quoted in the epigraph of this volume's introduction, as "terrible forebodings of impending disaster."[4]

In this chapter, we explore Tolstoy's intimation of future catastrophe and argue that, through his characterizations of the main protagonists in *Anna Karenina*, he contrasts the essentially ahistorical, peaceful, and circular worldview envisioned by Slavophiles to the more outward-looking, aggressive, and linear approach to Russian history embodied by the related ideology of Pan-Slavism. Tolstoy's fears of the growing militant mentality before and during the writing of *Anna Karenina* underscore the novel's apocalypticism; in the novel he outlines not only the crumbling of the old aristocracy and traditional family structure, but also Russia's changing sense of its role in history. Using the aforementioned description of Stiva as a starting point, we reconsider the relationship between Part VIII and the rest of the novel, arguing that Tolstoy, while portraying this character as an irresponsible philanderer, nonetheless also shows unexpected links between his instinctive behavior and Slavophile ideals. Tolstoy juxtaposes Oblonsky and the harmonious unity he embodies with other characters that either parallel this way of life or oppose it. In our view, Tolstoy demonstrates these different aspects of Russian identity in part by contrasting circular, unifying symbols to warlike, linear, apocalyptic images. The alternation of these symbols creates a sense of onrushing terror and disintegration that reflects fin-de-siècle anxiety in the novel. In this sense, the descriptions of Stiva that both open and close *Anna Karenina* are connected to substantive ruminations on Russia's destiny, and have much broader implications than the adultery theme with which the character is usually associated.

Tolstoy, Slavophilism, and Pan-Slavism

Although Tolstoy's initial intention in *Anna Karenina* was to write a novel far more confined in scope than its predecessor, *War and Peace* (1869), many of the same concerns about Russian nationhood and identity can be found in the later work. *Anna Karenina* explores the respective ideologies of Slavophilism and Pan-Slavism, both of which posit a Russia with ancient, longstanding virtues rooted in Orthodoxy and embodied best by the humble, pious lower classes. Where Slavophiles were content with an introspective adoption of these virtues, however, Pan-Slavists took a more messianic approach, justifying the aggressive exportation of these virtues to other parts of Europe.[5] Tolstoy's opposition of roundness and linearity throughout the novel corresponds symbolically to these contrasting peaceful and bellicose aspects of late nineteenth-century Russian identity.

Despite Tolstoy's initial lukewarm reception of Slavophilism as a young man in the 1850s, a renewed sympathy for the movement's principles can be encountered in *Anna Karenina*,[6] most noticeably in Levin's efforts to study Russian peasants' unique national traits instead of imposing Western agricultural methods on them.[7] As Richard Gustafson has demonstrated, Tolstoy's lifelong spiritual ideal involved a metaphysical unity of everything, a harmonious merging of parts with the whole, with all people participating together in the "song of life."[8] His unchanging conviction that brotherhood can only be achieved when people strive for happiness communally rather than individually resonates with the Slavophile doctrine of *sobornost'*, or a metaphorical church constructed on the basis of what Alexey Khomiakov called "free unanimity" – the voluntary submission to the larger whole without loss of individuality.[9]

The Slavophile utopian notion of Russian virtues rooted in the past and preserved in the peasantry was essentially backward-looking and, while privileging Eastern Orthodoxy, it did not generally promote an expansionist policy for Russia or even claim exclusive possession of spiritual truth.[10] Khomiakov, for instance, offered a universalist, non-nationalist conception of the Church, affirming that it "belongs to the whole world and not any locality; because she hallows all humanity and all the earth and not one particular nation or one country."[11] In the decade following the 1861 emancipation of the serfs, however, this static, peaceful unity gradually gave way to Pan-Slavism, a more aggressive, militaristic idea that Russia would be the savior of a decaying West.[12] This ideology found its most prominent and concrete expression in Nikolai Danilevsky's *Russia and Europe* (1869), which posited Russia as a unique civilization whose values were incompatible with those of a decaying Western Europe. Danilevsky argued that Russia was destined by Providence to establish a Union of Slavic Lands that would enter into battle with Europe: "A Pan-Slavic union," he asserted, "is the only firm soil on which we can develop our independent Slavic culture."[13] *Russia and Europe* was viewed by some commentators not so much as the statement of a new ideology as a continuation of Slavophilism; Strakhov, in his foreword to the third edition, called it "a complete catechism or codex of Slavophilism."[14] Thus, by the 1870s, the "classical" idea of Russia as home to a peace-loving Christian people living by the light of inner truth was gradually transformed into a more pragmatic, imperialist view. Exponents of Pan-Slavism such as Dostoevsky felt that the divine Russian mission justified force in the Ottoman Empire to support the struggle of Orthodox Slavs against the Turks: hence his famous riposte against Levin's (and Tolstoy's) pacifism in the July and August 1877 issue of the *Writer's Diary*.[15]

In 1872, while beginning *Anna Karenina*, Tolstoy was keenly aware of Pan-Slavism. In a letter from this time, he asked Strakhov to send him Danilevsky's recently published articles, "The Present War" and "Europe and the Russo-Turkish War."[16] As Olga Maiorova points out, there is a certain amount of convergence between *Russia and Europe* and Tolstoy's notion in *War and Peace* of Russian victory over Napoleon as an affirmation of the national spirit and moral supremacy.[17] However, Tolstoy became increasingly disturbed by the movement's nationalist fervor, corresponding with Afanasy Fet on the war beginning in 1875 and eventually making a trip to Moscow in November 1876 to learn more about the hostilities between the Russians and Turks. Since the Eastern Question thus concerned him before he completed *Anna Karenina*, the arguments about it in Part VIII were not the tacked-on afterthought that *Russkii vestnik* editor Mikhail Katkov and other contemporary readers assumed. Given Tolstoy's greater sympathy toward Slavophilism and his accompanying concern about the rise of militaristic nationalism, one can view *Anna Karenina* as a contrast between two strands of this body of thought: the "classical" Slavophilism of past generations and the ascendant Pan-Slavism of the 1860s and 1870s. If Danilevsky and other Pan-Slavists promoted an optimistic view of Russia as a solution to the fin-de-siècle anxiety affecting Europe, then Tolstoy reflects a more negative attitude toward Russia's future. In fact, he interprets Russia's aggressive turn in the 1870s as evidence not of triumph over a decaying Europe, but rather of falling victim to the same decline in moral stature.

Oblonsky's secularized *sobornost'*

Tolstoy establishes a pattern of linking characters to Russian national traits that symbolize different aspects of the respective ideologies from the very beginning of *Anna Karenina*. Although Levin is the primary representative of Slavophile ideals, Tolstoy also links the hero's frequent philosophical opponent, Oblonsky, to certain features of Slavophilism, some of them virtues embodied by Levin himself. This may seem somewhat surprising in light of Tolstoy's obvious distaste for Stiva's epicurianism. As John Bayley points out, Stiva's charming nature is essential to Tolstoy's plan, since it forces readers to identify with him, and thus, to put themselves in his sister's position as an adulterer later on.[18] Other critics, however, build on Dostoevsky's interpretation of Oblonsky as an embodiment of petty evil, emphasizing Tolstoy's ironic treatment of the character.[19] Gary Saul Morson argues: "[Stiva's] evil, hidden in everyday charm, spreads more widely and so proves even more destructive."[20] Stewart Justman notes that the narrator's ironic use of theatrical language to describe Stiva's ill-fated smile at Dolly when his adultery is discovered relates Tolstoy's moral castigation of Oblonsky, as he paints the character as an irresponsible player at life.[21] While Tolstoy's description of Stiva's self-satisfaction with his physique is relatively neutral, as Ani Kokobobo points out in the present volume, such enjoyment of one's own sexuality in his later works becomes imbued with the grotesque.

Not all readers, however, have focused on Stiva from the point of view of Tolstoyan morality. Radical critics of Tolstoy's time such as Pyotr Tkachev made little distinction between Levin and Oblonsky, finding each to be an egoist: one concerned purely with sensual desires, the other with family life.[22] More recently, other commentators have examined Stiva's complex origins, and his crucial impact on the morally upright Levin. Kathryn Feuer notes that by the novel's end, Levin has essentially internalized the lesson encapsulated in Oblonsky's mantra, "vse obrazuetsia," literally, "everything will shape itself."[23] Donna Orwin locates Oblonsky's origins in the kind of *samoudovletvorenie*, or self-satisfied joy in life, that earlier characters such as Pierre Bezukhov from *War and Peace* represent. She notes that Tolstoy still presents this egoistic type as positive in *Anna Karenina* in many ways, and that Stiva even makes good counter-arguments to Levin during their Part VI conversation on the problem of inequality between peasants and landowners.[24]

While Oblonsky shares Bezukhov's egoistic joy in life, he also has roots – surprisingly – in this character's spiritual mentor, Platon Karataev, "the personification of everything Russian, kindly, and round."[25] This peculiarly Russian quality, for Tolstoy, carries over into his portrait of Stiva, who, like Karataev, is described as having an almost feminine appearance, an amiable forgetfulness, and the capacity to adjust easily to changing circumstances. Tolstoy introduces a cluster of "roundness" motifs in his opening chapters that frame Oblonsky, like Karataev, as a figure from a static, unchanging Russian past.[26] These include his description of Stiva's "plump, well-tended body," long, curly whiskers, preference for round-shaped foods such as buttered rolls, and even his last name. In all cases, these circular images reflect an inner peace, happiness, and trust in chaos to "work itself out" that resonates with the Slavophile vision of a harmonious, integrated identity. At other points in the novel, these symbols are contrasted with weapons and other warlike, linear images that symbolize Pan-Slavism, apocalypticism, and Tolstoy's fears about Russia's future.

Stiva's physical traits and the internal harmony they reflect coexist with a peace-loving, tolerant, non-judgmental personality that similarly recalls certain Slavophile virtues, including the fundamental unity of Slavophile *sobornost'*. The narrator describes Stiva, a nobleman content with his position of privilege, as a person who unites people from all ends of the social spectrum, and who exhibits democratic tendencies, treating everyone equally, regardless of rank or position. Although Stiva's desire to subscribe to the views of the majority exposes his intellectual shallowness, it also reflects a premium on consensus that goes along with a desire to unite others as much as possible. The narrator's comment that "half Moscow and Petersburg were relatives or friends of Stepan Arkadych" indicates his connectedness with all parts of upper-class society.[27] His brilliant organization of the dinner party in Part IV, the high point of his capacity to bring diverse individuals together, depends in part on his unerring aesthetic tastes in composing the best possible arrangement of food, drink, guests, and conversation: Tolstoy describes Stiva as kneading the "social dough." Karenin and Koznyshev represent *la pièce de résistance*, and the fiery, eccentric Pestsov is compared to a gravy or garnish. Like a chef, Stiva livens up the "dish" by adding a pinch of salt, making subtle changes that heighten the atmosphere and overall enjoyment considerably. But there is also an ethical imperative to establish good relations between as many people as possible.[28] At the dinner, Stiva temporarily dispels Karenin's awkwardness by engaging him in lively discussion with Koznyshev and Pestsov. He also attempts to shield Karenin from Pestsov and Turovtsyn when they touch on the theme of cuckoldry that unwittingly cuts too close to the bone. Similarly, his seemingly casual placement of Levin opposite Kitty paves the way for a successful marriage proposal, allowing Levin to experience a temporary sense of all-encompassing unity similar to what Stiva feels on a regular basis.

Stiva's insistence on universal family and friendship, in fact, recalls the Slavophile emphasis on the harmonious interaction of all members of a community. When Karenin tells him that their relations have been severed as a result of Anna's adultery, Stiva simply smiles, and claims that this cannot be possible because both Anna and Karenin are "first-rate, splendid" people.

Similarly, he physically draws Levin and Vronsky together by asserting that both are friends of his and should make friends with each other as well: "I know that you will be friendly and intimate because you are both good fellows."[29] Stiva seems to intuitively create a kind of secular *sobornost'* in a harmonious society bound by universal, unending, interconnected feelings of brotherhood and friendship. His ability to bring seemingly disparate people together even transforms Levin for the better in some ways. By introducing Levin to Anna, for instance, Stiva indirectly persuades his friend to soften his judgmental attitude toward fallen women in favor of his own more sympathetic attitude.

Tolstoy's moral disapprobation and ironic description of Stiva, however, indicate that the character embodies a debased form of the harmonious, static, inward-looking values that characterized Slavophilism. Despite Oblonsky's conciliatory qualities, his vision of all-embracing unity ultimately goes too far, leading him into the adulterous embrace of governesses and ballet girls. Moreover, his striving for harmonious relations between all members of his community is neither realistic nor attainable. His desires are utopian in the sense that they involve the reconciliation of the mutually exclusive, as when he encourages both Levin and Vronsky to pursue Kitty, without considering the impossibility of both his wishes coming true. Tolstoy makes clear that this impossibility applies to his financial life as well: he is falling into greater and greater debt, and destroying his children's future through bad business decisions such as the sale of a forest to the merchant Riabinin for much less than its value. Stiva's enjoyment of European culture, lackadaisical attitude toward his family, and lack of anything more than pro forma religious belief directly oppose key Slavophile principles. His "Russian" virtues are divorced from his predecessor Karataev's piety and simplicity. What Tolstoy describes, thus, is a kind of secularization – and hence corruption – of traditional Russian ideals. Stiva represents a kind of transitional figure from the Russianness represented by Karataev (seen as a largely positive force in *War and Peace*) to a kind of backward, decaying force in *Anna Karenina*.

By allowing Stiva, who features in critical literature mainly as an adulterer and epicure, to embody aspects of a utopian ideal, albeit one he pursues in a comic and at times harmfully carefree way, Tolstoy creates a character that anticipates the textual strategies of decadence and fin-de-siècle prose. Decadent works have been described as unsettling critics for their "interfer[ence] with boundaries and borders (national, sexual, definitional, historical, to name but a few) that criticism normally relies upon to make its judgments, producing what we call a 'perennial decay' of those boundaries and borders."³⁰ Stiva has long baffled readers for being a genial character depicted largely sympathetically, despite violating Tolstoy's own morals. If, instead of trying to align Stiva with the author's ideology, we read him precisely as a figure that is simultaneously a compassionate utopian and an incorrigible adulterer who disturbs boundaries and reconciles quarrels, then the centrality of his role in *Anna Karenina* becomes even clearer. The novel is full of dissolving boundaries: Russian military might is moving west, the railway connects all lands and peoples, and traditional family boundaries no longer hold. Stiva, the unifier of disparate circles, simultaneously embodies the ideal of Slavophile unity and the crisis of a very modern and unsettling ambiguity.

The circular images that surround Stiva are attached to other characters as well, thus supporting the idea that Tolstoy is using them to reflect a broader Russian ideal of continuity and harmonious unity. Anna, like her brother, is often described – especially early in the novel – in circular terms: the similar roundness of her figure, the ringlets in her hair, the rings covering her fingers, and the circle of Dolly's children who gather around her when she visits to reunify Dolly and Stiva. Moreover, she shares her brother's unrealistic longing for the harmony of the mutually exclusive. Stiva's encouragement of both Levin and Vronsky as rivals for Kitty's love, and his reconciliation of his two friends at the party following the election, has a comic outcome. However, Anna's same desire for the unity of the mutually exclusive has the most tragic possible outcome. Her dream of taking both Vronsky and Karenin as her husbands, and her attempt to reconcile them at her bedside when she fears death after the birth of her daughter by Vronsky, are emblematic of her impossible longings for freedom and stability, family and self-determination – desires that cannot coexist and lead to her demise. Indeed, Anna's very choice of Vronsky underscores the futility of her strivings. As Edward Wasiolek suggests, in his ambitions for a brilliant career (which he sacrifices), and his desire for regularity, routine, and a stable position, Vronsky is quite similar to Karenin.³¹ Anna's affair offers only temporary relief from her stagnant life with her husband; but eventually, she is forced to confront Vronsky's own practical desires for legal marriage and patrimony. Anna's utopian dream thus engenders a nightmare in which the two entities she wishes could coexist are at odds. If Stiva's blithe vision of universal contentment among disparate individuals, as Tolstoy implies, is impossible to maintain in the long run, Anna's desperate search for harmony ends in precipitous destruction.

Utopian landownership

Such similarities, perhaps, are to be expected in Tolstoyan siblings. How-ever, some of the same characteristics also apply to Stiva's friend and moral and intellectual nemesis, Levin, who more directly exemplifies Slavophile tendencies. Many of the autobiographical qualities Tolstoy reflects through Levin, such as his attachment to his estate, hostility toward city life, and love of simple foods, can be seen as Slavophile values. Most importantly, his rejection of Western agricultural methods and emphasis on the importance of workers' cultural and social backgrounds reflect Slavophile thinking. As Levin thinks to himself while visiting the landowner Sviyazhsky: "We've been pushing ahead for a long time in our own [the nobility's] way, the European way, without asking ourselves about the properties of the work-force. Let's try to look at the workforce not as an ideal *workforce*, but as the *Russian muzhik* with his instincts, and organize our farming accordingly."[32]

However, while Levin's rural, estate-bound way of life is radically dif-ferent from Stiva's, the two share a longing for establishing harmonious relations among groups of people. In Levin's case, this longing bridges the distance between master and peasant, initiating an attempt to better under-stand, relate to, and work with the peasants on his estate. Levin's impulse to marry a peasant girl following Kitty's initial rejection indicates a desire to coexist harmoniously with other social groups, as does his friendship with Stiva, a very different sort of nobleman than himself. The famous hay-mowing scene, which provides Levin a temporary but healing sense of oneness with the world and everyone around him, features the scythe, a curved instrument that cuts in a circular, arc-like motion, a "curved semi-circle," thus paralleling the "roundness" motifs associated with Stiva and Anna. It also features a similar ecstasy in the achievement of unity within oneself, with nature, and with all other people in the world.

Levin and Stiva's moral opposition, thus, obscures a fundamental sim-ilarity in their approach to life. Each, in his different sphere of Russian society, embraces an old way of life and an essentially conservative outlook that resists large-scale change. Levin's resistance to the latest European mod-ernizations in agriculture parallels Stiva's blithe indifference to the growing prominence of the merchant class represented by Riabinin as an economic force. Each character is focused, in different ways, on the freedom of the individual within a harmonious collective, be it Levin's rural, agriculture-based community, or Stiva's social circles in Moscow and Petersburg. Both thus reflect a broader Slavophile conception of everyday life. It is no accident that, from the perspective of a radical like Tkachev, neither Stiva nor Levin do anything to improve the lives of others or their nation. The moral differences between the characters were seen as essentially irrelevant: both were relics of a past that had long ceased to exist. The desires of both Levin and Stiva to preserve their class's way of life, then, were equally utopian, rooted in quintessentially Russian traditions.

Apocalypse and violence in *Anna Karenina*

Throughout the novel, the static, utopian qualities and accompanying round symbols associated with Stiva, Anna, and Levin are continually opposed to a series of violent, dynamic, linear images connected with historical momentum and social change: the railway, the roadway, sweeping forces, and stretched strings. These apocalyptic symbols signal a move away from the harmonious, traditionalist vision of Slavophilism that Stiva's hospitality and peacemaking enact toward a more aggressive building of Slavdom, most visible in the public support for the Russo-Turkish War. Associated with danger and destruction, these symbols represent not only an ideological opposition to Stiva, Levin, and Anna's versions of *sobornost'* but an active threat to the traditional way of life that Tolstoy (at the time, at least) valued. Long before the outbreak of war in Part VIII, these symbols foreshadow a destructive trajectory for Russia.

Most notable among the novel's ominous linear images is the railroad, the site of death, disfigured bodies, and the disruption of family life. In addition to being a symbol of modernization, the railroad in *Anna Karenina* is associated with moral and political crises. In this sense, Tolstoy reflects broader concerns more associated with the end of the century, in both Russia and the West. As Mark Steinberg argues about the fin-de-siècle Russian mentality, "Russians had come to share the worries of earlier western European intellectuals that the brilliant promises of modern progress were an illusion and a myth."[33] The potential and actual violence encountered on the railroad intensifies toward the end of the book, both during Anna's suicide at the end of Part VII and as citizens bid farewell to the departing Russian troops in Part VIII. The soldiers packed in railway cars carry "linear" weapons such as rifles and swords, and embody a Pan-Slavic vision of Russia's historical destiny; in contrast to the harmonious, ahistorical vision of Slavophile *sobornost'*, the crowd at the platform supports aggressive intervention in international conflicts. The line of the railroad becomes the path along which Russian ideas and influence move into the Balkan conflict.

It is through the image of the railroad that Tolstoy brings the tensions between Slavophilism and Pan-Slavism directly to bear on fin-de-siècle anxieties. Daniel Pick describes fin-de-siècle Europe as torn between two teleological visions of humanity: on the one hand, evolution, mirrored by technical and social progress, and on the other degeneration or atavism marked by physical and moral decay. The "interlocking languages of progress and degeneration" that he sees in late nineteenth-century art and scientific literature meet in the semiotics of Tolstoy's railway in the Russian context.[34] Here the forward-looking, progressive, Pan-Slavic view diverges from the relatively backward- and inward-looking Slavophilism. At the same time, the engine of progress runs on blood-stained tracks. The linear train brings dismemberment, both literal and figurative: it plows blindly over Anna's body and the watchman's, it brings adulterous lovers together, and it carries soldiers toward possible death on the battlefield.

Other dynamic, linear symbols join with the railway to create a picture of progress and war as a great current, sweeping all levels of society toward an unknown fate. Koznyshev, describing the popular support for the war, speaks of an "elemental power" (*stikhiinaia sila*) that has "caught [everyone] up and is carrying them in one direction."[35] This power accomplishes on an abstract, historical level what the railway does physically: it carries Russia forward into war. Furthermore, just as the railroad unites members of all the classes, who are pulled along by the same engine, the elemental force unites the Russian people in support of the war. "Personal opinions mean nothing here," Koznyshev tells Levin and Prince Shcherbatsky. "It's no matter of personal opinions when all Russia – the people – has expressed its will."[36]

The sense of darkness and threat accompanying these dynamic images is reinforced by the violence and unpredictability associated with speed and forward momentum throughout *Anna Karenina*. This trend is displayed particularly clearly in a series of driving accidents that illustrate power slipping out of control. For example, Vronsky's lapse of judgment causes the death of his prized racehorse Frou-Frou, whose magnificent forward charge he throws off balance. Later, Veslovsky drives Levin's team into a swamp, unable to keep them on a safe course due to his inexperience. Such accidents plague trains as well as horses. The death of the watchman, crushed underneath the train in Part I, casts a pall over the entire narrative. Interestingly, even in the games that children play, the railroad is a site of deadly speed and ejected passengers. Tania and Grisha's "train" early in the novel tips over, spilling passengers from the roof, while the conductor in Serezha's train, later in the narrative, must be "brave and agile" to avoid being flung off.[37] The children's games comically mirror a graver trend, but they also reveal that an air of disaster has penetrated even the upper-class drawing rooms and nurseries.

The lesson of these wagons, trains, and horses run amok may easily be extended to political momentum. The elemental force that charges forward linearly sweeps all of Russia along, but whither does it bear the nation? Will the war end in Serbia? How many lives will it cost? Danilevsky, Dostoevsky, and other Pan-Slavists envisioned a new Slavdom with its capital at Constantinople. In *Anna Karenina*, however, there is no clear historical destination, only fervor and blind faith in the manifestation of the people's will. The elemental force and the trains of soldiers that hurtle blindly forward recall another, earlier image of Russia's runaway destiny, that of the apocalyptic troika in Nikolai Gogol's *Dead Souls* (1842):

> And you, Rus, do you not hurtle forward too, like some spirited troika that none can catch? A trail of smoke marks your passage, the bridges rumble, everything falls back and is left behind. On seeing this miracle of God, the onlooker stops in his tracks: what is this? – a bolt of lightning hurled from the heavens? And this terrifying onrush – what does it portend? And what unearthly power lies hidden in these unearthly steeds? . . . With a wondrous jingling the carriage bells ring out; torn into shreds, the air rumbles and turns to wind; every thing on this earth flashes by as, with an oblique look, other peoples and empires step aside to let her fly past.[38]

The transformation from Slavophile utopia into apocalyptic, hurtling vehicles reflects the dangerous political currents that Tolstoy observed in the 1870s.[39] Koznyshev borrows from Slavophile rhetoric in his oration about Slavic brotherhood and the people's will, but his vision is more aggressive and exclusive. There are no enemies or strangers in Stiva's utopia, where two rival lovers can both sincerely be wished success. In contrast, Koznyshev's Pan-Slavism, similar to Danilevsky's anticipated conflict between Slavs and the Romano-Germanic empire, includes a clear sense of self and other: Slav versus Turk. Though Koznyshev argues that the war is motivated by compassion, a Christian response to Turkish atrocities, his worldview contains an expendable "other," the enemy.

The darkness that Tolstoy inscribes in Koznyshev's vision derives not only from its violence but also from its facelessness. Koznyshev is interested in mass movements, in the will of an entire nation, but not in individual people. Just as he dismisses personal opinion in the comment cited above, he is also uninterested in individual identities. Koznyshev does not see the departing volunteers, for example, as people of interest in their own right: "Again the volunteers bowed and stuck their heads out the windows, but Sergei Ivanovich paid no attention to them; he had dealt with the volunteers so much that he knew their general type and it did not interest him."⁴⁰ To a man interested in historical forces and generalities, soldiers' faces are irrelevant details.

The facelessness of the elemental force and its destructive potential go hand in hand. A worldview that privileges the masses over the individual more readily justifies sending soldiers to kill and die than can a philosophy of individual conscience such as Levin's. Koznyshev is certain that he can understand the Russian people en masse through the expression of their historical will, an idea that Levin opposes vehemently. Levin contends that the "people" speaking in support of the war are only a vocal minority. Most of the peasantry, he believes, "like Mikhailych, not only don't express their will, but don't have the slightest notion what they should express their will about. What right then do we have to say it's the will of the people?"⁴¹

Slavophile *sobornost'*, in the sense of Khomiakov's "free unanimity," also values the collective; however, it does so without eclipsing the individual. As described above, "classic" Slavophilism is rooted in shared spiritual vision, for love of which individuals freely choose to put the collective good above their own. Pan-Slavism, by contrast, lacks both the element of individual discernment and the sense of moral absolutes. By declaring that "personal opinion means nothing" compared to the people's will, Koznyshev reveals a worldview that is not about individual choice but about taking averages, measuring the momentum of the masses, and being swept forward inevitably by the zeitgeist.

By contrast, Levin's moral epiphany at the novel's end is about individual revelation, and does not establish any connections to broader national impulses. Levin is inspired by a muzhik's comment about living "not for one's own needs but for God."⁴² Rather than abstractly pondering "the people," Levin speaks with one particular peasant, Fyodor, about their mutual acquaintance, Uncle Fokanych. Crucially, everyone involved in the scene is given a name, underscoring the opposition between Levin's focus on individuals and personal observation and the abstract mass that interests Koznyshev. Similarly, Levin's insight gives him a sense of harmony with all, and he applies it not to national destiny but to his own work, his marriage, and his personal relationships with peasants. In Levin's worldview, it is harder to justify taking another's life. What Koznyshev sees as the triumphant expression of the people's will is, to Levin, a faceless, violent surge.

The novel does not just embody these two competing visions of Russia's historical destiny, however; it also traces the destruction of one by the other.

The normally round, full Anna, for example, finds herself transformed into "a tightened string that is about to snap."[43] What Koznyshev describes is not merely an abstract idea but an active threat to the more harmonious way of life that Levin and Stiva attempt to preserve, each in his own way. For this reason, a sense of cataclysm penetrates even seemingly idyllic parts of the novel. Critics such as David Bethea and Robert Louis Jackson have noted the important role of various large-scale apocalyptic elements, such as the railroad, Anna's violent death, and even the epigraph.[44] Apocalyptic imagery, such as the lightning bolt that strikes near Kitty and her child, permeates even Levin's family life. Further, it can affect characters less aware of this conflict than Levin. For instance, the dream that Stiva recalls in the very first chapter has apocalyptic overtones. Stiva thinks only of the dream's enjoyable elements – the dinner party replete with wine, women, and song. However, the song he remembers at first, "Il tesorio mio" from Mozart's *Don Giovanni*, contains a message of apocalyptic retribution that recalls the Biblical epigraph, as Don Ottavio sings of avenging Donna Anna's father, killed by Giovanni. From the beginning, Stiva's utopian dream world is "infected" by apocalyptic imagery, although he is naïvely unaware of the threat. Perhaps more significantly, given this reading, the plush position Stiva covets and finally obtains in Part VIII involves service with the railways. The destructive, cataclysmic, all-embracing changes affect everyone as the currents of "progress" are recast as harbingers of destruction. However, unlike Levin and Koznyshev, Oblonsky remains blissfully unconscious of the watershed moment in Russian history that is taking place, or his own symbolic role in relation to it; hence, his growing irrelevance, culminating in the Princess's annoyed reaction to him in Part VIII.

* * *

Tolstoy famously argued in an April 23–26, 1876 letter to Nikolai Strakhov that an "endless labyrinth of linkages" melded *Anna Karenina* together, despite the seeming disunity of two main plotlines that intersected only once. As we have argued, this linkage is created in part through a complex strategy of character oppositions and symbols that connect the family and adultery novel plotlines with the content of Tolstoy's gradually developing anti-military political message and despair over the submerging and degradation of traditional Russian ways of life. The collision of utopian and apocalyptic visions at the novel's beginning serves as a unifying thread while simultaneously underscoring the transformation Tolstoy's conception of *Anna Karenina* underwent.[45] This commentary, seamlessly interwoven into detailed descriptions of the major characters – their

physical appearances, gestures, preferences, and inner conflicts – demonstrates Tolstoy's concern about the secularization and corruption of the
Slavophile utopia, and its transformation in the 1870s into an ideology
promoting a clash of civilizations. Together, these elements indicate despair
and pessimism regarding Russia's future a decade before the fin-de-siècle
mood blossomed in the rest of Europe.

NOTES

1 Leo Tolstoy, *Anna Karenina*, translated by Richard Pevear and Larissa
   Volokhonsky (New York: Penguin Books, 2000), 774. All citations from *Anna
   Karenina* are this translation.
2 See A. V. Knowles, "Russian Views of Anna Karenina, 1875–1878," *Slavic and
   East European Journal* 22:3 (1978): 301–312, for a summary of these readings.
3 Tatiana Kuzmic views Tolstoy as linking the Eastern crisis closely with the
   family novel, as he draws parallels between the Pan-Slavic idea of Russia as
   savior and intercessor for fellow Slavs and Vronsky's adulterous relations with
   Anna. "'Serbia: Vronskii's Last Love': Reading *Anna Karenina* in the Context
   of Empire," *Toronto Slavic Quarterly* 43 (2013): 40–66.
4 Berdiaev, *The Origin of Russian Communism*, 77.
5 There is some anticipation of the Pan-Slavist position in Slavophile writings.
   Despite Konstantin Aksakov's general indifference to Slavs other than Russians,
   as Andrzej Walicki points out, he was one of the first to link Slavophile ideas
   to a Pan-Slavic program in his essay "On the Eastern Question," written
   in 1854 during the Crimean War, as he called for Russian intervention in
   Moldavia and Wallachia, and a "war of liberation" leading to a "lasting alliance
   of all Slavs." See Andrzej Walicki, *The Slavophile Controversy: History of a
   Conservative Utopia in Nineteenth-Century Russian Thought*, translated by Hilda
   Andrews-Rusiecka (Oxford: Clarendon Press, 1975), 496–497. However, for
   the most part, "classical Slavophilism" tended toward a more enclosed, inward-
   looking vision of harmony within Russian borders. As Peter Christoff points
   out, "it would be a serious error to disregard [Aksakov's] major concerns and
   contributions to Slavophilism . . . and to highlight instead his pan-Slavism,
   a sporadic latecomer in his considerations and something peripheral to his
   thought." *K. S. Aksakov, A Study in Ideas* (Princeton University Press, 1982),
   270–271.
6 As Pål Kolstø points out, despite Tolstoy's initial contempt for Slavophilism,
   he frequently drew on their ideas throughout his career, especially at watershed
   historical moments such as the 1905 Revolution. See "Power as Burden: The
   Slavophile Concept of the State and Lev Tolstoy," *The Russian Review* 64
   (2005): 559–574.
7 See Donna Orwin, "Strakhov's *World as a Whole*: A Missing Link between Dostoevsky and Tolstoy," in *Poetics. Self. Place. Essays in Honor of Anna Lisa Crone*,
   edited by Catherine O'Neill, Nicole Boudreau, and Sarah Krive (Bloomington,

IN: Slavica, 2007), 473–493, for a discussion of how Strakhov's book *World as a Whole* impacted Tolstoy's work on *Anna Karenina*.

8 Richard Gustafson, *Leo Tolstoy: Resident and Stranger* (Princeton University Press, 1986), 9.

9 See Khomiakov, "Letter to the Editor of *L'Union Chrétienne*," 139.

10 Susanna Rabow-Edling, disagreeing with the traditional notion of Slavophilism as a conservative utopia, describes it as "a critical assessment of contemporary Russian society and a project for change." *Slavophile Thought and the Politics of Cultural Nationalism* (Albany: State University of New York Press, 2007), 2. Nevertheless, as she affirms, this transformation took place entirely in the cultural rather than political sphere.

11 Alexey Khomiakov, "The Church is One," in *On Spiritual Unity*, edited by Jakim and Bird, 33.

12 As Andrzej Walicki notes about the 1860s–1870s, "Orthodox *sobornost'* and ancient Russian 'spiritual wholeness' were outstripped by economic, social, and political issues." *The Slavophile Controversy*, 464.

13 Nikolai Danilevskii, *Rossiia i Evropa* (Moscow: Kniga, 1991), 397 (our translation).

14 Quoted in Walicki, *The Slavophile Controversy*, 504. As Robert MacMaster points out, however, Danilevsky was promoting Slavophile cultural ideas as a means to military expansion: "it becomes clear, in the last chapters of his book, that he wanted a Panslav Union not so much as a protected base for a cultural flowering, but more because its institution would bring on a war with Europe – a war that was providential in origin and liturgical in function." See *Danilevsky: A Russian Totalitarian Philosopher* (Cambridge, MA: Harvard University Press, 1967), 245.

15 If anything, Dostoevsky's views on the Eastern Question were even more extreme than Danilevsky's. In an otherwise laudatory review of *Russia and Europe*, he objected to Danilevsky's plan for Russia to share control of Constantinople with other Slavic nations. "How can Russia participate in the ownership of Constantinople on an *equal* basis with the Slavs if Russia in every respect is unequal to them – to each little nation separately and to all of them combined?" See *A Writer's Diary*, translated by Lantz, 1207–1208 (Dostoevsky's italics).

16 Barbara Lönnqvist conjectures that the title of Koznyshev's unsuccessful book, *An Essay in Survey of the Principles and Forms of Statehood in Europe and Russia*, may be an ironic hint by Tolstoy at Danilevsky's title. See "Geroi romana Anna Karenina v zerkale slavianskogo voprosa," in *Severnyi sbornik: Proceedings of the NorFA Network in Russian Literature 1995–2000*, edited by Peter Jensen and Ingunn Lunde (Stockholm: Almqvist & Wiksell International, 2000), 134.

17 Olga Maiorova, *From the Shadow of Empire: Defining the Russian Nation through Cultural Mythology, 1855–1870* (Madison: University of Wisconsin Press, 2010), 188–189.

18 John Bayley, *Tolstoy and the Novel* (London: Chatto & Windus, 1966), 205–206.

19 *A Writer's Diary*, translated by Lantz, 872–878.

20 Gary Saul Morson, *"Anna Karenina" in Our Time: Seeing More Wisely* (New Haven, CT: Yale University Press, 2007), 36.

21 Stewart Justman, "Stiva's Idiotic Grin," *Philosophy and Literature* 33 (2009): 432–433.

22 P. N. Tkachev, "Tkachov Attacks Tolstoy's Aristocraticism: 1875," in *Tolstoy, the Critical Heritage*, edited by A. V. Knowles (London: Routledge and Kegan Paul, 1978), 250–261.

23 Kathryn Feuer, "Stiva," in *Russian Literature and American Critics*, edited by Kenneth N. Brostrom (Ann Arbor: University of Michigan Press, 1984), 354.

24 Orwin, "Strakhov's *World as a Whole*," 473–493.

25 Leo Tolstoy, *War and Peace*, translated by Ann Dunnigan (New York: Signet, 1968), 1161.

26 In addition to Bezukhov and Karataev, Oblonsky calls to mind other possible prototypes. R. F. Christian notes that Tolstoy used his lifelong friend Perfilev (from whom he borrowed money while writing *War and Peace*) as a partial model for Oblonsky. See *Tolstoy's Letters*, edited and translated by R. F. Christian (London: Athlone Press, 1978), 16. Stiva also seems to have some traits of the incorrigibly lazy but lovable, quintessentially Russian Oblomov: a similarly circular surname, a fat, well-tended, somewhat lazy nature, and a genial personality that attracts others to him.

27 *Anna Karenina*, 14.

28 See, however, Helena Goscilo-Kostin, "Tolstoyan Fare: Credo à la Carte," *Slavic and East European Review* 62:4 (1984): 481–495, for a contrasting argument. For her, Tolstoy uses Stiva's fascination with the aesthetics of consumption to illustrate his immorality, as his consumption of various exotic foods parallels his similar incontinence in relation to women.

29 *Anna Karenina*, 627.

30 Liz Constable, Dennis Denisoff, and Matthew Potolsky, eds., *Perennial Decay: On the Aesthetics and Politics of Decadence* (Philadelphia: University of Pennsylvania Press, 1999), 11.

31 Edward Wasiolek, *Tolstoy's Major Fiction* (University of Chicago Press, 1978), 142.

32 *Anna Karenina*, 338.

33 Steinberg, *Petersburg Fin de Siècle*, 1.

34 Pick, *Faces of Degeneration*, 3.

35 *Anna Karenina*, 808.

36 Ibid., 806.

37 Ibid., 728.

38 Nikolai Gogol, *Dead Souls*, translated by Christopher English (Oxford University Press, 2009), 254–255.

39 Gogol's image of the hurtling troika anticipates the connection Russian fin-de-siècle writers make between the country's historical momentum and a more universal sense of impending catastrophe. For a more detailed discussion of Gogol's "formative influence" on the Russian fin de siècle, see Muireann Maguire's chapter in this volume.

40 *Anna Karenina,* 775.

41 Ibid., 807.

42 Ibid., 795.

43 Ibid., 427.

44 As David Bethea points out, Tolstoy outlines an apocalyptic plot in *Anna Karenina,* although the novel contains few references to the type of world-ending cataclysm described in Revelation. See *The Shape of the Apocalypse in Russian Fiction* (Princeton University Press, 1989), 77–79. Comparing *Anna Karenina* to *The Idiot,* Bethea notes the pattern of using horses and trains to prefigure a catastrophic ending: "Tolstoy, like Dostoevsky, prefigures his heroine's doom through a series of mechanical and equine images of relentless movement in a novel far more symbolically patterned than earlier works" (79). Jackson notes the introduction of apocalyptic images early in the novel, connecting it to broader national disaster: "All the crucial linkages have been broken [in the Oblonsky household]. The 'body' of the family, the household, 'home' – on the symbolic plane, the church – has been dismembered, its congregation scattered. The dismemberment of Anna, of course, is only the final representation of this tragedy, just as the 'disfigured corpse' of the guard at the railroad station is the first harbinger of Anna's death and of the general theme of family, social and economic breakdown in Russian life." See Robert Louis Jackson, "On the Ambivalent Beginning of *Anna Karenina,*" in *Semantic Analysis of Literary Texts,* edited by Eric de Haard, Thomas Langerak, and Willem G. Weststeijn (Amsterdam: Elsevier, 1990), 350–351.

45 Boris Eikhenbaum describes *Anna Karenina*'s development from a seemingly conventional work inspired by the adultery and family novel subgenres into a full-fledged ideological statement suffused with political commentary on the most urgent contemporary events of its decade. See *Tolstoi in the Seventies,* translated by Albert Kaspin (Ann Arbor, MI: Ardis, 1982), 111–126.

PART II

Destabilizing gender and sexuality

CHAPTER 5

"Mister Russian Beast"
Civilization's discontents in Turgenev

Emma Lieber

Turgenev does not immediately come to mind as a fin-de-siècle Russian writer, even avant la lettre. Often read as a poet of, if not exactly constitutional serenity, then at least achieved dispassion, Turgenev's poetics of temperance and the "well-lived life" seem anathema to the poetics of degradation, decline, and disease that define fin-de-siècle thinking.[1] In Turgenev, said D. S. Merezhkovsky, we have a "genius of measure and, hence, genius of culture";[2] to T. S. Eliot, Turgenev's works, with their controlled satisfactions, are distinctively satisfying to "the civilized mind."[3] Certainly, no one would characterize Turgenev as cheery. Yet most criticism on the author continues to center on the protective structures of civilized life that his works erect to stave off cataclysm and decay for individuals, communities, and texts: behavioral restraint, or upper-class gentility; the accouterments of culture; the stabilities and enclosing function of aesthetic form, or the well-made text.[4] Turgenev seems to promulgate and uphold all of these formations as a counter to destructive forces in an easily identifiable epic battle between nature and culture. Though undoubtedly ambiguous, the valence of this conflict is often taken as tentatively uplifting; feeble though they may be, cultural forms are, in the dominant critical understanding, an assertion of human composure against elemental degradation and decline, an enduring pronouncement of human dignity despite their questionable efficacy. Indeed, in the minds of many readers, Turgenev's texts, with their "absolute sanity," are models of narrative health.[5]

Precisely this sense of calm reserve led to Turgenev's fall from grace with the Russian reading public as the fin de siècle approached, when "utopian and apocalyptic" tendencies in Russian social and political thought, as Robert Louis Jackson writes, led the more "maximalist" leanings of Tolstoy and Dostoevsky to be favored.[6] Admittedly, these writers, with their "convulsed, terror-haunted" visions, are more readily classified as fin-de-siècle thinkers.[7] Dostoevsky himself famously voiced displeasure with Turgenev's

This research was assisted by a New Faculty Fellows award from the American Council of Learned Societies, funded by The Andrew W. Mellon Foundation.

restraint in his criticism of the execution scene in "The Execution of Tropmann" (1870) – in which the narrator averts his gaze from the beheading in a
demonstration of gentlemanly daintiness – and by pillorying that moment
in *Demons* (1872).[8] As D. S. Mirsky wrote, Turgenev was "replaced by
spicier food"[9] – and specifically, if we may consider a certain maximalism
a national inclination, by spicy food of a distinctively Russian flavor. If, as
this collection posits, the fin-de-siècle mentality found an especially comfortable home in Russia, then a study of Turgenev as a fin-de-siècle Russian
writer appears doubly or perhaps tautologically paradoxical: Russia's foremost champion of placidity and culture appears not only far removed from
the convulsions of fin-de-siècle thinking, but also distinctly un-Russian in
the first place.

But then perhaps the stakes of such a study are concomitantly high. If
fin-de-siècle agita creeps into even Turgenev's writing – burrowing itself
into, or perhaps leaking out of, the tightly buttoned personas of his characters – then it may indeed be an indigenous trait, bred somehow in the bone.
It is not for nothing that Nordau cites Lavretsky's return at the end of *A
Nest of the Gentry* (1859) as a characteristically fin-de-siècle scene.[10] Nordau
here offers a reversal of what has come to be the traditional formula among
scholars in his assessment of Turgenev's fin-de-siècle defeatism – Lavretsky
decays while nature blooms – whereas I would like to compound it. It
seems to me that in Turgenev's texts, culture and nature are symbiotically
entwined: that cultural forms serve as the instrument or medium of elemental violence rather than its obverse and bulwark, and that they enhance
destructive energies precisely in the act of reining them in. In these texts,
the human subject is composed of a complex of libidinal force and civilized
constraint, its troubles determined by their always-already enmeshment.
Thus, whatever quiet pessimism critics have begun to discern in Turgenev's
relationship to the cultural formations that he appears to valorize, I believe
that the situation in his texts is actually considerably worse. In this sense,
it seems to me that our reading of the valence of Turgenev's portrayal of
civilization and culture would do well to recognize the intensity of its fin-
de-siècle angst, by which primitive enactment and civilized form (both the
refinements of culture and the containments of narrative craft) are inex-
tricably bound, the latter enhancing the threat of the former, or perhaps
indistinguishable from it in the first place. Under this lens, Turgenev comes
into focus as very much a poet of civilization, but one for whom culture is
the problem rather than a fantasied cure, and in whose works civilization
commits its quintessentially fin-de-siècle misdeed: it makes us sick.

In many ways, the link I am forging between Turgenev and fin-de-
siècle discourse hinges on Freud. The connections between degeneration

theory as developed in the work of Nordau, B. A. Morel, Richard Krafft-Ebing, and others and early Freudian thought, much of which similarly located the origins of pervasive mental illness in hereditary degeneracy and biological models of decay, are by now commonplace in scholarship.[11] It might be noted that Freud and Nordau studied under the same mentor, Jean-Martin Charcot. Like these thinkers, Freud saw degeneracy as the quintessential ailment of civilization, and though his ideas would change throughout the course of his career, the widespread fin-de-siècle association between civilized life and emotional distress was central to his theory. His late work, *Civilization and its Discontents* (1929), charted the origin of modern disease in the inevitable conflict between individual satisfaction and the repressive action of culture, or the demands of social living. Thus Freudian theory represented "the many developments, repressions, sublimations and reaction-formations, by means of which a child . . . grows into what we call a normal man, the bearer, and in part the victim, of the civilization that has been so painfully acquired."[12] Freud further participated in the drama of masculinity that marked turn-of-the-century discourse in what Olga Matich calls his "thoroughly decadent castration theory," which, for him, stood at the center of so much of modern malcontent.[13] Later, Freud moved away from ideas of degeneration as diagnostic marker and epistemology, rejecting both the biological underpinnings of degeneration theory and the severity of its judgments – whose distinctly moralistic philosophy was predicated, in Sander L. Gilman's words, on the employment of "degeneracy" as "the label for the Other, specifically the Other as the essence of pathology."[14] The quintessential Freudian subject became, in Freud's mature thinking, not the degenerate but the neurotic, whose troubles are determined by unconscious conflict rather than biological and hereditary deterioration, and whose nomination is born of a considerably more democratic impulse. Unlike the degenerate in the theorizing of Nordau, Morel, and others – often visibly identifiable by cranio-facial markers or other deformities, and frequently the fantasied subjects of social quarantine – the Freudian neurotic is veritably everywhere.

Thus this chapter applies a psychoanalytic lens to Turgenev, the author of gentlemen whose "tightly buttoned overcoats" seem an iconic representation of the repressive action of civilized life.[15] All those suits and collars that are the building blocks of Turgenev's poetics – the costumes and manners and rules of etiquette by which so many of his characters live their lives – constitute, in this view, not a protective carapace from natural energies but a sick game. Indeed, one prime point of intersection between Freud and Turgenev is their interest, manifest in the former and often latent in the latter, in sexual malaise. In Turgenev, the representations of civilized refinement and restraint always carry with them the flavor of sexual disease, and the repressive action carried out by the accouterments of culture reflects, symptomatizes, and goes to make up the sexual formation of the subject. Having himself carried on a lifelong, unfulfilled romance with an opera singer, Turgenev was likely well acquainted with the erotic nature of cultured inhibition, not to mention its disappointments and dangers: the extent to which dainty reserve can mask, amplify, or stand in for far more primitive energies.

In what follows I would like to explore these Freudian notions of sexuality in one of Turgenev's *Sportsman's Sketches*, "A Living Relic" (1874), and in the novella *First Love* (1860), both of which feature characters whose difficulties trace back to a sexual disappointment in the prime of puberty: a troubled "first love." In certain aspects, the two texts may be seen as prefiguring the Freudian Oedipal complex, the place where primal desire and the prohibitions of culture converge, as well as its attendant phantasies in the primal scene and castration anxiety. Indeed both texts document the psychosexual origins of their own composition and of the authorial impulse generally, and they may be considered case studies in sexual pathology, in which the patient under consideration is simultaneously character, narrator, and author himself. "A Living Relic" further calls into question the structure of the therapeutic relationship as well as the gender dynamics that, in the early days of psychoanalysis, so often served as the foundation of that relation; the female invalid enunciates her sickness to the man, whose expertise in narrative is meant to cure her. By emphasizing not only the speaker's sexual malaise but also the listener's, and by revealing how that distress determines the assertion of narrative authority, "A Living Relic" puts to question the efficacy and the ethics of such efforts, and it suggests that Turgenev would have viewed even the talking cure with considerable skepticism. In this sense, he was perhaps outdoing Freud in fin-de-siècle defeatism, especially as it related to the possibility of healing. For Freud, some analyses may very well have been interminable; but Turgenev, as we will see, casts any potential for remediation as unlikely. *First Love* similarly documents not only the early formation of individual disturbance but also the extent to which disease, in modern civilization, is a universal endowment. Most broadly, both of these works center on characters located either at the margins of civilization or on the brink of entering it, and for whom initiation into human culture, or at least the possibility of re-entry, is a distinctly dangerous proposition. The language of disorder that permeates the texts is thus the byproduct of the attempted grafting of culture onto nature, however curative the intent of that application. Elaine Showalter observes of thinkers like Nordau that:

> In periods of cultural insecurity, when there are fears of regression and degeneration, the longing for strict border controls around the definition of gender, as well as race, class, and nationality, becomes especially intense. If the different races can be kept in their places, if the various classes can be held in their proper districts of the city, and if men and women can be fixed in their separate spheres, many hope, apocalypse can be prevented and we can preserve a comforting sense of identity and permanence.[16]

Like Freud, Turgenev participated in the language of degeneration without succumbing to these small-minded fantasies about the necessary reinforcement of cultural norms, since he understood that such muscular attempts, even in a more benign guise, were their own brand of pathology. For Turgenev, the well-lived life, like the well-made text, is anything but well.

* * *

Matich writes that fin-de-siècle degeneration theory "reveal[s] . . . an obsessive fascination with the decomposing . . . body."[17] "A Living Relic," in Turgenev's *Sportsman's Sketches*, certainly seems to fit that bill. Bedridden since an accident that left "something inside me – in the depths of my body – . . . broken"[18] and on a long decline toward death, the peasant Lukeria has veritably disintegrated, her singular body exploded into plurality by the process of decomposition: she has become a relic or, in the Russian, the plural "moshchi." Even her limbs are "not under her control,"[19] her bodily integrity shattered, we learn, by erotic excitement: sexual desire for another peasant caused her accident, a steep fall after a faulty step.[20] Sexuality has ruined, or made ruins of, Lukeria's body – a predicament reminiscent of eighteenth- and nineteenth-century fears of masturbation – leaving it prematurely aged and practically insensate.

In her ruined state, Lukeria exists beyond culture, and specifically beyond what many claim culture provides in Turgenev's fiction: the safety of enclosure, protection from the elements. She lies in a small shack, covered only by a thin quilt, and if, in so many readings of Turgenev's works, the sheltering function of cultural formation extends to efforts of textual organization – the forms of order provided by the various narratives and other symbolic arrangements that we create, and by which we lead our lives – then Lukeria is hardly privy to these either. A priest has denied her the ritual of confession, since her condition apparently prevents her from sinning; the doctors

who have visited her have difficulty naming her illness; she is unable to
hold a book, and the calendar she has been given for entertainment goes
unused. She is indeed almost entirely incapable of comprehensible communication, the ordering and organizing of transmissible language, since
the most noticeable result of her bodily decay is the disablement of her
mouth: her lips "c[an] barely be seen," and a smile finds itself "unable to
form."[21] One must sit close in order to hear her voice. What a perfect
opportunity for the sportsman, who comes across her shack during a hunting trip and who, like a good therapist, prompts her story, thus offering her
the benefits of his own salutary acuity for narrative organization and containment, as well as the possibility of narrative cure. In this sense, the story
evokes not only fin-de-siècle anxiety about bodily and moral deterioration
but also the correlative urging for its correction, to which Freud himself
subscribed, though with considerably more nuance and less bigotry than
Nordau. This is a curative endeavor, however, that Turgenev suspects not
only compounds the problem, but is also determined by complexes even
sicker than the original patient's disease.

For there is undoubtedly a violence inherent in the hunter's persona,
one that is lurking even in the very activation of narrative mastery that
makes up much of the sportsman's activity. As Elizabeth Cheresh Allen
writes, in the *Sportsman's Sketches* generally, "the sportsman emerges as a
character not merely hunting for game, or even simply hunting for new
experience, but as an individual hunting for a manner of *narrating*, that
is ... for ways of ordering and understanding what he perceives."[22] One
might reitalicize Allen's sentence – "an individual *hunting* for a manner
of narrating" – to underscore the brutality inherent in the act of epistemological probing. We are moved to ask what exactly the narrator gets
out of this arrangement, or in what way it gets him off. As we learn, he
had known Lukeria when he was sixteen, and found her attractive. It is
here, in the story's latent suspicion that the civilizing action offered by the
male aristocrat to the female peasant carries the seed of sexual aggression,
that Turgenev's wholesale fin-de-siècle melancholy comes to the fore. If the
narrator, in offering his ear, enables Lukeria's mouth, the transaction is in
point of fact coercive, since, though Lukeria seems happy for the opportunity to *talk* – and to take pleasure in working her oral faculties after a
long silence – she is actually loathe to *narrate* – that is, to organize her
life story by the application of some real or metaphorical calendar. Rather,
she has "trained ... [her]self not to think, and more than anything, not to
remember."[23] The narrator's solicitation of her tale, and his offering of the
possibility of composure, narrative shapeliness, and conceptual unity that is

otherwise unavailable to her decomposing self, resembles the actions of doctors who, in attempting to find a name for her affliction, "burnt my spine with hot irons... put me in lumps of ice... [so that] I got quite numb in the end."[24] When one physician finally is able to "t[ell] me the name of my disease – some wonderful long name," he promptly "[goes] away; and all my poor bones ached for a week after,"[25] just as the narrator, in his intrusion, intensifies the pain and then departs, leaving her with little more than shame over her disclosures. Lukeria never asked for a diagnosis, for her body to be prodded and named, her history plumbed and ordered. Coherence can be violating, especially when it is enforced. The hunter even probes into Lukeria's dreams. Does he even have her consent in passing along her story to us, or in enveloping it in his own?

The tale closes with news of Lukeria's death, which has perhaps been accelerated by the pain of these purportedly therapeutic invasions. A constable reports it, yet another authority figure exercising his own diagnostic prowess by pronouncing her not medically disordered but "stricken of God... for her sins, one must suppose." He insists that "no, we don't judge her," but his statement is undercut by his unbidden unearthing of a moral to her story. Lukeria appears unable to escape such authorings; her bodily paralysis makes her the perfect subject of scrutiny and framing. The story's last words are a report of Lukeria's dying impression, the sound of church bells unheard by anyone else; "probably she did not dare say," presumes the narrator, that the sound was coming "from heaven."[26] This is a manifestly uplifting finale, though it is unclear what justifies this conjecture, or this hasty filling-in of Lukeria's preferred silence. In her solitary existence, Lukeria is privy to a knowledge that comes from an eschewal of the forms of self-protection and narrative enclosure necessary to the narrator and his various stand-ins. Lying alone, unthinking, covered by a thin quilt that contrasts the hunter's protective gear, Lukeria can "feel that I'm alive... breathe... put myself all into that,... smell every scent, even the faintest!... [and]... hear everything – everything. If a mole burrows in the ground – I hear even that... I don't need to be told of it, even; I'm the first to know directly."[27] The narrator's condescending assumption about the simple piety reflected in Lukeria's last words thus gets the matter precisely backwards: in her responsiveness to her environment, Lukeria *actually hears* better than he does, and the unmediated experience that she gets in return is her great and only gift. How terrible for that gift to go unacknowledged by such a bad listener, who, deaf to the church bells, wraps up her story, and packages her free associations by putting banalities in her mouth that are easier for him to swallow. It is the narrator's inability to tolerate Lukeria's demurral from language and the comforts of meaning that truly enforces her voicelessness.

One is inclined, therefore, to read the story perversely, and to glimpse the pathology that the tale chronicles more in the gentleman-narrator than in the peasant-patient. The primary affliction that Turgenev narrates consists not in being abandoned by civilization, but in being all-too-firmly ensconced within it, and in repeating the enforcements and containments of culture as its minister. The narrator's opening words are a French proverb, "a dry fisherman and a wet hunter are a sorry sight,"[28] and his palpable satisfaction in the proverb's ability to package and make manageable physical experience reads like an anxiety-ridden attempt at compensation for the failures of his actual raincoat, which lets water through. In fact, the narrator seems almost compulsively tidy, offering a clean white handkerchief to Lukeria, though its use for her is unclear. We begin to see here why the narrator would want, by means of protective garments, cleaning apparatuses, the aesthetic experience, and other instruments of order and enclosure, to restrain an already paralyzed woman even further. In her decomposed state, Lukeria attains a communion with and access to her surroundings that the hunter, whose manifest travels only mask psychic confinement, can hardly muster. Envy lurks in his response to her metaphorical freedom of movement.

The narrator's intrusion is all the more troubling for the suggestion that he wishes to be insulated from investigation into the wildernesses in his own self; his interpellation of Lukeria becomes a defense against his own fear of exposure before readers and himself as much as from the rain and other elements. In the sketch's beginning, we are privy to the rather disturbing disclosure, by the narrator's peasant-guide, that the settlement to which they are retiring, which houses Lukeria and "the existence of which" the narrator "had not even suspected until then,"[29] belongs to the narrator's own mother. This revelation suggests that all the narrator's efforts at ordering and organizing the world around him may be a displaced response to, and an attempt to remediate, certain unresolved Oedipal confusions. As Freud would tell us, much of the Oedipal struggle involves the child's questions about sexual difference as evidenced in the parents (who has what organ?) as well as the sexual act itself (what do they do with them?). Given the narrator's apparent retention, even in adulthood, of ignorance regarding his parents' activities and possessions, some aspect of his own history seems to have gone untended. It could be said that the unwitting traversal of a property that turns out to be one's mother's evokes

Oedipus' unmentionable incestuous act, albeit in diluted form. Further-more, like the sexual aggression in the narrator's treatment of Lukeria, there is palpable rage underlying his efforts of authorship and other acts of control: forms of restraint that likely perpetuated the Oedipal mysteries (a little less delicacy and he might have learned what's what much sooner). Yet the more uninhibited sexuality of the lower classes appears no more promising, since Lukeria is equally doomed by eros. The various dangers of narration in the story are in fact compounded by the suspicion that the oral pleasure of speech is a renewal of the excitement that first got Lukeria into trouble, her acquiescence to the narrator's interview perhaps ushering her further decline. But whatever serene, silent access to nature she could achieve in the narrator's absence, we are hardly inclined to romanticize her position either way. Silence or speech, civilization or savagery – in this story all are equally damned, left with no hope of salvation or melioration, headed toward doom, and merely urging one another further along the path.

Like "A Living Relic," *First Love* is a disturbed production, a bleak case history of malaise born of its subject's initiation into culture, and a story in which every character is, one way or another, a carrier of disease. The etiology of the central, fundamentally sexual ailment is considerably more fleshed out in the novella, the Oedipal scenes and associations given actual, albeit often displaced, representation. If the peasant Lukeria's rel-ative exemption from the imperatives of culture – her class identity, her proximity to death – are vitiated by the sketch's narrator, the narrator of *First Love*, Vladimir Petrovich, is born into civilized living, though he also approaches cultural systems from the relative wilderness of childhood. Possibly for this reason the convulsions of this text are commensurately pronounced, permeated by the intensity of childhood longing and aggres-sion. In parsing the manifestations and obstructions of these impulses – the libidinal economy as created and compounded by cultural restriction – we witness the involuted pathologies that, for Turgenev, compose the human animal. If the fin-de-siècle mood is defined, from some perspectives, by a feeling of melancholic ineffectualness, then Turgenev's story documents the onset in the individual persona of that insufficiency, here literalized as sexual and intellectual impotence: the neurotic's characteristic struggle with desire. Once again, one of the condition's more persistent symptoms is expressed in the writer's craft, or in the very composition of a narrative that at once traces the ailment's source and represents its perpetuation – a fact that goes some way toward further indicating Turgenev's hopelessness vis-à-vis the question of cure.

In the novella's opening, two guests lingering after a dinner party are instructed by their host to share their first experience of love, or perhaps the more singular and autonomous experience of "first love." After the others say their piece, Vladimir Petrovich begs leave to write his account in privacy and then read it aloud – we are then privy to his narrative. The substance of what follows reveals the neurotic underpinnings of modern frame narratives that – unlike the more liberatory offerings of, for example, Boccaccio, in which the delights indulged in the tales are replicated in the sensualities of storytelling – gain their force from inhibited sexuality. Vladimir even denies himself the pleasures of spontaneous speech in his insistence on penning his history; if he is "no good at telling things,"[30] his impotence stems not from Lukeria's lack of authorial control but from a hypertrophied brand of it, a tense closeting of desire rather than a ruinous opening-up. We should see in the gender and class politics of this story as well, then, a certain envy underlying the manifest fear of Lukeria's position, in which feminine acquiescence and peasant forbearance converge, and whose indigenous openness to bodily and personal degradation offers the possibility for communion, however little she is left with in the end. For Lukeria, at least, desire had its day, however short and doomed. With regards to the gender negotiations, Turgenev's male characters are so characteristically passive perhaps as a result of this underground envy, though, in another turn of the screw, that identification is bound up with aggression toward or even violent outlashes against the source of that resentment. For Turgenev, there is no sexual relation.

The account that follows the opening frame, which chronicles the first stirrings of Vladimir's sexuality directed, at age sixteen, at his somewhat older neighbor Zinaida Zasekina, thus serves in part to document the inception of his later authorial behavior and the lock-down on desire that it expresses. In the Zasekins' garden, Vladimir joins a coterie of grown-ups, each possessing a title or another sort of professional self-definition – "count," "doctor," "captain" – who court Zinaida's favor with distinctly contrived enactments laden with sadistic undertones: games with "rules," "regulations," and even a "master of ceremonies," where the victor, according to procedure, receives a kiss from the coveted object. As in the case of the sportsman, adult sexuality expresses itself in its cultural ornamentations, its structures of containment and systems of organization, which grow into repositories of libidinal investment. The interplay between authority and subservience, the injunctions of regulation, rite, and role-playing, not only increase and prolong the pleasure, but become a source of enjoyment in their own right.

Vladimir, only recently a child, walks in on the whole seedy business, bleary-eyed and mutely aroused, his assigned title expressing his unbidden entrance into these adult doings: he becomes "monsieur le page."[31] In fact when, sitting at the garden's edge and experiencing the first stirrings of desire, Vladimir first sees Zinaida surrounded by her suitors and cries out in pleasure, he is laughed at mockingly by the grown men, his "dumb and secret longings"[32] instantly embittered by this education in repression. Acculturation indeed. In one game, each participant must confess his dreams, and the most original gets the prize; in another, called "comparisons," the men attempt to articulate likenesses among disparate objects; in a third, luck determines the victor in the form of a serendipitously chosen ticket. We should see in these enactments, especially those by which speech is enforced, regulated, and codified, the original of which the story's frame – "each of us is obliged to tell the story of his first love" – is a copy.[33]

Yet Vladimir's enmeshment in these proceedings may be less the source of his personality formation than an iteration of its development along an already-established path, a further solidification of libidinal economy. The only child of aristocratic parents, themselves emblems of restraint and composure, Vladimir springs from a hothouse of inhibition and control. It is a wonder his parents were able to find an opening in their "hard-skinned"[34] selves plastic enough to produce a child in the first place. His attraction to the goings-on next door may be determined by his history, the object of the tale's love story less Zinaida than the parents, or Zinaida as a figure for the parents. One should note that Vladimir's family composition forms a perfect Oedipal triangle of mother, father, and son, though the fact that Vladimir's desire is manifestly directed less at his mother than at his father, his passion for the man apparently enhanced because curbed by the latter's "restraining hand,"[35] goes some way toward indicating the complexity of the family pathology as introjected into the son. The notion of "first love" emerges all the more salaciously through its relation to earlier patterns, the early infantile attachments that shape the child's first romantic foray. As another guest in the story's outer frame says, "I didn't have a first love... but started straight off with my second," since "strictly speaking, I fell in love for the first and last time at the age of six" – though in his accounting it was with his nurse.[36] Repetitions have a way of multiplying, such that firsts are always seconds and seconds thirds. Love is always belated.

At this point, we have in Vladimir a picture of the determinants in love object choice, and of the costs wrought by the impossibility of fulfilling primal desires, worthy of a Freudian case study. Turgenev then compounds the problem by converging psychic pattern and blunt reality in the affair between Zinaida and Vladimir's father Pyotr, the Oedipal configuration replaced by the father–son–Zinaida love triangle. In true Oedipal fashion, Vladimir is merely a voyeur of the drama. He watches a tryst between the others in the garden, his alarm leading him to "drop . . . [his] penknife in the grass" after which he fails "to even start looking for it."[37] Later on, he witnesses an appalling scene in which his father strikes Zinaida with a riding crop – a representative act of dominion over nature that reveals such cultural efforts as constituting, at base, something like a sexual fetish. If Vladimir's loss of his penknife represents the castration the child fears in the face of the father, his taking up the pen in adulthood is small recompense for this emasculation, especially in its figuration as a stale replacement for the more immediate pleasures of speech, and for the impotencies that even its wielding cannot correct. In any event, the adult instrument has lost its force and its edge: pen rather than knife. At the culminating moment of the father's sadistic act, words fail the narrator in his attempt to describe Zinaida's facial expression – in part, surely, because, as a woman who claims to "need someone who would break [her] in two," she likely experiences as much gratification as fear.[38] The primal scene, with its confusion and seething force, has robbed the child of speech, a trauma retained by the adult. This is a father who, in insisting on possessing *all* of the narrative's women, cannot be overcome, and a son's potency that, one fears, will never be restored. Indeed, in the competition for Zinaida's affection, Pyotr Vasilievich's closest adversary is not Vladimir but another of the adults, Count Malevsky – who, of the group of men congregating next door, was the "only one who . . . kn[ew] how to bluff himself into our house and make himself very agreeable to my mother," a position he then uses to expose the affair.[39] In all of these adult exchanges and illicit pairings, Vladimir, bereft of both parental and female attention, is the only one left with "no one [to] love . . . me."[40] If the "first love" of the title has an ambiguous referent (who is its proprietor and who its object?), it becomes increasingly clear that the tale of its flourishing is one from which Vladimir is systematically excluded, unrecognized as a player by all of his various object-choices. The story of his first love, like that of Lukeria's suffering, is not his own.

Further evidence of the compacted intricacy of pathology – and of the complex involutions that convulse this strange configuration of cathecting subjects and cathected objects – exists in the notion that Malevsky, in replacing Pyotr vis-à-vis his wife, also replaces Vladimir as rival for Zinaida, becoming a stand-in for both father and son. In this shifting web, Zinaida acts both as Vladimir's mother, the object upon which both his own and his father's affections converge, and, by her own admission, as his sister: as she says, "I could be your auntie – well, no, not your auntie, but your elder sister."[41] The text itself then confirms this association by a coincidence of names; Zinaida's younger brother is also Vladimir, and the narrator, in a relegation indicative of his banishment to perpetual childhood, is at one point charged to play with him while the adults go about their business. One wonders if the energies that coalesce in this sibling identification have less to do with Zinaida's sisterly affection for Vladimir than with her erotic feelings for his father and her intuition that their requital, meaning the elder man's attraction to a much younger woman, hints in its own way of incest. In her own construction, Zinaida, not Vladimir, will make the Oedipal conquest and get the parent, and the Oedipal attachment metaphorically consummated is the one – father–daughter – that has nothing to do with Vladimir. This consummation brings pollution in the family bloodline even sadder and stranger, for Vladimir at least, than those that beset Oedipus himself: for if Oedipus, in making his mother his wife, becomes brother to his children, Vladimir, when the story intimates that Zinaida has become pregnant by Pyotr, becomes merely brother to his figurative and embryonic nephew or niece. As a child-onlooker on the drama, Vladimir has been subject to family pathology but has had no hand to play in it. His Oedipal demands are pushed to the background, with the compounded perversions of the situation resulting from the narrative's simultaneous double lens: the fact that, as with all young boys, he must share his love story with his father. He cannot even muster the appropriate rage – on behalf of Zinaida, his mother, or himself – when he witnesses the slap, instead admitting that his father "seemed to grow in my eyes":[42] as though the father had virtually transformed into the paternal swelling organ, at the expense of any comparable activity on the son's part. That Zinaida's pregnancy goes entirely unspoken in the story and perhaps, for the adult Vladimir, consciously unacknowledged, is further evidence of Vladimir's continuing impotence, here expressed as authorial and epistemological insufficiency. On the other hand, the convolutions of this kinship arrangement are so profound – the text even displaces the drama and has Zinaida die in childbirth years after her affair with Pyotr – that one can hardly blame Vladimir his difficulties.

Although we have strayed a bit from the analysis of how fin-de-siècle thinking relates to Turgenev's texts, the hothouse of convoluted pathologies that *First Love* constructs, and from which there appears no exit, should go far in indicating the novella's atmosphere of foreboding, as well as the extent to which the dainty aristocratic life in Turgenev is anything but serene. The refinements of civilization are symptomatic of a greater, primal malaise rather than a curative. When even the doctor calls himself "a queer sort,"[43] one indeed despairs of the possibility of cures of any kind, at least insofar as we are located in a culture so skittish that Nietzsche's and Freud's vision of healing at the hands of "doctors and nurses *who are sick themselves*" is unthinkable.[44] No less than Lukeria, the characters of *First Love* are hopelessly ruined, not despite, but because of, the regulatory measures that bind in order to deny more primitive energies. Pyotr, for one, is a monster of control whose corporeal outbursts, including the apoplectic fit that kills him, are conditioned by his ethic of repression as surely as they belie his own fantasy of absolute potency; it is Pyotr's wife, after all, who has the money. His one offering of paternal wisdom to Vladimir is the injunction to "learn how to express your will... and you'll be free, and you'll be in command."[45] And yet as with "A Living Relic," even the undertone of nostalgia for the natural, uncorrupted self, unsullied by civilized form and the noxious artifice of adults, offers little by way of salvation or possibility. For not only are the ecstasies of childhood and the abandon of unfettered sexuality not long for this world, but we have also seen the suggestion that those freedoms were absent from the beginning. Though the doctor warns Vladimir that "you could catch an infection"[46] from the sick enactments in Zinaida's garden, it may in fact be the gentile environment of Vladimir's own upbringing – the aristocratic hauteur, the marriage-for-profit, the erupting violence – that is the origin of contagion. The pivotal initiation dramatized is not that of Vladimir into Zinaida's garden, but that of Zinaida into Vladimir's world, the rules and restrictions of which turn out, in him, to be bred in the bone. Zinaida herself is described as a "mixture of cunning and carelessness, artificiality and simplicity, peacefulness and playfulness,"[47] however, and the Zasekin household is a grotesque composite of aristocratic pretension and base dilapidation. In this text, the confinements of civilization are always a primary constitutive factor, with all human personalities composed of a confluence of nature and culture, impulse and inhibition, and disorder and control – a condition emblematized by the nickname Zinaida gives to the hussar Belovzorov: "my dear Mister Beast" (*monsieur moi zver*).[48]

Thus like "A Living Relic," *First Love* documents the rotting of the human person, though here this deterioration is not only premature – the decomposing Lukeria was only thirty – but nearly a priori, occurring long before sexual consummation is even on the table, already resident in body, mind, and culture. The novella closes with the narrator recounting a visit he made in his early twenties, just days after hearing of Zinaida's death, to a dying old peasant woman who "had seen no joy in her life" but who visibly feared death nonetheless.[49] In repeating the sexual politics of "A Living Relic" – a gentleman watching the body of a peasant woman disintegrate – the ending also rehearses the hopelessness of the human predicament, in which those who renounce pleasure are no more saved than those who experience it and vice versa, and there is no escaping the scopic complex deeply entwined in the human disorder. We are all just watching each other die; when you die, there is always someone there to watch. Indeed, Turgenev may have been prescient here of his own corporeal fate, since, as Ilya Vinitsky shows in his contribution to this volume, the author's slow and painful death was itself thoroughly observed and documented, as his body grew as rotten as Lukeria's. That the narrative never returns to the opening frame of the dinner party enacts in miniature the various forms of ruination that the texts document while representing the impotence underlying the meaning-making compulsions of authorial composure. Just as surely as he has come to wear the collars and neckties that choked his father, Vladimir has been acculturated into that man's methods of domination and control – he just doesn't employ them very well.

In conclusion, I would like to return to Dostoevsky's famous polemic with Turgenev, centering on the latter's refusal to watch the beheading in "The Execution of Tropmann," as it relates to the other opening question of this examination, that of Turgenev's so-called fin-de-siècle angst, or, rather, his lack thereof – or, to put it admittedly reductively, the question of his "Russianness." Undoubtedly we admire Dostoevsky enormously for his insistence on looking at human suffering straight on.[50] Yet the question of the ethics of vision, not to mention the sexual implications of the gaze, that always haunts Turgenev's scenes of looking or not looking is not far from Dostoevsky's terror-stricken sensibility, however pious the latter's manifest attitude to the act of watching. What detractors and admirers of Turgenev alike tend not to appreciate is the extent to which for him both possibilities – the looking at or the looking away, the animal voyeurism or the civilized reserve – are equally pathological and, potentially, equally violent. In this sense Turgenev leaves us without even the vision of hope embodied in Dostoevsky's figure of the empathetic witness. Compare Raskolnikov's dream of a mare being whipped in *Crime and Punishment* – his outpouring of childish love for the victim evidence of the spark of divinity still resident in his adult person – and Vladimir's dream after Zinaida's beating, a vision that similarly evokes in him the horror that "they're whipping her... whipping her, whipping her"[51] and in which Belovzorov, covered in blood, threatens his father. One can hardly imagine a fantasy more terror-haunted, or one that leaves us with so little hope of resolution. Dostoevsky had at least his vision of grace, however infrequently it was achieved.

Dostoevsky is usually identified as the psychologist among nineteenth-century Russian writers, and he is the author whose insights are most frequently associated with Freud's. Yet the dream in Turgenev's text, with the identifications, projections, and displacements whose complexity is compounded by the absence of Vladimir from the dream-scene – for surely the rage to which the dream testifies is the dreamer's own – stands out as closer to Freud's vision. In the dream, Vladimir as voyeur recalls the unconscious with its drives and inhibitions, desires and resistances, and the extent to which its productions, existing beyond morality, tend to belie all forms of human idealism. It is this systematic refusal of any assurances that accounts for the disquiet that Turgenev's works so frequently evoke and that, perhaps, makes him a fin-de-siècle Russian writer par excellence.

NOTES

1 Jane Costlow, *Worlds within Worlds* (Princeton University Press, 1990), 14–15.
2 G. A. Bialyi, *Russkii realism ot Turgeneva k Chekhovu* (Leningrad: Sovetskii pisatel', 1990), 5.
3 T. S. Eliot, "Turgenev," *The Egoist* 4:10 (1917): 167.
4 See especially Costlow, *Worlds within Worlds*, and Elizabeth Cheresh Allen, *Beyond Realism: Turgenev's Poetics of Secular Salvation* (Stanford University Press, 1992), both of which argue that Turgenev valorizes civilization as a defense against the chaotic and destructive forces of the natural world.
5 Joseph Conrad, *Notes on Life and Letters* (Cambridge University Press, 2004), 42.
6 Robert Louis Jackson, "The Turgenev Question," *Sewanee Review* 93 (1985): 303.
7 Conrad, *Notes on Life and Letters*, 42.
8 For more on "The Execution of Tropmann" and how that text might contribute to a pessimistic reading of the valence of civilization in Turgenev's works, see Emma Lieber, "'Pardon, Monsieur': Civilization and Civility in Turgenev's 'The Execution of Tropmann,'" *Slavic Review* 66:4 (2007): 667–682.
9 D. S. Mirsky, "Turgenev's Prose," in *Critical Essays on Ivan Turgenev*, edited by David A. Lowe (Boston: G. K. Hall, 1989), 38.
10 Nordau, *Degeneration*, 3.

11 For a survey of Freud's use of the term "degeneracy" and its relation to theories of degeneration, see Sander L. Gilman, *The Case of Sigmund Freud: Medicine and Identity at the Fin de Siècle* (Baltimore: Johns Hopkins University Press, 1994), especially the chapter "The Degenerate Foot and the Search for Oedipus."

12 Sigmund Freud, *Five Lectures on Psychoanalysis* (New York: W. W. Norton, 1990), 37.

13 Matich, *Erotic Utopia*, 18. For further discussion of the crisis of masculinity that characterized fin-de-siècle thinking, see Connor Doak's contribution to this volume.

14 Gilman, *The Case of Sigmund Freud*, 162.

15 Ivan Turgenev, "Kazn' Tropmana," in *Polnoe sobranie sochinenii i pisem v dvadtsati vos'mi tomakh* (Moscow: Nauka, 1960–1968), XIV:153.

16 Showalter, *Sexual Anarchy*, 4.

17 Matich, *Erotic Utopia*, 18.

18 Ivan Turgenev, "Zhivye moshchi," in *Zapiski okhotnika* (Chicago: Bradda Books, 1965), 338.

19 Ibid., 342.

20 Gilman claims that limping and other forms of invalidity were often taken as symptoms of sexual malaise, and that the association of hysteria "with the impairment of gait can be traced back to the eighteenth century." *The Case of Sigmund Freud*, 126.

21 Turgenev, "Zhivye moshchi," 337.

22 Allen, *Beyond Realism*, 143.

23 Turgenev, "Zhivye moshchi," 340.

24 Ibid., 338.

25 Ibid., 342.

26 Ibid., 347.

27 Ibid., 339.

28 Ibid., 335.

29 Ibid., 336.

30 Ivan Turgenev, *First Love*, in *First Love and Other Stories*, translated by Richard Freeborn (Oxford University Press, 1989), 145.

31 Ibid., 188.

32 Ibid., 162.

33 Ibid., 144.

34 Ibid., 171.

35 Ibid., 163.

36 Ibid., 144.

37 Ibid., 190.

38 Ibid., 167.

39 Ibid., 187.

40 Ibid., 193.

41 Ibid., 182.

42 Ibid., 193.

43 Ibid., 171.
44 Friedrich Nietzsche, *On the Genealogy of Morality*, edited by Keith Ansell-Pearson and translated by Carol Diethe (Cambridge University Press, 1994), 92.
45 Turgenev, *First Love*, 164.
46 Ibid., 171.
47 Ibid., 166.
48 Ibid., 178.
49 Ibid., 202.
50 For example, as Jackson writes, unlike Turgenev's narrator at the execution scene, Dostoevsky's narrator in *Notes from the House of the Dead* refused to "avert his own face" from the horrors of the prison. See Robert Louis Jackson, "The Root and the Flower: Dostoevsky and Turgenev: A Comparative Esthetic," *Yale Review* (Winter 1974): 248.
51 Turgenev, *First Love*, 199.

CHAPTER 6

Masculine degeneration in Dostoevsky's Demons

Connor Doak

Dostoevsky's *Demons*, which had seemed a provincial nightmarish fantasy from the last century, now crawl around the world before our very eyes.

– Alexander Solzhenitsyn[1]

Of all the writers discussed in this volume, Dostoevsky is the most easily identified as a forerunner of the anxieties about degeneration that characterized the fin de siècle. His writing forecasts an imminent apocalypse: an 1881 diary entry predicts "the end of this century will bring a catastrophe of a kind never seen before" and his novels paint a picture of the spiritual sickness, social deprivation, and political ideas that pave the way toward a cataclysmic modernity.[2] Hence D. S. Mirsky calls him "the first and greatest symptom of the spiritual decomposition of the Russian soul."[3] The novel *Demons* (1871–1872) perhaps best exemplifies Dostoevsky's prophetic and pessimistic strain. Albert Camus speaks for many readers when he writes that *Demons* "heralds the nihilism of our age" and calls its characters "torn and dead souls . . . the very souls who populate our own society and spiritual world."[4]

This chapter highlights one aspect of these "torn and dead souls" that has hitherto been neglected: their masculinity. While it is a critical commonplace to discuss *Demons* in the light of the "fathers and sons" topos that runs through Russian literature, this chapter also attempts to map the genealogy of masculinities that accompanies generational change.[5] Broadly speaking, Dostoevsky derides the liberal men of the forties, represented in the novel by Stepan Verkhovensky and the writer Semen Karmazinov, as hysterical, effeminate, and ineffectual. Yet he critiques still more harshly the radical generation of "sons," particularly Pyotr Verkhovensky and Nikolai Stavrogin, for their brand of masculinity based on the fetishization of power and violence. Even Ivan Shatov, often considered the character who comes closest to Dostoevsky's own views in *Demons*, ends up as a cuckold celebrating his wife giving birth to another man's child. I read *Demons* as Dostoevsky's attempt to diagnose the failings of the models of masculinity extant in his time, and his frustrated search to imagine a character type that could combine masculinity with Christian love.[6]

I focus here specifically on degenerate *men* because Dostoevsky himself perceived Russia's problems in gendered terms. His journalism repeatedly affirms that Russian women possess superior qualities to men: an 1873 essay in *Diary of a Writer* suggests "our [Russian] women possess sincerity, perseverance, earnestness, and honor, the quest for truth and sacrifice. All these qualities have always been stronger in Russian women than in men."[7] In 1876, he articulates this gender binary even more strongly, suggesting that Russian women embody "our one great hope, one of the keys to our renewal" while disparaging Russian men because they have "succumbed terribly to the debauchery of avarice, cynicism, and materialism."[8] The notion that women provided the key to national redemption was common among mid- to late nineteenth-century Russian thinkers, as Jenny Kaminer demonstrates in Chapter 7 of this volume. Richard Avramenko and Jingcai Ying rightly point out how Dostoevsky's heroines provide such a redemptive role in *Demons*.[9] However, I turn my attention to the other side of the coin: the fact that Dostoevsky blames *men* for the nation's woes. While Nina Pelikan Straus has done pioneering work in locating a critique of masculine power and male violence in Dostoevsky's novels, my essay aims to situate Dostoevsky's anxieties about masculinity as part of a larger dialogue about degeneration in the European fin de siècle.[10]

Dostoevsky was not alone in expressing concerns about masculine degeneration in this period. Recent research on fin-de-siècle Europe emphasizes how discourses of degeneration often depended – implicitly or explicitly – on fears about a loss of masculinity. For example, Robert Nye has pointed to anxieties about masculinity in B. A. Morel's foundational work on degeneration in the 1850s: Morel worried that men were losing their physical strength, sexual potency, and suffering increasingly from sexual perversion.[11] Such perversion is a paramount concern in Richard Krafft-Ebing's *Psychopathia Sexualis* (1886), which identifies periods of "moral decadence" in modern civilization during which "effeminacy, sensuality and luxury" gain ascendancy, and men suffer from "monstrous perversions of the sexual life."[12] However, it was Nordau's *Degeneration* (1892) that popularized the concept of degeneration internationally. As Andrew Smith points out, Nordau was particularly worried by an "effeminate 'emotionalism' which constituted a key aspect of 'mental stigma of degenerates.'"[13] In response to this trend, Nordau called for the creation of a stoic, virile ideal: "men who rise early and are not weary before sunset, who have clear heads, solid stomachs, and hard muscles."[14]

Although I aim to situate Dostoevsky's *Demons* within this broader context, I emphasize that I am not concerned here with questions of influence. Krafft-Ebing and Nordau published their major texts after Dostoevsky's death, and it is doubtful that Dostoevsky knew Morel's work.[15] In Dostoevsky's Russia, "degeneration" (*vyrozhdenie, degeneratsiia*) in its medical sense was a term known only to specialists, and it would not be recognized as a sociocultural phenomenon until the 1880s.[16] Nevertheless, I plan to show here that Dostoevsky's *Demons* presents a cast of degenerate men, many of whom suffer from the specific ailments that would later be identified in works by Nordau and Krafft-Ebing. Yet, as we shall see, Dostoevsky offers a more nuanced evaluation of masculine degeneration than his European counterparts, often managing to avoid the essentialism that dominates their work, and seeing redemptive potential where they see only sickness and decay.

The liberal generation: Stepan Trofimovich's performance of degeneration

The opening chapters of *Demons* acquaint the reader with its central comic figure, Stepan Trofimovich Verkhovensky. As Joseph Frank and others have noted, Stepan Trofimovich appears to be an exaggerated, depraved version of the men of the forties that featured in novels by Pisemsky and the early Turgenev, among others.[17] Stepan Trofimovich outwardly professes the romantic idealism common in this period, along with its incumbent codes of masculinity: the privileging of ideas over actions, the valorization of art and beauty, self-sacrifice in love, and a chivalric respect for women.

However, Stepan Trofimovich carries these ideas to the extreme: he is not merely sensitive, but frequently hysterical. He is given not only to noble self-sacrifice, but also to masochism and self-humiliation; he is not merely an admirer of women, but slavishly enthralled by Varvara Petrovna.[18] His love letters are described as "the nervous outbursts of that most innocent of fifty-year-old babies."[19] During a period of absence, we are told these letters were "literally soaked with the tears of separation."[20] As a confidant of Stepan, the chronicler has to deal frequently with his friend's "hysterical fits and sobbing on [his] shoulders."[21]

One can draw an obvious parallel between Dostoevsky's Stepan Trofimovich and Nordau's portrait of the degenerate.[22] For Nordau, emotionalism was one of degeneration's key symptoms:

> Another mental stigma of degenerates is their emotionalism... He [the degenerate] laughs until he sheds tears, or weeps copiously without adequate occasion; a commonplace line of poetry or prose sends a shudder down his back; he falls into raptures before indifferent pictures or status; and music especially, even the most insipid and least commendable, arouses in him the most vehement emotions.[23]

Stepan Trofimovich would appear to be a textbook case. Describing his friend's decline at the beginning of Chapter 5, the narrator tells us that Stepan Trofimovich "was drinking more, had become more lachrymose, was suffering from weak nerves and had developed a hypersensitivity to art" (*k iziashchnomu*).[24]

Crucially, the novel draws a connection between Stepan Trofimovich's degenerate emotionalism and his liberal politics. The narrator speaks sardonically of how Stepan Trofimovich "suffered bouts of what we called 'civic sorrow' among ourselves... that is, he suffered from spleen."[25] The liberal circle's inflation of "spleen" into the high-minded phrase "civic sorrow" makes a mockery of Stepan Trofimovich's politics. Interestingly, Nordau also protests against building one's political convictions out of emotion. In *Degeneration*, he rails against "muddle-headed" people who "feel a leaning towards a sickly, impotent socialism" not from "sober scientific conviction" but rather from "a hysterical emotionality."[26] Nordau's language – *sickly, impotent, hysterical* – reveals the gendered connotations of basing one's political beliefs on emotion. Thus he suggests that only effeminate and defective men make their political choices based on emotion.

Stepan Trofimovich's effeminacy is revealed most clearly in the passages that describe Varvara Petrovna's attempt to arrange a marriage between him and Dasha Shatova, in order to cover up her own son's misdeeds. Varvara Petrovna explains that the plan will work because Stepan Trofimovich is himself a *baba*, an effeminate man whom she can control. When Varvara Petrovna relays this plan to Stepan Trofimovich, he objects at first, but his choice of words serves only to confirm the insult to his masculinity:

> "I... I never could have imagined that you would marry me off... to another... woman!"
> "You're not a young lady, Stepan Trofimovich. Only young ladies are married off. You're getting married yourself," hissed Varvara Petrovna poisonously.
> "Yes, I've mixed up the words," he said, switching to French, "but it's the same thing." He stared at her, looking lost.[27]

Tellingly, Stepan Trofimovich emphasizes his own effeminacy by borrowing a verb normally used for women, "vydat' kogo-nibud' (zamuzh)" or "to marry somebody off." This phrasing suggests his complicity with his own humiliation, his willingness to perform an effeminate role for his own masochistic pleasure. Indeed, when Stepan Trofimovich explains Varvara Petrovna's plan to the narrator, the narrator notes that "a smile of shame, utter desperation, yet, at the same time, some peculiar rapture" crosses Stepan Trofimovich's face.[28]

Masochism in Dostoevsky's novels is hardly a new topic for critics: Daniel Rancour-Laferrière in particular has written widely on this phenomenon.[29] For our purposes, however, it is crucial to note that the power dynamic in the Varvara Petrovna and Stepan Trofimovich relationship conforms closely to Nordau's definition of masochism as a symptom of degeneration:

> The man affected by this perversion [masochism] feels himself, as regards woman, to be the weaker party, as the one standing in need of protection, as the slave who rolls on the ground, compelled to obey the behests of his mistress, and finding his happiness in obedience. It is the inversion of the healthy and natural relation between the sexes.[30]

Thus in addition to Rancour-Laferrière's reading, which interprets Dostoevsky's explorations of masochism as part of the Russian national psyche, we can also consider the Stepan Trofimovich and Varvara Petrovna relationship as representing anxieties that are specific to the fin-de-siècle moment with its overturning of the gender norms that had appeared "natural" to Nordau.

Stepan Trofimovich not only indulges in contrived emotional outbursts with Varvara Petrovna, but also stages similar performances to negotiate his relationships with other characters. He relies on outbursts frequently when he fails to carry out a particular duty required by the social norms of masculinity. For example, he uses this emotionalism to disguise how he has neglected his fatherly responsibilities toward his son Pyotr Stepanovich. When Pyotr Stepanovich returns to town, Stepan Trofimovich publicly embraces him and offers a histrionic apology – half in Russian, half in French – with tears rolling down his cheeks.[31] Pyotr Stepanovich, belonging to the radical generation of the sons, behaves according to a different code of masculinity, and responds to his father's emotionalism with his own performance of stoic restraint. Pyotr Stepanovich even reprimands Stepan Trofimovich, telling his father to "cut out the drama" (*bez zheshtov*) in order to save face in front of Stavrogin, who has just entered the room.[32]

However, Pyotr Stepanovich need not worry on that score, because Stavrogin has long been familiar with Stepan Trofimovich's emotional outbursts. When Stavrogin was a boy, Stepan Trofimovich served as his tutor. Rather than fulfill his masculine responsibilities of providing a role model and an education, Stepan Trofimovich resorted to emotional out-bursts when caring for the boy. An intriguing passage sketches out their relationship:

> Stepan Trofimovich's whole secret lay in the fact that he was a child himself. Often, he would wake his ten- or eleven-year-old friend at night, with the sole purpose of pouring out his injured feelings in tears before the boy, or to reveal some family secret, without realizing that such actions were completely unacceptable. They would throw themselves into each other's embrace and cry...
>
> Stepan Trofimovich managed to touch the deepest heartstrings of his friend and to awake in him the first and as yet unclear feeling of that eternal and sacred longing, which any chosen soul, having tasted and known it, will never exchange later for a cheap satisfaction... But in any case, it was good that the teacher and pupil eventually went their own ways, even if their separation came too late.[33]

This passage has attracted much critical commentary, and the evasive language makes it intentionally difficult to pinpoint the nature of the transgression that took place. Some see it as a veiled account of child abuse, while others have suggested they indulged in mutual masturbation.[34] For our purposes, it is crucial to note that this passage again depicts Stepan Trofimovich as insufficiently masculine to restrain his emotions: he acts as if he too were "a child himself," rather than a man, "pour[ing] out his injured feelings in tears."

Even if one reads the abuse as primarily emotional in nature rather than sexual, there remains the problem of Stepan Trofimovich awakening in the boy that "eternal and sacred longing" that "he will never exchange later for a cheap satisfaction." This comment implies a peculiar kind of yearning for something different from coitus and leads the modern reader to consider affinities between Stepan Trofimovich and the decadent move-ment. Emerging toward the end of the nineteenth century, the decadent movement privileged forms of desire that focused on alternatives to het-erosexual intercourse and reproduction.[35] However, in Dostoevsky's novel, this "eternal and sacred longing" – the language of the high-minded Stepan Trofimovich – degenerates into a taste for sexual violence in the next gen-eration once Stavrogin becomes an adult.

The radical generation: Stavrogin as *homme fatal*

We can think of *Demons* as a terrifying hall of mirrors, where the degenerate features of the fathers, described in the text with some subtlety, become reflected as grotesque and monstrous among the sons. Thus the novel's vague inference of an inappropriate relationship between Stepan Trofimovich and the boy Stavrogin reappears in a more disturbing form in the censored chapter "At Tikhon's." In Stavrogin's confession, he reveals how he took perverse pleasure in watching the young girl Matresha flogged, and in eventually seducing her. Unlike the early chapters that treat Stepan Trofimovich's performances of his own effeminacy and masochism rather comically, Stavrogin describes his own sexuality in much darker, more violent terms. Thus he writes how he finds "elation in the tormenting knowledge of his own baseness" when watching Matresha being flogged, and describes the "rapture" he would feel if a French viscount whom he had insulted had seized him by the hair and forced him to surrender.[36]

While the effeminate Stepan Trofimovich derives pleasure mostly from his self-effacing masochism, Stavrogin couples this masochism with a sadistic streak, and, moreover, he possesses the virile good looks and charm to prove attractive to women and men who willingly make themselves his victims.[37] Even Matresha, at least according to Stavrogin, responds to his advances in "complete rapture" with passionate kisses of her own.[38] Stavrogin becomes an *homme fatal* in the most literal sense of this phrase: Matresha hangs herself after her encounter with Stavrogin, and she is one of many characters who fall victim to his charms.[39]

Of the men in the novel, it is Pyotr Stepanovich who falls most obviously for the charms of this *homme fatal*. Irene Zohrab has identified the homoeroticism in their relationship, and her suggestion that Dostoevsky may have drawn on the work of German sexologist Karl Ulrichs neatly dovetails with this chapter's claim that *Demons* reflects a fin-de-siècle worldview where gender and sexuality norms have been distorted.[40] However, I would also point out that Pyotr Stepanovich's confession of his feelings for Stavrogin forms a grotesque reprise of Stepan Trofimovich's earlier outbursts in front of Varvara. Consider the romantic clichés and masochistic overtones when Pyotr Stepanovich expresses his feelings to Stavrogin:

> "Stavrogin, you're beautiful!" cried Pyotr Stepanovich, almost in ecstasy. "Do you know that you're beautiful! . . . I love beauty. I'm a nihilist, but love beauty. Don't nihilists love beauty? It's only idols that they don't love, but I love an idol. You are my idol! . . . You are the leader, you are the sun and I am your worm."
> He suddenly kissed Stavrogin's hand. A shiver ran down Stavrogin's spine and he tore his hand away in fright.[41]

In confessing his love for Stavrogin, Pyotr Stepanovich appears aware here of a mismatch between these feelings and his revolutionary politics. "Don't nihilists love beauty?" Pyotr Stepanovich asks. "It's only idols they don't love, but I love an idol!" His implication is that a true nihilist would not idolize another human being. Indeed, according to the "Revolutionary's Catechism" (1869), attributed to Nechaev and Bakunin, the revolutionary was expected to be "stern with himself," "stern with others," and to repress any "tender, effeminizing feelings of kinship, friendship, love and gratitude" and replace them with "a total cold passion for the revolutionary cause."[42] As we saw earlier, Pyotr Stepanovich successfully plays the role of the stern, detached son during the reunion with his mawkish father, a performance perhaps staged for the benefit of Stavrogin. However, Pyotr Stepanovich ultimately proves unable to repress his feelings for Stavrogin and succumbs to the same kind of emotional, masochistic outbursts characteristic of his father. Moreover, this scene also suggests that Pyotr Stepanovich follows his father in committing the error identified by Nordau: we can say that Pyotr Stepanovich bases his radical political views not on "sober scientific conviction" but rather on "a hysterical emotionality."[43]

What attracts Pyotr Stepanovich to Stavrogin? When Stavrogin is first introduced, the narrator records his surprise at encountering a "very hand-some young man" when he had expected to meet "some dirty scruff, worn out from debauchery and stinking of vodka."[44] His fawning description goes on to extol the perfection of Stavrogin's physical features, but notes that there was nonetheless something repulsive about him:

> [H]is hair seemed somehow very black indeed, his bright eyes seemed some-how very calm and clear, the color of his face seemed very white and tender, his rosy cheeks somehow too bright and clean. His teeth were like pearls, his lips like coral. One would think him the very image of a handsome man, yet somehow he also seemed repulsive. People said his face resembled a mask; they talked too of his exceptional physical strength.[45]

On the surface, Stavrogin's perfectly regular features, robust health, and physical strength make him one of Nordau's ideal men with their "clear heads, solid stomachs, and hard muscles."[46] Yet there is also a hint of femi-nine beauty about Stavrogin: the rosy cheeks, the coral lips, and the pearly teeth add an element of gender ambiguity. Whereas Nordau sees a correla-tion between the healthy body and a healthy mind, Dostoevsky intention-ally decouples the two: the seemingly beautiful Stavrogin ultimately proves ambiguous in terms of gender, possesses a depraved sexuality, and becomes the book's greatest villain. Stavrogin abuses the magnetic power he holds over others, becoming the kernel around which all the novel's sexual and political conflicts revolve.

Through his depiction of Stavrogin, we see that although Dostoevsky and Nordau shared similar anxieties about the degeneration of masculinity, they did not posit the same solutions. For Nordau, the solution lay in returning to an essentialized system of virility that had been corrupted by the decadence of modern living. Yet Dostoevsky did not advocate such a simple solution. For him, the seemingly virile Stavrogin merely continues the system of sadomasochistic domination and abuse of power that had characterized the relationship between Stepan Trofimovich and Varvara Petrovna.

Shatov: An alternative masculinity?

If both Stepan Trofimovich's effeminate, masochistic behavior and Stavrogin's hypermasculinity prove unsatisfactory, then the reader of *Demons* must look elsewhere for a paragon of an alternative, defensible masculinity. The most obvious candidate for this role is Ivan Shatov, who breaks away from the revolutionary movement and struggles to believe in God, and who has been identified as "Dostoevsky's mouthpiece."[47]

Significantly, the early chapters depict Shatov as having a gruff exterior, "irascible" and ill at ease in society: "Awkward and clumsy, Shatov disliked sweet nothings. He gave the outward appearance of seeming rude, but inside he seemed most sensitive."[48] Shatov often appears inarticulate in his actions with others: in a conversation with Liza about Captain Lebiadkin, Shatov "*muttered,* as though involuntarily (*kak by nekhotia*)," that Lebiadkin is a good-for-nothing drunkard; when she tries to press him, he "*grimaced* and made for the door, having *growled* 'What's it got to do with me?'"[49] Implicitly, the narrative draws a contrast between the eloquent falsity of Stepan Trofimovich, who has learned to perform the emotional part allotted to him on stage, and the reserved Shatov, whose reluctance to articulate his feelings suggests a profundity of emotion Stepan Trofimovich lacks.

Moreover, Shatov appears as a non-violent and sympathetic man in his relationships with women; his kind of masculinity sharply contrasts with the behavior of the lady-killer Stavrogin. For example, Shatov offers a kind ear to Maria Lebiadkina, the disabled woman whom Stavrogin married and abandoned. Dostoevsky devotes several pages to a dialogue between Shatov and Maria in which he acts as her confidant.[50] Their relationship appears non-sexual, based on his sympathy rather than mutual affection. He listens attentively to her while she repeats her claim that she once gave birth and drowned the baby. He does challenge her, asking if her story is not simply a delusion, but she does not take offense at the question, even accepting he may be right.

This scene creates the possibility of a meaningful, non-sexual interaction between a sexually mature man and a child-like woman, and provides a counterpoint to Stavrogin's abuse of Maria (and his involvement or complicity in her murder) as well as the seduction of Matresha in the censored chapter. Interactions that mirror the Shatov and Maria pattern reoccur between Alyosha Karamazov and Liza Khokhlakova in *Brothers Karamazov*. Such scenes show Dostoevsky's attempt to articulate a counter-model to masculine degeneration, which depends on compassion and alternative forms of kinship, rather than a return to patriarchal domination, heterosexual romance, and the marriage plot.

Interestingly, Dostoevsky's notebooks reveal that he initially imagined Shatov – then Shaposhnikov – as a sexually active character. As Edward Wasiolek notes, one version imagined Shaposhnikov cuckolding Stepan Trofimovich (then Granovsky) and he was the lover, rather than brother, of Dasha.[51] On the other hand, Dostoevsky initially imagined Stavrogin (then the Prince) as the hero who would become a new man, repent of his sins, possibly after finding true love, although the notebooks depict him shooting himself after this revelatory moment.[52] Why then did Shatov, the novel's most redeeming character, eventually appear as asexual, and why did Stavrogin, initially planned as the convert, fail to repent? The answer may be that Dostoevsky found it impossible to imagine a masculinity that could unite an active sexuality with moral goodness in his fictional world.

Indeed, in Dostoevsky's world, the fact that Stavrogin has cuckolded Shatov plays in favor of Shatov rather than Stavrogin. One of the novel's most touching scenes takes place when Marie gives birth and Shatov becomes a surrogate father. Shatov unconditionally welcomes the boy as his son, even while fully conscious that the boy is a result of his wife's affair with Stavrogin. Shatov revels in fatherhood. The passage describing his joy on his wife giving birth uses high-register lexis and echoes the language of religious ecstasy:

> "Rejoice, Arina Prokhorovna ... It's a great joy," Shatov babbled with a blissful, idiotic expression ...
> "Where does the great joy come in?" asked Arina Prokhorovna happily, busying herself, clearing up and working like a convict.
> "The mystery of the appearance of a new creature. It's a great and inexplicable mystery, Arina Prokhorovna, and it's such a pity that you don't understand it."

Shatov was muttering in a disconnected, stupefied and ecstatic tone. Something seemed to rattle in his head and pour itself out of his soul without his volition.[53]

Here, for once, the usually reserved Shatov falls into rapture upon seeing the newborn. He celebrates the birth of his son unreservedly – even hysterically – despite the fact that the boy represents the fruit of his wife's extramarital union and therefore symbolizes Stavrogin's cuckolding of him. Yet unlike Stepan Trofimovich's feigned emotional outbursts in the early chapters, the text suggests that Shatov's hysteric behavior here is genuine, meaning it happens "without his volition," and is therefore depicted favorably by Dostoevsky. Thus I would suggest that Dostoevsky would agree with Nordau's later critique of emotionalism as a symptom of degeneration, but only in those cases when the emotion is feigned. Dostoevsky distinguishes between two kinds of emotional outbursts: those that are overblown and performative in nature, and those that are authentic.

Yet the novel encourages the reader to wonder whether the division between those two types of performance may be a porous one, to question whether Shatov's emotional outburst may also be feigned. Thus the masculinized Arina Prokhorovna, who carries out her role of midwife with clinical detachment, detects a note of ostentatious, self-serving charity in Shatov when she hears that he plans to adopt the boy and bring him up as his son. She accuses him of high-minded posturing, and tells him that he "needn't set himself up as a benefactor of the human race."[54] Her stinging comment draws attention to the performative aspect of Shatov's proclamation. The reader, already aware of Stepan Trofimovich's staged emotional outbursts, might well ask if Shatov is now engaging in the same kind of behavior, and whether the passage should be read ironically. Shatov's emotional outburst and his failed masculinity, though not performative in intention, are vulnerable to being misread as performative in a world where everyone else is performing. Thus the novel implies a potentially problematic congruence between the liberal hypocrisy of a Stepan Trofimovich and the apparently genuine charity of a Shatov.

Rowan Williams reads Shatov as a character through whom Dostoevsky honestly confronts the limitations of his own Christian worldview. Shatov cannot assert his belief in God, only in the Messianic potential of Russia, and he admits his fears that his ideology may simply be stale, recycled Slavophilism.[55] In terms of gender, Shatov proves similarly problematic. He initially seems to offer the hope of a different kind of masculinity: a new attitude toward women that includes neither the masochistic dependence of Stepan Trofimovich nor the violent predatory behavior of Stavrogin. However, his naïve optimism makes him easy prey for the radicals, while both his self-sacrificing behavior and his delight in children seem strangely reminiscent of the liberals. Ultimately, Shatov can be read as a test case where Dostoevsky experiments with a new kind of man, but finds even the new model imperfect.

Conclusion: The redemption of Stepan Trofimovich

The novel's conclusion switches back to focus on Stepan Trofimovich, who unexpectedly sets out on a pilgrimage and experiences a Christian conversion, an unlikely denouement in view of his former buffoonery. The reader is unprepared for this comic, middle-aged man who undergoes little character development in Parts I and II to occupy a central role so late in the novel. Moreover, aware of both the narrator's unreliability and Stepan Trofimovich's own penchant for lying and self-deception, the reader constantly questions the conversion's authenticity. Yet if Stepan Trofimovich's ultimate fate remains ambiguous, he undoubtedly fares better than Stavrogin, who is revealed to have hanged himself in the novel's conclusion.

I believe that Dostoevsky ultimately found it easier to redeem Stepan Trofimovich because of the two men's different paradigms of masculinity. As I mentioned previously, Dostoevsky's original plan for the novel involved the conversion and repentance of Stavrogin. If Stavrogin's active sexuality and his penchant for violence were factors in preventing him from becoming the convert, it also seems fair to add that Dostoevsky found it easier to reconcile the passive, effeminate, and masochistic masculinity of Stepan Trofimovich with his brand of Christianity and his vision for the nation, even if the author realized that the compromise was necessarily an imperfect one.

Here, I return to the comments that Dostoevsky made in his diary about the contrast between contemporary Russian men, who have succumbed to "avarice, cynicism and materialism," and Russian women, who have managed to preserve "sincerity, perseverance, earnestness, and honor, the quest for truth and sacrifice." While Stepan Trofimovich has frequently been insincere and untruthful in Parts I and II of the novel, he has at least paid lip service to these virtues, whereas the radical men of the sixties have abandoned them entirely. It is these qualities that come to the fore in Stepan Trofimovich during the conversion narrative.

Significantly, the conversion narrative in Part III involves Stepan Trofimovich taking a journey across the Russian land and encountering a maternal woman who professes feminine, Christian virtues of a type that the
masculinized liberal and radical women of the novel have forgotten. Sofia
Matveevna possesses "a certain honor, independence and yet at the same
time, a certain quietude."[56] She reads the New Testament to him, particularly the Sermon on the Mount and the Biblical account of the exorcism of
the swine. Moved by the Gospel, Stepan Trofimovich speaks of forgiving
his enemies and offers an apology for his transgressions that contains a
fairly accurate self-assessment:

> My friend, all my life I have lied. Even when I was telling the truth (*pravdu*).
> I never spoke for the sake of a higher truth (*dlia istiny*), but only for myself,
> I even knew that before, but I only see it now . . . *Savez-vous*, perhaps I'm
> even lying now, yes, I'm probably lying now. The main thing is that I believe
> myself when I am lying.[57]

In typical Dostoevskian fashion, Stepan Trofimovich recognizes that he
may still be lying even in his confession, an admission that both adds to
and detracts from its apparent authenticity. The narrative seems playfully
ambiguous at this point, marked with respect for Stepan Trofimovich's genuine attempt at repentance but perhaps recognizing that no confession can
be completely genuine or devoid of self-interest; no conversion experience
lacks an element of doubt. Just as Dostoevsky encourages his readers to
wonder whether Shatov is performing a role in his rapture in the birth
scene, so here we wonder whether Stepan Trofimovich's conversion might
simply be the latest performance of masculine failure.

Nevertheless, the reader now warms to Stepan Trofimovich's apparent
innocence and need for maternal affection. His feelings for the kind Sofia
Matveevna remain exaggerated, vaguely comic, and reminiscent of his old
masochistic desires for Varvara Petrovna, but the secret smiles of rapturous
delight have vanished from the text. It is hard to know whether to read
passages such as this one as ironic or earnest:

> "My savior!" he cried, folding his hands in reverence before her. He contin-
> ued in French: "You're as noble as a marquess! As for me, I'm a scoundrel!
> Oh, I've been dishonorable my whole life."[58]

On the one hand, certain clues point to an ironic reading, including the
exaggerated diction, for example "savior" and "marquess," the hand gestures, and especially the switch to French, which so often signals inauthenticity in Dostoevsky. On the other hand, Christian conversion narratives

do rely on such absolute rhetoric, including the confession of one's absolute depravity.

Significantly, the post-conversion Stepan Trofimovich does not undergo any change in his masculinity. He does not recover his virility, his physical health remains frail, and he remains prone to hysterical outbursts. By Nordau's standards, he is still a degenerate: he retains his emotionalism and exhibits great sensitivity to the Gospel stories that Sofia Matveevna tells him. His exaggerated respect for women also remains, and he stays dependent on them. Indeed, we can imagine that Nordau would dismiss his Christianity as "mysticism," which he considered a pathological symptom of degeneration.[59] Krafft-Ebing might have interpreted his religious fervor as a sublimation of "natural" forms of love:

> Love when weak is frequently turned away from its real object into different channels, such as voluptuous poetry, bizarre aesthetics, or religion. In the latter case it readily falls prey to mysticism, fanaticism, sectarianism or religious mania.[60]

Had Stepan Trofimovich been one of Krafft-Ebing's patients, we can imagine the psychiatrist would have viewed his conversion experience merely as another step in his degeneration. Dostoevsky, on the other hand, depicts Stepan Trofimovich's conversion not as mania but as an experience that allows for glimpses of goodness and truth, even as that truth must be undercut by nagging doubts about the conversion's authenticity. Similarly, Stepan Trofimovich's ambivalent masculinity and his emotional outbursts thus become valorized in these chapters, even as the reader remains unsure as to whether they should be read as performative.

Although Dostoevsky praises emotionalism when it has its origins in authentic feeling, the novel demonstrates his awareness of the difficulties in distinguishing between authentic and inauthentic feeling. However, the effeminate post-conversion Stepan Trofimovich and the cuckolded Shatov are presented as favorable alternatives to the terrifying Stavrogin, who gives the outward appearance of attractive virility but whose depravity runs deeper than that of any other character.

The fin de siècle presented a cultural moment of self-examination, a time when writers and thinkers tried to diagnose what had gone wrong with society and to propose a cure. As the title of *Demons* suggests, Dostoevsky perceived the problem primarily in religious terms, and was far from alone in doing so. However, he differed sharply from those fin-de-siècle thinkers in the West who contended that religion needed an injection of virility, such as Nordau's own call for a "muscular Judaism," or the "muscular

Christianity" that emerged in the Protestant Anglosphere.[61] Dostoevsky's
Demons ultimately shows his refusal to sign up to an essentialized definition
of masculinity, and his continuing interest in degeneration as a privileged
state for men. Where Nordau and Krafft-Ebing see only decline and degeneration, Dostoevsky recognizes the potential for redemption. Although the
opening chapters of *Demons* suggest that Dostoevsky shares the anxieties
of the era about the feminization of men, their growing emotionalism, and
their masochistic dependence on women, the novel ultimately becomes an
inquiry into whether those same qualities might be compatible with his
vision of Christian redemption.

NOTES

1 Aleksandr Solzhenitsyn, *Nobelevskaia lektsiia po literature 1970 goda* (Munich: Deutsch Taschenbuch Verlag, 1972), 21. All translations from the Russian are my own unless otherwise stated.

2 All Dostoevsky citations refer to F. M. Dostoevskii, *Polnoe sobranie sochinenii i pisem v tridtsati tomakh* (Leningrad: Nauka, 1972–1990), hereafter abbreviated as *PSS*. This quotation appears in *PSS* XXVII:50. On Dostoevsky as an apoca-lyptic prophet, see P. Travis Kroeker and Bruce Ward, eds., *Remembering the End: Dostoevsky as Prophet to Modernity* (Boulder, CO: Westview Press, 2001), especially Chapter 1.

3 D. S. Mirsky, *A History of Russian Literature from its Beginnings to 1900* (New York: Knopf, 1927), 358.

4 Albert Camus, "Prière d'insérer des *Possédés*," in *Théâtre, récits, nouvelles* (Paris: Gallimard, 1965), 1877. Cited and translated in Ray Davison, *Camus: The Challenge of Dostoevsky* (University of Exeter Press, 1997), 138. While Camus focuses on Dostoevsky's philosophical vision, others – such as Berdiaev – saw the novel as political prophecy: see the discussion in Joseph Frank, *Dostoevsky: The Miraculous Years: 1865–1871* (Princeton University Press, 1995), 435–438.

5 On the fathers and sons topos in *Demons*, see, inter alia, Frank, *The Miraculous Years*, 396–411; R. L. Busch, "Turgenev's *Ottsy i deti* and Dostoevskii's *Besy*," *Canadian Slavonic Papers* 16:1 (1984): 1–9; Miller, *Dostoevsky's Unfinished Jour-ney*, Chapter 5; Carol Apollonio Flath, *Dostoevsky's Secrets: Reading Against the Grain* (Evanston, IL: Northwestern University Press, 2009), Chapter 6.

6 *Demons* is not the only Dostoevsky novel that rewards reading through a mas-culinity studies framework. The contrast between the depraved, virile Rogozhin and the emasculated Myshkin in *The Idiot* would also make for a rewarding examination; so too would the varying different types of masculinity that the three (four?) brothers exhibit in *Brothers Karamazov*. However, the present study focuses on *Demons* because it is in this novel that typologies of masculin-ity are most obviously linked to shifting ideological paradigms in the mid- to late nineteenth century.

7 *PSS* xxi:127. Interestingly, Dostoevsky points out one particular flaw in the
   Russian woman: "her dependence on certain ideas that come from men, and
   her ability to adopt such ideas wholesale and believe in them unreservedly."
   In other words, it is when women take on the ideas of men – and become
   masculinized – that they lose their best qualities. Negative representations of
   female masculinity appear in *Demons* in Varvara Petrovna Stavrogina and Arina
   Prokhorovna Virginskaya.

8 *PSS* xxiii:28. We can also see this gender divide at play in Dostoevsky's comments on Onegin and Tatiana in his 1880 Pushkin Speech (*PSS* xxvi:136–149).
   Dostoevsky calls Tatiana "the apotheosis of the Russian woman" (140) and
   contrasts her magnanimous, self-sacrificing, and faithful nature with Onegin's
   spleen and his lack of belief in Russia's future.

9 Avramenko and Ying rightly suggest that the heroines "exemplify the Russian
   woman's striving to reunite the degenerated Russian man with Mother Earth"
   and also serve as the "followers of Christ from whom the Russian man will
   regain his faith in God." Richard Avramenko and Jingcai Ying, "Dostoevsky's
   Heroines: Or, on the Compassion of the Russian Woman," in *Dostoevsky's
   Political Thought*, edited by Richard Avramenko and Lee Trepanier (Lanham,
   MD: Lexington Books, 2013), 75–76. For a more comprehensive treatment of
   women in Dostoevsky, see Nina Pelikan Straus, *Dostoevsky and the Woman
   Question: Rereadings at the End of the Century* (New York: St. Martin's Press,
   1994).

10 In *Dostoevsky and the Woman Question*, Straus argues that Dostoevsky's oeuvre
   attacks "masculine notions of autonomy, power and rationality" in ways that
   "accord with some feminist insights" (17). She sees Prince Myshkin in *The Idiot*
   as an "alternative model for masculinity, as an antitype to male violence toward
   women personified by Rogozhin, and as an antidote to Western patriarchal
   rationality and secularism" (53).

11 For a reading of Morel and degeneration theory that emphasizes these anxieties
   about masculinity, see Robert A. Nye, *Masculinity and Male Codes of Honor in
   Modern France* (Oxford University Press, 1993), especially Chapters 5 and 6.

12 Richard Krafft-Ebing, *Psychopathia Sexualis*, translated by F. J. Rebman (New
   York: Rebman Company, 1894), 6–7. In outlining the history of sexuality,
   Krafft-Ebing takes a teleological view, seeing gradual progress toward more
   enlightened behavior over the centuries. Yet he also warns that prosperous
   civilizations are peculiarly vulnerable to decadence and sexual pathology, and
   names "Rome, Greece, and France under Louis XIV and XV" as "warning
   examples" of societies where moral decadence and sexual licentiousness led to
   political collapse (6).

13 Andrew Smith, *Victorian Demons: Medicine, Masculinity, and the Gothic at the
   Fin-de-Siècle* (Manchester University Press, 2004), 15.

14 Nordau, *Degeneration*, 541.

15 Although there is no evidence he knew Morel's work, Dostoevsky kept up with
   the emerging field of psychiatry. Critics have productively explored his work
   as an engagement with and critique of its tenets. See Harriet Murav, *Holy

Foolishness: Dostoevsky's Novels and the Poetics of Cultural Critique (Stanford University Press, 1992), especially Chapters 2 and 3.

16 Dating the arrival of degeneration theory in Russia, Daniel Beer cites Vasily Florinsky's 1866 *Improvement and Degeneration of the Human Race* (*Usovershenstvovanie i vyrozdhenie chelovecheskogo roda*) as an early landmark, but points out that this study went largely unnoticed. There are scattered references to Florinsky in Dostoevsky's notebooks and journalism, but none to this particular work. According to Beer, it is only from the 1880s that degeneration theory became more widespread in Russia, first in the context of institutional psychiatry, and then as a sociocultural phenomenon. See Beer, *Renovating Russia*, 38–41.

17 See Frank, *The Miraculous Years*, 453–459.

18 Miller points out the inversion of gender roles in Stepan Trofimovich's and Varvara Petrovna's relationship: "[H]is role is more feminine, hers more masculine." Miller, *Dostoevsky's Unfinished Journey*, 87. Varvara Petrovna exhibits the female masculinity that runs parallel to Stepan Trofimovich's effeminacy in Dostoevsky's vision of a degenerate Russia. Among the minor characters, the weak, cuckolded Virginsky and his assertive, masculinized wife parallel the inversion of gender roles found in Stepan Trofimovich and Varvara Petrovna.

19 *PSS* x:13.

20 *PSS* x:26.

21 Ibid.

22 Nordau was not well acquainted with Dostoevsky's work, but he devoted a whole chapter to a critique of Tolstoy and his "emotionalism." See *Degeneration*, 144–171.

23 Ibid., 19.

24 *PSS* x:52.

25 *PSS* x:12. Dostoevsky underscores the irony here by adding: "Later, he succumbed not only to civic sorrow, but also to champagne."

26 Nordau, *Degeneration*, 170. Nordau is speaking here of Tolstoy's followers in Germany. Although their political philosophy is distant from Stepan's idealistic liberalism, it is interesting to note that Nordau shares Dostoevsky's skepticism about individuals building a politics out of (false) emotion.

27 *PSS* x:61.

28 *PSS* x:86.

29 Daniel Rancour-Laferriere, *The Slave Soul of Russia: Moral Masochism and the Cult of Suffering* (New York University Press, 1995), especially 78–86 and 234–244.

30 Nordau, *Degeneration*, 414. Krafft-Ebing also devotes considerable attention to masochism in his *Psychopathia Sexualis*, 131–212.

31 *PSS* x:144.

32 Ibid.

33 *PSS* x:35.

34 John Williams suggests that the passage "indicates that Stavrogin has been the repeated victim of homosexually seductive behavior by his intellectual

mentor, if not of outright homosexual seduction." John S. Williams, "Stavrogin's Motivation: Love and Suicide," *Psychoanalytic Review* 69:2 (1982): 259. Miller suggests masturbation in *Dostoevsky's Unfinished Journey*, 91, as does Fusso in her *Discovering Sexuality in Dostoevsky*, 172, note 30.

35 On the movement in Russia, see particularly Matich, *Erotic Utopia*.

36 *PSS* XI:14.

37 Straus argues that Dostoevsky's depiction of Stavrogin unmasks the romantic image of the masculine Superman. Straus, *Dostoevsky and the Woman Question*, 81–96.

38 *PSS* XI:16.

39 The narrator writes "all the ladies went crazy" over Stavrogin; "some worshipped him while others hated him . . . but both groups went crazy over him." *PSS* X:37.

40 Irene Zohrab, "Mann-Mannliche Love in Dostoevsky's Fiction (An Approach to *The Possessed*): With Some Attributions of Editorial Notes in *The Citizen*. First Installment," *The Dostoevsky Journal: An Independent Review* 3–4 (2002–2003): 113–226.

41 *PSS* X:323–324.

42 The history of the catechism and the debates about its authorship appear along with an English translation of the text in Philip Pomper, *Sergei Nechaev* (New Brunswick, NJ: Rutgers University Press, 1979), 87–95. The passage quoted here appears on 91, and the translation is Pomper's.

43 Nordau, *Degeneration*, 170. Significantly, Stepan Trofimovich himself supports this hypothesis about his son's politics being based on feeling rather than conviction. Speaking of his son's generation, he explains, "socialism attracts them not because of its realism, but because of its sentimental, idealistic side, what we might call its religious quality, its poetry" (*PSS* X:63). Stepan Trofimovich's complaint about the politics of the men of the sixties is remarkably close to Nordau's complaint about the German Tolstoyans. Ironically, Stepan Trofimovich's criticism of his son's socialism applies equally well to his own liberalism.

44 *PSS* X:37.

45 Ibid.

46 Nordau, *Degeneration*, 541.

47 Ronald Hingley, *The Undiscovered Dostoevsky* (London: Hamish Hamilton, 1962), 155.

48 Shatov is thrice referred to as "irascible" (*PSS* X:52, 76, 90). The long quotation is from *PSS* X:34.

49 *PSS* X:106–107. Emphasis mine.

50 *PSS* X:114–118.

51 F. M. Dostoevsky, *The Notebooks for* The Possessed, edited by Edward Wasiolek and translated by Victor Terras (University of Chicago Press, 1968). On Shaposhnikov, see 104–105.

52 Ibid., 170–171.

53 *PSS* x:452. Shatov's enthusiasm shows Dostoevsky's willingness to imagine alternative families not based on biological bonds, a point that Fusso has stressed in her analysis of the family in Dostoevsky's work. See Fusso, *Discovering Sexuality in Dostoevsky*, Chapter 6.

54 *PSS* x:452. In the same section, she tells him "people can't get by without high-minded phrases."

55 Rowan Williams, *Dostoevsky: Language, Faith and Fiction* (London: Continuum, 2008), 21–23.

56 *PSS* x:488.

57 *PSS* x:497.

58 *PSS* x:496.

59 Nordau devoted an entire subsection of *Degeneration* to mysticism, which he viewed as a lack of lucid thinking resulting from abnormalities in the brain. See Book II, especially 56–60.

60 Krafft-Ebing, *Psychopathia Sexualis*, 12.

61 On Nordau as a key figure in the invention of muscular Judaism in the 1890s, see Todd Samuel Presner, *Muscular Judaism: The Jewish Body and the Politics of Regeneration* (New York: Routledge, 2007), especially Chapters 1 and 2. Muscular Christianity had its genesis in 1850s England and its heyday in America *c*. 1880–1920. See Donald Hall, ed., *Muscular Christianity: Embodying the Victorian Age* (Cambridge University Press, 1994), 3–16.

CHAPTER 7

The burden of superfluity
Reconsidering female heroism in Chekhov's
The Seagull

Jenny Kaminer

In 1860, the radical critic Nikolai Dobroliubov proclaimed the beginning of a "new phase" in the life of the Russian people. He identified a dramatic heroine – Katerina in Alexander Ostrovsky's 1859 tragedy *The Storm* – as the initiator of this collective rebirth through, ironically, her death by suicide in the Volga River. Katerina had chosen to flee what he famously termed the "kingdom of darkness," where a firmly entrenched familial despotism left her brutalized and despairing. In doing so, she embodied, for Dobroliubov, those positive qualities – purposefulness, resolve, a capacity for self-sacrifice – that distinguished her from the weak-willed and inert "superfluous" men plaguing nineteenth-century Russian literature and society.[1] Dobroliubov presented Katerina as a sort of antidote to the crisis of superfluity that he condemned in his earlier article, "What is Oblomovism?" (1859), where he identified the perpetually couch-ridden hero of Goncharov's novel *Oblomov* as the apotheosis of this uniquely Russian scourge. If earlier nineteenth-century female heroines, spanning the eras of sentimentalism, romanticism, and realism – from the eponymous "Poor Liza" by Karamzin, to Tatiana in Pushkin's novel-in-verse *Eugene Onegin* and Bela in Lermontov's *A Hero of Our Time*, to name but a few – had fallen victim to the inconstancy and fallibility of the superfluous man, now Katerina, in death, symbolized a female moral victory over the vice(s) of superfluity.

As any moderately astute reader of nineteenth-century Russian literature can observe, despite Dobroliubov's optimistic proclamation of a "new phase" initiated by Katerina's defiant act, the well-worn character of the troubled, ambivalent Russian male – with the faithful, morally superior Russian woman as his foil – continued to surface throughout the decades after the premiere of *The Storm*. As Connor Doak reveals in the present volume, masculine failure featured prominently in Russian works such as Dostoevsky's 1872 novel *Demons*. In fact, by the time of the fin de siècle, superfluity had become something akin to a "contagious disease."[2] The sense of alienation from a social order that characterized the nineteenth-century superfluous protagonist was replaced by a self-contained and self-generated predicament. Rather than responding to real-life circumstances, now "characters . . . internalize their feelings of separateness and live lives of misery only because they *believe* they are isolated" (original italics).[3] Or, as Mila Shevchenko explains, "while the literature of the first seventy years of the century exploits 'superfluity' mainly in terms of ideological and social category, fin-de-siècle theatrical discourse emphasizes the psychological and aesthetic aspects of the phenomenon."[4] In other words, rather than disappearing, as Dobroliubov had predicted, the category of the "superfluous man" began to be characterized by an internalized and intangible feeling of estrangement that coalesced with the more widespread, pan-European fin-de-siècle mood.

Although Dobroliubov's admittedly problematic reading of Ostrovsky's play elicited its share of opprobrium, his positing of a relationship between suicide, doomed romance, familial despotism, female heroism, and ultimate triumph is provocative.[5] These same elements that Dobroliubov foregrounded in his reading of Ostrovsky's play resurfaced on the Russian stage some thirty-five years later, in Anton Chekhov's far more internationally recognized play *The Seagull* (1896), which the author labeled a "comedy" despite the offstage suicide with which it concludes. With *The Seagull*, Chekhov upends fin-de-siècle expectations surrounding women, love, loss, and suicide. Like Katerina, Nina Zarechnaia, Chekhov's flawed heroine, transgresses accepted sexual morality and flees a domestic "kingdom of darkness," with tragic results – namely, abandonment by her lover and the death of her out-of-wedlock child. I will argue, however, that Nina more closely represents the realization of Dobroliubov's hopes for an "active" female to counterbalance the futility of the Russian male. Nina's transcendence of Katerina's fate may, in fact, be encoded in her surname, "Zarechnaia," which in Russian, roughly translated, means "beyond the river." This chapter will elucidate the details of how Nina "goes beyond" the tragic end of her female dramatic and literary predecessors – from both the realist and the romantic eras – as well as that of her former paramour, the suicidal Konstantin Treplev. It will claim that, in *The Seagull*, Chekhov presents the degeneration of the idealized Russian woman of nineteenth-century literary and cultural mythology, replacing her with an imperfect, probably unhappy, but nonetheless completely different kind of heroine.

***

Chekhov's challenging of traditional gender binaries in *The Seagull* resonates with the prevailing tone of "sexual anarchy" that characterized the fin de siècle. During the 1880s and 1890s – the years that Chekhov began his literary endeavors – a continent-wide anxiety about previously sacrosanct codes of behavior for men and women prevailed. As Elaine Showalter aptly describes, "during this period . . . all the laws that governed sexual identity and behavior seemed to be breaking down . . . New Women and male aesthetes redefined the meanings of femininity and masculinity."[6] This apprehension about shifting gender roles permeated the cultural output of the period, including in influential dramatic works by Chekhov's contemporaries, such as Ibsen's *A Doll's House* and *Hedda Gabler*, Strindberg's *Miss Julie* and *The Father*, and Shaw's *Mrs. Warren's Profession*.[7] In visual culture, the fear of "feminine evil" produced increasingly terrifying images of women untethered from the imperative to nurture and so doomed to gradual degeneration.[8] Woman became a "case study," both for artists and for scientists, "an object to be incisively opened, analyzed, and reassembled" in the search for the root causes of the New Woman's rejection of convention and social norms.[9] The reaction of Chekhov's audience members, who wrote him letters lamenting the "fundamental lack of the heroic" in his works, attests – among other things – to the unease engendered by the "sexual anarchy" contained in works such as *The Seagull*.[10]

For the nineteenth-century Russian woman, the accepted and familiar notions of heroism, the absence of which these audience members found so confounding, meant adhering to a moral burden that Barbara Heldt has famously termed a "terrible perfection." The idealization of Russian womanhood, which placed so much responsibility for both familial and national destiny on women's shoulders, was "frightening to men who could not match it in 'manly' action and inhibiting to women who were supposed to incarnate it, or else."[11] This glorified female personified the prized Russian value of "oneness" (*tsel'nost'*), which necessitated "a resourceful, patient, resilient stability" and precluded the possibility of "introspection, self-consciousness, skepticism."[12] In other words, a Russian woman busy ensuring individual and collective salvation could ill afford the philosophical indulgences, contradictions, and solipsism of male literary characters such as Dostoevsky's Raskolnikov, to cite but one example. Jehanne Gheith calls this heroine the "necessary woman," adding that she serves the dual function of embodying the superfluous man's most vaunted values while also revealing his fundamental impotence as he allows the idealized female to slip away, often into the arms of another man, as seen in both *Eugene Onegin* and *Oblomov*.[13]

The issue of gender in Chekhov's dramas has constituted something of a vexed question for critics of his work. On the one hand, Chekhov has been extolled for his skill at authentic characterization, as well as for his ability to reveal the unadulterated or demythologized essence of the human soul. At least one prominent critic has suggested that this praise cannot be equally extended to Chekhov's female characters, however. Identifying women as something akin to the playwright's Achilles heel, Donald Rayfield observes that "on the few occasions that Chekhov's characterizations risk being caricatures, we find they are always of women."[14] For John Tulloch, Chekhov's female characters lack the ability to "recognize the complexity of life," therefore projecting a false and overly simplistic "authenticity in a world where there cannot be one." This prompts them to "repeatedly seek sublime truths in abstract visions," attempts that doom these women to inevitable failure.[15] Critics of *The Seagull* have repeatedly singled out the play's female characters for their perniciously self-dramatizing and inauthentic behavior, criticizing them for an excessive emphasis on their own unhappiness.[16]

Among feminist theater scholars, a trepidation about the issue of gender in Chekhov often surfaces, and the notion that Chekhov's women characters have been "less gender-defined than those of other male playwrights in modern theatre, such as Ibsen, seems to prevail."[17] For example, in *Women in Modern Drama*, Gail Finney explains the decision to exclude Chekhov from her discussion by arguing that "the problems from which his characters suffer are existential and transcend gender boundaries, affecting men and women alike."[18] In a comparable vein, Heldt cautions against constructing any typologies of the "Chekhov heroine" because of the author's "humaneness, his willingness to assume that human beings are basically similar."[19] This chapter, then, also aims to contribute to a discussion about the nature of gender in Chekhov's drama by examining these seemingly conflicting conclusions – that gender either represents the "Achilles heel" of Chekhov's oeuvre or that his works transcend gendered categories altogether – more closely in the context of the characterization of women in *The Seagull*. It is my belief that this "vexed question" can be more fruitfully explored by considering how the playwright may have responded directly to the cultural and literary mythology of Russian womanhood, as well as fin-de-siècle disquietude about rapidly shifting gender roles, in his development of female heroism in the play.

***

A logical launching point for such a consideration is *Ivanov* (1887), Chekhov's second full-length play and the first to be performed. *Ivanov* provides a productive background against which to foreground the reworking of gender binaries that Chekhov undertook in *The Seagull* a few years later. With the work's title hero – a disenchanted, tormented nobleman languishing on his provincial estate – the playwright offered his most direct and purposeful dramatic contribution to the "superfluous man" tradition. The relationships between Ivanov and the women he loves and torments mainly adhere to the demands of "terrible perfection" that nineteenth-century audiences had come to expect. At the same time, the play anticipates the ways in which *The Seagull* will more significantly challenge this familiar and well-worn gender hierarchy.

Ivanov's ennui bears a distinct resemblance to numerous literary precursors, from both the Russian and European traditions. The interest in "Hamletism" was a fin-de-siècle phenomenon on the Western European stage, and Ivanov – as well as Treplev, later, in *The Seagull* – represents Chekhov's fusion of the "superfluous man" Russian literary type with this contemporaneous phenomenon. Ivanov himself acknowledges a self-conscious and meta-literary aspect to his particular breed of unhappiness, in Act Two, Scene VI: "I am dying from shame to think that I, a healthy, strong person, have turned into either a Hamlet or a Manfred or a superfluous man . . . into the Devil himself knows what! Some pathetic types are flattered when you call them Hamlets or superfluous, but for me it's a disgrace! It wounds my pride, shame overwhelms me, and I suffer."[20] In a letter to A. S. Suvorin from December 30, 1888, Chekhov described Ivanov as exhibiting symptoms of a uniquely Russian "excitability" (*vozbudimost'*), characterized by an inevitable preference for the past over the present, as well as the waves of exhaustion that follow the pursuit of "burdens beyond his strength." This leaves him tired, bored, and cynical before he's even had a chance to grow a decent mustache. Simply put, "men like Ivanov do not solve difficulties but collapse under their weight."[21]

The two main female characters together embody the traits of idealized Russian femininity. Ivanov's wife, Anna, is a Jew who has forsaken her family and heritage in order to marry Ivanov, only to watch him tire of her, while the young, strong-headed, and vital Sasha promises him regeneration through the power of her love. The relationship between Ivanov and his wife rests upon the foundation of a one-sided sacrifice, as Ivanov himself acknowledges: "'Anyuta is a remarkable, an exceptional woman . . . For my sake she converted to my religion, cast off her father and mother, turned her back on wealth, and if I'd demanded another hundred sacrifices, she would have made them without blinking an eye . . . there is nothing at all remarkable about me and I made no sacrifices at all . . . to make a long story short, I married when I was passionately in love and swore love everlasting, but . . . five years have gone by, she's still in love with me, while I . . . ' (*Splays his hands in a gesture of futility*)" (13; 30–31). Ivanov, in turn, refuses to sacrifice either monetarily by paying for the trip to the Crimea that offers his wife the only hope for overcoming certain death by consumption or emotionally by sparing his wife the grief that his nightly visits to another woman, Sasha, cause her. Ivanov confesses that the knowledge of his wife's imminent death leaves him feeling "just a sort of void, weariness" rather than "love and pity," and that he himself cannot comprehend what is transpiring inside of him (13; 31). Anna's unconditional sacrifice of family and identity and the constancy of her love for her husband despite his indifference highlight Ivanov's ignobility. Anna, in other words, clearly shoulders the burden of "terrible perfection."

By contrast, Sasha represents a new, more progressive generation of women, and Chekhov himself described her as "a young woman of the latest mold . . . well-educated, intelligent, honest."[22] Sasha shares many characteristics with her European counterpart, the New Woman, who would experience her literary heyday in the 1890s, notably in novels by writers such as Thomas Hardy and in plays by dramatists including George Bernard Shaw. The New Woman – independent-minded, physically vigorous, perhaps financially self-sufficient, and frank about matters of sexuality – defined herself primarily in opposition to the Victorian "old woman," whose life as a "household nun" was circumscribed by modest self-abnegation for her family.[23] This generational conflict is especially pronounced in the stark contrast that Chekhov draws between Anna and Sasha in *Ivanov*. Sasha, it would seem, heralded a new model of Russian womanhood. Indeed, the co-founder of the Moscow Art Theater, V. I. Nemirovich-Danchenko, referred to Sasha as a "transitional type" of Russian woman, standing halfway between the "Turgenevian" type and the "contemporary girl." By 1904, when Nemirovich-Danchenko made his observations, he expressed confidence that the new Russian girl of the early twentieth century was no longer wasting her efforts "on some Ivanov or other."[24]

Sasha, then, is a threshold figure, a woman on the cusp of two eras. It is her reproduction of certain "terribly perfect" traits, however, that ultimately dooms to failure any potential rebellion on her part against the generation of women represented by Anna. Whether for selfless or selfish motivations, Sasha espouses an unflinching belief in the power of "active" female love to transform the corroded male soul. She explains her beliefs to Ivanov in the following exchange, from Act Three, Scene VII:

Men just don't get it. Every girl prefers a loser to a success, because every
girl is attracted by active love . . . Don't you get it? Active. Men are involved
in business and so they shove love into the background . . . But for us love
is life itself. I love you, that means that I dream about how I'll cure you of
tedium, how I'll go with you to the ends of the earth. (58–59; 68)[25]

By declaring that she would follow Ivanov to the "ends of the earth," Sasha
evokes a paradigmatic image of female self-sacrifice from earlier in the
nineteenth century: that of the well-born wives of the Decembrist rebels
who voluntarily shared their husbands' harsh Siberian exile. Ivanov himself
wonders why Russian women inevitably seek out the emotionally stilted
man: "When a man is healthy, strong and cheerful, you ignore him, but
as soon as he starts sliding downhill and bemoaning his fate, you cling to
him. Is it really worse to be the wife of a strong, courageous man than to be
the nursemaid of some sniveling loser?" Sasha's reply to this query, "much
worse," constitutes something like the defiant declaration of the "terribly
perfect" woman (58; 67–68).

Ivanov, however, like many of his predecessors in the "superfluous man"
genre, cannot be redeemed through the devotion and selflessness of the
morally superior woman who offers "active love." Sasha herself acknowledges the failure of her mission in the final moments, confessing that she
had "wanted love to be active, not agonizing" (72; 79). Ultimately, her
blind devotion to Ivanov prevents Sasha from transcending the strictures
of the idealized nineteenth-century Russian heroine and embodying the
New Woman of a new era. The play ends on the eve of Ivanov's wed-
ding to Sasha, with the protagonist exiting the stage and shooting himself.
Although Sasha outlives Ivanov, this tragic ending presents a decidedly
ambiguous picture of the New Woman's fusion with the "terribly perfect"
one.

***

Ivanov's denouement, as well as its description of the hero's character
traits – his brooding, his dissatisfaction, his critique of a society in which
he seemingly can find no productive role to play – are, of course, quite
reminiscent of Konstantin in *The Seagull*. Chekhov's next full-length play,
The Seagull provides a more multifaceted and nuanced exploration of
the gender dynamics first examined in *Ivanov*. Whereas *Ivanov* marked
Chekhov's continuation of the "superfluous man" tradition and its gender
hierarchy, in *The Seagull* he openly deconstructs and perhaps even mocks
the genre. In other words, Chekhov reorders the binary opposition between

the superfluous man and the virtuous, long-suffering female in an original and unexpected way.

This becomes immediately evident in the opening scene, where the character of Masha famously declares that she wears black because she is in "mourning for her life," which Peta Tait aptly terms a "social performance of her unhappiness."[26] Masha might represent something of a prototypical "superfluous woman" in Russian literature, with her self-conscious and ironic melancholy and her indulgence in typically masculine habits, such as taking snuff and drinking vodka. This somewhat androgynous behavior links Masha with dramatic representations of the New Woman on the European stage, where women were shown riding a bicycle or smoking cigarettes.[27] Later, Masha asks Trigorin to make the inscription of his book out to her "who can't identify her family and lives in this world for no apparent reason," a motto that any superfluous man would be happy to adopt as his own (34; 161). These gestures constitute Masha's "parody of her own emotional state... [of] the excesses of her emotional imagination" and, by extension, Chekhov's gentle ridicule of the indulgences of performed superfluity.[28] The New Woman in plays by such dramatists as Shaw – who, in *Misalliance*, to name but one example, had a female character donning men's clothes and aviator goggles – contained similarly parodic elements.[29] Masha also engages in consciously self-destructive behavior by marrying the schoolteacher, Medvedenko, in a futile attempt to conquer her unrequited love for Konstantin, proclaiming "once I'm married, there will be no room for love" (33; 161). Masha's habits may be masculine, but the source of her unhappiness is typically feminine. If the Russian "superfluous man" of the realist tradition went off to fight in the Caucasus in anticipation of an almost certain physical death, so Masha's resigned acceptance of an unhappy marriage promises a more gradual but, nonetheless, inevitable spiritual death – a decline that coalesces with the fin-de-siècle mood. The cruelty that both she and her mother exhibit toward Medvedenko also hints at a reversal of the typical female victim and male victimizer dichotomy.

If Masha challenges established gender binaries while echoing larger trends in fin-de-siècle European theater, then the character of Nina, at least initially, offers the reassurance of familiarity. In the first three acts, Nina appears to embody certain qualities of the "terribly perfect" Russian woman: purity, honesty, idealism, readiness for self-sacrifice. First Konstantin and eventually Trigorin fall sway to these qualities. In Act Three, Trigorin pleads with Arkadina to let him experience the transformative effects of romance with the young woman who possesses these ideals: "A love that's young, charming, poetical, wafting me to a dream world – it's the one and the only thing on this earth that can bring happiness. I've never yet experienced a love like that" (41; 167). The affections of the "necessary woman" would allow Trigorin, he imagines, to escape the banality of everyday existence, bridging the gap between the quotidian and the transcendental. Although the successful Trigorin does not suffer from the burden of superfluity that plagued many of his predecessors in the Russian literary tradition, he nonetheless feels drawn to the transcendence that a romance with Nina promises – a promise that ultimately, and not surprisingly, proves illusory. Indeed, the medallion that Nina gives to Trigorin on the eve of his departure from the estate seems to foreshadow the tragic denouement of their relationship. Referring to the following line from one of Trigorin's texts – "If ever my life is of use to you, come and take it" – it serves as a declaration of readiness for self-abnegation that falls neatly within the tradition of the "necessary" Russian woman (40; 166).

Chekhov, however, introduces a new and complicating element into the gender dynamics in *The Seagull*, an element wholly absent from *Ivanov*: devotion to art. Nina's performance of Konstantin's play presents the possibility of a creative symbiosis between man and woman, of the elimination of the gulf that has traditionally left "superfluous men" such as Ivanov isolated from those around him. Medvedenko articulates this expectation in the play's very opening exchange, when he explicitly connects Konstantin and Nina's romantic relationship with their imminent artistic collaboration: "They are in love, and today their souls will merge in an attempt to present a joint artistic creation" (5; 137).[30] If the Russian literary tradition "insists on the lack of unity between heroes and heroines," then the creative alliance of Nina and Konstantin offers a challenge to this dictum and the gender division that it perpetuates.[31] The promise of this unity remains unfulfilled, of course, as succinctly revealed in Act Two, during the scene where Konstantin brings Nina a slain seagull, to which she responds: "Lately you've been so touchy, and you talk in code, symbols of some kind. And this gull is obviously a symbol too, but, forgive me, I don't understand it . . . I'm too ordinary to understand you" (27; 156). Konstantin now speaks in a language that Nina cannot decode, their failure to communicate highlighting the disappointment of the hopes for creative harmony raised in the play's opening scenes. Reinforcing the connection between their romantic relationship and their artistic one, Konstantin dates the former's deterioration to "that night when my play was a stupid fiasco" (27; 156).[32]

In her choice of Trigorin over Konstantin, Nina offers a direct rebuttal to Ivanov's assertion that women always choose the weaker male. She selects the successful and good-natured Trigorin over the neurotic and self-loathing Konstantin – another way that Chekhov reimagines the typical superfluous male and virtuous female plot that he had mainly reproduced in *Ivanov*. If "female victimization is dependent on the absence of choice," then Nina's rejection of Konstantin suggests her ability to "rise above the victim role."[33] Both Nina and Konstantin challenge familiar models of Russian masculinity and femininity, echoing the anxiety about evolving gender roles that characterized the fin-de-siècle years. While Konstantin's excessive displays of emotionality – his suicide attempts, his tortured relationship with his mother – render him "hysterical" and thus "aligned with... feminine weakness," Nina's preference for the perpetually fortunate and charismatic Trigorin indicates a rejection of the "necessary" woman's habitual predilection.[34] Unlike Ivanov, who wondered at the female preference for "losers," Konstantin unequivocally states that "women don't forgive failure" (27; 156). The sacrifice that her female predecessors from *Ivanov* readily made for love, Nina instead directs toward art, or at least toward the romanticized notions of art and fame that she nurtures in the first three acts. As she tells Trigorin in Act Two: "For the joy of being a writer or an actress, I would put up with my family disowning me, poverty, disappointment; I would live in a garret and eat nothing but black bread, suffer dissatisfaction with myself and realize my own imperfection, but in return I would insist on fame... real, resounding fame!" (31; 159). Whereas Sasha dreamt of "staying up nights copying [Ivanov's] papers" or "walking [with him] a hundred miles on foot" in exchange for nothing but the satisfaction of "active love" (59; 68), Nina imagines deprivations in the service of art and with the expectation of a concrete reward: fame.

Nina does, of course, make great sacrifices and suffer acutely, both for art and for love, during the play's timeline. These genuine sacrifices extend far beyond what either she or the idealistic Sasha had envisioned. The character of Nina contains elements of the "terribly perfect" and "necessary" Russian woman, but she transcends the unidimensionality of this archetype. Nor does her fate adhere neatly to the "female victim and male victimizer" category of the fallen woman so prevalent in both Russian and European nineteenth-century literature.[35] By infusing the character with a devotion to the art of acting – no matter how open-ended the question of her actual talent remains – Chekhov endows her "necessary" female characteristics, such as her self-sacrifice and fidelity, with a new significance. By Act Four, Nina's understanding of art and sacrifice has been denuded of all melodrama: "Now I know, understand, Kostya, that in our work – it doesn't matter whether we act or we write – the main thing isn't fame, glamour, the things I dreamed about, it's knowing how to endure" (58; 181). She exhibits a sober awareness of her own limitations as an actress, confirming Konstantin's earlier observations that she "became petty, trivial, acted mind-lessly... [without knowing] what to do with my hands" (58; 181). Nonetheless, Nina insists that she has subsequently attained a higher level in her performance, that she is now "a real actress" who plays with "pleasure and joy" and who experiences the daily growth of her "spiritual strength" (ibid.). The multidimensionality of her self-realization represents a challenge to the notion that Russian heroines must necessarily embody "oneness."

Both Nina and Sasha outlive the suicidal "superfluous men" in their respective plays, but it is Nina who transcends the limitations both of her circumstances – the restrictive parents who eventually disown her, her provincial upbringing – and her own misguided romanticism. Sasha survives, but Nina *endures* in a purposeful way and without a "fear of life," as she tells Konstantin during their final encounter (58; 181). It is this purposeful endurance not connected with any male that constitutes Chekhov's most significant reworking of the category of the "terribly perfect" Russian woman, even if the fate that awaits Nina as a peripatetic provincial actress is far from happy. If the river symbolizes both the external and internal limitations that Nina faces, then she does, in fact, embody the promise that her name evokes and that Dobroliubov had attributed to Ostrovsky's heroine some thirty years earlier.

Returning to Ostrovsky's *The Storm*, besides the prominence of the water imagery in both plays, numerous biographical similarities between the two heroines emerge. Oppressive domestic circumstances rendered both of their young lives a prison, from which each sought escape in sexual transgression.[36] Both faced the opprobrium and ostracism that inevitably greeted the nineteenth-century "fallen woman." In choosing death, however, Katerina reflected both the nineteenth century's "cultural obsession with women's suicide" and the "multivalent nexus between self-killing and familial despotism" that developed in Russian society and culture in the latter decades of the nineteenth century.[37] Dobroliubov viewed her suicide not only as the antidote to male inaction but also as a protest against the oppression of the Russian patriarchal family, which required such extreme self-sacrifice to be vanquished.[38] While Katerina sees premonitions of her imminent death throughout the play, equating her home with the grave, Nina, as mentioned above, describes the absence of a "fear of life."[39] Katerina's suicide also anticipated a trend in European theater during the nineteenth century's final decades, when seemingly every major playwright had to write a "fallen woman" play in an effort "to combine elements of the Ibsenite modern problem play with a familiar and crowd-pleasing genre."[40] Katerina's and Nina's European counterparts frequently ended their lives in suicide, their tragic circumstances serving a didactic and cautionary function.[41] Unlike those of her Ostrovskian predecessor and her European contemporaries, Nina's fate provides audience members with neither a clear resolution nor an identifiable moral lesson. While "late nineteenth-century convention" required that "the woman who truly loved a man must die," Nina refuses to do so, despite the tragic outcome of her affair with Trigorin, whom she continues to love.[42] Simon Karlinsky identifies *The Seagull* as the play that marked the Russian stage's "first liberation from both the conventions of Ostrovskian drama that had dominated since the 1850s and from the patterns and formulas of the Western well-made social play."[43] This "liberation" consists not only in the oft-acknowledged innovative aspects of Chekhov's dramaturgy – the lack of traditional action, the moving of dramatic events such as Konstantin's suicide offstage – but also in the challenging of gendered categories and the reconsideration of female heroism that the play's women, namely Nina, represent.

The reaction of those Russian audience members who wrote to Chekhov to express their distress over his works' "fundamental lack of the heroic" can be partially explained, with reference to *The Seagull*, through the play's gender dynamics. These Russian theatergoers were exhibiting symptoms of the same anxiety about "sexual anarchy" – a fundamental breakdown in previously sacrosanct codes for female and male behavior – that characterized the fin de siècle.[44] Nina's decision to pursue an autonomous – if undoubtedly precarious and probably unhappy – existence as an actress, a life not circumscribed by the domestic sphere, aligns her partially with the New Woman of playwrights such as Ibsen and Shaw. The future that awaited Ibsen's Nora, after the famous door slam with which she ends *A Doll's House*, was most likely no happier than Nina's, but her actions nonetheless represent a resounding break with dramatic and societal convention. In a similar vein, *The Seagull* problematizes notions of Russian heroism by reproducing some of the expected elements of the familiar superfluous man/"necessary" woman binary, while, at the same time, reordering those elements in an unexpected way.

The Seagull represents the culmination of the multifaceted dramatic exploration of female heroism that Chekhov began in *Ivanov*. Through the character of Masha, he shows how a woman can be as dissatisfied with life, self-destructive, and occasionally cruel as any man. Through the character of Nina, he offers a glimpse at how a woman may be relieved of the burden of "terrible perfection" through a difficult, imperfect, but, ultimately, transcendent devotion to art. Amidst the melancholy "kingdom of darkness" of the fin de siècle, Nina provides a distinct, if notably ambiguous, "ray of light." It is her arguably misguided allegiance to art, rather than Katerina's suicidal plunge into the Volga, that represents the realization of the hopes articulated by Dobroliubov some thirty-five years earlier for a heroine who could relieve Russian drama – and, by extension, Russian society – of the lingering burden of male superfluity.

NOTES

1 Nikolai Dobroliubov, "Luch sveta v temnom tsarstve," in *A. N. Ostrovskii, Teatr i zhizn': Izbrannye p'esy* (Moscow: Shkola-Press, 1995), 465–518. See the discussion in Susan K. Morrissey, *Suicide and the Body Politic in Imperial Russia* (Cambridge University Press, 2006), Chapter 9, "A Ray of Light in the Kingdom of Darkness," especially 238–241.

2 Ellen Chances, *Conformity's Children: An Approach to the Superfluous Man in Russian Literature* (Columbus, OH: Slavica, 1978), 147.

3 Ibid.

4 Mila B. Shevchenko, "Melodramatic Scenarios and Modes of Marginality: The Poetics of Anton Chekhov's Early Drama and of Fin-de-Siècle Russian Popular Drama" (PhD diss., University of Michigan, 2008), 5.

5 See, for example, D. I. Pisarev, "Motivy russkoi dramy," in *A. N. Ostrovskii, Teatr i zhizn'*, 519–527. Vera S. Dunham, in her classic essay, supports Dobroliubov's interpretation when she observes that "Katerina acts when driven toward fulfillment. Having enacted the storm of her life, she leaves her weak husband to his desolation and in envy of her courage. His love likewise is weak while in contrast Katerina's strength is monumental." See "The Strong Woman Motif," in *The Transformation of Russian Society*, edited by Cyril E. Black (Cambridge, MA: Harvard University Press, 1960), 464.

6 Showalter, *Sexual Anarchy*, 3.

7 See Gail Finney, *Women in Modern Drama: Freud, Feminism, and European Theater at the Turn of the Century* (Ithaca, NY: Cornell University Press, 1989).

8 Bram Dijkstra, *Idols of Perversity: Fantasies of Feminine Evil in Fin-de-Siècle Culture* (New York: Oxford University Press, 1986), 368.

9 Showalter, *Sexual Anarchy*, 128.

10 Carolina de Maegd-Soëp, *Chekhov and Women: Women in the Life and Work of Chekhov* (Bloomington, IN: Slavica, 1987), 77.

11 Barbara Heldt, *Terrible Perfection: Women and Russian Literature* (Indianapolis: Indiana University Press, 1987), 12, 5.

12 Dunham, "The Strong Woman Motif," 467.

13 Jehanne Gheith, "The Superfluous Man and the Necessary Woman: A 'Re-Vision,'" *The Russian Review* 55:2 (1996): 233.

14 Donald Rayfield, *Understanding Chekhov: A Critical Study of Chekhov's Prose and Drama* (London: Bristol Classical Press, 1999), xiv.

15 John Tulloch, *Chekhov: A Structuralist Study* (London: Macmillan, 1980), 154–155.

16 See the discussion in Peta Tait, *Performing Emotions: Gender, Bodies, Spaces, in Chekhov's Drama and Stanislavski's Theatre* (Aldershot, Eng.: Ashgate, 2002), 23–24. A more positive appraisal of *The Seagull's* female characters is offered by Nicholas Moravčevich, who argues that, beginning with this play, "the feminine characters in the Chekhovian drama begin, not only to match their masculine counterparts in terms of complexity and plasticity of portraiture, but at times even to outdistance them in terms of aesthetic appeal and stage presence." See Moravčevich, "Women in Chekhov's Plays," in *Chekhov's Great Plays: A Critical Anthology*, edited by Jean-Pierre Barricelli (New York University Press, 1981), 204.

17 Tait, *Performing Emotions*, 7.

18 Finney, *Women in Modern Drama*, 15. For an illuminating discussion of how Chekhov's female characterization may have marked his "interrogation of the melodramatic form," see Cynthia Marsh, "The Stage Representation of Chekhov's Women," in *The Cambridge Companion to Chekhov*, edited by Vera Gottlieb and Paul Allain (Cambridge University Press, 2000), 216–227. Another trend is represented by Toby Clyman who, in her article "Čexov's Victimized Women," details the unique hardships facing both peasant and aristocratic women in the author's works, where they "are confronted with factors which leave them open to abuse and exacerbate the existing aggravating conditions in life." See Clyman, "Čexov's Victimized Women," *Russian Language Journal* 28 (1974): 31.

19 Heldt, *Terrible Perfection*, 49.

20 A. P. Chekhov, *Ivanov*, in *Polnoe sobranie sochinenii i pisem*, edited by N. F. Bel'chikov et al. (Moscow: Nauka, 1974–1983), XII:37; hereafter referred to as *PSS*. Translated by Laurence Senelick, in *Anton Chekhov's Selected Plays* (New York: W. W. Norton, 2005), 51. All subsequent citations are to these editions and are noted in the text with the Russian page numbers followed by those in the translation. I have occasionally modified the translation. For example, Senelick translates *lishnii* as "redundant," which I have changed to the more accepted "superfluous."

For more on "Hamletism" during the fin de siècle, see John Stokes, "Varieties of Performance," in *The Cambridge Companion to the Fin de Siècle*, edited by Gail Marshall (Cambridge University Press, 2007), 215–218. John McKellor Reid contends that it is Ivanov's realization that he may be typed as a "Russian Hamlet" that provides the comedic "wit" of the play. See McKellor Reid, "Ivanov: The Perils of Typicality," *Modern Drama* 49:1 (2006): 81.

21 Chekhov, "Pis'mo A. S. Suvorinu," in *PSS* III:109, III.

22 Ibid., 113.

23 Finney, *Women in Modern Drama*, 195–196; I borrow the term "household nun" from Dijkstra, *Idols of Perversity*, Chapter I.

24 Quoted in de Maegd-Soëp, *Chekhov and Women*, 274. Chances pronounces a more critical judgment upon Sasha, characterizing her as a "thoughtless person devoid of compassion" and thus a poor "necessary woman" for the tormented Ivanov. See Chances, *Conformity's Children*, 146.

25 Chekhov's own view of Sasha, as articulated in his letter to Suvorin, emphasized her attraction to a man's "complaints, whining and misfortunes" rather than his "bravery and dexterity." He also observed that the true object of Sasha's love was not Ivanov himself but the "gratifying and holy task" of saving him. See Chekhov, "Pis'mo Suvorinu," 113–114. Chekhov thus introduces an element of self-interest into the "terribly perfect" woman's traditionally boundless self-sacrifice.

26 Chekhov, *Chaika*, in *PSS* VIII:5; in *Anton Chekhov's Selected Plays*, 136. All subsequent citations are to these editions and noted in the text with the Russian page numbers followed by those in the translation. I have occasionally modified the translation. Tait, *Performing Emotions*, 26.

27 Finney, *Women in Modern Drama*, 196.

28 Tait, *Performing Emotions*, 26.

29 Finney, *Women in Modern Drama*, 197.

30 As Michael Finke observes, it is a "staging meant to enact a coupling of sorts." See Finke, *Seeing Chekhov* (Ithaca, NY: Cornell University Press, 2005), 11. For a discussion of Treplev's play in the context of Chekhov's eschatological thinking, see Thomas Newlin's chapter in this volume.

31 Dunham, "The Strong Woman Motif," 481.

32 Arkadina, of course, plays a key role in disrupting this attempt at creative unity. Longing for his mother's approval, Konstantin, during the performance of his play, renders his mother's gaze "existentially determining" and allows her negative response to stimulate his "infantile, and terribly vulnerable" behavior. See Finke, *Seeing Chekhov*, 11.

33 Olga Matich, "A Typology of Fallen Women in Nineteenth Century Russian Literature," in *American Contributions to the Ninth International Congress of Slavists* (Bloomington, IN: Slavica, 1983), II:332.

34 Tait, *Performing Emotions*, 35.

35 Matich, "Typology," 327.

36 At the beginning of Act One, for example, Treplev observes that Nina's "father and stepmother watch her like hawks, and it's as hard to pry her loose from that house as if it were a prison" (7; 138).

37 Margaret Higonnet, "Speaking Silences: Women's Suicide," in *The Female Body in Western Culture*, edited by Susan Rubin Suleiman (Cambridge, MA: Harvard University Press, 1986), 68; Morrissey, *Suicide and the Body Politic*, 246.

38 Dobroliubov, "Luch sveta," 495.

39 A. N. Ostrovskii, *Groza*, in *A. N. Ostrovskii, Teatr i zhizn'*, 113.

40 Sos Eltis, "The Fallen Woman on Stage: Maidens, Magdalens, and the Emancipated Female," in *The Cambridge Companion to Victorian and Edwardian Theatre*, edited by Kerry Powell (Cambridge University Press, 2004), 227, 228.

41 Ibid., 224, 226. *The Seagull* was also written and performed during a period of heightened interest in sexual morality in Russia, in the aftermath of the debates spurred by Leo Tolstoy's story *The Kreutzer Sonata*. See Peter Ulf Møller, *Postlude to* The Kreutzer Sonata: *Tolstoj and the Debate on Sexuality in Russian Literature in the 1890s* (Leiden: E. J. Brill, 1988), especially Chapter 8, which focuses on Chekhov's contribution to this debate in his prose works.

42 Dijkstra, *Idols of Perversity*, 133. J. Douglas Clayton contends that Nina, nonetheless, faces imminent death from tuberculosis, and that her "optimism [in the play's closing act] is not optimism at all, but . . . a symptom of morbidity." See J. Douglas Clayton, "Diagnosis and Balagan: The Poetics of Chekhov's Drama," in *Adapting Chekhov, The Text and Its Mutations*, edited by J. Douglas Clayton and Yana Meerzon (New York: Routledge, 2013), 25.

43 *Anton Chekhov's Life and Thought: Selected Letters and Commentary*, translated by Michael Heim and edited by Simon Karlinsky (Evanston, IL: Northwestern University Press, 1973), 280. Newlin identifies the innovative dramatic structure of another of Chekhov's plays, *Uncle Vanya*, as one of that work's "decadent ecosystems." See Newlin's contribution to the present volume.

44 De Maegd-Soëp, *Chekhov and Women*, 77. For a discussion of the reception of Chekhov's representation of women by Russian women themselves, see Jane Gary Harris, "Image Criticism Revisited: Chekhov's Reception in the Early 20th Century Russian Women's Periodical Press," *Essays in Poetics* 31 (2006): 234–257.

PART III

Generic experimentation and hybridity

CHAPTER 8

The fall of the house
Gothic narrative and the decline of the Russian family

Katherine Bowers

"There are families over which an inescapable fatalism seems to weigh," observes Mikhail Saltykov-Shchedrin toward the end of *The Golovlev Family* (*Gospoda Golovlevy*, 1875–1880). He continues:

> This is especially the case among the petty gentry, who have no occupation, no connection to the common life, and no administrative meaning, who first huddled in the shelter of serfdom, scattered across Russia, but now are living out their final days on crumbling estates without protection.[1]

Saltykov-Shchedrin's novel focuses on one doomed family, but the unhappy Golovlevs are hardly unique in Russian literature. Across the long nineteenth century we see them in works ranging from Fonvizin's play *The Minor* (1782) to Chekhov's last drama, *The Cherry Orchard* (1904), from the declining estates in Gogol's *Dead Souls* (1842) to Tolstoy's famous meditation on unhappy families in *Anna Karenina* (1877). Serfdom's abolishment in 1861 led to a shift in the role of Russia's landed gentry class, but, as Saltykov-Shchedrin suggests, the family was in a declining state even before Alexander II's reforms. Family decline narratives became increasingly prevalent in Russian realism as the fin de siècle approached, gothic elements in them marking portrayals of familial and social breakdown.[2]

The decline of a family is not a uniquely gothic plot,[3] but it is closely associated with the genre as the gothic has a long history of "fall of the house" narratives. The narrative convention derives its name from Edgar Allan Poe's 1839 story "The Fall of the House of Usher," although the plotline within the gothic canon predates Poe's tale considerably.[4] In the gothic variant, the family is cursed in some mysterious and yet palpable way. Transgressions that occurred in the family's history drive their current circumstances. Gothic tropes such as live burials, imprisoned innocents, villainous guardians or patriarchs, suggestions of the supernatural, and a fascination with fear, terror, and dread abound. Unsurprisingly, in the end, the cursed family is doomed or destroyed outright.

The gothic motifs that appear in nineteenth-century Russian family novels are symptomatic of a heightened sense of anxiety related to decline and degeneration, a key feature of the fin-de-siècle mood as we see in the present volume's chapters on family degeneration (Holland), decadent ecosystems (Newlin), and masculine degeneration (Connor Doak), among others. Describing the fin de siècle, Mark Steinberg observes that "'falling' and 'ruin' were common terms in what was often a melodramatic account of modern sickness," and describes an obsession with "excess, sickness, and decline."[5] While Steinberg discusses the experience of the individual in the city, the anxiety he identifies permeated Russian life – both urban and rural, as many scholars note.[6] The gothic genre enabled writers to access an array of tropes and conventions that combine melodrama, enhanced fear, and a backdrop of social breakdown to portray this feeling of overwhelming anxiety. Robin Feuer Miller and Ani Kokobobo's chapters in the present volume on the Christmas story and the grotesque, respectively, demonstrate similar examples of realist generic utility. In this vein, the gothic mode enables a way of describing the world that relies not only on a fascination with the gloomy or macabre, but also on the anxiety that emerges from encounters with these elements and the related psychologies of dread and fear.

The gothic "fall of the house" plot, then, is a narrative of family decline, but one that also incorporates an emphasis on dread and anxiety more closely associated with fin-de-siècle atmosphere. This chapter will examine this "fall of the house" narrative in three works – Sergei Aksakov's *The Family Chronicle* (*Semeinaia khronika*, 1856), Saltykov-Shchedrin's *The Golovlev Family*, and Ivan Bunin's *Dry Valley* (*Sukhodol*, 1911) – and the way gothic elements in each effect this fin-de-siècle mood, in the first two cases, avant la lettre. From early to late realism, each describes a family in a different stage of its life cycle, each oppressed in some sense by an "inescapable fatalism." Aksakov's work chronicles a new dynasty's foundation and its first three generations, but gothic episodes hint at the family's underlying problems, while Saltykov-Shchedrin's novel uses gothic tropes to show a family in the process of decline across multiple generations. Bunin's novella rounds out the trilogy, describing a house that has already fallen, drawing on the gothic mode to create an atmosphere of gloomy nostalgia and anxious destruction.

The gothic's emphasis on looking backward initially seems at odds with the fin de siècle's anxious fascination with modernity. However, upon closer examination, the gothic mode and especially the "fall of the house" plot particularly resonate with fin-de-siècle anxieties about decline, degeneration, and destruction. While some recent studies have demonstrated specific connections between gothic writing and fin-de-siècle culture,[7] this chapter aims to show that, in Russia, gothic motifs appeared as an expression of fin-de-siècle anxiety avant la lettre. Indeed, episodes from the histories of Aksakov's Bagrovs, Saltykov-Shchedrin's Golovlevs, and Bunin's Khrushchevs demonstrate that the themes so prevalent at the fin de siècle – gloom, destruction, and fatalistic thinking – had already seeped into Russian realism in the guise of the gothic. The prevalence of these themes in the nineteenth-century Russian family novel points to the "inescapable fatalism" hanging over Russian society, exposing latent anxieties about family legacy and decline, the estate system, and Russia's alleged backwardness in the face of a rapidly modernizing Western Europe.

Gothic elements and family decline in the early realist text

Aksakov began writing the sketches that became *The Family Chronicle* in the early 1840s, urged by Gogol to create a new literature based on life.[8] Gogol's own novel of the early 1840s, *Dead Souls*, evocatively depicts a conniving civil servant visiting a series of estates featuring "perverted or distorted forms of domesticity."[9] Pliushkin's home, the last stop on Chichikov's journey in Part I, has degenerated so much that it appears like "a vast, decrepit invalid . . . amidst impenetrable gloom," set within the "picturesque desolation" of its overgrown garden.[10] Where Gogol's novel seems at times preoccupied with decay and corruption, Aksakov's work appears to take a more positive line. *The Family Chronicle* tells the Bagrov family's story across multiple generations, beginning with the establishment of Novoe Bagrovo, the family's estate. The family's patriarch, Stepan Mikhailych, resembles a legendary creator figure, and the work's early parts describe Novoe Bagrovo in nearly mythical terms. Life there becomes an ideal for the work's narrator, Stepan Mikhailych's grandson and heir to the estate. The *Chronicle* ends on a hopeful note with the narrator's birth, seen as both a continuation of the family's legacy and an affirmation of its blessing.

Yet while the novel's structure and narrative voice do seem affirmative, the dysfunctional marriage of Stepan Mikhailych's ward Praskovia Ivanovna in Part II sharply contrasts with the Russian pastoral idyll established in Part I. The narrative takes a Gogolian turn as it describes improbable extremes such as imprisonment and starvation, and even suggests devil worship. While not a true "fall of the house" narrative as the family eventually rallies and revives, the episode's preoccupation with disharmony and decline undermines Aksakov's idyll. The Part II gothic motifs highlight underlying anxieties, which center on notions of heredity and legacy, a theme that constantly emerges in "fall of the house" gothic writing.[11] While in *The Golovlev Family* and *Dry Valley*, as I will show, family houses decline and fall, *The Family Chronicle* presents a strong family, but one in which gothic motifs in one episode illustrate the anxiety surrounding the potential "fall of the house," with ramifications for our understanding of the work as a whole.

In Part II, fortune hunter Mikhail Kurolesov tricks fifteen-year-old heiress Praskovia Ivanovna into marrying him. Despite Stepan Mikhailych's displeasure, the young couple is happy at first. Kurolesov takes Praskovia Ivanovna's neglected estates in hand, making them prosperous again, and is admired in the district for his good management. However, as time passes, Kurolesov's tendencies toward violence and alcoholism become habit, and horrors escalate:

> Gradually rumors began to spread that the Major was not just severe as before, but actively cruel . . . that he had gathered together a company with which, carousing, he committed abominations of all types, but the worst offense was the merciless violence he inflicted on his serfs while intoxicated; it was said two men had already died under torture.[12]

Later, Kurolesov's behavior intensifies:

> [H]is continuous cruelty eventually developed into an insatiable thirst for torture and human blood. Spurred on by the fear and deference of those around him, he quickly lost all sense of humanity.[13]

Kurolesov's decline from respected landowner to cruel tyrant stems from his misplaced desire for material wealth and amusement, as well as his tendency toward alcoholism. Aksakov's narrator notes that hard work distracts Kurolesov, but, growing bored, he spins more wildly out of control.

Conversely, Stepan Mikhailych runs Bagrovo well and prospers, precisely because of his obsessive interest in continuing the family line. He chooses a wife for her bloodlines, not her fortune, and he puts the estate and wellbeing of his family above all. Although Stepan Mikhailych's relatives and retainers fear his temper, his honorable character sharply contrasts with Kurolesov's villainy. However, Kurolesov's striking similarities to Stepan Mikhailych – his authority, temper, and potential for cruelty – reveal the thin line between noble patriarch and destructive wastrel.[14] In this light, the gothic horror that colors Kurolesov's story emphasizes latent anxiety about the family's potential decline just as significantly as the deaths of the second generation's children in infancy. If, even one generation removed from the strong founder figure, destruction of estate and legacy is possible on such a scale, the family is undermined.

As the gothic episode continues, Praskovia Ivanovna eventually discovers her husband's activities and sets out to deprive him of authority over her estates.[15] Kurolesov beats her and locks her in the cellar to starve until she signs her property over to him. Stepan Mikhailych comes to rescue his former ward:

> You can imagine what Stepan Mikhailych was like when he heard of [it] . . . Parasha, beaten nearly to death by her villainous husband, Parasha locked for three days in a dungeon – perhaps already dead – the image appeared so vividly in his imagination that he sprang up like a madman.[16]

The gothic vision in this episode emphasizes the striking difference between Stepan Mikhailych's and Kurolesov's understanding of and loyalty to family. It takes an unnatural death to resolve the situation; ultimately Kurolesov is poisoned with a mixture of arsenic and kvass, thus freeing Praskovia Ivanovna and returning her lands to the Bagrov family's holdings.

In the character of Stepan Mikhailych, Aksakov puts forward a Slavophile agenda, calling for a return to moral and religious law, ancestral tradition, and the primacy of the right and just over the state's written laws.[17] Although Stepan Mikhailych represents order and wisdom, maintaining his estates justly and prosperously, the episode serves to emphasize his limitations, another source of anxiety. Praskovia Ivanovna has inherited his sense of duty and justice, as well as his honor and courage, but she is unable to act, oppressed by both her husband and the legal system that gives him power over her. Stepan Mikhailych's desire to continue his line depends not only on his will, but also to some extent on chance, on the influx of others into the family by marriage, and on the personalities of his descendants; ultimately, he is unable to control all aspects of his legacy.

These gothic plot elements, although sequestered in the second sketch, carry an ominous shadow. They appear out of place amidst the affirmative foundation narrative and pastoral idyll described in the *Chronicle*. Although the situation ends happily for Praskovia Ivanovna, who is rid of her husband and returns to Novoe Bagrovo, and for the Bagrov family patrimony, which regains her estates, the episode carries a hint of potential decline and degeneration. In this sense, the gothic mode in Aksakov's *Family Chronicle* can be read as an early indicator of the fin-de-siècle motifs that became pervasive in later Russian realism. While the novel's conclusion valorizes the family, the work as a whole seems to reject the grim present, characterized by marital discord, in favor of an idealized mythical past and bright future. However, the gothic anxiety that emerges in relation to marriage and legacy in Praskovia Ivanovna's sketch problematizes notions of family continuity and stability, and undermines the work's affirmative ending. While *The Family Chronicle* ends on an optimistic note, Aksakov's gothic interlude echoes intellectual rumblings against the family in Western Europe,[18] and informs Saltykov-Shchedrin's *The Golovlev Family*, a strong indictment against the contemporary family packaged neatly in a "fall of the house" narrative frame.

The fall of the house of Golovlev

The prevalence of family novels throughout the nineteenth century points to a broader discourse about the family underway generally in Russia and Western Europe at this time. As the century progressed, the rise of industry led to a separation between home and workplace and, consequently, a shift in family values. Champions of the traditional family, such as Hegel, put forward its economic strength and its moral stability as a societal unit. Leftists such as Marx and Engels spoke out against the traditional family as an institution. For them, the family stood for inequality because of the uneven division of labor between the sexes, and also represented an unsustainable economic unit. In *The Communist Manifesto* (1848), they call for the bourgeois family's abolition, writing, "The bourgeois family will vanish as a matter of course when its complement vanishes, and both will vanish with the vanishing of capital."[19] Upheaval in the family unit was a particular cause for concern in Russia where the traditional family provided the backbone of the estate system.[20]

The Golovlev Family stands as a biting satire on the family problem and an examination of the social ramifications of degeneration theory, as Holland's chapter discusses. Thematically and structurally linked with Aksakov's novel, *The Golovlev Family* provides a family chronicle across three generations.[21] Where Aksakov's novel ends on an optimistic note, however, Saltykov-Shchedrin's novel narrates the Golovlevs' decline and degeneration, ending with their doom. Despite this bleak subject matter, Saltykov-Shchedrin's scathing satirical pen imbues the novel with dark humor. The work significantly undermines the traditional family novels that Saltykov-Shchedrin despised.[22] He equates these "false" family novels and their insincere portrayal of society with the Russian countryside's stagnation. The gothic elements in *The Golovlev Family* serve a dual function. On the one hand, gothic exaggeration strikes a humorous note, parodying the sincerity of the traditional family-oriented novel and adding to the work's overall satiric quality. On the other hand, Saltykov-Shchedrin's novel exploits the gothic conventions of the "fall of the house" plot to offer an ideologically charged indictment of Russian society and an implied call for change.

Saltykov-Shchedrin's Golovlevs are doomed from the start, "cursed" in the gothic literary tradition. While the narrator never gives specific details about this curse, the matriarch, Arina Petrovna, and her son, Porfiry, also known as Little Judas (*Iudushka*), seem preoccupied with this possibility. We learn that Arina Petrovna can curse Little Judas and others in the family, and she takes this power seriously.[23] Spreading out from interactions with Arina Petrovna, the fear of an unknown power permeates the novel, informing the family members' relations with each other. However, *The Golovlev Family* lends itself especially well to the gothic sensibility, even beyond its "fall of the house" narrative structure.[24] Family interactions are conducted through a veil of fear, exposing the dysfunction and disintegration of maternal and sibling bonds.

As relationships are perverted, the gothic mode signals their degeneration. For example, when Pavel first describes his brother, Little Judas appears as a monster, a basilisk.[25] Fear and dread characterize their relationship, and ultimately underscore the trajectory of the family's disintegration as this fear appears in gothic-tinged passages recounting other Golovlevs' degeneration or deaths. As some family members spiral into death, they become fixated on the idea that the Golovlev estate itself represents a tomb. Anninka, Arina Petrovna's granddaughter, perceives the estate itself as a harbinger of death:

> Golovlevo, that is death itself, malicious, spiritually empty; it is death always lying in wait for a new victim. Two uncles died here. Here two brothers, her cousins, received "especially serious" wounds, the consequence of which was death. Finally, Liubinka as well . . . the beginning of [her] "particularly serious" wounds doubtlessly lay in Golovlevo. All the deaths, all the poisons, all the pestulant sores – everything originated here.[26]

Golovlevo not only foreshadows deaths, but also causes them; return to the ancestral home figures in the death of nearly every family member. Like a monster waiting to devour its victims, even from afar, the estate becomes an object of fear and a catalyst for growing anxiety among family members.

Although they all live together in the same house, each lives in isolation. First Stepan, then Pavel, then Little Judas become wrapped up in their own affairs and lock themselves away. A tendency to forgetfulness allows this isolation to grow. Stepan becomes an alcoholic and drinks himself to death in the estate office; no one checks on him until it is too late. Similarly Pavel wastes away with his fatal disease alone, until the family members recall that they must arrange his affairs. Little Judas becomes so embroiled in petty busy work that he has little awareness of the outside world, even as his sons die one by one. He seems to give little thought to the disintegration of his legacy, or the loss of descendants who should be his heirs. Whereas, in *The Family Chronicle*, Stepan Mikhailych is concerned to the point of obsession with preserving his family legacy for future generations, the second-generation Golovlevs not only view their legacy with apathy, but they actively neglect it, ignoring the third generation or driving it away.

As the passage quoted above shows, this isolation is not only a character-istic of Golovlev family life, but another manifestation of the family home's destructive and anxiety-inducing properties. In a similar vein, earlier in the novel, the narrator describes a deathly silence that follows family members:

> The dining room emptied; everyone dispersed to his room. The house gradually stilled, and a deathly silence crept from room to room and finally reached the last refuge where ritual life persisted longer than in other secluded corners, the study of the master of Golovlevo.[27]

This "deathly silence" persists, mentioned again and again as the novel draws to a close. Similarly, the narrator constantly describes the house as plunged in darkness or playing host to an "impenetrable gloom." The silence, here a symbol of the family curse, pervades the space, eventually enveloping each Golovlev, and Little Judas last of all. The passage under-scores a phenomenon widely reported in the early twentieth century as a symptom of modernity and the fin-de-siècle atmosphere: an "emptiness of solitude," to use Grigory Gordon's 1909 phrasing.[28]

Not surprisingly, given both the "fall of the house" trajectory and fin-de-siècle anxiety, eventually the house of Golovlev falls. Unlike Aksakov's *Chronicle*, which hints at decline in its central gothic episodes, this "fall of the house" narrative has an absolute end:

> Everywhere, from each corner of the hateful house, the dead seemed to crawl out. In every direction, wherever one turned, the gray ghosts stirred. There's Papa, Vladimir Mikhailovich in a white nightcap, sticking out his tongue and quoting [vulgar poems]. There's brother Styopka-the-Dunce and near him Pashka-the-Silent; and here's Liubinka; and here are the final offspring of the Golovlev family: Volodka and Petka . . . drunkenness, wantonness, torment oozed blood . . . And above all these phantoms hovered a living ghost, none other than Porfiry Vladimirych Golovlev, the last representative of the empty line.[29]

The scene is reminiscent of the House of Usher's spectacular collapse in Poe's story. That story revolves around siblings Roderick and Madeline, last descendants of the Usher family. The family's final moment is anticipated by various escalating events: Roderick buries Madeline alive, Madeline escapes and attacks Roderick, and the two fall into a deadly embrace. The narrator, a passing traveler, flees, but looks back to see the house collapse and sink into the ground, dark water covering its last traces. In Poe's tale, both family and house are destroyed together, the one precipitating the other. However, instead of physical destruction, when Golovlevo falls, the house undergoes a metaphysical collapse, crumbling under a pile of family ghosts.

The lost Golovlevs, the family curse's victims, haunt Little Judas in the end. Here Saltykov-Shchedrin uses a hybrid gothic-satire genre to lighten the terrible scene with humor. The narrator lists the early curse victims almost gaily, as though they spend their time flitting about the estate without a care. While, earlier in the novel, these transgressions merely accumulated without consequences for their perpetrators, in this last scene, the victims return to haunt the living. As the list grows, the tone becomes more somber and, finally, the image of blood oozing from the family's transgressions lends an atmosphere of true horror and tragedy to the tableau. Little Judas's role as a "living ghost" (*zhivoi prizrak*), too, becomes humorless and bleak when we consider him as the doomed family's final representative. Tormented by conscience, this scene prompts the reconciliatory behavior that leads to his own demise: he begs his victims' forgiveness and begins a journey to his mother's grave, freezing to death on the way. And so Little Judas, the "living ghost," follows the other Golovlev phantoms in fear and anxiety, and, eventually, death.

Saltykov-Shchedrin's gothic use seems odd because, as a rationalist and materialist, he did not believe in the metaphysical. In his gothic realism, terror has a concrete cause, and the spiritual hierarchy relied upon by gothic writers such as Radcliffe or Lewis is absent. This materialism brings Saltykov-Shchedrin closer to the decadence – in the sense of spiritual emptiness – explored by fin-de-siècle writers such as Oscar Wilde, Aubrey Beardsley, or Joris-Karl Huysmans.[30] The phantoms that haunt, for example, Wilde's Dorian Gray or Huysmans's Jean des Esseintes are more in the line of psychological or existential torments than supernatural specters. Similarly, as Ilya Vinitsky observes, "Shchedrin's phantoms come from within, rather than outside, historical reality: the supernatural here has social, economic, psychological, and biological causes."[31] As an example of the "fall of the house" narrative, *The Golovlev Family* evinces the gothic's role in the theme, but simultaneously showcases its fin-de-siècle preoccupations, exposing their presence in the ideological realist novel.

Dry Valley: Gothic nostalgia at the fin de siècle

Building on Saltykov-Shchedrin's novel, thematically linked "fall of the house" works appear with increasing frequency in the Russian cultural context as the nineteenth century draws to a close. Milton Ehre names a few: "*The Golovlyovs* stands with Goncharov's *Oblomov*, Bunin's *Dry Valley*, Chekhov's *Cherry Orchard* as one of the great Russian literary epitaphs upon a dying social order."[32] Ehre's identification of the works as "epitaphs" plays on the idea of memorialization, a theme we see expressed in the particular nostalgic tone used throughout *Dry Valley*. This tone sets Bunin's work apart from Aksakov's or Saltykov-Shchedrin's family novels. Aksakov's novel rejects the present for the legendary past and the promise of an unknown but idealized future, paying homage to the family's past greatness while acknowledging its future potential. In Saltykov-Shchedrin's novel neither the past nor present merit accolades, and the future seems bleak. In Bunin's *Dry Valley*, however, the narrative's emphasis shifts: it mourns the demise of a way of life, even as the gothic motifs describing it emphasize its inevitable decline.[33]

Dry Valley tells the story of the Khrushchev family and its ancestral estate, Sukhodol, through the eyes of its last descendants. In the beginning, the narrators are children, but, as the novella continues, they grow up. Accordingly, their initially naïve descriptions and retellings of Sukhodol's legends and history become increasingly tinged with awareness. At first, the narrators engage nostalgically with the image of Sukhodol's past glory: "Our passionate dreams of Sukhodol were understandable: for us it was a poetic image of the past."[34] The Khrushchev family chronicle, related by Natalia, a peasant on the estate, enthralls the house's young descendants, who clamor to hear more stories from "olden times." Characterized by violence, transgression, greed, and betrayal, these bygone days seem exciting and important to the children. The young Khrushchevs take pride in their legacy, boasting of their father's status as heir to Sukhodol and extolling their family's importance:

> My sister and I lived for a long time in the steady tow of Sukhodol, lived under the spell of its antiquity . . . But it was always our ancestors, of course, who ruled that family, and we felt this through the ages. The history of family, kin and clan, is always subterranean, convoluted, mysterious, often

terrifying. But it's that long past, those dark depths and legends, that often give a family strength.[35]

Pride in family for them includes pride in family secrets, transgressions, and fears; these trappings of legend become a source of strength, a way of binding a family together.

Hints of the supernatural attend the estate, contributing to this idea of legend. When the Khrushchev children first travel to Sukhodol, they meet Aunt Tonia, who appears suddenly, mystically from darkness, terrifying the children. Although she later becomes a beloved folk feature of the estate experience, the fear they feel is palpable in the moment. Their account of Tonia's appearance represents the first indication that Sukhodol's reality may contradict the stories told to the children. Similarly, other events tied to folklore carry a connotation of fear. A local sorcerer called in to cure the ailing mistress uses folkloric magic to provoke terror. Later the devil seems to haunt the house. Finally the constant discussion of thunderstorms reveals that several family members have died under mysterious circumstances during storms. In these instances, the family's legend seems to combine with some unnatural, destructive, and terrifying force.

The family's place in local society preoccupies the children as they repeat Natalia's tales, and, through their naïve assumptions, a picture of hierarchy and hegemony emerges. Natalia tells the children that Khrushchev, in the early days of the estate, carried a whip, a symbol of his authority. The children look forward to one day, also, carrying whips, thus continuing the family legacy, although they seem to have little understanding of the whip's meaning. Natalia's story further reinforces this point. The affectionate children at first see the peasant as a pseudo-family member and enjoy her jolly Sukhodol stories, but in adulthood they feel sadness and guilt when they hear Natalia recount her "broken" life spent at Sukhodol. For the children, the family and estate are legendary, but the adult narrators realize their oppressive role in the lives of the peasants they admired as children. This awareness adds to the anxious undercurrent that accompanies the story's gothic narrative.

As Joost van Baak remarks in his study of the house in Russian literature, "The disappearance of a way of life is accompanied by the inevitable dissolution of the spaces that supported it. Empty or derelict houses are 'read' by the reminiscing narrator as metonymic material images of the former inhabitants, often his direct ancestors, and the ways in which they lived."[36] For van Baak, it is the house and estate themselves, decaying and crumbling, that symbolize the transience of time and the dissolution of the way of life they supported. As in Poe's "The Fall of the House of Usher," the destruction of the decaying Sukhodol estate and the Khrushchev family's demise are linked. However, the "fall of the house" of Khrushchev is not spectacular as in Poe's story or *The Golovlev Family*:

> And now the Sukhodol estate is completely empty. All those mentioned here have died, as have their neighbors and their peers. And sometimes you think: Is it true? Did they really live on this earth? It's only at the graveyard that you feel they really did exist – feel, in fact, a frightening proximity to them. But even for that you must make an effort; you must sit and think beside a family headstone – if you can find one. It is shameful to say, but impossible to hide: we don't even know where the graves . . . lie.[37]

The peasants who worked the estate are entirely forgotten, and the Khrushchev graveyard is so overgrown and decayed as to suggest that the family lives on only in the stories told by the novella's narrators. From the narrative's beginning, the estate has been in a state of decay. The air smells of it, and the narrators describe the house's physical dilapidation, its rotting gardens and sagging balconies. But it is only in this moment in the graveyard that we understand that the family, too, has died out. The narrators' nostalgic ruminations reinforce this point:

> No knight's descendant could ever say that in half a century an entire class of people vanished from the earth. He could never speak of such great numbers of people who deteriorated, who committed suicide and drank themselves to death, people who went mad, let go of everything, just disappeared. He could never admit, as I confess here, that the lives of not only our ancestors but even the lives of our great grandfathers are a complete and utter mystery to us now . . . ![38]

Like its decaying estate, the Khrushchev family has become a sad husk that exists only in remembered stories, and those memories are growing dim. Here the narrators identify the true tragedy of a noble house's fall as its loss of identity and structure. They mention some causes of this malaise: suicide, alcoholism, madness. These, however, are the symptoms of a larger problem, caused by generations of decline. Unlike Aksakov, whose work is set in the present but idealizes the past and future, or Saltykov-Shchedrin, who sees only darkness and decay in the past, present, or future, in Bunin's novella there is no future; the family's gothic past has built a legacy of nothing, its estate crumbling and its legends forgotten. In an expression of fin-de-siècle anxiety par excellence, the Khrushchevs' end has already come, and all that remains afterwards are emptiness, melancholy, and the unknown. Despite its nostalgic tone and lack of overt violence, *Dry Valley* is the most destructive and bleak of the three "fall of the house" narratives examined in this chapter.

***

Made rotten by stagnation and greed, the noble families of Russian literature collapse with increasing frequency as the twentieth century approaches. In chronicling the Golovlev family's downfall, Saltykov-Shchedrin invents an extreme case study, emphasizing what he sees as the gentry's problems – or transgressions. Whereas Saltykov-Shchedrin's *The Golovlev Family* stands as a model "fall of the house" narrative, Aksakov's *The Family Chronicle* is more ambiguous, contrasting the notion of the idealized happy family with a model for an unhappy, disintegrating one. For these writers, the gothic provided a means of accessing or describing a palpable fin-de-siècle mood, not yet articulated in the Russian cultural climate. Eventually, when *Dry Valley* takes up the plot as a lens through which to reflect upon a vanishing way of life, the gothic, with its historical emphasis, emphasis on destructive forces, and fascination with nostalgia, gloom, and death, seems a natural mode of expression.

The "fall of the house" plot cannot avoid its ending, and its inevitable trajectory symbolizes destruction and doom, striking a chord with the fin de siècle's emphasis on ending. The Golovlevs' and other families' curses, in this sense, become the curse of late tsarist Russia: the feeling of "inescapable fatalism" and approaching cataclysm, the mystery of moral transgressions committed but never confessed, stagnation, and decline over generations. And, indeed, reinforced by socioeconomic and historical circumstances, these gothic elements promoted a cultural climate in Russia that manifested in fin-de-siècle anxiety, revolutionary violence, and eventually led to what could be described as a much larger "fall of the house."

NOTES

1 M. E. Saltykov-Shchedrin, *Gospoda Golovlevy*, in *Sobranie sochinenii v dvadt-sati tomakh*, XIII:251. Hereafter *SS*. All translations are my own unless noted otherwise.

2 My research identifies three key characteristics that, together, define any gothic work: (1) the narrative focuses on a mystery's solution: curiosity propels the reader to continue turning pages, anticipating horrors hinted at but constantly deferred; (2) the narrative revolves around a transgression or broken taboo, the repercussions of which inform the work as a whole; and (3) the narrative is preoccupied with psychologies such as fear, dread, and revulsion – both their representation in the text and emotional impact on the reader – which give

rise to a sense of anxiety that permeates the text. This definition builds upon
the work of David Punter, Fred Botting, and Muireann Maguire. See Punter,
The Literature of Terror: The Modern Gothic (London: Longman, 1996), 146;
Botting, *Gothic* (London: Routledge, 1996), 2–3; and Maguire, *Stalin's Ghosts:
Gothic Themes in Early Soviet Literature* (Oxford: Peter Lang, 2012), 10–14.

3 Joost van Baak discusses the "House Myth" in *The House in Russian Literature:
A Mythopoeic Exploration* (Amsterdam: Rodopi, 2009), including numerous
examples of families in decline (69–75, 164–165). According to van Baak,
"fall of the house" narratives depict cyclic routine and order "disrupted by
catastrophic or fatal plot developments, especially where a family disinte-
grates or dies out, bringing their house to an end – the Death of the House"
(261).

4 The "fall of the house" topos appears in the first gothic novel, Horace Walpole's
The Castle of Otranto (1767), and reoccurs frequently in the genre. Aside from
Walpole's novel and Poe's story, the plot features in Clara Reeve's *The Old
English Baron* (1777), Ann Radcliffe's *The Castles of Athlin and Dunbayne* (1789)
and *A Sicilian Romance* (1790), Matthew Lewis's *The Monk* (1795), and Charles
Maturin's *Melmoth the Wanderer* (1820), among others. For more information
about the "fall of the house" plot in gothic fiction, see Anne Williams, *Art
of Darkness: A Poetics of Gothic* (University of Chicago Press, 1995), 38–48
(on houses and patriarchal systems), and 87–96 (on families and legacies).
For an in-depth look at the "fall of the house" plot and domestic space, see
Kate Ferguson Ellis, *The Contested Castle: Gothic Novels and the Subversion of
Domestic Ideology* (Urbana: University of Illinois Press, 1989), especially 3–17,
33–52.

5 Steinberg, *Petersburg Fin de Siècle*, 157.

6 Nordau's discussion of the decline of culture in *Degeneration*, citing works by
Turgenev and Tolstoy, points to this trend, as does the work of scholars such
as Thomas Newlin, who concludes *The Voice in the Garden: Andrei Bolotov
and the Anxieties of the Russian Pastoral, 1738–1833* (Evanston, IL: Northwestern
University Press, 2001) with a discussion about the anxiety of disillusionment
in the pastoral by writers such as Tolstoy, Chekhov, and Blok (187–190).
In *This Meager Nature: Landscape and National Identity in Imperial Russia*
(DeKalb: Northern Illinois University Press, 2002), Christopher Ely claims
that the combination of "the abiding negation of the Russian landscape"
(compared to Europe) and an "emerging tendency to celebrate a special, even
virtuous, Russian misery . . . paradoxically made attractive an image of the
Russian land as a uniquely grim and unappealing space" (135). This aesthetic
view translates into anxiety in Russian novels chronicling gentry life. See, for
example, Amy Singleton's argument that Oblomov's family estate becomes
"an anxiety-provoking land of the dead" (77–79) in *No Place Like Home: The
Literary Artist and Russia's Search for Cultural Identity* (Albany: State University
of New York Press, 1997).

7 Studies that explore the correlation between fin-de-siècle degeneration and
gothic themes include Kelly Hurley's *The Gothic Body: Sexuality, Materialism,*

and Degeneration at the Fin de Siècle (Cambridge University Press, 2004) and Andrew Smith's *Victorian Demons*. Both focus on the British tradition, arguing that Victorians' interest in technology, science, medicine, and sexuality resulted in an outpouring of gothic works toward the century's end, including Bram Stoker's *Dracula* (1897) and Robert Louis Stevenson's *The Strange Case of Dr. Jekyll and Mr. Hyde* (1886). Both Hurley and Smith link the fin-de-siècle obsession with degeneration back to the gothic imagination.

8 See S. T. Aksakov, *Istoriia moego znakomstva s Gogolem, s vkliucheniem vsei perepiski, c 1832 po 1852*, in *Sobranie sochinenii v piati tomakh* (Moscow: Pravda, 1966), III:384–385.

9 van Baak, *The House in Russian Literature*, 155.

10 Nikolai Gogol', *Mertvye dushi*, in *Polnoe sobranie sochinenii v chetyrnadtsati tomakh* (Moscow: Pushkinskii Dom, 1951), IV:111–112. Trans. English, 110–111.

11 For example, in *The Castle of Otranto*, the main action is dictated by the family's curse, but sparked by the patriarch's obsession with building his legacy. For more information about the perils of legacy building and an overview of this theme in gothic literature, see Allan Hepburn, *Troubled Legacies: Narrative and Inheritance* (University of Toronto Press, 2007), 8–11.

12 S. T. Aksakov, *Semeinaia khronika*, in *Sobranie sochinenii*, I:100–101.

13 Ibid., 104.

14 In contrast, Richard Gregg claims that, while Stepan Mikhailych's terrible temper establishes him as a gothic villain, the family's ability to come together in the end neutralizes his anger and prevents his decline. See "The Decline of a Dynast: From Power to Love in Aksakov's *Family Chronicle*," *The Russian Review* 50:1 (1991): 35–47.

15 Andrew Durkin presents Praskovia Ivanovna as an oppressed gothic heroine. Aksakov's fascination with the gothic does not extend to its obsession with psychologies such as fear, Durkin notes; instead, this gothic episode serves to bring the work's inherent moral judgment into sharper focus. See *Sergei Aksakov and Russian Pastoral* (New Brunswick, NJ: Rutgers University Press, 1983), 114–168.

16 Aksakov, *Semeinaia khronika*, 114.

17 For more information about Aksakov's Slavophilism, see Peter Christoff, *An Introduction to Nineteenth-Century Russian Slavophilism: K. S. Aksakov* (The Hague: Mouton, 1982), 148–149. Additionally, see Michael Hughes, "The Russian Nobility and the Russian Countryside: Ambivalences and Orientations," *Journal of European Studies* 36:2 (2006): 115–137, especially 128–130.

18 Although Aksakov was writing within a largely conservative Slavophile tradition, his critical depiction of violence against women within marriage bears certain similarities with the critique of marriage emerging among his socialist contemporaries in Western Europe, such as Charles Fourier and Robert Owen, who rejected the family unit as a significant hindrance to their visions of a socially equal society.

19 Karl Marx and Friedrich Engels, *Manifesto of the Communist Party and Selected Essays* (Rockville, MD: Arc Manor, 2008), 19. For more information, see

Richard Weikart, "Marx, Engels, and the Abolition of the Family," *History of European Ideas* 18:5 (1994): 657–672.

20 For more information, see Richard Stites, *The Women's Liberation Movement in Russia, 1860–1930: Feminism, Nihilism, Bolshevism* (Princeton University Press, 1978), especially 29–115.

21 Many critics argue that *The Family Chronicle* is a precursor to and inspiration for Saltykov-Shchedrin's later work, including Durkin, *Sergei Aksakov and Russian Pastoral*, 244; van Baak, *The House in Russian Literature*, 162; Todd, "Anti-Hero," 102; Kramer, "Satiric Form," 455.

22 Kramer argues that *The Golovlev Family* parodies the conventional, family-oriented novel. See "Satiric Form," 453–464.

23 Jenny Kaminer examines Arina Petrovna's maternal instincts (and lack thereof) in "A Mother's Land: Arina Petrovna Golovlyova and the Economic Restructuring of the Golovlyov Family," *Slavic and East European Journal* 53:4 (2009): 545–565.

24 As Ilya Vinitsky argues, Saltykov-Shchedrin forges a "realist-gothic" aesthetic, and his novel operates within the gothic's realm. Vinitsky uses his gothic interpretation of *The Golovlev Family* as a way into the work's resonance with spiritualism. See Vinitsky, *Ghostly Paradoxes: Modern Spiritualism and Russian Culture in the Age of Realism* (University of Toronto Press, 2009), 113–116.

25 "He hated little Judas but at the same time feared him. He knew little Judas's eyes oozed an enchanting poison, that his voice would creep into your soul serpent-like and paralyze your will." *SS* XIII:67.

26 *SS* XIII:249.

27 *SS* XIII:118–119.

28 Gordon writes, "Now and at every step one meets individuals who are weak and without will, who feel alone and isolated amidst the very noise and intensity of life. They cannot find ideals to pursue. Always and everywhere they find themselves surrounded by the emptiness of solitude." Steinberg discusses Gordon's observation and the isolation of the self in society as part of a broader feeling of pathological melancholy symptomatic of fin-de-siècle anxiety. See Steinberg, *Petersburg Fin de Siècle*, 252.

29 *SS* XIII:256.

30 For more information about decadence and its roots in darker genres of romanticism such as the gothic, see Mario Praz, *The Romantic Agony* (Oxford University Press, 1978). Praz catalogues romantic tendencies, such as Byronism, that grew into widespread ennui and emptiness in fin-de-siècle decadence.

31 Vinitsky, *Ghostly Paradoxes*, 114.

32 Ehre, "A Classic of Russian Realism," 9.

33 For a gothic reading of Bunin's novella, see Dale Peterson, "Russian Gothic: The Deathless Paradoxes of Bunin's *Dry Valley*," *Slavic and East European Journal* 31:1 (1987): 36–49.

34 I. A. Bunin, Sukhodol, *in* Sobranie sochinenii v piati tomakh (Moscow: Pravda, 1956), II:III. All Bunin translations are from *Ivan Bunin: Collected Stories*, translated by Graham Hettlinger (Chicago: Ivan R. Dee, 2007), here 19–20.

Subsequent citations provide the Russian edition page number first, followed by the English edition.

35 113; 22.
36 van Baak, *The House in Russian Literature*, 244–245.
37 153–154; 72–73.
38 152; 71.

CHAPTER 9

Corpses of desire and convention
Tolstoy's and Artsybashev's grotesque realism

Ani Kokobobo

The last decade of tsarist Russia has been described as an "era of possibility and crisis, marked by an often desperate search for meaning of the present and a sense of the future."[1] According to historians, this sense of crisis in Russia under Nicholas II was precipitated by profound socioeconomic changes during the end of the nineteenth century and the tension they evoked between the economic push toward Western-style political development and the tsarist regime's efforts to cling to autocracy.[2] No more comfortable with economic change and Westernizing trends, average Russians also worried about the repercussions of modern civilization and industrial progress. As Mark Steinberg argues, during this time, the Russian "[v]ocabulary became filled with talk of catastrophic disintegration, decline, groundlessness, sickness, disenchantment, and uncertainty."[3]

In this chapter, I address two Russian realist authors writing at the turn of the century – Leo Tolstoy and Mikhail Artsybashev – and consider how they adjusted to the social transition by using the lens of the grotesque to supplement their realism. Described as a style "preeminent in periods of great social upheaval and cultural instability,"[4] the grotesque allows for a reconceptualization of familiar worlds in a new light through its ability to estrange reality. This estrangement often entails a dehumanization of individuals by stripping them of their spirituality and reducing them to their bodily selves. In his purest form, the grotesque individual is a mere physical shell, resembling a walking corpse or an objectified man devoid of spirituality; he may look like a normal man, but he is a normal man estranged, deprived of his spiritual essence.

The fin de siècle was the perfect time for the grotesque, which had appeared in the work of earlier authors like Gogol and later ones like Saltykov-Shchedrin and Dostoevsky.[5] Its preoccupation with the body and sexuality made the revival of the grotesque during the fin de siècle particularly appropriate. Seen as a "perilously risqué [time] in attitudes about sex, sexuality and sexual identity," the fin de siècle brought to the forefront all kinds of debates on sexuality, including discussions of homosexuality during Oscar Wilde's trial for sodomy in England,[6] which illustrated how much sex had become a public affair in fin-de-siècle Europe. In fact, so pervasive was the question of sex that the English novelist George Gissing described the fin de siècle as a period of "sexual anarchy."[7]

In the Russian context, sexuality similarly received a great deal of attention during this period; as Laura Engelstein argues, sexuality was essential to the public discourse of the time and tied to questions of civic order and political authority. When the 1905 Revolution produced only meager political results, the disappointment led intellectuals and professionals to refocus their efforts on sexual themes, "in compensation for lost civic hopes and as a challenge to the puritanical anti-individualism of the radical left."[8] Olga Matich similarly brings up the importance of sexuality in her study of Russian decadents – a group obsessed with mortality and physical decline that used sexuality to counteract these processes. In decadent fashion, individuals like Dmitry Merezhkovsky, Zinaida Gippius, and others believed they could defeat death through sexual abstention, "resisting nature's procreative imperative and reject[ing] traditional notions of gender."[9]

Among fin-de-siècle realists, Tolstoy and Artsybashev emerge as particularly important voices in debates over sexuality. A core realist, Tolstoy remained active as a writer well into the fin de siècle and his later works exemplify the darkening of the realist canon as it approached the century's end. In particular, during this period, questions of sex became more prominent in Tolstoy's writings, and works such as the notorious novella *The Kreutzer Sonata* (1889) provoked increased discussion of sexuality in Russian public discourse.[10] A decade later, Tolstoy followed the novella with *Resurrection* (1899), which similarly placed sexuality to the fore.

Belonging to a later generation than Tolstoy, Artsybashev came into his own during the fin de siècle, gaining prominence as a realist writer by exploring sexual themes. In particular, his novel *Sanin* (1907), which transformed the conventional realist gentry protagonist into a sexual hedonist, was a "cultural event of enormous importance" in fin-de-siècle Russia, inspiring lectures with large audiences, mock trials, and several monographs refuting the "novel's gospel of 'free love.'"[11] Unlike Tolstoy, who depicted sexuality as a force for moral corruption and juxtaposed sexual desire with his own Christian moral code, Artsybashev condemned society's repressive and hollow morality and wholeheartedly embraced sexuality.[12] In this sense, Artsybashev may be said to fit with larger fin-de-siècle European trends, as reflected in the work of Max Stirner and Friedrich Nietzsche, who challenged repressive sexual morality and professed the "life-affirming and individualistic philosophy of life that legitimized the pursuit of sensual pleasure."[13]

Despite their great ideological differences, works by Tolstoy and Artsybashev reflect the significance of sexuality during the fin de siècle, while also displaying overarching pessimism about both the present and future. For one author, Tolstoy, sexuality motivates the failure and decay characteristic of the fin de siècle, whereas for the other, Artsybashev, sexuality provides a means to overcome fin-de-siècle despair. In this chapter, I consider discussions of sexuality in both Tolstoy's non-fiction and fictional works like *The Kreutzer Sonata* and *Resurrection* and in Artsybashev's *Sanin*. Despite their conceptual differences, these last two realist novels converge in their similar aesthetic devices, illustrating the evolution of Russian realism during the fin de siècle. As I argue, while Tolstoy condemns sexuality and praises Christian morality and Artsybashev praises sexuality and criticizes societal repression, both authors use the grotesque style to depict their respective visions of the world. A natural evolution of and complement to realism during the fin de siècle, the grotesque invades this style, becoming a means for both Tolstoy and Artsybashev to capture the heightened sexuality and despair of the era.

The grotesque at the fin de siècle

When we think about the role of the grotesque during the fin de siècle, the style's overall ability to reconceptualize a familiar world in a new light is one of its more important features for writers. A foundational figure in Russian realism, Tolstoy returned to the novel genre in *Resurrection* armed with new religious beliefs and aiming to shed new light on the familiar worlds of his earlier novels. Although the character Nekhliudov had already appeared in Tolstoy's earlier fiction most notably in *A Landowner's Morning* (1856), Tolstoy refined his realism through the lens of the grotesque, casting Nekhliudov and his world in a new light. Similarly, the grotesque was a means for Artsybashev to reimagine the nineteenth-century realist canon from his own perspective, transforming Sanin, who has all the makings of a traditional gentry hero, into a great voluptuary. In considering how these authors managed to degrade the earlier world of the realist novel into a reality driven by the body and sexual desire, we must first define the grotesque style that allowed this transformation.

Uncertain in origin and marginalized in aesthetic theory, the grotesque evolves over time and is highly resistant to definition. The two foremost theorists of the grotesque and their major works on the subject, Wolfgang

Kayser's *The Grotesque in Art and Literature* and Bakhtin's *Rabelais and His World*, disagree wildly on the style – one views it as a dark and ominous distortion, while the other as a happy and comic upturning of reality. One thing that could be said for certain about the grotesque, however, is that its essence is in the eye of the beholder, built upon the reader or viewer's expectations of how things should be. "THE GROTESQUE IS THE ESTRANGED WORLD," writes Kayser (emphasis in the original).[14] Unlike the fantastic, which is driven by its own esoteric laws, the grotesque does not completely remove the reader from reality, but simply renders the worlds we know unreliable. It is this core philosophical principle that underlies the style.

The importance assigned to the body as a site of sexual desire during the Russian fin de siècle greatly influences the nature of grotesque estrangement we encounter in its texts. While we normally expect human life to be a mixture of spirituality and physicality, in the novels by Tolstoy and Artsybashev all life is often reduced to the level of the body. Bakhtin's definition proves helpful in establishing some of the more specific philosophical principles guiding the style, especially as it appears in both Tolstoy and Artsybashev. He defines the grotesque as a style that "turns [its] subject into flesh."[15] As he asserts, "the essential principle of grotesque realism is degradation – the lowering of all that is high, spiritual, ideal, abstract; it is a transfer to the material level, to the sphere of earth and body."[16] Connecting the grotesque to sex, Bakhtin suggests that: "To degrade also means to concern oneself with the lower stratum of the body, the life of the belly and the reproductive organs; it therefore relates to acts of defecation and copulation, conception, pregnancy, and birth."[17] Although Bakhtin was writing about the comic Rabelaisian grotesque, the basic philosophy he outlines remains significant in the Russian fin de siècle's darker grotesque. Bakhtin's view of the grotesque as a style of degradation is especially valuable in the extensive discussions of sexuality we encounter in both *Resurrection* and *Sanin*.[18] This underlying philosophy of the grotesque appears in both novels, helping shape the style, even before its poetics become manifest.

Poetically, it is bodily degradation, rather than supernatural deformity, that breeds hints of monstrosity in the realist grotesque. Judging by the paintings found underneath the Baths of Titus in Renaissance Italy that gave the style its name (1480), the grotesque was visually and poetically characterized by an "unstable mixture of heterogeneous elements"[19] and an affront of "classificatory systems."[20] The discovered paintings defy normalcy by unnaturally mixing unrelated phenomena, showing human and animal forms emerging from plant stems. Victor Hugo similarly highlights the hybridity underlying the grotesque in his "Preface to *Cromwell*." "It is the grotesque," he writes, "which scatters lavishly, in air, water, earth, fire, those myriads of intermediary creatures which we find all alive in the popular traditions of the Middle Ages; ... which gives Satan his horns, his cloven foot and his bat's wings."[21] The implication behind these statements is that the violation of boundaries in the grotesque generates monstrosities: "misshapen, ugly, exaggerated, or even formless" images and characters.[22]

For the realist author, however, the deformity of the grotesque is hardly as obvious as in the person of Hugo's Satan or in the frescoes underneath the Baths of Titus. With its empirical bent, realism could not accommodate the original deformations of the grotesque. Instead of genuine monstrosity and violations of natural boundaries, in realism we encounter the *appearance* of monstrosity and of violation; instead of reaching for a supernatural body, the realist relies on the human body, with all its natural unnaturalness, to create the grotesque and cast hints of monstrosity.

As the body is degraded and sexualized, it is also lowered to the level of an object or an animal – it becomes a means for the violations of boundaries we notice in the beginnings of the grotesque. Under the lens of the fin-de-siècle realist grotesque, a human being morphs into a hybrid creature – part object, part man, or part animal, part man. In the realist's canvas the process of hybridity is not literal or even fully physical; it occurs on a psychological level. As both Tolstoy and Artsybashev show by foregrounding the body, people can become so focused on bodily pleasure that they lose their spirituality and humanity in the process.

Tolstoy's grotesque theology and fiction

Tolstoy's adoption of the grotesque seems only natural given his long-standing artistic investment in depictions of the body and the impact of physicality on the human personality and interpersonal interaction. Tolstoy's ability to capture human beings in all their bodily peculiarities has been long recognized by scholars and readers alike; in a well-known critical adage going back to Dmitry Merezhkovsky, Tolstoy is referred to as a keen "seer of flesh." For much of his career, the concreteness of Tolstoy's texts has been linked to his realism. "If the world could write by itself," observed Isaac Babel, "it would write like Tolstoy."[23] When a work of fiction is described as equivalent to the world, then it must recreate this world in all its local color and intricacies. Within the bounds of this realist canvas, the individual body is especially prominent, thus laying the foundation for a poetics of the body that transformed into a poetics of grotesque physicality in Tolstoy's later years.

This transformation occurs during Tolstoy's later years, following his so-called religious conversion, when the body, which had formerly been a neutral presence and a shape for realist rendition, assumed a negative role. In theoretical writings like *Harmonization and Translation of the Four New Testament Gospels* (1881), the body becomes the basis for Tolstoy's later grotesque poetics. In this work, Tolstoy evokes the ideology of the grotesque by comparing the life of the body, particularly when this life centers on sexual pleasure, to animal existence and death. These comparisons do not exist on a purely metaphorical level, but instead suggest a plurality behind human life, showing body-oriented individuals possessing traits of either the animal or the corpse and in violation of fundamental, normally inviolable boundaries.

Tolstoy's description of bodily life as a form of death comes from his own heavily redacted translation of a remark by Jesus in John's Gospel. "Let the dead bury the dead," says Jesus in Tolstoy's Gospel, "God is the God of the living, and not of the dead." Tolstoy interprets this comment idiosyncratically, as meaning that "by relying on the source of temporal life, believing in it, man is destroyed, dies."[24] The alternative to this death-bound life is the life of the spirit, which entails a connection to God and results in "non-temporal, indestructible life." Life on earth is either a form of living death or simply leads to death. "What we call earthly life is death," writes Tolstoy. "Today, tomorrow, it will come to an end."[25] Following this reasoning, our life on earth, especially when devoted to bodily pleasures like sex, emerges as a state of living death with the body as the sarcophagus of the soul. This state suggests a hybridity between the living body and the corpse that recalls the violation of boundaries essential to the grotesque.

In the later essay *On Life*, Tolstoy highlights the other kind of hybridity, that between animal and man, which similarly evokes the ideas underlying the grotesque. Tolstoy describes two layers of human existence: the life of the self not grounded in time and space but connected to the spirit of God, and the personal life tied to time and space, synonymous with animal existence. "Man is born, the dog, the horse, are born, each has a special body," writes Tolstoy. "This body lives a certain time and then dies, decomposes, passes into other beings, and ceases to be . . . The heart beats, the lungs act – the body does not decompose, the man, the dog, the horse, live. The heart ceases to beat, respiration is arrested – the body begins to decompose; the animal is dead."[26] Although he does not call man an animal in this statement, through his intentionally reductive reasoning, Tolstoy equates human life to animal life, which coexists with and even displaces a person's humanity.

In reducing human life to the beating of a heart or the decomposing body, Tolstoy evokes the conceptual basis of his realist grotesque, which facilitates violation of boundaries and monstrosity through degradation to the level of physicality. Reduced to their flesh, human beings can appear as lower hypostases of themselves – a person can appear as an animal, or a corpse-like being with little animation.

As is clearly illustrated in Tolstoy's later fiction, sexuality and sexual attraction constitute the most propitious settings for fostering this type of grotesque degradation and hybridity. If Tolstoy's theoretical writings reveal the potential for the grotesque in abstract terms, Tolstoy's later fiction shows the sexualized body closely resembling the animal or the corpse. For instance, in *The Kreutzer Sonata*, grotesque degradation and hybridity are apparent in several ways. As implied in Pozdnyshev's narrative, male sexual desire prompts the degradation of women. Pozdnyshev articulates that men can only have a sexual interest in a woman and are unburdened by concern for her personality. In his seemingly interminable rant, Pozdnyshev degrades women, calling them an "instrument for acting on [male] sensuality" and asks that this "object [women] be removed and put away" by the police.[27] Although visually the grotesque does not make much of an appearance in *The Kreutzer Sonata*, the ideas behind the style – in particular the idea of lowering everything to the level of body – are present throughout. Boundaries between animate, human existence, and material things are broached as women are depicted simultaneously as human beings and inanimate things, instruments for male sexual arousal and sexual satiation.

Beyond the description of women as dehumanized subjects, Pozdnyshev also articulates another hybrid similarly rooted on sexuality – that of woman as subject and animal. Pozdnyshev's diatribe on human sexuality begins with the suggestion that men and women are "created like the animals,"[28] and he interprets human interactions from this perspective. "I only know her as an animal," he declares after seeing his wife flirting with the musician who becomes her lover. Once he sees his wife in this light, Pozdnyshev realizes that nothing can prevent her from satisfying her animal appetites. "[N]othing can or should restrain an animal," he exhorts while watching his wife and her soon-to-be lover communicate through "the animal in each of them." Sexual corruption is inevitable in this scenario. Indeed, while bearing witness to it, Pozdnyshev is drawn in by an animal pull as well. "No, she is not a human being," he declares in a final touch of grotesque degradation. "She is a bitch, a terrible bitch (*suka*)!"[29] In her betrayed husband's eyes, Pozdnyshev's wife is degraded to her animal nature. She may not be a full-blown monster, but she is certainly not fully human either. It is this grotesque degradation of his spouse to the level of a "bitch" with no human attributes that could be said to facilitate her eventual murder at the hands of her jealous and equally animalistic husband. By depriving characters of their humanity, grotesque degradation and depersonalization render murder more palatable to the perpetrator; it is only when his wife begins to speak of what he has done that Pozdnyshev comes to terms with his crime.

Grotesque realism in *Resurrection*

The grotesque sexuality ideologically sketched out in *The Kreutzer Sonata* assumes poetic form in Tolstoy's last novel, *Resurrection*. Sexuality is at the center of *Resurrection* and greatly maligned as the root cause for both societal evils and individual sorrows. It is certainly sexual desire that motivates Nekhliudov's relationship with his aunts' ward Maslova, the "original sin" in the novel that precipitates Maslova's prostitution and jail sentence. Tolstoy verbally articulates the evils of unchecked sexuality throughout the narrative of *Resurrection*, raging against wanton lasciviousness and erotic desire, whether consummated or not. Yet in addition to this rhetoric, Tolstoy's most useful tool for condemning sexual impulses is also his poetics, which revolve around the body, an entity morphing into a grotesque hybrid at the first hint of sexual desire.

The most obvious grotesque body in *Resurrection* to display this type of hybridity is the corpse of the lecherous merchant who was a client at the brothel and whom Maslova is accused of killing. The merchant's corpse, which is presented as material evidence in the trial, functions as a focal point for the grotesque in *Resurrection*; it spills out from every orifice, breaching boundaries between the inside and the outside and "poison[ing] the air of the whole novel."[30] This grotesque body is painstakingly described down to its smallest anatomical details, rendered piecemeal as a medical artifact – an assortment of pus, enlarged organs, and rotting skin – that almost cannot add up to an actual, whole human being. By means of this nameless, hybrid body, part human and part object, this *it* whose identity is reduced to a pound of flesh, Tolstoy powerfully captures and gives physical form to the evils of sexuality. The body of the merchant who dies soliciting a prostitute functions as a metonymic reflection for the moral corruption in society and the degradation of women and all individuals for the sake of sexual fulfillment.

Traces of the merchant's fleshy rot are scattered throughout the world of the novel, seemingly contaminating characters who have not renounced the sin of sexuality. As a prostitute who engages in socially sanctioned, meaningless sex, Maslova herself is shown in a state of living death, stripped of all spirituality. "This woman is dead (*mertvaia zhenshchina*)," thinks Nekhliudov to himself when he first sees Maslova at the jail.[31] This same association between sexuality and death comes to his mind again when he is confronted with the anatomy report of the dead merchant and cannot help but find it equivalent to the post-coital body of the seduced and later hyper-sexualized Maslova; her puffy and ill appearance evokes the swollen, dead merchant. With her bloated face and demeanor of sexual depravity, Maslova exemplifies the image of the objectified woman that Tolstoy describes in *The Kreutzer Sonata*. Like the merchant's corpse, she is a grotesque being, a sexually objectified woman who lowers herself, in Pozdnyshev's words, "not to the level of an animal but to the level of a thing."

This grotesque degradation is not limited to the prostitute Maslova but rather marks a collective societal malaise; for, after all, as we learn in *The Kreutzer Sonata*, it is society that encourages spiritually debasing sexual intercourse. While Maslova is in court, many of the jurors are busy thinking about their own sexual escapades and simultaneously take note of her attractiveness; in prison a male prisoner even sexually assaults her. The only time Maslova stops being a grotesque body and her identity as a spiritual human being is restored is when she is around political prisoners like Simonson, who is celibate and loves Maslova with a pure, Platonic love.

The grotesque in *Resurrection* is not limited to the prostitute's defiled body; countless gentry characters who could have been protagonists in Tolstoy's earlier works are similarly cast in a grotesque light. Nekhliudov himself, prior to his spiritual resurrection, begins the novel cleansing and pomading his plump body in a nearly fetishistic way that evokes the grotesque. Unlike Tolstoy's neutral portrayal of Stiva Oblonsky as self-satisfied with his own physique in *Anna Karenina*, Nekhliudov's grooming rituals are repulsive and the mark of someone lacking in conscience, who only lives for the body. His acquaintances, the Korchagins, are likewise objectified. When visiting the Korchagins after Maslova's trial, Nekhliudov witnesses an alien and grotesque side to them. "At that moment," writes Tolstoy about Nekhliudov, "strange images (*strannye obrazy*) [rose] in his imagination for some unaccountable reason."[32] These strange images take the shape of singled out body parts that infiltrate Nekhliudov's field of vision. The false teeth and lidless eyes of old Korchagin, his red face and smacking lips, stick out. Like the dead merchant, old Korchagin is a collection of unappealing appendages extracted from the whole of him that protrude outwards menacingly; he is a grotesque hybrid, part man, part thing.

From the merchant's dead body, to Maslova's "exorbitant body,"[33] to the whole social body, *Resurrection* stands out as a novel where individuals are depicted and treated first and foremost as bodies. Yet these bodies are by no means normal human bodies; through Tolstoy's aesthetics of the grotesque, they appear as monstrous hybrids, intermediary creatures that are part human and part inanimate beings. If in *The Kreutzer Sonata* we see the ideological conception of the grotesque sexual hybrid, in *Resurrection* these hybrids are both theoretically and poetically constructed through narrative depictions. As a result, when viewed in a certain light, individuals who are sexual and act on sexual impulses produce the grotesque effect and appear nearly monstrous even though realism does not permit literal monstrosity.

As we learn in *Resurrection* and earlier in *The Kreutzer Sonata*, Tolstoy's solution to the grotesquery of sexuality is total celibacy. In *The Kreutzer Sonata* this notion is discussed in purely theoretical terms: human society, according to Tolstoy, could function a bit like a beehive where all life is collective and asexual. Yet in *Resurrection* Tolstoy gives more grounding to this argument. After years of prostitution, Maslova escapes the grotesque world of sexuality through the company of political prisoners who refuse sexuality for purely spiritual connections. The unusual attitudes of sexual restraint among the prisoners resonate powerfully with the ideas floating around during the Russian fin de siècle, a time when sexual restraint could be as prominent as sexual promiscuity. Sexuality and sexual liberation were important facets of the period, but abstention from sexual fulfillment was equally important for fin-de-siècle artists and thinkers. As Olga Matich argues, the Russian symbolists obtained a strange elation from sexual restraint.[34]

On the other hand, Tolstoy's version of sexual restraint also reinforces the sense of dejection characteristic of the fin de siècle. As Nordau points out in his discussion of *The Kreutzer Sonata* as a fundamentally fin-de-siècle work, Tolstoy's unreasonable ethics of sexual repression would ultimately lead "humanity to die out with the present generation."[35] Tolstoy's theory of sexual abstinence is thus an eminently fin-de-siècle doctrine that could precipitate the end of the world through total population evisceration.

Sexuality and the ideology of the grotesque in *Sanin*

While, for Tolstoy, the body became the site of the grotesque and encroached upon and deadened the soul with its animal sexuality, for Artsybashev, the life of the body was a healthy display of individuality. Unlike Tolstoy, who commences *Resurrection* appalled at Nekhliudov's bath rituals, Artsybashev provides a largely positive rendition of his protagonist, Sanin, taking enormous joy in his body, stretching and flexing his muscles "with pleasure."[36] Different characters have different attitudes toward the body in the novel, but Sanin, who seems to serve as a mouthpiece for the author, considers sexuality eminently healthy and an essential component of the life impulse. As a natural and positive part of life, not only does sexuality not deny an individual's spiritual identity, but any attempt to repress the sexual for the sake of what appear to be artificial spiritual concerns also represses individual identity. If in *Resurrection* we get the sense that society encourages sexual degradation and validates or at least does not deter the view of individuals as sexual beings, Artsybashev conceives of society as repressive of natural sexual impulses. Thinking about human society early in the novel, the protagonist Sanin believes that many people want "to transform the whole world into a kind of monastic barracks, with one set of rules for everyone based on the annihilation of all personality and the subordination of its power to some mysterious group of elders."[37] The "monastic barrack," which would in effect erase all human sexuality and, indirectly, all human personality, serves as a metaphor for society and its persistent repression of sexuality's life-giving force. In this sense, then, in contrast to Tolstoy, who sees the free reign of sexual impulses as a denial of individual personality and spirituality, Artsybashev recognizes sexuality as the site of the self.

These preliminary comparisons paint a stark contrast between Tolstoy and Artsybashev and their position on sexuality. Yet if we construe Artsybashev as an anti-Tolstoy of sorts, then he can only assume such a role through the original author's influence. Core ideological differences aside, both writers pay sexuality major attention and Artsybashev's novel cannot be approached without observing the Tolstoyan precedent. "Artsybashev's preaching proceeds directly from Tolstoy," writes D. S. Mirsky in a discussion of *Sanin*, "only it is Tolstoy the other way round, and Tolstoy without genius."[38] Whether one agrees with Mirsky's dismissal of Artsybashev's talent, the link he suggests between the authors is worth exploring.

When identifying what is Tolstoyan about *Sanin*, Mirsky suggests that the novel "can be reduced to one pattern, borrowed from Tolstoy; he (or she) thought he wished this and that, but in reality he only wished quite another thing – that is, to quell his sexual desire, which is the only human reality."³⁹ Of course, as other scholars like Ronald LeBlanc have noted, the comparison between Tolstoy and Artsybashev, or Tolstoyism and Saninism, can be carried out on multiple levels, some of them entirely unrelated to sexuality.⁴⁰ Yet Mirsky's remark draws attention to a fundamentally fin-de-siècle feature of *Resurrection* and *Sanin*: the inordinate attention paid to the sexual impulse. Other common themes between the authors, like non-resistance to evil through violence, are ultimately dwarfed by the great emphasis on sexuality.

The focus on the body and sexuality, and their designation as the site of human individuality, produce key traits of the grotesque in *Sanin*. The grotesque, as defined by Bakhtin, emerges as a style that celebrates phys-icality. While Tolstoy darkens the grotesque by denigrating the body and bodily impulses, Artsybashev applauds bodily life. Discussions of sexuality constitute the core of human existence in *Sanin*, and everything outside of them is deemed stilted and artificial by both Artsybashev and his protag-onist. Even Tolstoy, who criticized *Sanin* as an unoriginal novel, notes its significant grotesque ideological makeup, by arguing that *Sanin* eloquently describes the "reduction of the human being to the level of an animal."⁴¹

Indeed, the power of sexuality is vividly rendered and palpable through-out the novel. In one telling scene, even Yuri Svarovich, an idealist and a counterpoint to Sanin, is seemingly overwhelmed by sexual desire after descending into a primal underground cave with his romantic interest, Karsavina. While the two are alone in the cave, Yuri realizes that he can have his way with Karsavina and can think of nothing but letting this desire loose on the woman's body. When repression ultimately quashes his natural desire, Artsybashev implies the unnaturalness behind this rejection of desire. Instead of "doing what he wanted to do more than life itself, that which filled his whole body with strength and passion," Yuri abides by contrived societal values, which construe sex as a taboo.⁴² In this scene, everything in life is reduced to sexual impulses, which are described as the most powerful and more important force in a person's life, almost superseding life itself. Through this neglect of philosophy and spiritual-ity for the sake of bodily drives, Artsybashev evokes the ideological basis of the grotesque found in Tolstoy's *The Kreutzer Sonata* and religious writings.

In fact, the power of sexuality can be witnessed throughout the novel as many characters choose their bodily selves over their more repressive social selves and succumb to sexual desire. The most obvious example of someone embracing their primal impulses is the novel's greatest voluptuary, Sanin, who is frequently attracted to women, at times even viewing his own sister sexually. Although he may serve as the novel's ideological mouthpiece on matters of sex, Sanin is not the only character with an active sex drive. Sanin's sister Lida is shown in the passionate embrace of the crass officer Zarudin, and her longing for the consummation of their relationship is so powerful that she is said to fall into an abyss of desire. Similarly, Karsavina is pleased to sense Yuri's desire in the cave when he voices what they are both thinking and asks whether she is afraid of being alone with him in an isolated place. Later in the novel, after societal repression once again thwarts the consummation of her relationship with Yuri, Karsavina gives herself to Sanin instead and experiences great pleasure despite her initial hesitation. In Artsybashev's novel, much as in *Resurrection* and *The Kreutzer Sonata*, sexual impulses are dominant and, indirectly, all life is lowered to the ideological level of the grotesque and the body.

Yet Artsybashev does not simply recreate the ideological underpinnings of the grotesque, he also partly recreates the poetics of its style. Although the grotesque in *Sanin* is not as visually prominent as in *Resurrection*, it nevertheless appears. In fact, we might argue that aside from borrowing the sexual theme from Tolstoy and thus perpetuating the fin-de-siècle emphasis on it, Artsybashev also borrows the grotesque poetics Tolstoy used to represent sexual desire.

Artsybashev himself acknowledges his intellectual debt to the style of Tolstoy and other Russian realists in a 1915 preface to an English edition of his novel *The Millionaire*. "I am an inveterate realist," he writes, "a disciple of the school of Tolstoi and Dostoevsky, whereas at the present day the so-called Decadents, who are extremely unfamiliar, not to say antipathetic to me, have gained the upper hand in Russia."[43] Indeed, not only is Artsybashev, by his own admission, a realist, but we might see him as closer to the late Tolstoy whose works are rich in fin-de-siècle themes; Artsybashev, who once declared that the artist in Tolstoy "overpowered" him,[44] borrowed the late Tolstoy's grotesque realism.

Death as the real grotesque

Looking at the poetics of *Sanin*, it is worth noting that Artsybashev constructs the grotesque by recreating the hybridity we find in Tolstoy's fiction between the human body and the corpse. But whereas, for Tolstoy, sex was a form of spiritual death, and the sexualized body a hybrid between the living human being and the corpse, Artsybashev's grotesque is firmly rooted in death. The sexualized body, though it intersects with the ideological standards of the grotesque, is never rendered unappealing through the grotesque aesthetic. Instead, the grotesque is centered on death and dead bodies.

One important, early glimpse of the grotesque in *Sanin* appears in connection with female suicide, an act constructed as the feminine response to being seduced and abandoned. For instance, when Yuri asks what she would do if he had allowed his passion to override his reason in the underground cave, Karsavina declares that she would probably have drowned herself. The drowning motif reappears later in Lida Sanina's plotline. After her sexual escapades with Zarudin, Lida becomes pregnant and must confront her transgressions. Following a brief conversation, it becomes apparent to her that Zarudin has no interest in marriage or fatherhood, which means that she must handle her predicament all on her own. Driven by her perception of societal condemnation, in a moment of desperation, Lida considers drowning as an escape and makes her way toward the river. Her brother Sanin, who instinctively follows her, watches Lida seemingly involuntarily submerging herself deeper into the water. Though she may not want to die, Lida feels that death is the only escape from the societal shame she will incur as an unmarried mother. Eventually, Sanin manages to prevent Lida's suicide by convincing her that she can redeem her social status by marrying Novikov, who has long been enamored with her.

After indirectly saving Lida's life, Sanin points out how illogical it is to consider suicide simply because one engaged in the natural act of sexual intercourse. In Sanin's view, such a death would only mean that artificial societal restrictions have resulted in the loss of a beautiful woman with much life and love left. "Neither your body or your soul is worse as a result of the act," he tells Lida, as he suggests marriage to Novikov.[45] When Lida questions his arguments, Sanin evokes death. "Well, and what would happen if you drowned yourself," he asks Lida. "Good and evil would suffer no loss or gain. Your bloated, disfigured corpse would be covered with silt, then fished out of the water and buried."[46] While Tolstoy depicts the sexualized body in the guise of the corpse, Artsybashev considers sex a key component of the life impulse and at odds with death.

Unlike the merchant's corpse in *Resurrection*, the bloated corpse in *Sanin* serves as a metonymical reflection of societal repression, which functions as a grotesque death-dealing force. The grotesque nature of sexual repression becomes apparent when Lida imagines the slimy river bottom and grows "terrified and disgusted."[47] The grotesquery of death and sexual repression is later confirmed by Sanin, who explains societal repression of sexuality to

Karsavina: "We've stigmatized our sexual desires as bestial, we've become ashamed of them, and cloaked them in humiliating forms."[48] A bit further, he directly ties this stigmatization to death: "Man is a harmonious combination of body and spirit, until that combination is destroyed [by] . . . the approach of death," he says. Unlike Tolstoy, who believed that indulging in the life of the body precipitated a form of spiritual death for the individual, Artsybashev sees the body's devastation as the only type of genuine death.

It is perhaps unsurprising, therefore, that Semenov dying at the novel's beginning should also represent a key instance of the grotesque in *Sanin*. A group of key characters are by his bedside as he is dying, a process described as slow, painful, and inevitable. Looking at the gravely ill Semenov, the narrator states, "Although he still had the same facial features as when he was alive and the same limbs as other people had, it now seemed as if both his features and his body were somehow especially terrifying and immobile. What animated and moved the bodies of other people so simply and comprehensively seemed not to exist for him."[49] Semenov's body is no longer driven by any internal spiritual agency on his part, but rather reduced to a frozen, immobile state. While he may look like other bodies, this sickly body is an estranged version of a normal body; Semenov is a grotesque double of who he was.

Whereas in Tolstoy's *Resurrection* sexual beings emerge as spiritually dead and are painted through a grotesque aesthetic that conflates them with corpses, in *Sanin*, the immoralist protagonist appears healthy and more generous than individuals who refrain from satisfying their sexual appetites. It is Sanin's lack of preconceived notions about sexuality that allows him to save Lida's life as she is trying to drown herself. His sexuality does not interfere with his spiritual love for others; in fact, his sexuality highlights his appreciation for life and all living things. When confronted with the image of dead birds shot by hunters, Sanin is viscerally upset that the beautiful creatures have been destroyed. Semenov's dead body and Lida's suicide attempt produce similar reactions in him. Unlike the world of societal repression, which is painted through the grotesque and invites fin-de-siècle despair and hopelessness in *Sanin*, sexuality and the body ultimately provide an avenue to a healthier and happier life. Characters like the novel's namesake find the last hope for a better life in sexual satisfaction, all the while knowing that perceptions of sexuality are permanently impaired by societal repression.

* * *

When referring to the fin de siècle as a "Dusk of Nations," Nordau paints a devastating picture: "all suns and all stars are gradually waning, and mankind with all its institutions and creations is perishing in the midst of a dying world."[50] This sense of a dying world full of perishing institutions was a key component of the fin-de-siècle mood that defined the end of the nineteenth and the beginning of the twentieth century in Russia. This mood, exacerbated at the century's end, permeated Russian realism and provoked many changes therein. As the contributions by Edith Clowes, Katherine Bowers, and Kate Holland in this volume indicate, styles like abject realism, the gothic, and naturalism supplement the realist's palette during this period. The grotesque is another manifestation of realism's evolution as it entered the fin de siècle. The forebodings and "deepening gloom" of the period – the "Dusk of Nations" as Nordau called it – led to a darkening of realism itself, which is made apparent in the works by Tolstoy and Artsybashev.[51] Through its ability to capture the familiar in a strange new light, the grotesque allowed realist authors like Tolstoy and later Artsybashev to portray the despair of the fin de siècle.

Indeed, this despair is apparent in both *Resurrection* and *Sanin*. Though Tolstoy and Artsybashev use the grotesque to convey two different perspectives on sexuality, they also employ its devices to express their own negative perception of social reality. At the end of both novels, we are confronted with protagonists – Nekhliudov and Sanin, respectively – who stand outside their social worlds. They find these worlds either morally corrupt or too repressive and are ultimately left alone at a crossroads. While it may be possible for Nekhliudov and Sanin to navigate life outside the bounds of their respective social realities, the endings of both novels exude an unmistakably negative impression of Russian fin-de-siècle social reality. While Tolstoy may see sexuality as the reason for the dying world, and Artsybashev may see it as its salvation, both authors are deeply embedded in the fin-de-siècle mood of their time.

NOTES

1 Steinberg, *Petersburg Fin de Siècle*, 1.
2 Sarah Badcock, "Autocracy in Crisis: Nicholas the Last," in *Late Imperial Russia: Problems and Prospects*, edited by Robert McKean and Ian Thatcher (New York: Manchester University Press, 2005), 9–10.
3 Steinberg, *Petersburg Fin de Siècle*, 1.
4 Robert Helbling, *The Power of "Negative" Thinking: The Grotesque in the Modern World* (Salt Lake City: Fredrick William Reynolds Association, 1982), 5.
5 The grotesque's reappearance is examined at length in my monograph *Freakish Others and Monsters Within: Russian Realism and the Grotesque, 1869–1899*, forthcoming.

6 Richard Kaye, "Sexual Identity at the Fin de Siècle," in *Cambridge Companion to the Fin de Siècle*, edited by Marshall, 53.

7 Quoted in Showalter, *Sexual Anarchy*, 3.

8 Engelstein, *The Keys to Happiness*, 1.

9 Matich, *Erotic Utopia*, 4.

10 For a detailed discussion of the public debate prompted by *The Kreutzer Sonata* in Russia and in Europe, see Møller, *Postlude to* The Kreutzer Sonata.

11 Eric Naiman, *Sex in Public: The Incarnation of Early Soviet Ideology* (Princeton University Press, 1997), 47.

12 Alexei Lalo, *Libertinage in Russian Culture and Literature* (Leiden: Brill, 2011), 145.

13 Otto Boele, *Erotic Nihilism in Late Imperial Russia: The Case of Mikhail Artsybashev's* Sanin (Madison: University of Wisconsin Press, 2009), 11.

14 *The Grotesque in Art and Literature* (New York: McGraw Hill, 1966), 184.

15 *Rabelais and His World*, translated by Helene Iswolsky (Bloomington: Indiana University Press, 1984), 20.

16 Ibid., 19.

17 Ibid., 21.

18 As Bakhtin argues in *Rabelais*, the grotesque reappeared during romanticism but lacked the joyous qualities of its original Rabelaisian version (36–37).

19 Kayser, *The Grotesque*, 53.

20 Geoffrey Harpham, *On the Grotesque: Strategies of Contradiction in Art and Literature* (Princeton University Press, 1982), 5.

21 Victor Hugo, "Preface to *Cromwell*," in *The Harvard Classics*, edited by Charles W. Eliot (New York: P. F. Collier & Son, 1910), XXXIX: 347.

22 Harpham, *On the Grotesque*, 5.

23 Quoted in Richard Pevear, "Introduction," in Leo Tolstoy, *War and Peace*, translated by Richard Pevear and Larissa Volokhonsky (New York: Vintage Classics, 2008), vii.

24 All references to Tolstoy's works are to the *Polnoe sobranie sochinenii v 90 tomakh, akademicheskoe iubileinoe izdanie* (Moscow: Khudozhestvennaia literatura, 1928–1958), henceforth *PSS*, here XXIV:752. All translations from Tolstoy are my own.

25 *PSS* XXIV:531.

26 *PSS* XXVI:331–332.

27 *PSS* XXVII:26.

28 *PSS* XXVII:34.

29 *PSS* XXVII:70.

30 Bayley, *Tolstoy and the Novel*, 258.

31 *PSS* XXXII:149.

32 *PSS* XXXII:97.

33 Harriet Murav, "Maslova's Exorbitant Body," *Tolstoy Studies Journal* 14 (2002): 35.

34 Matich, *Erotic Utopia*, 4.

35 Nordau, *Degeneration*, 164.

36 All references pertain to the Russian edition of *Sanin* (St. Petersburg: Zhizn', 1908). English translations are from *Sanin*, translated by Michael Katz (Ithaca, NY: Cornell University Press, 2001), 19. In subsequent citations, Russian page numbers will be provided first, followed by the translation.
37 15; 27.
38 D. S. Mirsky, *Contemporary Russian Literature, 1881–1925* (New York: Knopf, 1926), 140.
39 Ibid.
40 See Ronald LeBlanc, "Saninism Versus Tolstoyism: The Anti-Tolstoy Subtext in Mikhail Artsybashev's *Sanin*," *Tolstoy Studies Journal* 18 (2006): 16–31.
41 Quoted in LeBlanc, "Saninism Versus Tolstoyism," 16.
42 37; 47.
43 "Introduction," in *The Millionaire* by Michael Artzibashef, translated by Percy Pinkerton (New York: B. W. Huebsch, 1915), 8.
44 "Introduction," in *Sanin*, translated by Katz, 9.
45 118; 125.
46 Ibid.
47 Ibid.
48 231; 232.
49 61–62; 71.
50 Nordau, *Degeneration*, 2.
51 Ibid., 6.

CHAPTER 10

The little man in the overcoat
Gogol and Krzhizhanovsky

Muireann Maguire

In 1932, Maxim Gorky was asked to critique a selection of unpublished short stories by a virtually unknown writer, Sigizmund Krzhizhanovsky (1887–1950). Gorky, soon to be elected first Chairman of the All-Union Congress of Soviet Writers, frequently intervened personally, on behalf of younger writers, mentoring future authors of what would become Socialist Realist literature. In this instance, the attempt to enlist Gorky's support backfired badly: his commentary uncompromisingly defines Krzhizhanovsky's chief offense against Soviet literary aesthetics:

> [I] cannot analyze Mr. Krzhizhanovsky's ironical compositions (*sochineniia*) in terms of their philosophical value, but they appear to me to be sufficiently interesting and it is probable that they would have been quite successful in the 1880s. In those days idle lucubration (*prazdnomyslie*) was in vogue among intellectuals, and friendly arguments around the samovar on whether our knowledge of the world may or may not be trusted formed a favorite entertainment... To me it seems that in our tragic age, when the entire world awaits a great and inescapable catastrophe, that cunning wordplay (*lukavoe prazdnoslovie*) is out of place, even if it happens to be sincere. The majority of mankind were not made for philosophy, whether expressed lyrically, satirically or even, as is usually the case, dully and obscurely. In our age a new system of knowledge is being created, based on actions, and not on perceptions, on facts and not words. Hence I believe that Mr. Krzhizhanovsky's compositions are unlikely to find a publisher. And even if one is found, they will undoubtedly confuse more than a few young minds, and for whom is that necessary?[1]

Gorky here implies that Krzhizhanovsky had committed the worst sin that could be imputed to a Soviet writer: self-indulgent untimeliness. His work failed to reflect the ethos and the reality of his own era. Love of wordplay and indulgence in philosophical allegories precluded any contemporary relevance.[2] Gorky's dismissal guaranteed continued obscurity for Krzhizhanovsky, a Kiev-born, ethnically Polish intellectual who had been seeking his literary fortune in Moscow since 1918. Krzhizhanovsky wrote prolifically, accumulating six story anthologies and three novellas between 1919 and his death in 1950; only nine short stories were published in his lifetime, however. Despite the admiration and support of diverse figures in Moscow's cultural intelligentsia, Krzhizhanovsky's idiosyncratic style largely failed to convince reviewers and publishers. Occasional concessions to Socialist Realist literary norms such as "Room of Joy" (1933), or the story cycle "Moscow During the First Year of the War" (1943–1949), had little effect, although his supporters' influence did gain him admission to the Union of Writers in 1940. As a result, Krzhizhanovsky relied precariously on non-academic criticism and part-time editing for income until a stroke in 1949 ended his career.

Yet Gorky was perfectly correct: Krzhizhanovsky *was* very much a nineteenth-century writer. The only Soviet peers to (briefly) share his ironic neo-romanticism were members of the ephemeral, early 1920s group, the Serapion Brothers.[3] Krzhizhanovsky had many fin-de-siècle influences: the symbolist poet M. A. Voloshin was an important mentor, and in 1923 he adapted G. K. Chesterton's *The Man Who Was Thursday* (1908) for Alexander Tairov's 1923 Kamernyi Theater production.[4] However, Krzhizhanovsky's aesthetics were inspired by two nineteenth-century writers who largely defined Russian symbolism: Nikolai Gogol and Edgar Allan Poe.[5] In homage to Gogol, Krzhizhanovsky's stories abound in grotesque and hyperbolic satire, fantastic interludes, Hoffmannesque motifs, "speaking names," metonymy to indicate character, frame narratives, and improvised soliloquies.[6] An early short story, "The Runaway Fingers" (1922), describes the consequences when a pianist's hand escapes from its owner – a playful variant on Gogol's "The Nose." In the mid-1920s, when Krzhizhanovsky composed the stories discussed here, new adaptations of Gogol's work were in vogue: notably Meyerhold's 1927 version of *The Inspector General* and Bulgakov's "The Adventures of Chichikov" (1925).[7] Given his open sympathy with Poe and Gogol, two of Russian symbolism's key predecessors, Krzhizhanovsky's fiction can be read as a late fulfillment of that movement's rather pessimistic precepts, many of which are implicit or inchoate within his fiction.

Although neither Gogol nor Krzhizhanovsky were fin-de-siècle writers, comparison of their fiction demonstrates how fin-de-siècle prose influenced, and changed the course of, Russian fantastic realism. This chapter offers new readings of Gogol's classic "The Overcoat" ("Shinel'," 1842) and Krzhizhanovsky's recently rediscovered modernist short story "Quadraturin" ("Kvadraturin," 1926), respectively precursor and legatee of Russian symbolism, as essays in fantastic realism, a subgenre considered character-istic – although not exclusively so – of fin-de-siècle fiction. As Nicholas Ruddick argues, the "successful break" with traditional realism achieved by integrating fantastic elements in prose was "one of the great literary achieve-ments of the fin de siècle."[8] Yet fantastic realism predated and outlasted the era of symbolism and decadence; in Russian literature in particular, fantas-tic realism is linked with Dostoevsky, specifically his use of "almost fantastic and exceptional" incident and plot to convey what he considered "the very essence of the real."[9] This understanding of fantastic realism as hyperreality is represented in Gogol's prose by grotesque exaggeration of detail, and in Krzhizhanovsky's primarily by the literalization of figures of speech. Both writers also exploit the more conventional, post-Todorovian definition of fantastic realism as the intrusion of a supernatural element into a realist context, causing the reader to "hesitate" and suspend disbelief.[10] Fantastic realism, in both these guises, is ubiquitous in fin-de-siècle fiction. Even ear-lier, however, fantastic realism, as practiced in fiction by Dostoevsky and others, was one of several literary approaches that prefigured fin-de-siècle preoccupations. See, for example, Yuri Corrigan's investigation of the crisis of self in *The Adolescent* or Connor Doak's analysis of Dostoevsky's role as precursor of degeneration anxiety in the present volume.

Both "The Overcoat" and "Quadraturin" correspond structurally, the-matically, and even semantically, as I shall show; both are "untimely," in the sense that they were radically misunderstood by critics of their own time. Both plots feature an implicitly demonic pact, a fatal moral compro-mise with materialism, and a psychologically vulnerable, socially isolated hero. Crucially, both tales are framed by the literature and criticism of the Russian fin de siècle, over which Gogol's fantastic realism exercised a for-mative influence and with which Krzhizhanovsky's story shares an aesthetic heritage. I begin, therefore, by comparing Gogol and Krzhizhanovsky as fantastic realist authors. The three chief correspondences between their stories are all also defining themes of fin-de-siècle artists and writers, not only in Russia: the role of the Devil and of material desire as agents of moral corruption, the function of physical space in provoking spiritual ter-ror, and the destabilization of personal identity – here, the self-destruction of the "little man" archetype. The chronologically authentic fin-de-siècle tale, Fyodor Sologub's "The Little Man" ("Malen'kii chelovek," 1907), demonstrates the transition between "The Overcoat" and "Quadraturin"; "The Little Man" recapitulates Gogol's themes and characterization whilst foreshadowing the darker psychological outcome of Krzhizhanovsky's plot. Additionally, Sologub's tale enables us to fix the moment when fantastic realism becomes self-annihilating, rather than self-liberating, for the unfortunate "little man" at its core in the fin-de-siècle period.

Gogol, Krzhizhanovsky, and (fantastic) realism

"The Overcoat" and "Quadraturin" were received very differently by realist critics. The former, despite its fantastic conclusion, was initially (mis-)read as social realism. Most of Gogol's contemporaries, including Belinsky, Chernyshevsky, and Dobroliubov, insisted on flying "The Overcoat" as the "banner (*znamia*) of the [natural] school," a misinterpretation only reversed by symbolist and formalist re-readings half a century later, then reinstated by Soviet critics.[11] Although the plot of "Quadraturin" is clearly indebted to "The Overcoat," Soviet editors dismissed the story as too fantastical to print. Krzhizhanovsky's attempt to authenticate his own fiction in the reflected light of Gogol's realist reputation, if deliberate, failed dismally.[12] Gogol's realism is a Tasmanian tiger of a topic, even more elusive than Krzhizhanovsky's. What Gogol's contemporaries mistook for realism, or at the very least libelous satire, was in fact a specious specificity: his ability to pass off repulsive grotesques as psychologically authentic individuals.[13]

In an unpublished open letter to P. A. Pletnev in 1846, Gogol dismissed his own characters as "caricatures," which writers bent on moralizing should not imitate.[14] Writing to his friend Pogodin after *The Inspector General*'s stormy premiere, Gogol complained that audiences took "the individual for the general, the accident for the rule. Whatever is said truthfully (*verno*) and vividly they immediately consider a libel (*paskvil*). Bring a couple of rogues out on stage, and a thousand honest folk will get worked up, saying 'We're not rogues.'"[15] Vasily Rozanov wrote in 1906 that "there are no living characters" in Gogol's plays, only "tiny wax figurines, but they make such artful faces that we wonder for a long time whether they truly move."[16] Half a century later Nabokov would refer more indulgently to Gogol's characters as "incomparable goblins."[17] Gogol's genius – as the writer himself, late in life, would fatally forget – was for typology, not teleology, and certainly not for the vatic role in which Belinsky and Chernyshevsky cast him. The symbolist Dmitry Merezhkovsky was among the first critics to describe the triumphant, ominous formlessness that both frames and animates Gogol's heroes: Akaky Akakievich is simultaneously phantom and corpse (*prizrak-mertvets*), existing in a world of "mendacity, madness and death."[18] Similarly, Krzhizhanovsky's characters are "phantasms," minus-people, or living corpses.[19] All these manifestations of hideous hyperreality identified by Gogol's critics – the marionettes, goblins, and animated corpses – are better understood as Dostoevskian fantastic realism: the writer's attempt to demonstrate the true (moral) nature of reality by exaggerating the most grotesque aspects of his characters' physicality.[20] In "Quadraturin," Krzhizhanovsky achieves a similar psychological effect by stretching the nature of his character's environment, rather than his physical form, to its limits.

Fantastic realism shapes or warps the plots of all three stories. Gogol's Akaky, Krzhizhanovsky's Sutulin, and Sologub's Saranin are all textbook "little men" – the natural school's archetypal hero.[21] In each story, however, the "little man" undergoes a fantastic peripeteia. The ordinary, even insignificant protagonist is exposed to some fantastic, more or less annihilating adversity, causing his mundane reality to collapse into supernatural chaos. The true narratological and even historical interest of all three stories lies not in their naturalistic beginnings, nor in their grotesque denouements, but in the psychological insight generated from the gap between the fantastic and the real. Krzhizhanovsky called this narrative device "experimental realism," illustrating his concept with the scene in Shakespeare's *Macbeth* where Macbeth and Banquo are forced to respond in real time to the witches' fantastic apparition. Macbeth's reaction to the weird sisters and their prophecies is "entirely real, simply hyperbolized, raised to maximum tension, brought to the 'super-naturalism' of the naturalist's laboratory."[22] Modern critics have borrowed the term to describe Krzhizhanovsky's own fictional strategy of literalizing metaphors, hyperbole, and other figures of speech: a lover literally trapped in his beloved's eye, an anatomical dummy that gives "birth" to a monster.[23]

Krzhizhanovsky's "experimental realism" does not significantly differ from other "strategies of indirection and constraint" which critics classify as fantastic realism;[24] indeed, in 1927 he declared – fittingly, within a fantastic tale – his intention to produce "a cycle of 'fantastic' short stories."[25] Like many fin-de-siècle writers, he identified Poe as a major influence; like Baudelaire before him, he praised Poe for his ability to combine philosophical conundrums with chilling psychological insight and for the eccentricity and experimentalism of his prose – a potential model, as Krzhizhanovsky suggested in a commemorative essay, for Socialist Realist fiction. Baudelaire praised Poe as a "jongleur"[26] while Krzhizhanovsky's essay uses the metaphor of a trampolinist leaping toward the stars. Poe was more than a literary model for Krzhizhanovsky: he was a companion in the artistic dislocation condemned by Gorky. Poe, argued Krzhizhanovsky, "inhabited a nation and a time poorly suited to his turn of mind (*umonastroenie*)."[27]

The remainder of this chapter will examine three fantastic realist tropes, common to all three stories, and also common tropes of fin-de-siècle literature: the presence of the demonic, spatial instability, and psychological disintegration. My aim is to show how the Russian fin de siècle's unresolved legacy of "perversity, despair and collapse" distorted the inherently liberating effect of the fantastic into a darker, self-annihilating ethos.[28]

"Quadraturin": Room without a view

I begin with a brief recapitulation of the plot of "Quadraturin," which, unlike "The Overcoat," is unlikely to be familiar to most readers. The hero, Sutulin, works in a Soviet city, probably Moscow, in the mid-1920s. Similarly, Gogol's Akaky Akakievich is a copying clerk in a government institution in St. Petersburg. Sutulin, like Akaky, is an archetypical "little man," a middlebrow individual lacking any social status or ambition, physically insignificant and psychologically torpid. Note Sutulin's neo-Gogolian "speaking name," from the adjective "sutulyi" meaning "hunched," prefiguring the story's theme of claustrophobic compression. Like Krzhizhanovsky himself, Sutulin inhabits a ludicrously cramped room within an overcrowded communal apartment. He is tormented by careless neighbors who slam the bathroom door, quarrel in the corridor, and capriciously redecorate.[29] The ominous Room Re-Measuring Committee is empowered to survey his room's dimensions and force his door, if necessary, in order to guarantee he has no more and no less space than that due to every Soviet citizen. No physical barrier, least of all a locked door, itself a questionable infraction of communal values, can exclude all of these social and psychological pressures. When the Room Re-Measuring Committee demands access, Sutulin buys time by breaking the circuit of his electric light and plunging his room into abysmal, if temporary, darkness. Sutulin's desire for privacy is inappropriate according to the communal values of his world. Aware of his own difference, his key priority is concealment.

Even before Sutulin becomes conscious of his tiny room's inadequacy, the narrative anticipates his discontent. An anonymous vendor appears at his door with an advertising sample of "Quadraturin," a paste that supposedly expands the internal surface area of rooms. Following the printed instructions, Sutulin applies it to his walls, but he accidentally drops the unsealed tube before treating the ceiling. The spilled paste instantly evaporates. This accident is analogous to the theft of Akaky's new overcoat in Gogol's story. Both misfortunes transform a material benefit into an excessive psychological loss: Akaky's grief over his coat far exceeds its value, while the spill's consequences are disproportionately disastrous for Sutulin. The Quadraturin acts overnight, transforming the cramped apartment into a good-sized room. Yet the room continues relentlessly expanding over the next two days. Bizarrely, this expansion cannot be perceived from the exterior. Inside, the ever-receding walls and ominously low ceiling evoke a coffin's interior.

Both Sutulin and the narrator unquestioningly internalize the idea that revising a room's dimensions is an unforgivable act of individualistic opportunism; as in other Soviet fiction of the period, bureaucracy overwrites miracle.[30] Rather than marveling at his luck, Sutulin lives in paranoid terror that his neighbors, his landlady, the Re-Measuring Committee, or even his ex-lover will discover his illegally expanded room. "Quadraturin" ends with Sutulin's dying screams inside the "four-cornered, inexorably growing and proliferating darkness,"[31] as neighbors gather in perplexity outside his closed door. This climax unites many general themes beloved of fin-de-siècle authors: estrangement and anxiety as qualities of modern urban existence, the untethering of the soul from untenable reality, and the consequent "apocalyptic rupture" on contact with the ideal.[32] The same sense of extreme anxiety and "apocalyptic rupture" is provoked by the fantastic incidents discussed in the following sections.

Sympathy for the Devil: Faustian plots

While "The Overcoat," "The Little Man," and "Quadraturin" share many fin-de-siècle fantastic features, the underlying structural formula for all three is the Faustian bargain. Whether by analogy, as in Wilde's *The Picture of Dorian Gray* (1890) or Stevenson's *The Strange Case of Dr. Jekyll and Mr. Hyde* (1886), or via an historical approach like Briusov's *The Fiery Angel* (1908), fin-de-siècle authors constantly explored the topos of demonic transactions, gifts, and technologies. Russian writers arguably acquired this infernal fascination from Gogol: Merezhkovsky called the Devil "[t]he sole subject of Gogol's art,"[33] while the formalist critic Dmitry Chizhevsky placed Satan at the center of the narrative of "The Overcoat."[34] In the basic Faustian formula, a duplicitous vendor offers a material or magical advantage to the often initially reluctant hero. Thus Gogol's Akaky, who wants his old coat repaired rather than replaced, actually curses himself for visiting Petrovich the tailor when the latter is sufficiently sober and alert to insist on the latter course. Sutulin is effectively "cold-called" by an insistent vendor.

The benefit thus obtained stimulates the hero's long-suppressed desires for material comfort. Exhorted by Petrovich, Akaky pays eighty rubles for a new overcoat with a cat-fur collar "that from a distance could always be taken for marten," fine silk seams, and "high-quality calico."[35] Chizhevsky has identified Petrovich's demonic attributes: principally, his smoke-filled flat, his wife's use of the term "one-eyed devil" to describe him, and his snuffbox with the portrait of a faceless general.[36] Just as Akaky is oblivious to these ominous features, Sutulin fails to note the Quadraturin agent's demonic aspects. In the story's first lines, for example, he raps twice on Sutulin's door; the second knock is "a bit louder and bonier (*kostistee*)," as if delivered by skeletal knuckles.[37] The time of day at which he appears and his vaguely spectral aura intensify this supernatural indication: "On the threshold, head grazing the lintel, stood a tall, grey man the color of the dusk seeping in at the window."[38] Although not explicitly faceless, like the general on Petrovich's snuffbox, the stranger's features are never described apart from his "fixed unblinking stare."[39] The agent's grayness suggests the "strange gray man" of Adelbert von Chamisso's "Peter Schlemiel" (1814), a deceptively benign demon who offers Fortunato's purse in exchange for the hero's shadow. The final point is – literally – damning; he takes Sutulin's signature in exchange for the Quadraturin sample, evoking the traditional Mephistophelian contract signed in the client's blood.

In the Faustian formula, once each man has exchanged his former state of contented deprivation for the advantage offered by the disguised Devil, his moral dissolution is assured, whether by natural or fantastic means. Akaky and Sutulin are led by their semi-supernatural tempters along a deceptively natural hierarchy of material pleasures and vanities, culminating in complete psychological transformation. The shy, incoherent Akaky pursues a prostitute and blasphemes on his deathbed; Sutulin loses his own identity within the physically realized void of his fears and self-destruction. Sologub's "The Little Man" is a linear descendant of "The Overcoat" and covers similar territory.[40] Its hero, Saranin, is a diminutive clerk who marries his plus-sized wife for her dowry, thus provoking his colleagues' mockery.[41] He decides to rectify matters by shrinking his wife and, through a chance encounter he fails to recognize as supernatural, obtains a magic potion from a mysterious Armenian vendor. Unfortunately, his wife innocently swaps their glasses at a crucial moment, causing Saranin to drink the potion intended for her. As a result, Saranin, already pint-sized, dwindles to invisibility; he suffers his supernatural fate as a direct consequence of meddling with fantastic forces.

Dangerous dimensions: Space invasions

The representation of spatial discontinuity in narrative through a fantastic distortion of nature appears often in fin-de-siècle literature, often as the image of the "abyss" beloved of symbolists. Russian symbolist critics found this abyss, rather like Pascal's portable precipice, everywhere in Gogol's prose.[42] Briusov, for instance, observed, "Gogol's entire life was a road that ran between two chasms, each of which pulled at him."[43] Similarly, Bely pictured Gogol's emotional problems in spatial terms: "His soul yearned for Gogol, and Gogol yearned for his soul, but an *abyss* lay between them; and the light, for Gogol, went out."[44] My concern is with the fantastic *action* of space upon characters, rather than the allegorical or symbolic functions of space(s).[45] The literalization of spatial dynamics within each narrative connects to symbolist figuration of space as an animate, often hostile force.[46] In all three stories, the main character is affected – unpleasantly – by space. The fateful theft of Akaky's overcoat occurs in "an endless square which, with houses on the far side that were almost invisible, looked like a terrible desert"; reinforcing this topographical tension is Akaky's impression that a distant policeman's booth seems to be "at the very edge of the world."[47] Even more acute spatial discontinuities occur throughout Gogol's fiction. As Merezhkovsky observed, "Gogol's world is a stupefying and soporific fog, a fantasy-mirage created by the Devil."[48] At the end of "The Portrait" (1835), the usurer's Satanic complexion is mysteriously replaced on the canvas by "a certain unfamiliar landscape."[49] The fog that repeatedly veils the action in "The Nose" also mocks the integrity of narrative itself by obscuring the storyteller's traditional omniscience. And in his lyrical conclusion to the first part of *Dead Souls*, Gogol once again implies the uncanniness of landscape:

> It is as though some unknown force has gathered you up on its wing, and you are flying, and everything flies with you . . . the road itself flies away into the unknown, fading distance, and there is something terrifying in this flashing by of objects, so swift that they fade from sight before they can be distinguished.[50]

Even while describing Chichikov's "rapturous and wondrous" flight into the distance, Gogol hints ambiguously at the horror implicit in the sheer expanse of nature. In their chapter in the present volume, Alexander Burry and S. Ceilidh Orr explore this scene's apocalyptic quality. Chichikov's speed is expedited by an "unknown force" (*nevedomaia sila*) – the preceding line refers tongue-in-cheek to the Devil – and the very scenery rushing past conceals "something terrifying" (*chto-to strashnoe*). The verb "propadat'," used twice here to mean "to vanish" or "to disappear," can also mean "to perish." Readers may be too distracted by Gogol's robust comparison between Chichikov's speeding troika and Russia's blind flight through history to notice that Chichikov is simultaneously disappearing into Russia herself. Perhaps it was because Gogol himself overlooked his protagonist's indirect "death" by vanishing that he vainly struggled to resurrect him for the second volume of *Dead Souls*. Death by landscape, or more precisely by spatial disproportion, is already implicit in the Gogolian narrative formula.

Where Gogol's characters are threatened by the fantastic danger of urban squares and rural landscapes, Krzhizhanovsky's fiction examines the potential of "minus-space," as he called his indoor topographies. Poe's influence is likely: the way Sutulin perishes – psychologically dissolving within an inexorably extending room – reverses the scenario of Poe's "The Pit and the Pendulum," in which the hero, held captive by the Inquisition, is all but crushed to death by his cell's moving walls. Rabinowitz suggests that Sologub's incredibly shrinking Saranin "is literally realizing the metaphor of the 'small man'";[51] Krzhizhanovsky, as Leiderman argues, does much the same thing.[52] This is how Sologub's Saranin, whose diminution has gradually continued throughout the narrative, finally disappears:

> Then suddenly . . . just after putting on his tiny new trousers, he became utterly tiny. He plunged through the tiny trousers. And yet he was already the size of a pinhead. There was a puff of wind, a mere draught. Saranin, minute as a speck of dust, rose up in the air. He spun around, mixed up with the cloud of dust-motes dancing in a ray of sunlight. And he vanished. All searches were in vain. Saranin was nowhere to be found . . . How was Saranin's disappearance to be expressed? Finally, after referring it to the Academy of Sciences, they decided to record him as having been sent on a scientific mission. Then they forgot about him. Saranin was no more.[53]

Krzhizhanovsky documents the same process of dissolution, but on a psychological rather than a physiological plane.[54] Sutulin's plight resembles that of another Krzhizhanovskian character who describes the sound of his own soul "dissolving in the emptiness . . . I gave this phenomenon a special name: *psychorrhea*. Meaning 'soul seepage.'"[55]

"Dying in the wilderness": The death of the little man

"Little men" like Sutulin and Saranin are by definition muted, pusillanimous figures. Take "The Overcoat." Akaky struggles to formulate connected phrases, and the strain of speaking to Petrovich or the Significant

Person reduces him repeatedly to grunts or wordless ellipses. But his speech assumes mock-heroic concision, if not eloquence, in the "humane passage" when he tells his colleagues: "Let me be. Why do you torment me?"[56] When his overcoat is stolen, he applies (albeit timidly) to the Significant Person for justice and when rebuffed, he dies – but not without lustily profaning the latter's name during his final paroxysms. In the fantastic final section, Akaky returns as a sort of spectral Robin Hood – pilfering overcoats from the wealthy until his vengeance is satisfied by the theft of the Significant Person's own cloak. Thus Akaky, although lexically incoherent, is capable of both self-expression and revenge when needed (admittedly, post mortem). Sutulin, like Akaky, is a "speaking mute":[57] he never utters a complete sentence to the "Quadraturin" vendor, and even his interior monologue is delivered in self-contradictory shorthand: "Hmm . . . Let's try it. Although . . . "[58] At two points in the text, Sutulin voices an appeal comparable to Akaky's plea for peace. First, when he decides to flee his quadraturinized apartment:

> Right now, while everyone's asleep. Collect my things (only the necessaries) and go. Run away. Leave the door wide open. Let *them*. Why should I be the only one? Why not let *them*?[59] (215)

Like Akaky cursing the Significant Person, Sutulin has finally turned against "them," the invisible authorities who circumscribe his actions and decisions. But while Akaky's rebellion is posthumously enacted, Sutulin's insurrection fizzles out. His final apostrophe, the scream in the dark that summons his neighbors, is wordless; dying, Sutulin lacks even language.

> In their sleep and in their fear, the occupants of the quadratures[60] adjacent to citizen Sutulin's eighty-six square feet couldn't make head or tail of the timbre and intonation of the cry that woke them in the middle of the night and compelled them to rush to the threshold of the Sutulin cell: for a man who is lost and dying in the wilderness to cry out is both futile and belated: but if even so – against all sense – he does cry out, then, most likely, *thus*.[61]

Although Akaky's life is lived in the shadow of senior officials, and he almost expires from terror in the Significant Person's presence, his relationship with these higher beings is at least marginally mutual: they dispense bonuses, salary advances, and occasional charity. Sologub's Saranin, victimized and eventually dismissed by his departmental superiors as his shrinking is viewed as politically suspect, falls halfway between Gogolian innocence and later paranoia. Krzhizhanovsky's Sutulin has no superiors to supply or deny justice; more damningly, he lacks the moral autonomy to enforce his own. When he decides to flee his haunted apartment, he cannot even find the door to leave. Unlike Gogol's Chichikov, lucidly and willingly absorbed by greater Russia, Sutulin becomes lost in an endless interiority he can neither map nor navigate. Akaky's and Sutulin's radically opposed responses to the intrusion of the fantastic mark a major intervening shift in cultural consciousness, which, I suggest, was crystallized by the writers of the Russian fin de siècle and their obsession with fear.

Conclusion: "Talk of horror"

For Gogol, fear was a positive enabler, perhaps the only route to cognition. He even suggests this in his early prose, such as the following passage from "Thoughts on Geography" in 1835:

> I have often had occasion to observe a child, . . . listening, completely engrossed, to some talk of horror, and on his almost lifeless face, previously unenlivened by any feelings of participation, signs of agitation and fear have suddenly erupted. Surely it would not be impossible to coax such an imagination to be of use to science.[62]

The decline in Gogol's productivity in his last decade, particularly his failure to write the second and third parts of *Dead Souls*, was probably caused by his blindness to the fact that fear – not optimism or moral prescriptiveness – was the prerequisite for his peculiar genius. While Gogol's fantastic, grotesque, and surreal scenarios subjected his characters to extraordinary torture, they also permitted extraordinary self-assertion: the fantastic facilitated individual rebellion, as in Akaky's larcenous adventures.

Yet the "little man" of the twentieth century has lost this capacity for fantastic rebellion. The Stalin-era hero of Daniil Kharms's *The Old Woman* (1939) assumes guilt for a death of which he is innocent; the extraterrestrial narrator of Abram Tertz's *Pkhents* (1956) sequesters his fantastic identity in the banal squalor of a communal apartment. When writers like Kharms and Krzhizhanovsky update Gogol's trope of the beleaguered "little man" to reflect Soviet reality, some autobiographical intent is implicit. Stories such as "Quadraturin" are, to some extent, allegories of the increasing alienation of creative intellectuals within Soviet society. The "little man" no longer represents a comfortably ridiculed underclass: the author *is* the "little man." But it would be facile to believe that historical factors alone underlie this character's increased vulnerability. These cannot explain the twentieth century's attrition of the "little man's" subjectivity, the leaching away of his consciousness as per Krzhizhanovsky's concept of "psychorrhea," as well as his physical being. This attrition even becomes a structural feature of the narrative. Of the fantastic interludes in the three stories discussed here, Sutulin's is the only one to lack "objective" intradiegetic corroboration. Akaky's ghost is seen by dozens; Saranin dwindles away in a display window; but there is no narrative evidence that Sutulin's nightmare transpires anywhere outside the cage of his own mind.

Of these three stories, only in Gogol's "The Overcoat" does the fantastic have a liberating effect. Akaky is literally dis-mantled by life's injustice. Fantastic realism, however, allows him a supernatural afterlife and an opportunity for effective revenge. In Sologub's "The Little Man," the fantastic deceives, humiliates, and finally dematerializes the hero, but the reader suspects that his suffering is determined by supernatural justice: Saranin is not a nice "little man." Only in "Quadraturin" is the action of the fantastic unsolicited, unjustified, and apparently random in its choice of victim. Where the fantastic facilitates self-expression for Akaky or for his ghost, at least, in "Quadraturin" it becomes the decisive factor in Sutulin's psychological disintegration. Why should the fantastic apparently lose its ability to produce restitutive, often transgressive, sometimes joyous renewals in the characters it affects? This loss was not universal – the carnivalesque fantastic of much of Mikhail Bulgakov's fiction proves the opposite. If, however, we read Krzhizhanovsky's story as a late expression of fin-de-siècle malaise, our question is answered.

In Russian fin-de-siècle texts, the fantastic is often a precursor to the symbolists' favored themes: death and fear of death, madness and the dread of madness. Both the self-destructive protagonists and the change in the haunting's locus from exteriority to interiority are prefigured in tales such as Sologub's "He Who Summons the Beast" (1906) or Briusov's "In The Mirror" (1903) – or, indeed, on a wider canvas, Wilde's *The Picture of Dorian Gray* or Arthur Machen's *The Three Impostors* (1895). Sutulin's death by mental attrition is foreshadowed by Sologub's infamous *nedotykomka* in *The Petty Demon* (1902), or the epidemic of "psychic distemper" (*psikhicheskoe rasstroistvo*) which ravages Briusov's "Republic of The Southern Cross" (1903). There are many more possible examples. Sutulin's pathetic end, like the deaths of other literary outsiders in Soviet prose, is not a consequence of fantastic realism per se but of its refraction through a pessimistic fin-de-siècle prism. Where fin-de-siècle influence is not felt, fantastic realism returns to its liberatingly transgressive roots and fantastic motifs in Russian literature continue, like Akaky Akakievich's ghost, to carriage-hop between genres and centuries, waylaying unwary writers and readers.

NOTES

1 M. A. Gor'kii in a letter to E. Lann, dated August 17, 1932, cited by Vadim Perel'muter in "Posle katastrofy," in Sigizmund Krzhizhanovskii, *Sobranie sochinenii v piati tomakh* (St. Petersburg: Symposium, 2001–2010), 25–26. Hereafter referred to as *SS*.

2 Karen Link Rosenflanz investigates Krzhizhanovsky's philosophical and linguistic wordplay in *Hunter of Themes: The Interplay of Word and Thing in the Works of Sigizmund Krzhizhanovskij* (New York: Peter Lang, 2005).

3 See Gary Kern and Christopher Collins, eds., *The Serapion Brothers: A Critical Anthology* (Ann Arbor, MI: Ardis, 1975).

4 For more on this adaptation, see Mariia Malikova, "'Sketch po koshmaru Chestertona' i kul'turnaia situatsiia NEPa," *Novoe literaturnoe obozrenie* 78 (2006). http://magazines.russ.ru/nlo/2006/78/mm2.html (accessed March 13, 2013).

5 On Poe's influence, see Joan Delaney Grossman, *Edgar Allan Poe in Russia: A Study in Legend and Literary Influence* (Würzburg: Jal-Verlag, 1973). Robert Maguire's volume *Gogol from the Twentieth Century: Eleven Essays* (Princeton University Press, 1974) presents symbolist, formalist, and Soviet essays on Gogol; Maguire's Introduction (3–54) discusses Gogol's influence on Russian symbolists (16–20).

6 Krzhizhanovsky mentions Gogol three times: in *Munchausen's Return* (*Vozvrashchenie Miunkhgauzena*, 1927–1928), *Postmark: Moscow* (*Shtempel': Moskva*, 1925), and *Someone Else's Theme* (*Chuzhaia tema*, 1929–1930). See I. B. Delektorskaia, "Gogolevskie motivy v tvorchestve Sigizmunda Krzhizhanovskogo," in *Gogol' i mirovaia kul'tura*, edited by V. P. Vikulova (Moscow: Universitet, 2003), 122–128. On the influence of Hoffmann in Krzhizhanovsky's fiction, see N. L. Leiderman, "The Intellectual Worlds of Sigizmund Krzhizhanovsky," *Slavic and East European Journal* 56:4 (2012): 520–521.

7 See Delektorskaia, "Gogolevskie motivy," 124.

8 Nicholas Ruddick, "The Fantastic Fiction of the Fin de Siècle," in *The Cambridge Companion to the Fin de Siècle*, edited by Marshall, 189.

9 Dostoevsky in a letter to N. N. Strakhov, cited by Jackson in *The Art of Dostoevsky*, 264. Dostoevsky's definition of the fantastic was notoriously variable. For more on Dostoevsky's "fantastic" and "fantastic realism," see Malcolm V. Jones, *Dostoyevsky After Bakhtin: Readings in Dostoyevsky's Fantastic Realism* (Cambridge University Press, 1990), especially 1–31.

10 See Tzvetan Todorov, *The Fantastic: A Structural Approach to a Literary Genre*, translated by Richard Howard (Ithaca, NY: Cornell University Press, 1975), 25–27. Rosemary Jackson draws on Todorov to define "fantastic realism" in the nineteenth-century novel as an "uneasy assimilation" of gothic–fantastic motifs and tropes with realist conventions, where "self-conscious confrontation" between the human and the inhuman is always immanent. See Jackson, *Fantasy: The Literature of Subversion* (London: Methuen, 1981), 123–140.

11 G. A. Gukovskii, *Realizm Gogolia* (Moscow and Leningrad: Khudozhestven-naia literatura, 1959), 345. For the background to the reception of "The Over-coat" as a naturalist and/or realist text, see Richard Peace, *The Enigma of Gogol: An Examination of the Writings of N. V. Gogol and their Place in the Russian Literary Tradition* (Cambridge University Press, 1981); Paul Debreczeny, "Nikolay Gogol and his Contemporary Critics," *Transactions of the American Philosophical Society* 56 (1966): 1–68; and Julian Graffy, *Gogol's "The Overcoat"* (London: Bristol Classical Press, 2000), 13–20.

12 I consider Russian naturalism and realism here as a continuous literary move-ment, agreeing with Richard Lehan that "[t]here is no Realism (with a capital 'R'), only realisms, which are brought into being by changing narrative conven-tions that are in turn the product of a changing historical reality. Naturalism is another form of realism – a sterner realism." See *Realism and Naturalism: The Novel in an Age of Transition* (Madison: University of Wisconsin Press, 2005), 35.

13 This is the "strange paradox" of Gogol's characters: "creatures apparently with-out psychology, who contrive to exhibit psychological problems." See Richard Peace, "Gogol and Psychological Realism: *Shinel'*," in *Russian and Slavic Lit-erature*, edited by Richard Freeborn, R. Milner-Gulland, and Charles A. Ward (Cambridge, MA: Slavica, 1976), 65.

14 Debreczeny, "Nikolay Gogol and his Contemporary Critics," 51.

15 Gogol', in a letter to M. A. Pogodin, May 10, 1836, in Gogol', *Sobranie sochinenii v shesti tomakh* (Moscow: Khudozhestvennaia literatura, 1952–1953), VI:300.

16 Vasilii Rozanov, "Pushkin i Gogol'," in *O Gogole* (Letchworth, Eng.: Prideaux Press, 1970), 13.

17 Vladimir Nabokov, *Lectures in Russian Literature* (London: Weidenfeld & Nicolson, 1981), 6.

18 Dmitry Merezhkovsky, "Gogol and the Devil," in *Gogol from the Twentieth Century*, edited and translated by Maguire, 61–62.

19 See Leiderman, "Intellectual Worlds," 520–526.

20 See Jones, *Dostoyevsky After Bakhtin*, 1–31.

21 For a good overview of the "little man" in Russian fiction, see Elizabeth Shepard, "Pavlov's 'Demon' and Gogol's 'Overcoat,'" *Slavic Review* 33 (1974): 288–301. This archetype, often associated with petty clerks in particular, preceded Gogol's Akaky by at least a decade; Shepard singles out Nikolai Pavlov's *The Demon* (1835) as an influential precursor to "The Overcoat," which nonetheless displaced it as "the exemplary chinovnik story in Russian fiction" (292). The idea of the "little man" archetype as a link between Gogol and Krzhizhanovsky has already been proposed in Maguire, *Stalin's Ghosts*, 85–86, and by Leiderman in "Intellectual Worlds," 523–526.

22 "Fragmenty o Shekspire" (1939), in *SS* IV:377. Interestingly, given his exclusion from Soviet literary practice, Krzhizhanovsky's analysis of *Macbeth* argued that the Soviet system was not intrinsically inimical to the fantastic. Instead, Bolshe-vik theorists programmatically literalized "experimental realism," by enacting its "principle of exaggeration" in daily life through radically, even unfeasibly,

revised outputs and targets (377). Whereas Krzhizhanovsky's fantastic approach exposed the contingency of the real, Socialist Realism converted fantasy into reality.

23 See Leiderman, "Intellectual Worlds," 522. The stories referred to are "In The Pupil" (1927) and "The Phantom" (1926).

24 Ruddick, "The Fantastic Fiction of the Fin de Siècle," 192.

25 "Trinadtsataia kategoriia rassudka," in *SS* III:281. On Krzhizhanovsky in the context of other twentieth-century fantastic realists like Borges and Calvino, see Adam Thirlwell's Introduction to *Autobiography of a Corpse*, translated by Joanne Turnbull (New York Review Books, 2013), x–xv.

26 Charles Baudelaire, "Notes nouvelles sur Edgar Poe" (1857), in *Selected Critical Studies of Baudelaire*, edited by D. Parmée (Cambridge University Press, 1949), 52.

27 "Edgar Allan Po: 90 let so dnia smerti," in *SS* IV:571.

28 Kirsten Lodge, "Introduction," in *The Dedalus Book of Russian Decadence*, edited by Kirsten Lodge (Sawtry, Eng.: Dedalus, 2007), 18.

29 Sigizmund Krzhizhanovsky, "Quadraturin," translated by Joanne Turnbull, in *Russian Short Stories from Pushkin to Buida*, edited by Robert Chandler (London: Penguin, 2005), 209.

30 The classic example is Bulgakov's *Heart of a Dog* (*Sobach'e serdtse*, 1925). As the miraculously reconstructed dog-man Sharikov tells his maker, "A person without documents is strictly forbidden to exist!" Mikhail Bulgakov, *Sobranie sochinenii*, edited by V. I. Losev (St. Petersburg: Azbuka-Klassika, 2002), III:283.

31 "Quadraturin," 214.

32 Matich, *Erotic Utopia*, 9.

33 Merezhkovsky, "Gogol and the Devil," 57.

34 Chizhevsky, "About Gogol's 'Overcoat,'" in *Gogol from the Twentieth Century*, edited and translated by Maguire, 315.

35 Gogol, "The Greatcoat," trans. Chandler, in *Russian Short Stories from Pushkin to Buida*, 50.

36 Chizhevsky, "About Gogol's 'Overcoat,'" 319–321.

37 "Quadraturin," 208.

38 Ibid.

39 Ibid.

40 See Graffy, *Gogol's "The Overcoat"*; Stanley Rabinowitz, "Fedor Sologub and his Nineteenth-Century Russian Antecedents," *Slavic and East European Journal* 22:3 (1978): 331; and Eric Laursen, "Transformation as Revelation: Sologub, Schopenhauer, and the Little Man," *Slavic and East European Journal* 39:4 (1995): 552–567.

41 Saranin's "speaking name" may derive from *sarancha* (locust).

42 Baudelaire's poem "Le Gouffre" in *Les Fleurs du Mal* (1857) enshrined the abyss in symbolist mythography. Steinberg notes that the "abyss" was a favorite trope of Russian writers. In Steinberg, *Petersburg Fin de Siècle*, 9.

43 Valery Briusov, "Burnt to Ashes," in *Gogol from the Twentieth Century*, edited and translated by Maguire, 131.

44 Andrei Belyi, "Gogol'," in *Kritika, estetika, teoriia simvolizma* (Moscow: Iskusstvo, 1994), 1:311 (Bely's italics).

45 V. N. Toporov discusses Krzhizhanovsky's concept of "minus-space" in "'Minus'-prostranstvo Sigizmunda Krzhizhanovskogo," in *Mif, ritual, simvol, obraz: issledovaniia v oblasti mifopoeticheskogo* (Moscow: Kul'tura, 1995), 548.

46 For example, Bely's eponymous *Peterburg* (1913) or any of Kafka's cityscapes.

47 "The Greatcoat," 54.

48 Merezhkovsky, "Gogol and the Devil," 71.

49 Gogol, "The Portrait," in *Arabesques*, edited by Carl Proffer and translated by Alexander Tulloch (Ann Arbor, MI: Ardis, 1982), 97.

50 *Dead Souls*, trans. English, 254.

51 Rabinowitz, "Fedor Sologub and his Nineteenth-Century Russian Antecedents," 331.

52 Leiderman develops this point with regard to Krzhizhanovsky's novella *The Wandering "Strangely"* in "Intellectual Worlds," 523–524.

53 Fedor Sologub, *Sobranie sochinenii v shesti tomakh* (Moscow: Intelvak, 2000), 1:630–631.

54 My interpretation of *Quadraturin* is more materialistic than Karen Link Rosenflanz's. She suggests that Sutulin's fate is metaphorical, representing a failed "experiment in higher order thinking." See Rosenflanz, "Overturned Verticals and Extinguished Suns: Facets of Krzhizhanovsky's Fourth Dimension," *Slavic and East European Journal* 56:4 (2012): 543.

55 *Autobiography of a Corpse*, 9 (translator's italics).

56 "The Greatcoat," 40.

57 Donald Fanger, *Dostoevsky and Romantic Realism: A Study of Dostoevsky in Relation to Balzac, Dickens and Gogol* (University of Chicago Press, 1965), 117.

58 "Quadraturin," 209.

59 Ibid., 215.

60 The translator's rendering of *kvadratura* (quadrilateral).

61 Ibid., 216.

62 "Thoughts on Geography (For Children)," trans. Tulloch, in Gogol, *Arabesques*, 202.

CHAPTER 11

Icons, eclipses, and stepping off the train
Vladimir Korolenko and the ocherk

Jane Costlow

Steam boats and locomotives are without doubt quite marvelous means of transportation, but whatever their advantages they have one major drawback: they distort perspective, and while they bring separate points closer together, in general they take us farther from a country . . . But all you have to do is get off the train or the steamboat – and immediately your perspective changes: . . . you're there, and you feel that around you something different is beginning . . . how much there is that's compelling, and of interest . . . [1]

– Vladimir Korolenko, "Gone"

Vladimir Korolenko has become a bit like the hamlets and fords he refers to in this passage: someone we are likely to know only in passing, someone we catch a glimpse of on our way elsewhere, to the land of Gorky or Chekhov. It's fairly unlikely that we've stepped down from the train, dusted off our boots, and set out to wander the byways of his diverse and capacious body of work. He is the author of a much-anthologized story, "Makar's Dream" (1883), and a three-volume autobiography that extends the nineteenth-century tradition of writers' memorialization of their lives. He is the great public intellectual of late Imperial Russia: involved in court cases defending the rights of minorities, shipped off to Siberia as a young populist, a hearty, bearded figure who sparred in the last year of his life with the Bolsheviks' Commissar of Enlightenment, Anatoly Lunacharsky. But as a writer he seems consigned to the ranks of lesser lights, someone whose stories get assigned in high school or a survey course and then forgotten, eclipsed by a host of other late Imperial figures: Gorky, Bunin, and Chekhov, to say nothing of the less publicly minded decadents and symbolists.

And yet Korolenko deserves our attention, particularly in the context of this volume, with its discussion of fin-de-siècle realism. In a volume that engages directly with the moods of apocalypticism, spiritual exhaustion, and pessimism of the late Imperial decades, Vladimir Korolenko seems like a bizarrely robust outlier, encountering rural Russia with humor,

generosity, and probing intelligence. The passage quoted above, from a
story called "Gone," is representative. First begun in 1890, the story was
published after the author's death; Sofia Korolenko, the writer's daughter,
introduces it in a volume that extended Korolenko's memoirs into the
period he spent in Nizhnii Novgorod (1888–1896). She suggests that the
passage represents a kind of "idiosyncratic philosophy of travel by foot."[2]
Korolenko's imaginative trekking off along the dusty pathways of Russia
does indeed suggest that something in the physicality and situatedness of
experience changes one's perspective, and that without such immersion we
are led into false assumptions. Our vision of things from the train becomes
too simple. Korolenko's words valorize the situated nature of understanding, chipping away at what one thinks one knows from a distance. If it is
a philosophy of walking, it is also a statement about what we might call
ambulatory or phenomenological realism.

No brief essay can begin to come to terms with the vast legacy of this
extraordinary man. What I hope to accomplish here is a consideration of the
kind of realism Korolenko practiced during the years he spent in Nizhnii
Novgorod, and how the sketches he wrote as he traveled the backroads
of the central Volga laid the ground for longer works that are hybrids
of documentary and reflective observation. Questions of genre have been
key in accounts of Korolenko's work: while scholars have conventionally
organized his output by the categories of journalism, publicistics, and belles
lettres, his writing is in fact a complicated map of fiction, non-fiction, and
memoir, in which the author's own subtitles proliferate to dizzying effect:
there are sketches and études, observations and reminiscences, legends
and *esquisses*. "Makar's Dream," probably the author's most famous short
story, is subtitled "A Christmas Story"; "Sokolinets" (1885) – an adventure
tale about a band of convicts escaping from Sakhalin in the Russian Far
East – is subtitled "From the Stories about Vagabonds." Other stories are
described as "from childhood reminiscences" ("In Bad Company," 1885);
"a Polessia legend" ("The Forest Sounds," 1886); and "a study (*etiud*)"
("The Blind Musician," 1886). The *ocherk* or sketch forms a key location
on this map of literary possibility for Korolenko, sometimes referring to
work that is construed by readers, and probably by the author himself,
as what we would call non-fiction; sometimes referring to works that are
fictional. Many if not most of these *ocherki* were underwritten by the
author's notebooks, journals he began keeping at least as early as his exile
in Siberia – journals that contain snippets of observation and dialogue
along with pencil drawings that are in their way as astutely observed as
his verbal descriptions, evidence of a visual sensibility that is abundantly

manifest throughout his work, but particularly in the *ocherki* of his Nizhnii period.[3]

Classic accounts of the *ocherk* have often involved historical considerations, including the genre's indebtedness to writers like Balzac, the essentially urban and characterological focus of 1840s physiological sketches, and the genre's transformation by radical writers of the 1860s and 1870s into what the authors of the *Soviet Literary Encyclopedia* call the "enlightenment sketch," suggesting an essentially didactic or educational function.[4] Critics and historians have also pointed to more intrinsic and stylistic aspects of the genre, often including a consideration of how a *sketch* might differ from a *story*. These include a focus on description of individuals that maintains an eye to a given character's "typicality," the relative unimportance of plot, the presence of the author as someone who enters into the course of events, a relatively free "grouping of material," the extent to which material is based on actual events or "made up," and the potential inclusion of "scientific" or statistical material.[5] One recent account argues for the genre's enormous importance for Russian literature, and in particular for understandings of realism and the real. The form has lent itself to a huge range of instantiations, and can be seen as an essentially intermediate genre, straddling the worlds of artistic literature and publicistics; it is best considered less in terms of one mega-genre (the *ocherk*) than in terms of prefixed subgenres: the portrait sketch, the sketch of daily life, the problem sketch, the travel sketch.[6] Finally, we might consider the sketch as something like an essay, modulating authorial voice so as to engage the reader in an essentially free-form exploration.[7] Each of these considerations points to the *ocherk*'s originating and organizing impulse – observation of personality and of place, improvisation of an idea and its associative potential, instruction, and voice – the last being key to the reader's experience and engagement. In the *ocherk* a sense of reality and observation trump the set of anticipations, anxieties, and resolutions associated with action and plot.

The sketches Korolenko wrote in the years he lived in Nizhnii Novgorod have been variously categorized sometimes as fiction, sometimes not,[8] – but they are by and large all excellent examples of the kind of undertaking the writer envisions in the passage from "Gone." Georgy Bialyi, writing in the late 1940s, links much of Korolenko's writing in Nizhnii to "practical struggle," but specific politics and struggles against corruption only account for some of what Korolenko wrote in these years; the *ocherki*, taken as a group, are intentionally open-ended and wandering, experimenting with ways of writing about locale and local lives. In their open-endedness Korolenko's sketches become vehicles not of resolution, but ways to leave questions unanswered: they are narratives that school the reader in the kind of open-hearted, non-judgmental, non-ideological curiosity that the author/narrator exemplifies. We step with him "off the train" to get a different perspective on Russia and the people of Russia's backroads. Just how he does this is what I will try to show below, based on examples from the sketches Korolenko wrote in the years 1887–1893.

Bialyi gives a careful accounting of the range and variety of writing that Korolenko did in his Nizhnii Novgorod years, from journalistic reporting on corruption to a rich array of narratives informed by his treks throughout the central Volga regions. Bialyi emphasizes, on the one hand, an immersion in the "minutiae" of provincial life that the Soviet literary scholar for some reason finds surprising; he redeems Korolenko's attention to "petty" details of everyday life as examples of his ongoing interest in "popular worldview."[9] Beyond the journalistic reporting of these years, Korolenko produced a range of works that Bialyi places on a continuum from "publicistics" to "belles lettres," much if not all of it inspired by his wanderings. In June of 1887 Korolenko followed the traditional pilgrimage route to the Oranki Monastery some fifty kilometers south of Nizhnii Novgorod; by September a story based on the trip had appeared in *Severnyi vestnik*. The same summer, August found Korolenko traveling up the Volga to Iurevets in the Kostroma region to observe a full solar eclipse; his account of the eclipse was published in October in *Russkie vedomosti*.

Both "After the Icon" ("Za ikonoi," 1887) and "At the Eclipse" ("Na zatmnenii," 1887) describe encounters with back-country Russia, and while both have strong ethnographic elements – dialogue rendered in local vernacular, detailed descriptions of crowds and striking individuals – they are much more than *just* descriptions. "After the Icon" takes the path of the pilgrimage as its structuring dynamic, lacing together conversations, incidents both harrowing and comic, evocative description, and moments of rumination on faith. At one point Korolenko inserts an account of the building of the monastery and the monks' relationship to the local indigenous people, the Mordva. The story's final section involves a lengthy and obscure disputation between two different groups of pilgrims on matters of faith and authority. "At the Eclipse" on the other hand limits itself to a brief time frame, using the cycle of the eclipse along with the village's topography to present a study in contrasts, between foreign astronomers assembled with their telescopes on the heights, and village folk alternately cowering and threatening to destroy both "astro-namers" and their heretical contraptions.[10] Here as in the earlier sketch Korolenko alternates passages of dialogue with descriptions of place and deeply atmospheric accounts of light and darkness. Both sketches can be read as studies of popular religious faith, seen as credulous and primitive but also oddly, undeniably powerful. As sketches these narratives stand alone, but they can also seem like steps toward the more complex narratives that Korolenko would publish in 1890 and 1893. *In the Wild and Empty Places* (*V pustynnykh mestakh,* 1890) takes a more extended kind of journey, both pilgrimage and river trek into the forests north of the Volga, including one of the great sacred sites of Old Belief – Svetloiar, site of the hidden city of Kitezh; *In the Famine Year* (*V golodnyi god,* 1893), an explicitly investigative journey to the district of Lukoianov in the Nizhnii region, shows Korolenko applying all of his skills as a writer to uncover and elucidate just what "famine" looks like. Korolenko also calls *In the Famine Year* "sketches" – attributing to himself a series of roles, from "accidental observer-belletrist" to "correspondent" and undertaker of "observations and practical work."[11] *In the Wild and Empty Places* similarly conjoins various kinds of narrative, including inserted stories that function almost as separate tales (and are in fact sometimes published on their own).[12] We might then either read the two earlier sketches as staging grounds for the later, more complex works – or, the better option seems to be that we might see in all these narratives an intentional effort to capture the fragmentary, the fleeting, the episodic, aiming quite explicitly not at conclusion but at impression and the open-ended question. As a group they are characterized by an improvisational or fluid quality,[13] by particular shapings of character and voice including the narrator-author's, and by remarkably resonant endings – which often seem to spurn closure intentionally.

If we take the two sketches from summer 1887 together, we are struck by how they contrast two very different rituals of watching, icon veneration and observation of solar phenomena, which seem to encapsulate an almost clichéd juxtaposition of tradition and modernity, faith and science. But the situation in Korolenko's hands is more complex, and opens up a meandering set of considerations about what and how we see. His interest in icons might seem to be occasioned in obvious ways by their cultural importance, and by icons' role as visual stimuli for powerful emotion. Korolenko's interest in icons and images in relation to his own talents as an artist is also worth considering, however. The *sketches* in Korolenko's notebooks are visual as well as verbal. His notebooks from the late 1880s include a series of simple and nicely rendered Volga scenes – small boats, some at anchor and others under sail, high banks with a church and bell tower – and others of the chapel and lake at Svetloiar, rendered in what looks like a mixture of pencil and water color (Figure 1).[14] A more than capable artist, Korolenko

Часовня у озера Светлояр

Рис. В. Г. Короленко
23 июня 1905 г.

Figure 1. The Chapel at Svetloiar, 1905. Scanned by Bates College Imaging Center

had used his talents to support himself and his family as a student; while studying at the Technological Institute in St. Petersburg he was hired to color plates for N. Zhivotovsky's botanical atlas, hailed as "one of the most remarkable works in natural science from pre-revolutionary Russia."[15] When Korolenko transferred to the Forest Institute in Moscow, he took Zhivotovsky's recommendation to the botanist Kliment Timiriazev, who went on to employ Korolenko making illustrations for his lectures.[16] All of this – along with Korolenko's critical reviews of contemporary artists – suggests not just serious interest in visual art, but the eye of a practitioner, someone practiced at "sketching" reality in multiple media.[17]

The titular icon of the 1887 story is, presumably, the Oranki icon of the Mother of God, whose yearly journey from Nizhnii to the Oranki Monastery commemorates its role in a miraculous cure of plague in the eighteenth century. Korolenko's title may not in fact be referring to that particular icon, however: intriguingly, the story might be less about following after the icon than moving beyond the icon – or considering what is on the icon's "other side." The Russian preposition "za" allows a variety of different readings, and we could find support for any one of them in Korolenko's text. While the icon's journey from one place to another leads Korolenko and his companion on this trek, the icon itself is not actually described in any particular detail. The closest thing to an actual description of the icon comes in a scene of mass healing and veneration. The passage is worth quoting at length:

> The day was really heating up. The icon got going again around ten o'clock. We set out early, but it was hard walking. Our legs didn't want to move, our whole bodies complained. But gradually the tiredness seemed to pass.
>
> Here and there the shade of a small wood hid us from the sun's heat, but for the most part on either side there was ripening rye. Sometimes a lane from a neighboring village ran out to meet the road, and village icons stood by small crossroad chapels . . . The icon stopped at each chapel and prayers were said. Then there was a crush around the icon. People shoved forwards to kiss the casing . . . Among these broad fields, by the small chapels, amid scattered and subsiding crowds the icon seemed closer, more accessible. Here it was surrounded by a tight cluster of genuine pilgrims. Tormented, suffering, sickly, and sorrowful folk engulfed the icon like a living wave lifted up by some force. With no mind for the others, heedless of all the shoves, they all looked in one direction . . . The half-extinguished eyes, withered hands, crippled backs, faces disfigured by pain and suffering – all turned toward one center, where a gold raiment shone from glass and frame bindings, and the head of the Mother of God bent like a dark blotch toward the child. The icon was particularly impressive in the depths of its casing. Rays of sunlight penetrated the glass and made soft, shining ripples on the gold of her crown; the crowd's motions moved the icon ever so slightly, the ripples of light ebbed and flared, gliding about, and the bent head seemed to move above the unsettled crowd . . . A kind of breath passed over the faces, smoothing shades of suffering, channeling them into a shared expression of kindness. I watched this picture not without emotion . . . Such a wave of human grief, of human longing and hope! . . . And such a great mass of common spiritual movement, engulfing, removing, erasing each separate suffering, each personal grief, like a drop that has drowned in the ocean! Is it not here, I thought, in this mighty current of human longing, singular faith, and similar hopes – that the source of this healing power lies?[18]

At the heart of this remarkable scene of adoration is the "dark blotch" of the Mother of God. What are we to make of Korolenko's phrasing? Is it simply an articulation of sensory limitation, marking what the eye cannot distinguish at a distance? If so, then this is an interesting example of Korolenko's refusal to insert what he knows, the face familiar to all Russians through the ubiquity of icons, for what he sees. Or do we read the blotch in ideological terms, an intentional denigration of the most holy of images? Surely the first is closer to the spirit of this passage. The real focus of Korolenko's attention here is not the icon but what he calls a *picture*. His prose highlights acts of seeing, acts so allied to the physical motion of bodies here that the object of veneration itself seems to come alive. The icon is represented in this passage at the intersection of the physical thing itself with sun's rays and the mobility of the crowd, in turn both physical and emotional. Everything, including Korolenko's own gaze, is in motion. And part of the passage's mobility, or animation, is the question with which it ends. In posing the question of whether it is faith of a certain sort that animates the icon and becomes the source of healing Korolenko might be said to mark his distance from the proceedings: he asks a question that no one in the crowd of faithful would ask. But the question does not register skepticism. Standing at some distance (but not too much), reminding us of his own aching limbs, open to experiencing some version of the waves of emotion that sweep over the crowd, Korolenko leaves us with no particular judgment about what he sees, but with a question, left unanswered, to be pondered as the pilgrimage moves on. Is the mighty current of human longing itself the source of healing?

An earlier encounter in the narration gives us an intriguing counterpart to this icon and the picture Korolenko creates around it. Here Korolenko describes an elderly pilgrim in considerable detail: "To one side along the footpath an old woman wove her way, leaning on a walking stick, quite bent over. It was obvious that she managed each step with enormous difficulty. Her hunched back shook, her head trembled as it hung low on her neck, her legs had trouble moving. She didn't lift her eyes, concentrating her gaze just ahead, measuring step by step her overwhelming journey."[19] The exchange that Korolenko and his companion Andrei Ivanovich have with this woman is quite brief: Andrei hails her as "mother" (*matushka*), and she responds with an affectionate "sweetie" (*kasatik*). She wants to know how far it is to the place where pilgrims can rest for the night, and they share her incredulity when she cannot believe it is still "so far." As is typical of these exchanges in Korolenko's work, the woman's voice is transcribed in vernacular Russian: "Akh, *batiushki*, it's far!.... Go along, go along, sweetie. Don't look at me, I'm an old woman... Nothing to look at... your legs, they're lively, but mine, you see, are just tuckered out... You go along, now, dear ones, go along."[20] The two men move on, encountering other – more obnoxious – pilgrims, and ultimately reach their night's rest. When they arrive, they are exhausted, and the section ends with a reminiscence that brings the old woman before us again:

I wonder how the old woman's doing? – Andrei Ivanovich sounds preoccupied as we pass through the village, with its illuminated windows where you can see samovars on tables and pilgrims relaxing. In my mind's eye the old, hunched figure appears, still toiling along in the darkness. Now no one will disturb her difficult, voluntary labors with unasked-for sympathy. Only the rye whispers on either side, as the moon looks down from the sky on the old and obsolescent one, exhausted beyond all strength.[21]

Here the questions that accompany the image are not just Korolenko's, they are his companion's as well. Just after the encounter with the woman Andrei was driven to exclaim, "Can it all be pointless? . . . Do you think there's really some reward up there? Can't be, it's all rubbish," seeming to wonder at the purpose of the woman's superhuman penance. Andrei's question is the kind of theological murmuring that interests Georgy Bialyi, for example, for the ways it seems to indicate a development in the character's attitude toward the story's central "action," the journey of faith in the wake of the icon.[22] But Korolenko as author doesn't dwell on Andrei's emergent crisis of faith, if indeed that is what it is; instead he brings us back to the image of the woman, with deep compassion for a figure who now seems almost mythic in her endless travel and travail. We might think here of the eternal journey of the suffering in "Makar's Dream" – but the impressionistic, fragmentary quality of the woman in "After the Icon" might equally gesture forward, toward a very different aesthetic: one thinks of Andrei Platonov's heart-wrenching juxtaposition of icons and old women in "The Motherland of Electricity" ("Rodina elektrichestva," 1939) – or his woman-bent-down-with-suffering in *Soul* (*Dusha*, 1935).[23] Korolenko does not match Platonov's more expressionist, even grotesque, rendering of human suffering but asks us to hold an image of the woman in our mind, not in the service of ideology, but as a memento of deep suffering and forbearance.

In both these scenes the passage of description, with vividly rendered images at its center, creates a kind of enigmatic pause within the longer narrative. It is the kind of pause Korolenko also uses to great effect in describing the landscape of their journey. One particular example intersects nicely with one of Korolenko's drawings from this period, one of a boat under sail on the Volga, while the account in "After the Icon" takes place on the Oka – as though the artist's sketch has surfaced in the writer's narrative (Figure 2). On the first day of their journey, Korolenko witnesses a different crowd scene as a suffering peasant woman is brought out to the icon to be healed. This healing of a woman "possessed" – a *klikusha* – occasions sharp disagreement among the pilgrims, some of whom think she's "faking it."

ВОЛЖСКИЙ ВИД

Figure 2. Small sailboat on the Volga, 1887. Scanned by Bates College Imaging Center

Following this dramatic event, Korolenko's companion decides to go for a swim. They descend to the river, and Korolenko gives us a kind of verbal miniature, a landscape that closes part two of the *ocherk*:

> A quiet bank. The crest of the bluff has hidden the crowd with its talk and movement. Now and then colorful figures appear up there, alone and in pairs, but they're fewer and farther between. The river laps against the rocky shore. To the right, about ten versts away, the buildings and churches of Kanavin are visible beyond the clearing mist. On our side, smoking from its high stacks, the factory labors away, soundlessly. After the bustling river traffic of the Volga her neighbor Oka makes a strange impression. How quiet it is here! Far away on the other side a sailboat slips along the sands. Beneath the bluff (a "yar" as they call them here) a dark splotch moves along the shore. It's haulers, who you almost never see anymore along the Volga, dragging a small barge. The smudge seems to stand in one spot, and it's only after long intervals that you see that they're getting smaller, moving away and up river. A miserable Oka steamboat is running from Nizhnii, its wheels making a hollow, slapping sound against the empty banks. You can't see anybody on deck; even on the ladder it's empty. The only thing visible is the lonely figure of the pilot, almost imperceptible by the wheel.[24]

Compared with the icon scene's intense emotions, this one is remarkable for its emptiness and quiet. We are tempted to say it is less emotional, since

Korolenko dispenses with the rolling waves of adjectives, paring the syntax down to a spare minimum. But in reality, the emotion here is just muted, embedded in landscape rather than human form: there is an extraordinary and uncanny power in the juxtaposition of visual images – the factory, the barge haulers, the "lonely figure of the pilot" on an almost empty boat. We come down from the bluff, with its melodrama and strife, only to find the absence of sound and a blurry image. Again Korolenko refers to that *dark splotch*, referring here to the haulers rather than the Mother of God. Just what we are seeing here is not quite clear, either to Korolenko or to us, and not just because the barge haulers are little more than a "spot" on the river; precisely what is happening is unclear in a deeper sense. Beyond whether or not that smudge depicts haulers lies the question implicit in the description itself: the river is simultaneously a place for a cooling swim, a site of factory smokestacks, and a landscape with (vanishing) brutal labor. There is an almost cubist assemblage of visual elements here, icons in another sense of nature–industry–labor, assembled in an enigmatic vision of "Russia."

The collage of impressions and images that Korolenko uses to such effect in scenes like this is connected to the way his own voice both appears and disappears. Sometimes we have a sense of Korolenko as the perceiving subject, the one through whom these impressions coalesce: in the icon scene we receive repeated reminders that Korolenko is the one watching, even if his attitude toward what he sees remains ambiguous. The question at the end of that passage draws the *volneniia* – the turbulent emotion – of the scene into a form of closure that does not draw a conclusion or pass judgment. The collage of images in the river scene above functions similarly, gathering impressions into a kind of question, one the reader must articulate for him or herself: what is this place; what is Russia; what am I to make of this remarkable and contradictory scene?

This same intermingling of description, dialogue, and authorial reserve shapes the *ocherk* Korolenko wrote later that same summer, "At the Eclipse." Subtitled "A sketch from nature," the story combines humor, dialogue, and reflection set in descriptive passages that bring us into Iurevets in the middle of a misty night, then take us through the early morning eclipse itself. Korolenko wanders through the village and relays his own fascination with the way the eclipse changes the quality of light – the contours and shadows of the visible world – surprised, finally at how powerfully the sun's return affects him. The story's dynamic rests in some sense on the contrast between the foreign "astro-namers" and the villagers, the former wholly engrossed with their instruments, the latter a mixture of terrified superstition and more sanguine curiosity. It would be easy to think of the story as a simple juxtaposition of superstition and "enlightenment," but, despite Korolenko's clear affiliation with those who can predict the planets' movements,[25] the "shadows" that he longs to dispel are more complicated: "And just how soon will the day come in Holy Russia – I thought suddenly . . . the day that disperses illusions, hostility, and mutual misunderstanding between the ones who look through telescopes and study the sky, and the ones who can only fall to the ground, seeing in *study* offense to an angry god?"[26] Put this way, the story's central conflict is not between knowledge and ignorance, but between worlds that do not listen to each other; the "astro-namers" are as guilty of this as the fearsome faithful crouching behind closed doors. After the eclipse, when the crowd grows lively and inquisitive, the astronomers brush off their questions. The "crowd dialogues" that Korolenko relays as unattributed fragments of conversation and observation suggest a diverse array of responses to the event – not just superstition and fear, but curiosity and, once the eclipse is over, delight. Striking in its absence is any attempt on Korolenko's part – as a character in the story – to explain anything to the various people he comes in contact with. There seems an almost studied effort not to take on the persona of pedagogue; rather than militating for enlightenment or adopting a didactic tone or its obverse, an insistence on the value of popular wisdom, Korolenko uses humor and his own fascination with the proceedings to describe a world in which curiosity and the evidence of the senses hang in the balance with fearsomeness and a scientific elite that has other things on its mind than educating the public.

The longer works that Korolenko went on to write during his years in Nizhnii Novgorod expand the *ocherk* into more comprehensive forms: *In the Wild and Empty Places* is a hybrid of cultural commentary and back-country trek; *In the Famine Year* is an explicitly polemical account of the famines of 1891–1892, in which Korolenko continues to use a "hybrid" genre – mixing dialogue, investigative reporting, statistical analysis, and descriptions of place. Both of those longer works are indebted to the earlier *ocherki*, and not just because the pilgrimage to Oranki or the eclipse at Iurevets helped Korolenko understand the region. Those sketches also helped him work through his thinking about observation and seeing, and the ways in which cultural icons can become vehicles of blindness. At the beginning of *In the Famine Year* he talks at some length about how readers' expectations of what famine looks like are wrong. Famine is not, he insists, just when "mothers devour their children." Many of the villages most ravaged by famine would appear to the "unschooled eye" as quite normal. Korolenko imagines readers expecting famine to look a certain way asking their own puzzled question: "But where's the famine?"[27] Part of his task in this reportage is to challenge an assumed image, and to find ways to replace it with a more complex understanding. Similarly, in his account of Svetloiar, Korolenko makes a bemused observation on the disappointment he felt upon first seeing a lake he had expected to look different. His expectations, he lets us know, had been formed by the mythologizing representations of an earlier author, Pavel Mel'nikov-Pechersky. The Svetloiar Korolenko experiences does not look like Mel'nikov-Pechersky's. "That's it?" he asks. But his final impression of what is indeed a tiny lake is not disappointment. On his second visit, Svetloiar proves wholly captivating, and he is reminded, interestingly, of "primitive, ancient icons."

> There was a sort of strangely attractive, almost magical simplicity about it. I tried to remember where I might have seen something similar before. And then I remembered. Bright little lakes like this, and rounded little hummocks and birches like these, show up on old, old icons of unassuming manner. A monk kneels in a round glade. A green oak wood had approached him on the one side, as if listening in on the words of human prayer; and in the background (if there is a foreground and background in such pictures) within green banks as in a chalice, is a tiny lake just like this. The awkward hand of the pious artist knows only simple, naïvely correct forms: an oval lake, round hills, trees that form a ring, like children for a folk dance. And over it all the air of "mother-pustynya," the very thing these simple-hearted supplicants were seeking.[28]

Our understanding of anything – person, place, or country – seemingly cannot dispense entirely with images; but nor should we take the images themselves as final or authoritative representations of phenomena, which, like life itself, are constantly changing. Both realism and reality emerge as dynamic processes, filtered through expectations but also potentially capable of constant revision and reimagination.[29]

What fascinates in this pair of *ocherki* from 1887 is how they register a perceptive, compassionate intelligence, that of a man of great humor and insight, responding to a Russia that is "endless . . . hard . . . distracted . . . difficult," but also "compelling and interesting," with its pilgrims, villages, haulers, and old women, all moving along dusty paths invisible from the highroad. "The work of the imagination," Korolenko wrote in 1888, "is images and pictures. Therefore we don't expect clear, purely logical definitions from an artist, but we're in our rights to expect points of view. Only a well-chosen point of view gives true perspective, in which shadows and light are realistically displayed. That's when we can see where the light is coming from and where the various hidden paths may lead."[30] Polemicizing here with Hippolyte Taine and his Russian followers who insisted that literature was solely a "reflector" or mirror of society, Korolenko gropes for language to express in expository fashion what the sketches illustrate so well. That "life is elusive; from the forms of the past it is constantly flowing into the forms of the future, while the present is a kind of fiction, and in our concept of it we grab a bit of the past and a bit from the future, whose interaction and conflict are what we call the contemporary."[31] The images Korolenko renders in his narratives seem to capture that elusive "present" but only for a moment. The artist who drew sketches in a notebook turned ultimately not to the visual, with its powerful illusion of stasis, but to narrative, with its resolute, unforgiving, and endlessly compelling movement.

What might this suggest about Korolenko's practice of realism? Korolenko's sketches of the late 1880s and early 1890s are open-ended and focused in their observations, grounded in the writer's peregrinations but also in his artistic practice. They eschew didactic tone and closure, are more likely to raise questions than answer them, and often use a kind of proto-cubist or impressionistic juxtaposition of visual elements. Their overall stance is fundamentally a matter of tone and composition, exploratory and energetic in ways that are related artistically to the author's physical exploration of the region. The Estonian scholar Lea Pil'd suggested two decades ago that Korolenko was particularly interested in "forms of mental process," a narrative process she situates in his characters; as she reads him, Korolenko viewed conventionalized thinking and reactions based on "established assumptions" as a major ethical, political, and psychic stumbling block for Russian efforts to move beyond the mentalities of serfdom.[32] Something similar might be said about Korolenko's narrators and the narratives as a whole, along with the process they initiate in the reader: points of view in his sketches are not polemical, but rather phenomenological, designed to get us thinking about established assumptions and how "forms of mental process" become stuck or stagnant, and how they can start to change. Vantage point and voice are key to this project – as is getting off the train, trekking along the dusty road, and striking up conversations. Throughout his life Korolenko was a principled and public advocate – someone arguing passionately for the rights of Russia's minority populations, someone who labored endlessly to expose corruption and hypocrisy – but his voice in these sketches is neither combative nor judgmental. Instead, he practices a voice of restrained humanity and humor, with lots of time for pondering and questions, leaving readers to draw their own conclusions. In this I think Korolenko engages in a kind of education, but in a manner that is deeply non-didactic and fundamentally respectful – both of his readers and of the people he encounters along his way.

NOTES

1 "Ushel," in *Sobranie sochinenii v desiati tomakh* (Moscow: Khudozhestvennaia literatura, 1953–1956), 417–418. This volume is hereafter referred to as *SS*. All translations are my own.
2 S. V. Korolenko, *Desiat' let v provintsii* (Izhevsk: Udmurtia, 1966), 85.
3 "Since adolescence I've been in the habit of rendering my impressions in words, seeking the best form for them, not content until I've found it," V. G. Korolenko, *Istoriia moego sovremennika*, quoted in the commentary to Korolenko's Siberian notebooks. *Zapisnye knizhki (1880–1900)* (Moscow: Khudozhestvennaia literatura, 1935), 417.
4 See "Ocherk" entry in *Literaturnaia entsiklopediia* (Moscow: Sovetskaia entsiklopediia, 1929–1939), VIII:381–388. The "enlightenment *ocherk*" of the 1860s and 1870s "gave rich factual material and significantly more correct [when compared with earlier 'bourgeois' sketches] renderings of the social situation of the exploited masses." The editors' examples of authors of such "enlightenment" *ocherki* are Reshetnikov, Levitov, and N. Uspensky.
5 Ibid.
6 See T. A. Kostyleva and S. R. Nemtseva, "Programma elektivnogo kursa 'Ocherk v russkoi literature: zhanrovaia spetsifika, istoriia razvitiia,'" *Literatura* 14 (2011). http://festival.1september.ru/articles/419022/ (accessed July 27, 2014).
7 Morson, *The Boundaries of Genre*, 15–16. Morson quotes the Soviet scholar Zhurbina who in turn quotes Korolenko on the particular qualities of the sketch: "Whatever has flashed before the author in the vague outlines of a future truth, he pursues passionately, not waiting while it is formed by itself in his soul into a clear, self-finished image . . . the reader is forced to live with him through his search, his disappointments, and all his preparatory work, as if apartments were let out when the wood for their construction had not yet been gathered."
8 Georgy Bialyi calls "Za ikonoi" a *rasskaz* but "Na zatmenii" an *ocherk*. See *V. G. Korolenko* (Moscow and Leningrad: Khudozhestvennaia literatura, 1949), 182, 184. Radha Balasubramanian, in the only English-language monograph on Korolenko's literary work, includes fifteen sketches in her listing of Korolenko's "stories" – including "During an Eclipse" but not "After the Icon." See *The Poetics of Korolenko's Fiction* (New York: Peter Lang, 1997), 24.
9 Bialyi, *V. G. Korolenko*, 178.
10 "Astronomy" becomes to the locals "ostroumy": sharp wits instead of namers of stars.
11 *V golodnyi god, SS* IX:100–102.
12 *V pustynnykh mestakh* is composed of eight sections, several of which are in turn divided into short, numbered sections. The third section of the work,

"Priemysh" ("The Adopted Child"), has been frequently published separately. I have contributed to this process of extraction with my translation of section II, "Svetloyar," published in *The Russia Reader: History, Culture, Politics*, edited by Adele Barker and Bruce Grant (Durham, NC: Duke University Press, 2010), 222–236.

13 The first term is my own, the second is one that Korolenko courts with his accounts of rivers and his analogy of literature to a "river pole" in "O naznachenii literatury," in *Vospominaniia. Stati'i. Pis'ma*. (Moscow: Sovetskaia Rossiia, 1988).

14 Reprinted in volume iii of the ten-volume edition from the 1950s. See "illiustratsii" segment following *V pustynnykh mestakh*. http://ruslit.traumlibrary. net/book/korolenko-ss10-03/korolenko-ss10-03.html (accessed July 27, 2014).

15 Zhivotovsky's botanical atlas has recently been reissued in a facsimile edition by Belyi Gorod Press. See S. I. Ivanov, *Botanicheskii atlas N. P. Zivotovskii* (Moscow: Belyi Gorod, 2013). http://www.belygorod.ru/catalog/119324/ (accessed January 16, 2015).

16 An account of this can be found in Korolenko's *Istoriia moego sovremennika*.

17 Korolenko's published writing on art includes several reviews of exhibits in Nizhnii in the late 1880s. See L. A. Gessen and A. G. Ostrovskii, eds., *Russkie pisateli ob izorazitel'nom iskusstve* (Leningrad: Khudozhnik RSFSR, 1976).

18 "Za ikonoi," *SS* iii:28–29.

19 *SS* iii:23.

20 *SS* iii:13–14.

21 *SS* iii:29.

22 Bialyi, *Russkii realism*, 183–185.

23 For a brief discussion of possible connections between the work of Korolenko and Platonov, see Thomas Seifrid, *Andrei Platonov: Uncertainties of Spirit* (Cambridge University Press, 1992), 233.

24 "Za ikonoi," SS iii:13–14.

25 Korolenko has brought with him his own simple observational device, and uses his watch to tell a local when the eclipse will start to pass.

26 "Na zatmenii," SS iii:53.

27 *V golodnyi god*, *SS* iii:101.

28 *V pustynnykh mestakh*, SS iii:129.

29 I give a more extended reading of *In the Wild and Empty Places* in Chapter 4 of *Heart-Pine Russia: Walking and Writing the Nineteenth-Century Forest* (Ithaca, NY: Cornell University Press, 2013).

30 "O naznachenii literatury," 296.

31 Ibid., 294.

32 Lea Pil'd, "Tipy narodnogo soznaniia v proze V. G. Korolenko 1880-x – nach. 1890-x gg," *Trudy po russkoi i slavianskoi filologii* (1994): 146. http://www .ruthenia.ru/reprint/trudy_i/pild.pdf (accessed July 7, 2014).

PART IV

Facing death and decay

CHAPTER 12

Decadent ecosystems in Uncle Vanya
A chorographic meditation

Thomas Newlin

Sometime in 1936 the poet Osip Mandelstam, banished to the backwater city of Voronezh, went to see a performance of *Uncle Vanya* at the local theater. He returned home and jotted down his thoughts, which were trenchant and grumpy. It was the play itself, rather than the provincial production, that annoyed him:

> Chekhov. Dramatis personae of *Uncle Vanya*: Serebriakov, Alexander Vladimirovich, a retired professor. Yelena Andreeva, his wife, 27 years old. Sofia Aleksandrovna (Sonia), his daughter from a first marriage. Voinitskaya, Marya Vasilevna, a privy counselor's widow, mother of the professor's first wife. Voinitsky, Ivan Petrovich, her son. Astrov, Mikhail Lvovich, a doctor. Telegin, an impoverished landowner. Marina, an old nanny. A worker.
>
> To make sense of the underlying relationships (*vnutrennie otnosheniia*) between these various characters, as systems, you have to study Chekhov's cast list inside out, pretty much memorize it. What an inexpressive and drab conundrum. Why are they all together? How is the privy counselor related to anybody? Try and determine the kinship or connection between Voinitsky, the son of the privy counselor's widow who was the mother of the professor's first wife, and Sofia Alexandrovna, the professor's daughter by his first marriage. In order to establish that one person is another person's uncle, you have to analyze the whole roster. I for one have an easier time understanding the spiraling schema of Dante's *Commedia*, with its circles and pathways and spherical astronomy, than this two-bit census-bureau twaddle.
>
> A biologist would call this Chekhovian principle ecological. Cohabitation (*sozhitel'stvo*) is the determinant factor in Chekhov. There's no action in his drama, there's only adjacency (*sosedstvo*) with its ensuing unpleasantnesses.
>
> With his specimen net Chekhov scoops up a sample of the "marsh mud" of humankind, the likes of which were never seen before. People live together and simply can't manage to go their separate ways. That's all. Just hand them some train tickets – to the "three sisters," for instance – and the play'll be over.[1]

While it is not entirely clear what Mandelstam means by the term "eco-logical," and while his jibes may seem gratuitously hostile, he nonetheless manages to put his finger on one of Chekhov's central points, even as he misses or willfully rejects that point entirely.[2] *Uncle Vanya* is, indeed, a deeply "ecological" play, both in its themes, which are evident enough, and in its structure, which is less evident. That is to say, *Uncle Vanya* explores, after its own fashion, "the interrelationships among organisms and between organisms, and between them and all aspects, living and non-living, of their environment."[3] More precisely, and to Mandelstam's annoyance, it explores – and models – the failure of these various "interre-lationships." In this sense, it is, by deliberate design, a centrifugal work of art, as the centripetally inclined Mandelstam senses so keenly: it gestures insistently toward the breakdown of the various structures, "systems," or ecosystems – social, environmental, artistic, corporeal – that underpin its fragile, spiraling universe. Because of its refusal to cohere in a traditional fashion, the play can seem disjointed or even ugly by the norms of the more classical poetics to which Mandelstam adhered, and it is hardly surprising that someone who just a few years earlier had called film "the metamorph of the tapeworm" felt a similarly visceral distaste for Chekhov's montage-like series of "scenes."[4] But *Uncle Vanya*'s preoccupation with fragmentation and degeneration is, of course, precisely what makes the work at once dis-tinctly realistic and distinctly modernist. It is also what makes it a peculiarly provocative leap of the dramatic and the ecological imagination.

This chapter will attempt to map out the "underlying relationships" between several of the many degraded or decaying "ecosystems" that were on Chekhov's mind as he wrote the play, first in the late 1880s, in its original iteration as *The Wood Demon* (*Leshii*), and then in the mid-1890s, when he refashioned *The Wood Demon* into *Uncle Vanya*. By exploring these "deca-dent ecosystems" more closely, I hope to show that the broad eschatolog-ical drift that characterized fin-de-siècle Europe metamorphosed in *Uncle Vanya* into a distinctly Russian version of "environmental apocalypticism," and that there is a close connection between Russians' gnawing anxiety at the century's end about their own cultural, moral, and social degeneration, and their concomitant unease over the ever-accelerating despoliation of the natural world.[5]

The word "ecosystem" – shorthand for "a discrete unit that consists of living and non-living parts, interacting to form a stable system" – was not a part of Chekhov's vocabulary: the term did not exist until 1935, when it was coined by the British ecologist A. G. Tansley.[6] "Ecology," a neologism first used in 1866 by the German scientist Ernst Haeckel, was likely not a part of it either. Indeed, the definition of "ecology" in the 1904 Brokhaus-Efron dictionary as "that part of zoology dealing with animals' dwelling-places – i.e., burrows, nests, lairs, etc." suggests just how narrow the Russians' understanding of the word still was at the time of Chekhov's death.[7] But "the study of ecology," as Donald Worster has noted, "is much older than the name," and "thinking ecologically" – that is, making connections between wholes and parts – is what artists have been doing since time immemorial.[8]

I am well aware, for sure, of the pitfalls – as well as the payoffs – of applying twentieth-century concepts and frameworks to a late nineteenth-century work. In an essay written in the early 1990s, Gary Saul Morson cautioned against cherry-picking certain "detachable parts" of *Uncle Vanya* that resonate strongly with present-day sensibilities and taking them at face value, thereby imposing a simplistic and anachronistic "green" reading on a work that is deeply ironic rather than earnestly exhortative.[9] Certainly Chekhov offers up no easy prescriptions or solutions in *Uncle Vanya*, and the environmental messaging that goes on in the play is invariably complicated and undercut by its problematic delivery. But the messaging is there nonetheless, and it reflects the real and growing concern, generally untempered by irony, that Chekhov and his contemporaries in Russia felt about the rapid degradation of the natural world around them. It is in no sense anachronistic to speak of both a burgeoning environmental awareness (a concern with human impacts on nature) and a burgeoning ecological awareness (an increasingly sophisticated understanding of the intricate web of "interrelationships" in nature) in late nineteenth-century Russia, as a spate of recent scholarship has demonstrated.[10] *Uncle Vanya* embodies and explores, in a complex and sometimes ironic way, both types of awareness.[11]

Worster has pointed out that "the men who drew the map for the freshly christened science of ecology" in the late nineteenth century were primarily geographers.[12] Although his focus is on the American and Western European ecological tradition, what he says holds true with regard to the Russian tradition as well: it was figures like the climatologist and geographer Alexander Voeikov and the soil scientist and geographer Vasily Dokuchaev who were doing the most important ecological thinking in Russia at the end of the century, even if it was not yet called that.[13] It is no coincidence, then, that maps play an important role in *Uncle Vanya*. In exploring the play's "decadent ecosystems," I pay particular attention to these maps, and to the subtle ways in which the ecological and the cartographic imagination become intertwined.[14]

It seems to me that we can distinguish between at least five "decadent ecosystems" at work in *Uncle Vanya*. They can be viewed, roughly, as a series of concentric circles.

On a metaphorical level the first and most fundamental of these "decadent ecosystems," as Mandelstam suggests, is the play itself – that is, its very structure as a work of art. And the list of characters that Mandelstam scrutinized with such distaste on the playbill that evening in Voronezh might be seen as the first of the play's various maps: it is a shorthand figuration of the play's formal disjuncture or "decadence," a subtle early warning or guide that sketches out the shape of things to come.

In his bid to create a new dramatic form, one commensurate with the increasingly fractured reality that he sought to represent, Chekhov took an axe to the time-honored and organically harmonious ecosystem of traditional drama – what Mandelstam, citing the example of the eighteenth-century Italian playwright Goldoni, referred to as "a flowering unity."[15] In late 1889 and early 1890, when *The Wood Demon* first came to the stage, critics lacerated Chekhov for his indifference to theatrical conventions: "Chekhov does not recognize the laws of drama," one critic opined. "The spectator can't make head or tail of his own impressions. He gets angry at the play."[16] Others remarked on the play's utter lack of "stageability" (*tsenichnost*), and complained – justifiably enough – that it was impossibly overloaded with characters and scenes.[17] One of the more generous and perceptive reactions came from N. P. Kicheev, editor of *The Alarm Clock*, to which Chekhov had contributed a number of his early stories. "Here we have a whole society infected with a 'pandemic' disease," he commented, using language that is very much marked by the specific anxieties of the fin de siècle. "This disease is a will toward destruction, an unthinking egotism, an utter incapacity for altruism, for the desire to do good for others... It is to this diseased 'vein' of contemporary society that Mr. Chekhov's new play is dedicated." But Kicheev did not see a link between the play's thematic preoccupations (disease and dysfunction) and its form, or apparent lack thereof: "I see in it only a series of *scenes*, overly drawn-out and short on action, though indisputably rendered in a fresh and talented way."[18] In reimagining *The Wood Demon* as *Uncle Vanya* six years later, Chekhov drastically pared down the cast of characters and the number and length of the "scenes" (*stseny*); he also did away entirely with the traditional textual markers that segmented each act into scenes (*iavleniia*). But while this streamlining made the play substantially more "stageable," it simultaneously worked to bring the jerky, episodic nature of its structure into sharper relief, rather than smoothing it over. Chekhov announced his intentions and responded directly to his earlier critics – that is, he at once echoed, accommodated, and challenged them – in the new play's subtitle. *The Wood Demon* had been "A Comedy in Four Acts"; *Uncle Vanya* became "Scenes from Country Life in Four Acts." By incorporating Kicheev's notion of the play as a mere "series of scenes" in its very title, Chekhov explicitly privileged fragmentation and randomness over unity. Curiously, when *Uncle Vanya* first appeared as a separate offprint in 1902 (it had originally been published as part of a collection of Chekhov's plays in 1897), the title-page description "Scenes from Country Life" (*Stseny iz derevenskoi zhizni*) became the more soothingly cohesive "A Scene from Country Life" (*Stsena iz derevenskoi zhizni*).[19] This was almost surely a kind of Freudian typographical slip on the part of the publisher – one that revealed deep-seated cultural assumptions and expectations about what a work of art should do and how it should hold together.

More open-minded audience members gave the "episodic quality" (*epizodichnost'*) of the refashioned play a positive spin. The theater critic Alexander Kugel', for instance, commented that "Chekhov feels, thinks, and takes in life episodically, by way of its bits and pieces, its flotsam and jetsam – and, it might be said, by way of endless parallels that never inter-sect, at least on any visible plane."[20] But others were less impressed. Tolstoy attended a performance of *Uncle Vanya* at the Moscow Art Theater in 1900, and though no stranger himself to formal experimentation, he came away "exasperated." His reaction was similar in tone and spirit to Mandelstam's several decades later: he griped that the play lacked any drama or discern-able center and simply "spun its wheels." And if Mandelstam facetiously recommended a few train tickets as an easy way to cut short the agony of these "scenes from country life," Tolstoy – somewhat less facetiously, and perhaps with classical comedy in the back of his mind – suggested pairing off Vanya and Astrov with some peasant girls as a quick solution to their malaise.[21] The pique felt so keenly by both Tolstoy and Mandelstam reflects, of course, their relatively conventional conception of how drama should unfold. Their vexed experience as spectators of the play is akin to the vexed experience of Serebriakov (a professor of literature, not coinci-dentally) within the play. "I don't like this house," he grouses. "A regular labyrinth. Twenty-six enormous rooms, everyone wanders off in different directions, you can never find anyone" (98). With these words Chekhov, we might say, at once announces the architecture of his deliberately drab, drafty, and disjointed play, and preempts his many future critics.

This brings us to the second "decadent ecosystem" that Chekhov con-fronts us with in *Uncle Vanya*: the gentry "nest" where the action of the play takes place – or what we might alternately refer to as the gentry *oikos* – to use the Greek word, meaning "household," "family," or "estate," from which the term "ecology" is derived.

Chekhov's "ecological" play presents us with an *oikos* in crisis. It is an *oikos* whose natural rhythms have been upended: breakfast is in the afternoon, lunch in the evening, and the whole household is up in the middle of the night. It is an *oikos* where meaningful work has stopped, and where the samovar – that symbolic heart of nineteenth-century Russian home life – has gone cold, both literally and figuratively. It is an *oikos* that is biologically at a dead end, where even the youngest men are middle-aged, depressive, and alcoholic, where no one, not even the twenty-one-year-old Sonya, seems to be in full bloom, where no one is happily in love, where no one even ever seems to have sex. It is an *oikos* made up of people who are themselves, like the play, "episodic" or "transient," as Elena bitterly complains (*A ia nudnoe, epizodicheskoe litso*; 89), and who remain, for all intents and purposes, alone together: they live as one household, but their relationship is indeed one of mere "cohabitation" or "adjacency," as Mandelstam so pithily puts it, rather than one of genuine interaction, communication, conviviality, or commiseration – and they are almost all *miserable*. A great deal of talking takes place in the play, as in all plays, but the characters here almost always talk past rather than to each other, as in all of Chekhov's plays, and as critics invariably point out.

It is worth noting that Chekhov was already well aware of Nordau's *Degeneration* when he began reworking *The Wood Demon* into *Uncle Vanya* in the mid-1890s.[22] In their general behavior – a cocktail of pessimism and idealism, passivity and aggression, egomania and abnegation – and in their relentless self-analysis, the various inhabitants of this particular *oikos* implicitly seem to confirm Nordau's theories, even as they also call to mind their own home-grown literary-genetic provenance: the robust lineage of familial buffoonery, grotesquery, and decadence represented by Saltykov-Shchedrin's Golovlevs and Dostoevsky's Karamazovs.[23]

If we move outwards from the dysfunctional hothouse of the estate, we enter the third "decadent ecosystem" of the play – the surrounding district or "uezd." This realm is linked even more explicitly to Nordauian discourse: Astrov's series of hand-drawn maps document the steady "degeneration" (*vyrozhdenie*) over half a century of the local ecosystem – its rivers, forests, fauna, and human settlements. It is this third, regional ring in our series of concentric circles, and its relationship with the fourth and fifth rings, that will concern me in the remainder of this chapter. The fourth ring I have in mind is the global ecosystem, the planet earth – and

I will argue that Chekhov evokes this global ecosystem, cryptically and enigmatically, in the last act of the play. The final, shadow ring of the play – and what might at the same time be seen as the "decadent ecosystem" that lies at its very core – is Chekhov's own body, which was slowly succumbing to tuberculosis even as he wrote *The Wood Demon* and *Uncle Vanya*.

We will recall that in the stage directions for the final act of *Uncle Vanya* Chekhov off-handedly hangs a map of Africa, "evidently of no use to anyone," on the wall of Vanya's office-cum-bedroom. We also recall that Chekhov once remarked, famously, that if you hang a rifle on the wall in a play, then it had better go off at some point. Maps, of course, don't go bang. But they can help us, less spectacularly, to situate ourselves or to find our way; they can also help open up our imagination. So why is Chekhov's pointedly "useless" map of Africa there on the wall, and where, if anywhere, does it lead us? For most of the final act it simply hangs there, mutely incongruous, and it is finally invoked more actively in the play's closing moments: Astrov, the humanely misanthropic, vodka-tippling medico and lothario who moonlights as tree-planter, ecological activist, and ecocartographer, stops and stares at it, as if noticing it for the very first time: "It must be a real scorcher now in this here Africa – an awful business!" (*A, dolzno byt', v etoi samoi Afrike teper' zharishcha – strashnoe delo!*), he muses absentmindedly (114). With that he takes a last shot of vodka, bids everyone a cursory adieu, and walks off stage. We see him no more.

Maxim Gorky, for one, thought this moment splendid: "In the last act," he wrote to Chekhov, "when the doctor, after a long pause, talks about the heat in Africa, I shuddered with delight over your talent and with fear for human beings, for our colorless and impoverished life."[24] But if Astrov's words function as the figurative equivalent of that requisite pistol shot (the map finally "goes off," so to speak), they are hardly climactic, cathartic, or revelatory. In fact Chekhov was at pains to dampen the scene's emotional energy: he told Olga Knipper in a letter that the mood of the whole fourth act needed to be "quiet and muted" rather than stormy, and that Astrov should address Elena not as an impassioned lover, but "in the same tone that he talks about the heat in Africa."[25] Astrov's parting salvo – if we can call it that – deepens rather than explains the enigma of the map.

The map acquires greater relevance and resonance if we think of it as being in silent dialogue with the three-part "cartogramme" that Astrov shows Elena in the previous act. His mapping of the district's ecological "degeneration" takes place, not coincidentally, under the direct gaze of the orphaned map of the terribly hot Africa. He tells Elena: "I have my own desk here, in Vanya's room. When I'm completely worn out, numb from fatigue, I drop everything and hustle over here, and then I amuse myself with this thingamajig for an hour or two. Vanya and Sonya click away at their abacuses, and I sit right by them at my desk and daub away. The cricket's chirping, it's cozy and peaceful" (94). It is of course paradoxical that the process of mapping the region's "decadent ecosystem" is restorative for Astrov: indeed his evocation of his "daubing away" is one of the few truly idyllic moments in a relentlessly unidyllic play. In Act One Astrov remarks that when he hears the rustling of the young forest he has planted, he "recognizes that in some small way he has power over the climate" (73). His mapmaking, like his tree planting, gives him a perhaps illusory sense of reassurance and control in a world that seems to be going to pot: they are both ways of fixing and shaping a landscape he loves. But the cartographic evocation of a blazingly hot Africa in the last act – eliciting as it does something between resignation and despair – seems to challenge that sense of hope and agency, undercutting the naïve notion that we can simply "plant a tree and save the world."

In his provocative book on maps and landscape painting, the philosopher Edward Casey foregrounds the important distinction, first made by the Greek geographer Ptolemy in the second century AD, between cartography and chorography. The two terms imply very different ways of imagining, representing, and experiencing the world. Cartography is a designation for macromapping – "a representation in picture of the whole known world," as Ptolemy put it. Abstract in its global scale, yet predicated on mathematical precision, cartography is planar and delineative, rather than topographic and descriptive. Chorography, on the other hand – from the Greek *chora*, a specific region – is a form of micromapping executed on a local scale: it encompasses the landscape that a human being takes in naturally with the sweep of the eye. In its richness of detail and its concern to convey the shape or "feel" of the land, chorographic mapping comes close to landscape painting. It is intimate, subjective, and manifestly aesthetic in a way that cartography is not.[26]

Although it contributes, in its idiosyncrasy and incongruity, to the chorographic particularity of the place where it hangs, the map of Africa in *Uncle Vanya* is cartographic, both for the play's audience, which necessarily sees it only from a distance, and for Astrov, who imagines the continent monolithically and abstractly, and fills the whole of its empty outline with a single distinguishing feature: heat. Astrov's own maps, on the other hand, gesture toward chorography.

They are chorographic, first of all, simply because they are emphatically homemade, and reflect, in multiple ways, the place they come from. They are also, after a fashion, works of art: Astrov has evidently lavished a great deal of attention to them on an aesthetic level, and refers to them as his "painting" (*zhivopis'*, 93); in his directions for Act Four Chekhov is at pains to include Astrov's paints and drawing implements, as opposed to his various medical instruments, as stage props. Most importantly, the maps do not merely delineate or evoke, rather they *describe* – indeed, unlike most maps, they actually narrate a whole history. It is true that they encompass a relatively large area – a district (*uezd*) in Russia can scarcely be taken in with the sweep of an eye, or quickly traversed – and they generalize many features of the landscape: Astrov explains that he uses dark and light green shading to indicate forested areas, green with red crosshatching to indicate "where elk and wild goats roamed," blue to show pastureland for cattle and horses (94). It is also true that the play's audience never really sees them, at least in a meaningful way: they exist as a visible prop on the stage, but their content is revealed ekphrastically, through Astrov's emotionally charged descriptions, and it is not always entirely clear what is actually on them and what is mere verbal elaboration on his part. But the abundance of detail that they contain – "Besides the villages and hamlets, you see, here and there are scattered various settlements, little farmsteads, old believer monasteries, watermills" (94) – is unambiguous, and they clearly reflect an intimate, chorographic knowledge on Astrov's part of a territory that he has crisscrossed repeatedly, for more than a decade, on his medical rounds.

We do not know what specific prototypes Chekhov had in mind when he first envisioned Astrov's maps. We do know, however, that in the spring of 1899 he wrote and asked his long-time friend Pyotr Kurkin, a zemstvo doctor in Serpukhov near Melikhovo, the estate Chekhov owned from 1892 to 1899, to find or prepare a suitable "cartogramme" for the Moscow Art Theater's production of *Uncle Vanya*. Kurkin duly drew one up, as he later put it, "from blank maps of Serpukhov district, with the village Melikhov in the center." Chekhov liked it and the theater used it.[27] The link between Astrov's cartogramme and Serpukhov district, Melikhovo, and Kurkin is revealing on several counts. The provenance of the map-as-stage-prop grounds the play concretely – or, we might say, chorographically – in a particular locale, and underscores the role that Chekhov's sojourn at Melikhovo played in the refashioning of *The Wood Demon* into *Uncle Vanya*. In 1892, during his first summer at Melikhovo, Chekhov worked side by side with Kurkin in a local effort to stave off the cholera epidemic that was engulfing parts of southern Russia, and he traveled tirelessly over the sector – some twenty-five villages – that had been assigned to him. Whenever he was at Melikhovo, he regularly received and treated the local peasantry.[28] He appears to have modeled Astrov on himself, in part, and perhaps also on Kurkin.[29] Kurkin was a pioneering figure in the development of public health statistics in Russia, and like Astrov he "personified the Moscow zemstvo physician whose tasks included the correlation of disease with geographic factors."[30] Kurkin, in fact, was doing much the same kind of collecting and compiling of data that Chekhov had undertaken at Sakhalin in 1891 – only in Moscow's back yard, rather than thousands of miles away.[31]

Catherine Evtuhov, in her groundbreaking study of Nizhnii Novgorod province in the second half of the nineteenth century, examines the extraordinarily thick descriptions done in the 1880s, under the aegis of the Nizhnii Novgorod zemstvo, of both the natural history of the province (Vasily Dokuchaev's astoundingly detailed survey of soil types there, complete with district-by-district "soil cartogrammes") and its socioeconomic complexion.[32] Chekhov was probably not directly aware of this work, but the medical-geographic-ethnographic surveying and describing that he undertook on Sakhalin was in the same spirit, and was part of a larger trend in Russian intellectual and public life at the end of the century toward "reading" and mapping the hinterlands in a manifestly "chorographic" way. Jane Costlow's investigation of Vladimir Korolenko's peripatetic slow readings of the backwoods of Nizhnii Novgorod province in the 1890s points to one example. Another was the work of Chekhov and Kurkin as zemstvo doctors: they were engaging in a kind of thick reading of the social, medical, and environmental conditions of the Serpukhov district. Kurkin distilled his data into a series of statistical studies of Moscow province.[33] Chekhov distilled his into Astrov's cartogramme, and, we might say, into *Uncle Vanya* as a whole: the play is an act of descriptive mapping at an even more local scale than Astrov's, an attempt to chart the complex physical and metaphysical ecology of a particular household or *oikos*, and to take measure of its "climate" and health, both figuratively and literally.

While Astrov's chorogaphic impulses reflect the particular ethos of the 1880s and 1890s, they have deeper roots as well. Both in its elaborate artistry and in its descriptive density, Astrov's cartogramme would seem to harken back to a tradition of cadastral mapping in Russia from the eighteenth century and earlier.[34] While Chekhov is unlikely to have laid eyes on many pre-nineteenth-century landholding maps, since few of them were ever published, his cartogramme has affinities with them that suggest some kind of common cultural lineage. Particularly intriguing is the way in which Astrov's maps partake, after their own fashion, in a distinctively Russian cartographic and toponymic practice of systematically marking and memorializing not just presence in a landscape, but also absence and disappearance. Seventeenth- and eighteenth-century cadastral maps consistently recorded the sites of abandoned settlements or *pustoshi* (singular *pustosh'*, from the word "empty"), usually in the form of blank circles with explanatory annotations.[35] Astrov does not specifically use the word *pustosh'* in presenting his cartogramme to Elena. But he makes it abundantly clear that the district is in effect riddled with *pustoshi* – that is, with areas that were once inhabited by people, animals, and birds, but are now empty. One of these places, in fact, is on the Serebriakov estate itself: a two-line exchange between Sonya and the old nanny in Act One – seemingly just a throw-away detail that is every bit as random as the map of Africa in Act Four – reveals that some local peasants have stopped by, evidently not for the first time, to petition about a particular "pustosh'" or "abandoned area" (*Vsë to zhe, opiat' vsë nashchët pustoshi*; 71).[36] In a play that is for the most part claustrophobically confined to the indoors – even Act One, set on the terrace, hews close to the house – this is one of the few, tantalizing glimpses we have of the dynamics of the estate's landscape. As a body of land, as a habitat, it would seem then that this estate, like the vast house full of empty rooms, closely mimics the larger pattern of depopulation and "degeneration" besetting the district. Indeed we might say that *pustoshi* of various sorts – demographic, environmental, psychic, verbal, narrative – are one of the play's defining tropes. These disinhabited spaces are at first flush invisible – mere blanks – but once we look more closely we see their traces everywhere.

While the cartogramme was already present, at least in embryonic form, in *The Wood Demon* (Act Four, Scene Six), the map of Africa was not: it figures only in *Uncle Vanya*. It would seem to be a kind of metonymic marker for Chekhov's increasingly complex and wide-angled anxiety, at the century's close, about climate, environmental degradation, and various impending ends – the end of the gentry "nests" where his plays are set, his own end, the world's end. Chekhov's vision had in a sense panned out – artistically, intellectually, existentially, experientially – between the writing of the two plays: he had developed a much broader – one might even say cosmic – view of the world. This shift is implicit in the metamorphosis of Khrushchev, the original "wood demon" or "leshii," into Astrov: a *leshii* is a manifestly chorographic figure, a woodland spirit or household deity; the name "Astrov," conversely, suggests a much more cosmic, global, or "cartographic" mode of perception.[37] Certainly between the late 1880s, when he wrote *The Wood Demon*, and the second half of the 1890s, when he recycled it into *Uncle Vanya*, Chekhov had become more of a global citizen: in 1890 he traveled by land across Russia to Sakhalin Island, where he spent several months studying convicts, and returned by boat via Hong Kong, Singapore, Ceylon, and the Red Sea, whence he gazed on Mount Sinai in Egypt. In March of 1891, just a few months after his return from Sakhalin, he set off with Suvorin on his first trip to Western Europe, where he would return in 1894, 1897, and 1900; throughout that decade he made vague plans that were never realized to travel to Africa, India, and even the Chicago World's Fair. He was also well aware of the intensifying debate among Russian scientists as to whether climate change in central Russia was anthropogenic (caused by man) or autogenic (natural and cyclical), and by 1890 he had read and reacted enthusiastically to Alexander Voeikov's 1884 book *The Climates of the Globe and of Russia in Particular*.[38]

That said, we can only guess at what Chekhov projected – beyond heat – onto that map of Africa. Chekhov's multiple assertions in various letters throughout the 1890s of his intent to travel to Africa suggest that the continent loomed large in his imagination. He was gripped by romantic fits of wanderlust throughout the decade, and Africa seems to have occupied the same kind of outsized place in his mind that America did in the minds of the young protagonists of his 1887 story "Boys" ("Mal'chiki"). In his paean to Przhevalsky, he mentions Livingstone and Stanley in admiring terms, and he was evidently familiar with the Russian translations of Stanley's *How I Found Livingstone: Travels, Adventures, and Discoveries in Central Africa* (1873) and the follow-up volume *In Darkest Africa* (1890).[39] We cannot help but wonder whether a fantasy along the lines of "Dr. Chekhov, I presume" ever crossed his mind. But we might also wonder if the enormous, distant, overheated continent that strikes Astrov as such "an awful business" represented a kind of Sakhalin Island writ large for Chekhov – that is, as he put it in his letters, "a complete hell," a vast existential and epistemological void, a Kurtzian "heart of darkness."[40] Certainly Chekhov had felt lost, at least in a figurative sense, on Sakhalin – and no Stanley had come looking for him.

Even before traveling halfway around the world, and before writing *The Wood Demon*, Chekhov seems to have been meditating on the possibility of catastrophic ecological "degeneration" on a global scale. In "The Reed Flute," a relentlessly dreary and unironic little story from 1887 that reeks of fin-de-siècle pessimism, the local "disorder in nature" that a peasant shepherd describes – the decline and disappearance of birds, fish, bees, and wild and domestic animals; the drying up of rivers and wetlands; the destruction and withering away of forestlands – takes on broad, apocalyptic significance: "The time has come for God's world to perish," the shepherd intones. "It may be that the world will end soon."[41] It would be absurd, of course, to suggest that Chekhov simply absorbed, uncritically, the religious-apocalyptic worldview of his peasant forbears. But a more modern and no less existentially fraught, fin-de-siècle type of eschatology – grounded in newly revived notions of "deep time" that came out of revolutionary advances in eighteenth- and nineteenth-century geology and biology – runs through a number of Chekhov's works in the 1890s.[42] Indeed, Astrov thinks a mere one hundred (64) or one thousand (73) years ahead; others peered into the more distant and numbing future. In "Ward Six" (1892), for instance, Ragin takes "deep time" to its gloomiest extreme: "Why brain centers and convolutions, why sight, speech, self-awareness, genius, if it is all doomed to sink into the ground and in the final end to cool down along with the earth's crust and then whirl around without sense or purpose, for millions of years, with the earth around the sun?"[43] A few years later, in the famous play-within-a-play in *The Seagull* (1895), Treplev proposes to "dream about what life will be in two hundred thousand years":

> Humans, lions, eagles, and partridges, horned stags, geese, spiders, the silent fish that dwell in the water, starfish, and those invisible to the naked eye – in short, all life forms, all life forms, all life forms, their sad cycle complete, are now extinct . . . Already thousands of centuries have gone by since the earth bore a single living creature, and this poor moon in vain doth light her lantern. No longer does the meadow awaken to the cry of the cranes, and the mayflies sound no longer in the linden groves. Cold, cold, cold. Empty, empty, empty. Awful, awful, awful.[44]

The words are incantatory and poetic – they sound like something by Velimir Khlebnikov – and they limn a delicate line between solemnity and utter ridiculousness. Like Ragin's tortuous musings, they come, of course, from Chekhov's pen, not from his mouth. But it is striking nonetheless that long before Bill McKibben, Chekhov was actively and not *just* ironically imagining "the end of nature," and that long before Alan Weisman, he was meditating on the largest dilemma of the fin de siècle, on "a world without us" – indeed, without any life at all.[45]

In 1895, just a year before Chekhov began refashioning *The Wood Demon* into *Uncle Vanya*, the German physicist Wilhelm Röntgen discovered the x-ray. By the early 1900s it would be widely used as a diagnostic tool in medicine. If x-rays had been taken of Chekhov's lungs during the 1890s, they would have produced a series of images – maps, if you will – that told a story of "degeneration" (*vyrozhdenie*) and "emptying out" (*opustoshenie*) not unlike the one told by Astrov's cartogramme. They would have shown a once healthy natural system that has become increasingly riddled, over time, with dead tissue and tuberculous cavities.[46] "Overall, a picture of gradual and indisputable decline," as Astrov puts it, "which will apparently take another ten to fifteen years to be complete." In Chekhov's case, it didn't even take that long. Though he was loathe to admit to others during that last decade or so of his life that he was dying, the doctor in him no doubt knew the score well enough: he was trapped within the decadent ecosystem of his own consumptive body.[47]

Generally we each cope with thoughts of our own death by assuring ourselves that it is not imminent: our ends somehow remain comfortably deferrable and abstract. For most of his relatively short adult life Chekhov did not have this psychological luxury. As he once put it to Gorky, "Living knowing that you'll end up dying is no picnic, but living knowing that you're going to die before your time – now that's completely absurd."[48] This constant existential pressure, this awareness of his all too imminent end, certainly shaped the way he thought, lived, and wrote. If, as Frank Kermode has suggested, plays and novels and stories are one of the important ways we model and manage our mortality – if they constitute, as he puts it, "the shapes which console the dying generations" – then Chekhov's fictions offer up only an odd sort of consolation.[49] Certainly Mandelstam found scant comfort in *Uncle Vanya*, with its "two-bit census-bureau twaddle," but perhaps in 1936 the play cut too close for comfort. Like Chekhov, he may have intuited the imminence of his own end, which came just two years later. Mandelstam, of course, was living in truly apocalyptic times – when communication and trust had collapsed, when the cultural and social ecosystem was truly decadent, when Russia, like Astrov's maps, would suddenly empty out, full of blank spaces, absences, *pustoshi*. It is no wonder the play put him in a bad mood.

NOTES

1 Osip Mandel'shtam, "O p'ese A. Chekhova 'Diadia Vania' (Nabrosok)," in *Collected Works/Sobranie sochinenii*, edited by Gleb Struve, Nikita Struve, and Boris Filipoff (Paris: YMCA Press, 1981), IV:107–109. In translating this passage I have consulted Anton Chekhov, *The Complete Plays*, edited and translated by Laurence Senelick (New York: W. W. Norton, 2006), 811–812, and *Chekhov's Uncle Vanya and The Wood Demon*, translated by Donald Rayfield (London: Bloomsbury, 1995), 68.

2 See Iu. I. Levin's astute remarks about Mandelstam's "principled non-acceptance" of Chekhov's approach to drama in his note "Zametki k stat'e Mandel'shtama o Chekhove," *Russian Literature* 5:2 (1977): 174–175.

3 "Ecology," in *A Dictionary of Ecology*, 2nd edn., edited by Michael Allaby (Oxford University Press, 1998), 136.

4 Osip Mandelstam, "A Conversation about Dante," in *The Complete Critical Letters and Prose*, edited by Jane Gary Harris (Ann Arbor, MI: Ardis, 1979), 398. Donald Davie suggests that Mandelstam's "classical" and "profoundly traditional" conception of form precluded "the finding of beauty in the discontinuous and asymmetrical." See "Mandelstam's Classicism" in his book *Slavic Excursions: Essays on Russian and Polish Literature* (University of Chicago Press, 1990), 287–289.

5 On "environmental apocalypticism," see Chapter 9 of Lawrence Buell, *The Environmental Imagination: Thoreau, Nature Writing, and the Formation of American Culture* (Cambridge, MA: Harvard University Press, 1996), 280–308.

6 *A Dictionary of Ecology*, 136.

7 See Simon Karlinsky, "Huntsmen, Birds, Forests, and Three Sisters," in *Chekhov's Great Plays*, 150–151, and 158, note 11; "Ekologiia," in *Brokgaus-Efron Entsiklopedicheskii slovar'*, vol. XL/LXXIX, edited by Ivan Andrievskii (St. Petersburg, 1904), 256. The entry was written by Vladimir Mikhailovich Shimkevich (1858–1923), a biologist. For an account of how the word "ecology" gradually accumulated its "complicated burden of meaning," see Donald Worster, *Nature's Economy: A History of Ecological Ideas* (Cambridge University Press, 1985), 190–193.

8 Worster, *Nature's Economy*, 378.

9 Gary Saul Morson, "*Uncle Vanya* as Prosaic Metadrama," in *Reading Chekhov's Text*, edited by Robert Louis Jackson (Evanston, IL: Northwestern University Press, 1993), 225. For a subtle discussion of the mix of exhortation, understatement, and irony at work in the play's treatment of environmental themes, see Jane Costlow, "Imaginations of Destruction: The 'Forest Question' in Nineteenth-Century Russian Culture," *The Russian Review* 62 (2003): 114–116.

10 See, for instance, Thomas Newlin, "At the Bottom of the River: Forms of Ecological Consciousness in Mid-Nineteenth-Century Russian Literature," *Russian Studies in Literature* 39:2 (2003): 71–90; Costlow, "Imaginations of Destruction" and *Heart-Pine Russia*; David Moon, "The Debate over Climate Change in the Steppe Region in Nineteenth-Century Russia," *The Russian Review* 69 (2010): 251–275, and *The Plough That Broke the Steppes: Agriculture and Environment on Russia's Grasslands, 1700–1914* (Oxford University Press, 2013).

11 There is substantial overlap in Russian between the concepts "environment" and "ecology." "Environment" is the somewhat awkward "okruzhaiushchaia sreda," while the adjectival form "environmental" is typically rendered as "ekologicheskii."

12 Worster, *Nature's Economy*, 193.

13 On Voeikov and Dokuchaev see Moon, "The Debate over Climate Change."

14 On Chekhov's knowledge of and interest in geography, climate, and the environment, see Ian M. Matley, "Chekhov and Geography," *The Russian Review* 31:4 (1972): 376–382; and Karlinsky, "Huntsmen, Birds, Forests, and Three Sisters."

15 Mandel'shtam, "O p'ese A. Chekhova 'Diadia Vania' (Nabrosok)," 107.

16 S. Vasil'eva (the pseudonym of S. V. Flerova), "Teatral'naia khronika," *Moskovskie vedemosti* 1, quoted in *Letopis' zhizni i tvorchestva A. P. Chekhova*, edited by I. Iu. Tverdokhlebov (Moscow: Nasledie IMLI, 2004), 11:311–312.

17 Chekhov, *Polnoe sobranie sochinenii i pisem*, edited by N. F. Bel'chikov et al. (Moscow: Nauka, 1974–1983): *Sochineniia* XII:385, 392. References to this edition will hereafter be indicated as *PSS* for *Sochineniia* or *PSP* for *Pis'ma*, followed by volume and page number. All references to *Uncle Vanya* in vol. XIII of the *PSS* will be indicated in the body of the text by page number only, in parentheses.

18 *PSP* XII:391.

19 Reproduced in *PSP* XIII:111. The summary account in the *PSS* of the publishing history of the work (XIII:387) does not reproduce or comment on this mistake.

20 *PSS* XIII:419.

21 *PSS* XIII:413–414.

22 See Aleksandr Krinitsyn, "Problema 'vyrozhdeniia' u Chekhova i Maksa Nordau," in *Chekhov v Germanii*, edited by V. B. Kataev and R.-D. Kluge (Moscow: Universitet, 1996), 165–170.

23 See the chapters by Holland and Bowers in this volume.

24 *PSS* XIII:409.

25 *PSP*, September 30, 1899; VIII:272.

26 Edward S. Casey, "Cartography and Chorography," in *Representing Place: Landscape Painting and Maps* (Minneapolis: University of Minnesota Press, 2002), 154–157, 169.

27 *PSS* XIII:396.

28 M. P. Chekhov, *Vokrug Chekhova: vstrechi i vpechatleniia* (Moscow: Moskovskii Rabochii, 1980), 81, 203–204.

29 K. M. Vinogradova, *Chekhov v Melikhove* (Moscow: Moskovskii Rabochii, 1959), 104.

30 Nancy Mandelker Frieden, *Russian Physicians in the Era of Reform and Revolution* (Princeton University Press, 1981), 93.

31 See Conevery Bolton Valenčius, "Chekhov's *Sakhalin Island* as a Medical Geography," in *Chekhov the Immigrant: Translating a Cultural Icon*, edited by Michael C. Finke and Julie de Sherbinin (Bloomington, IN: Slavica, 2007), 299–314.

32 Catherine Evtuhov, *Portrait of a Russian Province: Economy, Society, and Civilization in Nineteenth-Century Nizhnii Novgorod* (University of Pittsburgh Press, 2011), 19–20, 165–181; color plates 1, 4, and 6 reproduce several of Dokuchaev's district "soil cartogrammes" (*pochvennye kartogrammy*).

33 See, among other works, his *Detskaia smertnost' v Moskovskoi gubernii i ee uezdakh v 1883–1897 gg.* (Moscow, 1902) and *Statistika boleznenosti naseleniia v Moskovskoi gubernii za period 1883–1902 gg.* (Moscow, 1907).

34 See M. A. Tsvetkov, "Cartographic Results of the General Survey of Russia 1766–1861," in *Essays on the History of Russian Cartography 16th to 19th Centuries*, edited and translated by James R. Gibson, Supplement No. 1 to *Canadian Cartographer* (University of Toronto Press, 1975), XII:91–104; XII:1–7; L. A. Shaposhnikova, *Izobrazhenie lesa na kartakh* (Moscow: Akademiia nauk, 1957), 5–14; and especially Chapters 3 and 4 of Valerie Kivelson, *Cartographies of Tsardom: The Land and Its Meanings in Seventeenth-Century Russia* (Ithaca, NY: Cornell University Press, 2006).

35 See Kivelson's fascinating discussion of "empty lands" in seventeenth-century Muscovite maps. *Cartographies of Tsardom*, 67–72, and plates 2–14.

36 English translations of the play generally do not render the word *pustosh'* in a way that conveys its precise meaning. It is worth noting that Chekhov plays with variations on the root for "empty" (*pust*) throughout the play. Early on (72) Astrov uses the verb *opustoshat'sia* (literally, "to become empty") to underscore the habitat destruction resulting from the felling of Russian forests; toward the very end of the play (110) he uses the related noun *opustoshenie* ("devastation" or, literally, "emptying") to describe the damage Elena and her husband would wreak if they were to remain on the estate.

37 The name also hints at the problematic arrogance that sometimes accompanies what Morson calls "apocalyptic or utopian" vision and rhetoric (Morson, "*Uncle Vanya* as Prosaic Metadrama," 226). Astrov admits that when he drinks he feels god-like, that he conjures up his own "philosophical system" and views his fellow human beings as "microbes" (82).

38 See his letter of March 22, 1890 to Suvorin, in which he requests a copy of A. Voeikov, *Klimaty zemnogo shara v osobennosti Rossii* (St. Petersburg, 1884). On Voeikov and nineteenth-century Russian views on climate change, see Moon, "The Debate over Climate Change."

39 *PSS* XVI:236. Genri Stenli, *Kak ia nashel Livingstona*, Pts. 1–2 (St. Petersburg, 1873); Genri Stenli, *V debriakh Afriki*, Pts. 1–2 (St. Petersburg, 1892). He refers to the first work in his story "A Reporter's Dream." See "Son reportera," *Budil'nik* 7 (1884): 86–87; the latter work is mentioned in a kartoteka he compiled in connection with his book on Sakhalin (*PSS* XV:897).

40 See Cathy Popkin's provocative essay "Chekhov as Ethnographer: Epistemological Crisis on Sakhalin Island," *Slavic Review* 51:1 (1992): 36–51.

41 *PSS* VI:323–324, 328.

42 On "deep time" see Stephen Jay Gould, *Time's Arrow, Time's Cycle* (Cambridge, MA: Harvard University Press, 1987).

43 *PSS* VIII:90. Translation from Anton Chekhov, *Selected Stories*, translated by Richard Pevear and Larissa Volokhonsky (New York: Random House, 2000), 188.

44 *PSS* XIII:13.

45 I refer here to Bill McKibben's book *The End of Nature* (New York: Anchor, 1989), which played a key role in raising public awareness of the imminent threat of anthropogenic climate change, and Alan Weisman's *The World Without Us* (New York: St. Martin's Press, 2007), a best-selling account of what would happen to the planet if the human race suddenly disappeared from it entirely.

46 It is worth noting that nineteenth-century medicine approached the body cartographically. One of the texts that Chekhov used as a medical student was titled *Descriptive and Topographical Human Anatomy: An Atlas* (*Opisatel'naia i topograficheskaia anatomiia cheloveka: Atlas*). See S. Balukhatyi, "Biblioteka Chekhova," in *Chekhov i ego sreda*, edited by N. F. Bel'chikov (Leningrad: Akademiia, 1930), 335.

47 Michael Finke has explored with great subtlety Chekhov's vexed relationship, as a consumptive and a doctor, with the scientific-medical discourse of "degeneration" as it applied to himself and his family. See his *Seeing Chekhov*, Chapter 3, and "Heal Thyself, Hide Thyself: Why Did Chekhov Ignore His TB?," in *Chekhov the Immigrant*, 285–297.

48 Maksim Gor'kii, "A. P. Chekhov," in *A. P. Chekhov v vospominaniiakh sovremennikov*, edited by N. I. Gitovich (Moscow: Khudozhestvennaia literatura, 1986), 453.

49 Kermode, *The Sense of an Ending*, 3.

CHAPTER 13

The mute body
Leonid Andreev's abject realism

Edith W. Clowes

[T]he abject has only one quality of the object – that of being opposed to *I*. If the object, however, through its opposition, settles me within the fragile texture of a desire for meaning, which, as a matter of fact, makes me ceaselessly and infinitely homologous to it, what is *abject*, on the contrary, the jettisoned object, is radically excluded and draws me toward the place where meaning collapses.
                                            – Julia Kristeva, *Powers of Horror*[1]

Beyond conveying credible scenarios of Russian life to their readers, realist writers debated and satirized injustice and inhumanity and set forth arguments for social change. To the degree that famous works of literary realism spurred passionate debate and inspired progress, those claims were historically justified. By the 1890s, however, "high" realism as a style had itself become the object of debate and parody. As such, it offered grounds for fresh experimentation. Among the most aesthetically radical and widely read and debated experiments were the truly fin-de-siècle stories of the young Russian neorealist, Leonid Andreev.

At the turn of the century an array of new directions branched from the realist tradition – Chekhov's "impressionist" stories of private despair; Gorky's rebellious tales of ragged heroes from the formerly invisible "lower depths" of Russian society; Merezhkovsky's, Gippius's, and Sologub's symbolist novels that sought historical and mythical regeneration but found dark disintegration; Andreev's psychological realism that bordered on nightmare; and the popular sex and society novels – Verbitskaia's six-volume *Keys to Happiness* and Nagrodskaia's *Wrath of Dionysus* – that popularized all of these elements. For the first time in Russian history, a rapid expansion of literacy at the turn of the century caused a complex layering of the readership into elite, highly educated readers; middlebrow readers thirsty for the themes, if not the difficult prose, of elite literature; and mass readers interested in easy adventure tales. Developing in part from experience with social commentary and feuilleton journalism, younger realists, first

Chekhov, and later Gorky, Bunin, and Andreev, wrote stories immediately accessible to newer, less cultivated readers.[2] In the twentieth century's first decade, these new forms of realism – historico-mythic, impressionist, revolutionary realist, and allegorical – tore at the fabric of moral and social convention, behavior, and belief. To this complex "neorealist" texture Andreev added a radically despairing tone that both generated a dark view of a disintegrating society and enhanced an already existing mood of anxiety and distress in its readers.

This chapter investigates Andreev, this most extreme of realists, not because he was unusually innovative but because he was a literary celebrity directly at the turn of the century. His early stories were enormously popular and sold in multiple editions. In many ways his writing – so different from others' sometimes hopeful, sometimes resolute search for principles of social and spiritual renewal – lay at the very heart of the fin-de-siècle mood that is this volume's focus. Contemporary writers, especially the more esoteric symbolists, often viewed his writing as derivative and exaggerated.[3] However, his writing style and themes resonated among newer, more credulous readers – particularly the younger generation of students. Andreev was one of Russia's first middlebrow writers, a literary popularizer who opened crucial social, philosophical, and psychological themes to the rapidly increasing Russian readership.[4] Some stories even became case studies for professional doctors and psychologists at the Academy of Medicine in St. Petersburg.[5] Widely viewed as expressing the anxieties of the turn of the century, Andreev's art both reverberated with and strengthened a mood of despair among his readers.[6] His stories embodied the fin-de-siècle mood – a mood of deep metaphysical doubt, decline of social and sexual mores, utter dejection and loss of belief in social and political progress. Written and published in Andreev's most popular period, three provocative stories and novellas – "The Abyss" (*Bezdna*, 1902), "The Red Laugh" (*Krasnyi smekh*, 1904), and "Seven People Hanged" (*Rasskaz o semi poveshennykh*, 1907) – capture the essence of this fin-de-siècle dilemma.

Critics have tended to see Andreev as a bridge figure between realism and symbolism, a generalization that is true enough but stops short of concrete definition of his style. When German expressionism became known in Russia in the 1920s, in a 1928 article, "Expressionism in Russia: Leonid Andreev's Plays," the Viatka scholar K. V. Driagin immediately recognized Andreev as a Russian expressionist avant la lettre.[7] The "expressionist" reading of Andreev can be solidified by focusing on his treatment of the abused human body in a variety of forms – sexual, military, and social-political. Like the late Tolstoy and Artsybashev, who, as Ani Kokobobo argues in this volume, sought to reinvent conventional realism through the grotesque, Andreev radicalized defining features of classical nineteenth-century realism to peel away social taboos and expose the horror of human existence. He did so, I argue, through an entirely expressionist style I will call "abject realism."

In her by now classic treatment, *Powers of Horror: An Essay on Abjection*, Julia Kristeva defines the abject as both a liminal condition and a form of consciousness, situated in feelings of loathing and dread. The abject "it," in her view, is "neither subject nor object," both "me" and "not me."[8] It is expressed variously in figures of bodily waste such as nail parings, feces, menstrual blood, the decaying body, and – perhaps most powerfully for Kristeva's purposes, though not for Andreev's – the powerful psycho-symbolic figure of the mother, embedded in the viewer's consciousness, from which the viewer strains to but can never fully detach himself or herself. The abject is a formless "jettisoned object" that is the stuff of taboo.[9] Beyond its clear repulsive force, the abject, importantly, has a fascination for "me," the subject. The abject consciousness has the fundamental power to undermine canonized systems of value and belief. If the "object" answers my "desire for meaning," the abject dangerously attracts me "toward the place where meaning collapses."[10]

Andreev's abject realism, then, treats the protagonist's transgression of laws governing taboo and his life-changing confrontation with the abject. In the three stories under discussion the dominant figure of the abject is the "mute body," that body that appears human but cannot speak for itself or respond in a recognizably "human" way. For Andreev, communicating through language is the basic, defining characteristic for being human. As poorly as his characters understand one another, it is nonetheless the very act of speaking that assures them, and us, that the human spirit is alive and responsive, and that there is hope. In Andreev's fiction the abject is symbolized by the silenced, "mute" human body that has somehow been abused. In this figure we stand on a disturbing border between the physical body, as such, and the body infused with mind and spirit. It is the violated body – the "mute body," either dead or near the edge of death – that represents the abject. The abject body can no longer articulate human sensibility. This concept of the abject offers us the focal point of Andreev's "realism," which draws us to the place where existential meaning, no matter how it is framed – as religious faith, social project, or philosophical system – is always shown to be a construct that will fail. The "real," in Andreev's work, is no longer found on the playing field of social interactions, as it is in classical nineteenth-century realism. Social convention is always a mask, a surface phenomenon, which Andreev compulsively strips away to probe the repressed "real" lying beneath.

In "On Realism in Art" (1921) and "Two Aspects of Language" (1956) Roman Jakobson defined realism as featuring a "syntagmatic" dominant, defined through relations of "contiguity." In this definition, the terms of a literary image – i.e., "thing or person x" resembles in some fashion "image y" – function on a figurative "horizontal" plane. Here by "horizontal plane" we mean social-psychological and material relations in the physical world where both terms are accessible to the five human senses and to human reason. This plane is conveyed through the device of precise, so-called "scientific" observation on the part of a relatively "objective" narrator. And, in Jakobson's definition, the poetics of literary realism is dominated by the figure of metonymy with its focus on images of part for whole and relations of contiguity between a character and the objects around that character.[11] Other classic definitions, such as Ian Watt's in *The Rise of the Novel* (1957), forego the poetic definition but focus on the narrator's claim to "objective" observation and the narrative's seamless imitation of sensory actuality as the dominants defining realist art.

Nineteenth-century Russian realism soon subverted both of those definitions, creating instead metaphorical emblems of psychological experience that cannot be perceived through the five senses alone. Starting with Dostoevsky's *Notes from Underground* (1864), in Garshin's "Red Flower" (1883) and, most scandalously, in Tolstoy's *Kreutzer Sonata* (1889), thematic "radicalization" revolved around the unconventional treatment of sex, violence, and madness that goes beyond traditional euphemisms. The surface of traditional social mores and moral consciousness is penetrated to probe violent unconscious urges.[12]

All of these works radicalize realism in a number of ways. As implied in both Jakobson's and Watt's realist concept of "observation," – the Latin etymology of which means "watching over" – the traditional realist world is conveyed through figures of sight. In contrast, both *Notes from Underground* and *Kreutzer Sonata* prefer the auditory, the vocalization of subliminal drives traditionally hidden from polite speech. All three works challenge the metonymic dominant traditional to realism and deepen the work's aura of actuality on a vertical or "paradigmatic" plane, creating an allegory of the unconscious in *Notes from Underground*; a symbol of hidden evil in Garshin's image of the red flower; and a work of music, Beethoven's "Kreutzer Sonata," as the emblems of or gateways to the unconscious. By contrast, Andreev's realism appeals to touch and feel, as well as sight, to probe unconscious fears.

Among the hotly debated aspects, particularly of Tolstoy's late realism, was the dehumanization of the female body. In his long essay, "The Meaning of Love" (1892), the philosopher Vladimir Solovev discredited contemporary male fetishizing of the female body, reconceiving this perception as the destructive effect of male egoism. Implicit in his critique was a poetics of prevalent social attitudes that foregrounded synecdoche. For example, as he observed, "in many people, almost always of the masculine sex, [sexual] feeling is mainly, and sometimes exclusively, aroused by one or the other part of the anatomy of the opposite sex (for example, hair, hand, foot), or even . . . certain pieces of clothing."[13] Through such views, Solovev argued, the female body is deprived of its independent, integral humanity and is reduced to a mere object that pleases the male sexual drive. Instead, Solovev offered metaphors of the spiritualized and transfigured body, seeing women as integral humans who have a voice, participate actively in building the ideal relationship of love, and are endowed with selfhood.

A number of critics have pointed out the importance of some anatomical synecdoches in Andreev's work, particularly eyes and hands.[14] Importantly, Andreev responded to the debate on love and sex in his most scandalous stories, "The Abyss" and "In the Fog" (*V tumane*).[15] Here he intensified the treatment of the metonymized female body as the site of violated humanity. In later works Andreev extended similar strategies to address issues of war, abuses of government power, and capital punishment – taking all these themes beyond the traditional realist treatment of social issues to reveal an existential horror at the human condition.

Critics' negative response to these stories made Andreev into an instant celebrity. While Gorky defended "The Abyss," the co-director of the Moscow Art Theater, Vladimir Nemirovich-Danchenko, called it a "monstrosity," "of which there is quite a lot in life."[16] Answering the charge that the stories were little more than vulgar pornography, Andreev joked that, in contrast to "Graf" Tolstoy (Count Tolstoy), he had become the "Porno-Graf," or Count Porn.[17] In surveys of student readers, both men and women, most respondents particularly liked "The Abyss" but uniformly saw it, if not directly as pornography, then as very disturbing. The story, in the view of many, forced readers to probe the psychology of desire rather than directly increasing sexual desire.[18] Andreev would take his stylistic and thematic approach far beyond the sexual atomization of these early stories to deal with war, political terror, and government oppression.

Even while popularizing motifs from Tolstoy, Dostoevsky, Nietzsche, Schopenhauer, and others, Andreev's achievement in these early twentieth-century works was to develop abject realism in order to lift the mask of social convention – first to unmask traditional ideals of young love, and, in later works, the ideals of valor in war and the justice of capital punishment. Before examining the functions of abject realism, it will help to summarize the three stories, since they are no longer widely known and read in the English-speaking world. Using the form of an existential allegory, "The Abyss" treats the gang rape of a young woman, Zinaida Nikolaevna, and its impact on the psyche of her beloved, Nevedomsky. The pair are out walking at sunset and come into an unfamiliar suburban wasteland inhabited by tramps and prostitutes. Three tramps pummel the young man and attack the young woman, leaving her unconscious. The young man, half-conscious, attempts to revive and comfort his beloved, only then himself to ravish her unconscious body.

"The Red Laugh" deals with a young officer's experience of war, inspired by the Russo-Japanese War. The first of two parts is a series of fragments from the officer's diary that convey the visceral horrors of war. The second part consists of a narrative by the officer's brother after the officer's return home. The brother depicts the officer's death – he has lost both legs and is a cripple – and meditates on the officer's experience and the possibility of heroism in war. The novella ends with the brother's own fantasies about death and unhinged mental state, brought on by reading his officer-brother's war diary.

"Seven People Hanged" deals with the anticipation of death. Inspired by the Grand Duke's assassination in 1905, the novella first treats a government minister's fearful anticipation of his own assassination, imagining his body grotesquely exploded to bits. Most of the work is devoted to the meditations on death of five revolutionaries and two ordinary criminals as they wait in prison in the days before their execution. The effect of the novella is to celebrate the revolutionaries as the most spiritually elevated of all the characters.

Drawing on Kristeva's definition of the abject as the "jettisoned object," which we dread and loathe, that both psychically adheres to us and repels us, we can see that the characters in all these stories are drawn against their conscious will to that liminal "place where meaning collapses."[19] In Andreev's works the abject is marked by the physical body – violated, debilitated, or dead – while psychologically the abject can refer to taboo urges and fears in the unconscious of the protagonist. For Andreev, the emblem for this condition is the abused and mute corporeal body, which is both "me" and "not me," "mine," and a loathed "not mine," with which the speaker identifies and from which he (it is always a male character) is repulsed.

Andreev uses a number of tactics that narrow perspective and generalize temporal and spatial context in order to focus attention on the abject. His narratives often teeter on the edge between traditional realist description and psychological allegory for the life of the unconscious.[20] He creates a generally recognizable setting but without specific social or historical identifiers, bringing the story close to an allegory. The narrative perspective often features one moral consciousness without reference to other perspectives or points of reference. Through some form of physical and psychological trauma his characters become alienated, dysfunctional, and, in some cases, insane.

Andreev's three stories convey what we may call the "narrative" of the abject body. Here screens raised by social conventions fail and fade to reveal the brute physical and psychological "real," an "It" that Andreev struggles to name.[21] In "The Abyss" the protagonist resists the reality of the abject, first treating the mute female body as still alive and capable of consciousness, only then to succumb to his hitherto suppressed sexual urges and further abusing and repulsing the body, making it abject. "The Red Laugh" creates the atomized, abject male body that contrasts to and undermines a traditional narrative about the glories of war. In "Seven People Hanged" Andreev literally explodes the metaphorical, though no less oppressive, "political body," rendering it abject. The narrator then resists the inevitable death of the revolutionaries, putting their meditations on death in poignant contrast to their ultimately loathsome bodies, as they are loaded onto a cart after execution.

The indeterminate nature of their settings makes these works generally allegorical. Temporally and spatially liminal, "The Abyss" sets the two young lovers' walk, the thematic treatment of sexual mores, and the sexual body in a transitional time of day, evening, with a bloody red sunset followed by darkness; the story's odd landscape could be anywhere, featuring woods and a wasteland with pits inhabited by marginal human figures.[22] The lack of specific features in this inner landscape makes it physically and psychically difficult for the characters to find their way. One soon senses that this evening stroll is more than a walk in the suburbs; it is an existential walk through the thickets of life, and, ultimately, the "place where meaning collapses."

In an extreme form "The Abyss" enacts the attitude taken from Schopenhauer and Tolstoy that love is an epiphenomenon, masking sexual drive and a will to control the other. The mask of romantic love is gradually peeled away to reveal the abject. To start with, the protagonist Nemovetsky is dishonest with himself and the increasingly worried Zinaida Nikolaevna: in order to preserve the appearance of his authority, Nemovetsky lies about knowing the path to safety.[23] As the pair enter the wasteland and encounter poorly dressed female figures, Zinaida Nikolaevna becomes more fearful. Nemovetsky lies to her, claiming not to know who these "dirty women" are, although, in fact, he knows very well that they are prostitutes, whom he has visited.[24]

In this world daylight rather stereotypically symbolizes the rule of reason and consciously held moral values, and darkness is the realm of the unconscious. The abject – the suppressed sexual drives in Nemovetsky's psyche, of which he is ashamed and about which he lies – emerges only after dark. Even in daylight, Nemovetsky's perception of his beloved is corporeal and synecdochal, echoing Solovev's image of the egotist, concerned with his own sexual needs. Thinking about her, he isolates hair, hand, leg, eye – never embracing the whole person. More disturbing, subliminally he wants to cause pain to Zinaida Nikolaevna, all the while imagining to himself that he is offering her support. While chatting with her about literary lovers, he finds himself wanting to "squeeze [Zinaida's] quivering little hand till it hurt."[25] Although Nemovetsky's behavior remains gentlemanly until night falls, he still thinks of Zinaida Nikolaevna in atomized, metonymizing terms. He is disturbed by Zinaida's white petticoats and "shapely leg" but, ashamed, "with an unconscious effort of will stifle[s]" his imagination.[26]

It is worth noting, too, that Zinaida Nikolaevna also thinks of the strangers they encounter in metonymies. In a rare switch to her perspective, she thinks about the so-called "dirty women" in the wilderness they are traversing.[27] She is struck by the "hopelessness" of their condition, conveyed in her metonymic consciousness by the dirty hem of the thin dress worn by one of the prostitutes.[28] At this point her fascination with and repulsion from the prostitutes add to the atmosphere of the abject.

Zinaida Nikolaevna is lively and responsive before sunset, but becomes increasingly mute after twilight. Muteness or unresponsiveness become her physical attributes; for example, Nemovetsky lets go of her "mute (*nemoi*) hand."[29] After the rape she loses consciousness, and her body is described a number of times as "this voiceless (*bezglasnyi*) female body."[30] It has lost its personhood. Zinaida's body becomes fully abject only through Nemovetsky's response of visceral loathing: "His hand hit upon the bared body, smooth, firm, cold, but not dead and with a shudder he jerked it away."[31] When he refuses to accept the humanity of this naked, abused, now mute body, Nemovetsky has completed the process of abjection. He cannot bear the implication of his own human fragility and rejects Zinaida as its physical embodiment.

"The Abyss" caused a public uproar when it first appeared early in 1902. In a letter to the editor of *Novoe vremia*, Countess Sofia Tolstaia accused Andreev of undermining public morals.[32] In response, Andreev perversely wrote his own letter to his editor at *Kur'er*, signing it from the story's protagonist, Nemovetsky. In this letter the abjection of the female body becomes irrepressible when "Nemovetsky" writes: "She became physically repugnant to me, disgusting and completely alien. I made an involuntary move to push her away and, when my hand touched her naked shoulder, I felt her chilled body's cold, and it suddenly struck me that this body was not just cold but covered with some sort of revolting, cold slime."[33] While, in the story, Nemovetsky the character offered to marry Zinaida and defend her honor, now that character, "defending himself," intends to abandon her and never see her again.

In "The Red Laugh" Andreev turns to the abject male body, stripping away the conventional justifications of war. Too obvious for informed readers, Andreev made this theme riveting for a younger, more recently literate reading public. For example, Andreev's nameless narrator, writing in his diary, conveys the nature of war in the story's first line: "madness and horror," adjectives that quickly became trite reminders of Andreev's style.[34] The narrator of journal fragments, a young officer, sees the soldiers as already half-crazed: "we moved, did our business, talked and even laughed, and we were just like – lunatics. Our movements were sure and swift, the commands were clear and their execution precise – but if all of a sudden one were to ask a soldier who he was, he would be hard pressed to find the answer in his confused brain."[35] Although everything in the army goes according to precise plans, underneath it all there is no sense of firm identity and no clear justification for the actions being taken. For Andreev, those failures of definition mark the onset of mass insanity.

War in this story is no longer about patriotism, heroic deeds, and the protection of the homeland. One soldier dreams only of taking a bath and getting rid of skin infections.[36] The doctor in the military clinic observes that war has inculcated soldiers with a love of killing and destroying, and has driven the public mad: "A merry, carefree band of brave men – we'll destroy everything [belonging to the enemy]: their buildings, their universities and museums; merry fellows, full of fiery laughter – we'll dance on their ruins. I proclaim the mad house to be our fatherland; and anyone who is still sane – our enemies."[37] In the name of glory, war has unleashed a powerful subliminal drive to tear everything apart, which ultimately can destroy the very order it initially proposed to defend.

The creation of the abject male body depends on the body's liminal nature and the viewer's double response of simultaneous fascination and revulsion, the familiarity of the human and dehumanizing alienation. The Kristevan border space, in which the cognizing subject's desire for meaning confronts the collapse of all meaning, is the rotting human body: "his back is red, as if he were alive, and only a slight yellowish pall, like that of smoked meat, gives a hint of death. Though I want to move away from him, I have no strength and, unsteady, I watch the endless, ghostly lines of men swaying as they walked. From how my head feels, although I know that I am having sunstroke, I react calmly."[38] Depicted through radical metonymy, the abject body, stripped of its social meaning, is linked to a number of oppositions – living versus dead; human versus edible food. The narrator compares the soldier's corpse to smoked meat, although, in his view, its red color makes it seem alive. As in "The Abyss," the protagonist's response confirms the abject condition – the protagonist is simultaneously drawn enough to the body to describe it and revolted by it. He himself is the victim of trauma, mentally – the shock of massive human destruction, and physically – a sunstroke.

Violently destroyed bodies in war soon become ghastly, only then to be fully dehumanized as grotesquely distorted body parts, under the aegis of the "red laugh" of death, itself a strange synecdoche, at once visual and auditory. In the second fragment, one soldier's face is blown off, replaced by a Quentin Tarantino-like image of blood gushing lavishly from the severed neck, like champagne from a bottle. In this image the narrator sees the horrifyingly real vision of a symbolic, even "supernatural," "red laugh" of death: "At that moment something happened – incomprehensible, monstrous, supernatural. A warm breeze blew on my right cheek and almost made me tumble, and before my very eyes something short, blunt, red replaced the pale visage, and blood poured from it as if from an uncorked bottle, the ones you see on a badly painted signboard. And in this short, red, flowing thing you could continually see a kind of smile, a toothless laugh – the red laugh."[39]

Mangled bodies pierced by stakes on the battle line now absurdly resemble dancing dolls, as the narrator loses his own sensitivity to pain: "Some of [the soldiers], as if blind, slipped into deep, funnel-like pits and pinned by their stomachs on sharp spears, jerked and danced, like toy clowns; new bodies pressed onto these ones, and soon the whole pit was filled to the brim with bloodied bodies, living and dead."[40]

The last event of this clearly antiwar story is the encroaching insanity of the dead officer's brother who ends the story with a nightmarish vision of the fallen lying in straight, even rows on the street. The humane idea motivating this vision is the desire that not one of the dead be forgotten. The brother, however, fears for his own life as the ever-increasing numbers of corpses filling the city, now claiming floor space in his own house, squeeze and suffocate him. When all the room on the street is taken, the corpses appear in their regular rows in the officer's family's house, from which it now becomes impossible to escape. Pity and honor of the dead will strangle the living. The abject here becomes apparent in the brother's conflicting responses – both his desire to honor the dead, and thus to find meaning in the horror of war, and his utter horror at the prospect of being buried alive by the encroaching masses of corpses. There is no way to control the slaughter of war. This site of abjection is another place where "meaning collapses." There is no empathy. All that remains is madness.

Andreev begins "Seven People Hanged" with the government minister's anticipated assassination and his vision of his own exploded body and then deals with each of the seven prisoners' anticipations of his or her own death, most of which now resist abjection. The minister most clearly becomes abject. To start with, he views himself as powerful and surrounded by impenetrable security, until he is alone in bed in the dark in a strange "safe house." I quote at some length to give the full sense of the minister's self-abjection:

> He remembered all the recent horrors, one after the other, when bombs were being thrown at people of his high estate, and even higher, and bombs ripped the body into festoons, spewed brains across the filthy brick walls, broke teeth out of their sockets. And from these memories his own ill, obese body, splayed on the bed, seemed to him already to be alien, already experiencing the fiery force of the explosion; and he imagined that his arms and shoulders were separating from his body, his teeth were falling out, his brain was falling into pieces, his legs were losing feeling and lay obediently, toes up, like a corpse.[41]

Here, in the terrified minister's imagination, his own abject, silenced body loses its political presence, turned into a series of synecdoches. In the exploded body we encounter a radical trope we might think of as synecdoche without metonymy, without social or other contiguity. The effect is radical abjection. As a further step in the process of abjection, the minister becomes a mere human being. As such, he realizes that he is revolted by his own body: "his short, fat neck horrified him, and it was unbearable to look at his swollen short fingers, to feel how short and how full of mortal fluid they were."[42] There is nothing powerful or vital in this corporeal image.

"Seven People Hanged" stands in contrast to much of Andreev's writing. Although the revolutionaries here generally resist the power of the abject even as they contemplate their imminent deaths, ultimately, no one can overcome the abjection of the human body – even through total, ascetic devotion to the spirit. Of particular note is the experience of the tough young revolutionary Musia whose preparation to die resists the power of the abject. She is thoroughly ascetic, rejecting the allure of the body, the unconscious, and their subliminal drives. Her body is white, almost transparent: "She was very pale, but not pale like a corpse; her body had the special burning white paleness produced by that powerful flame burning inside a person; when the body shows translucent like fine Sèvres china."[43] This transparency suggests her deep ascetic control over her body. Although not yet directly related to Orthodox iconography, but rather to the Western image of Sèvres bone china, the translucence shows a body that is the opposite of abject. Here Musia's spirit shines through her body; her mind has taken control over matter. And she embraces the death that so many want to escape. In that condition she finds admirable strength – and, in fact, may be among the strongest of Andreev's characters.

Interestingly, in her ascetic embrace of death, like many historical Russian revolutionaries, Musia invokes a number of Orthodox spiritual values. By overcoming the horror of physical death, she can overcome the abject.[44] In Chapter 7, titled "There Is No Death," we find a rare vision of overcoming physical death and fear of death. Importantly, here we encounter the full desexualization of the female body. Musia owns a ring with a skull, bones, and a wreath of thorns around them, clearly symbolizing Christ's crucifixion. While in "The Abyss" the female hand is a synecdoche of the sexualized body, the fact that Musia wears this ring removes sexual connotations from her hand and shows her devotion to a higher ideal. In short, the ring returns spiritual autonomy to her body. Musia finds joy in dying and embraces her impending death. Aspects of Orthodox belief buttress her belief in her own death, and we find the vocabulary of Orthodoxy in her thinking – words such as martyr (*muchenik*), blessed (*blazhennyi*), and joy (*radost'*). She thinks of herself as too young to have achieved anything:

> Musia . . . justified herself with the idea that she – a young, insignificant, unaccomplished woman, not a hero, was being subjected to the same honorable and sublime death that real heroes and martyrs before her had suffered. With unshakeable belief in human goodness, empathy, love she imagined to herself how anxious people were for her, how they were suffering, and how

they were pitying her – and she felt so guilty she started to blush. It was as if by hanging on the gallows, she was committing a great impropriety.[45]

Death is liberation, and Musia believes in immortality. In corporeal death a person can be transformed and illuminated. There is no abjection here because her dread of the taboo has been conquered:

> And an ineffable joy overwhelms her. There is no doubt, no wavering, she is accepted into the lap [of God], she has the right to join the ranks of the illuminati (*svetlye*), who over the centuries ascended to high heaven, enduring the stake, torture, and execution. Transparent peace and calm and limitless, quietly glowing happiness. It was as if she had already left the earth and was approaching the unknown sun of truth and life and was floating disembodied in its light. "So that is death. What kind of death is that?" thinks Musia enraptured.[46]

The young and naïve Musia possesses the inner fortitude to find heroism in death. Although clearly uplifted by Musia's meditations, the narrator makes clear that avoiding death and the abject body is impossible in the end. The living are left with the ultimate human reality of the abject human body: "the corpses were laid in a box. And then transported away. With extended necks, crazily popped eyeballs, a swollen blue tongue, which protruded like some fanciful awful flower out of the lips, speckled with bloody foam."[47] Finally, material life that ends violently must founder in the abject. Although inwardly, one overcomes the abject by sublimating and transcending violent drives that command most human life, the violated material body is grotesque.[48]

What did Andreev's extreme treatment of the abject accomplish and how did it change the nature of realism? Kristeva notes that the abject functions as the sign of muddled, deformed proscriptions. We might conclude that the overwhelming popularity of the abject in Andreev's fiction in the first decade of the twentieth century points to the fragility of Russia's social order. Andreev's stories captured and magnified the Russian fin-de-siècle mood. He pushed its darkest tones to their limit, or beyond, for some, more discriminating readers becoming something of a self-parody. However high-minded they might be, his characters always meet an abject fate, affirming the failure of the existing social order and its laws and rules to manage senseless violence and abuse.

Kristeva can help us to conceptualize the link between Andreev's figure of the abject "mute body" and its enormous popularity in the larger social body with its laws and proscriptions. Kristeva speaks of the abject's social and political function as neither confirming nor renouncing but corrupting rules and laws. The abject, in her view, is "perverse" in that it "neither gives up nor assumes a prohibition, a rule, or a law; but turns them aside, misleads, corrupts; uses them, takes advantage of them, the better to deny them."[49] The abject lens, as we have seen, muddles social convention through its simultaneous attraction and revulsion to what is taboo, what has been "jettisoned" as dangerous. Responses of both loathing and pity muddy the emotional landscape and make it difficult unequivocally to uphold core social strictures. Sexual prohibition, so central to religious belief – male authority and female moral strength – melts away in the face of raw sexual drive. The glory of war becomes instead the gore of war. The heroism and self-sacrifice of the radical cause is negated and perverted by reducing everyone, even the most saintly, to grotesque corporeality of the violently ended life.

"Why," Kristeva asks, "does corporeal waste, menstrual blood, and excrement, or everything that is assimilated to them, from nail-parings to decay, represent . . . the objective frailty of symbolic order?"[50] In his stories Andreev offers image after relentless image that performs the function of grinding away at the Russian social order – and perhaps offers an answer, as well, to Kristeva's question. Physical secretion and violently deceased, decaying bodies are markers of the ultimate purposelessness of human life – the ultimate "red laugh," that mask that grins at all human efforts to create a higher order to bring meaning to the chaos of human nature.

Neorealism after Andreev is marked by its emphasis on corporeality and its appeal to what some might call the "lower" senses. Beyond the visual dominant of nineteenth-century realism, neorealist work particularly appeals to smell, feel, and touch. Andreev contributed to that corporeal focus, though in a quite fastidious vein. However, far from celebrating the fullness of sensory experience, Andreev's stories exhibit a strongly ascetic disgust of the body. In the end his is a grotesque vision that focuses on the distorted and dismembered body and denies human endurance and, ultimately, human goodness.

NOTES

1 Julia Kristeva, *Powers of Horror: An Essay in Abjection* (New York: Columbia University Press, 1982), 1–2.
2 Jeffrey Brooks, *When Russia Learned to Read: Literacy and Popular Literature, 1861–1917* (Princeton University Press, 1985); Edith W. Clowes, "From Populist to Popular Art: Superman and the Myth of Self-Determination," in *The Revolution of Moral Consciousness: Nietzsche in Russian Literature, 1890–1914* (DeKalb: Northern Illinois University Press, 1988), 83–113.

3 In 1902 Anton Chekhov remarked that Andreev's stories were like "the singing of a fake nightingale." Quoted in Valerii Ivanovich Bezzubov, *Leonid Andreev i traditsii russkogo realizma* (Tallinn: Eesti Raamat, 1984), 117. See also Dmitrii Merezhkovskii, "V ob'ezianykh lapakh (O Leonide Andreeve)," in *V tikhom omute* (Moscow: Sovetskii pisatel', 1991). In this 1908 article Merezhkovsky mocked Andreev with the thought that "I'm not afraid of the things Andreev uses to scare me." See http://philology.ruslibrary.ru/default.asp?trID=233& artID=316 (accessed July 4, 2013). In his article, "The New Russian Prose" (1923), Zamiatin implied that Andreev's writing was a bad influence, luring young writers to use too many heavy words, mainly adjectives starting with the prefix "bez-," for example, *bezdna* (abyss), *bezdonnyi* (bottomless), or *bezumnyi* (insane), and thus "pay for Andreev's sins." See Evgenii Zamiatin, *Sochineniia* (Moscow: Kniga, 1988), 427.

4 Clowes, "From Populist to Popular Art," 81, 85.

5 James B. Woodward, *Leonid Andreev: A Study* (Oxford University Press, 1969), 77.

6 G. I. Chulkov, ed., *Pis'ma Leonida Andreeva* (Letchworth, Eng.: Prideaux Press, 1977), 34.

7 Stephen Hutchings, *A Semiotic Analysis of the Short Stories of Leonid Andreev, 1900–1909* (London: Modern Humanities Research Association, 1990), 2. Acknowledgment goes to Megan Luttrell, who, in my Russian Modernism seminar at the University of Kansas, wrote a thoughtful paper on Andreev and expressionism, which spurred my interest in this topic.

8 Kristeva, *Powers of Horror*, 1.

9 Ibid., 2.

10 Ibid.

11 Roman Jakobson, "Two Aspects of Language and Two Types of Aphasic Disturbances," in *On Language: Roman Jakobson*, edited by Linda Waugh and Monique Monville-Burston (Cambridge, MA: Harvard University Press, 1990), 130. See also his "On Realism in Art," in *Readings in Russian Poetics: Formalist and Structuralist Views*, edited by Ladislav Matejka and Krystyna Pomorska (Cambridge, MA: MIT Press, 1971), 38–46.

12 For thorough treatments of this topic, see Møller, *Postlude to* The Kreutzer Sonata; Laura Engelstein and Stephanie Sandler, eds., *Self and Story in Russian History* (Ithaca, NY: Cornell University Press, 2000).

13 Vladimir Solov'ev, *Chteniia o bogochelovechestve* (St. Petersburg: Khudozhestvennaia literatura, 1994), 331.

14 James B. Woodward, "Devices of Emphasis and Amplification in the Style of Leonid Andreev," *Slavic and East European Journal* 9:3 (1965): 247–256, especially 248–250; Veronica Makarova, "Stylistic Features in the Novella 'Darkness' by Leonid Andreev," *Russian Literature* 68:3–4 (2010): 327–344, especially 332–333.

15 Bezzubov, *Leonid Andreev i traditsii russkogo realizma*, 27.

16 Quoted in Leonid Andreev, *Sobranie sochinenii v shesti tomakh* (Moscow: Khudozhestvennaia literatura, 1990), 1:617.

17 Ibid., 26.
18 Engelstein, *The Keys to Happiness*, 374.
19 Kristeva, *Powers of Horror*, 2.
20 Hutchings, *A Semiotic Analysis*, 184.
21 Ibid., 103.
22 Possible parallels in expressionist visual art might be found in two paintings by the Norwegian pre-expressionist, Edvard Munch, the well-known *Scream* (1893) and *Ashes* (1894), showing a man and woman in a woodland picnic scene who have clearly just had sex and are very upset.
23 Andreev, *Sobranie sochinenii* (1990), 356, 360.
24 Ibid., 359.
25 Ibid., 356.
26 Ibid.
27 Ibid., 359.
28 Ibid., 360.
29 Ibid., 362.
30 Ibid., 365.
31 Ibid.
32 Bezzubov, *Leonid Andreev i traditsii russkogo realizma*, 24.
33 Andreev, *Sobranie sochinenii* (1990), 615.
34 Leonid Andreev, *Sobranie sochinenii v shesti tomakh* (Moscow: Knigovek, 2012), II:37.
35 Ibid., 41.
36 Ibid., 48.
37 Ibid., 62.
38 Ibid., 39.
39 Ibid., 43.
40 Ibid., 44.
41 Ibid., 412.
42 Ibid., 416.
43 Ibid., 419.
44 Berdiaev, *The Origin of Russian Communism*, particularly 19, 45–52, 75.
45 Andreev, *Sobranie sochinenii* (2012), 448.
46 Ibid., 449.
47 Ibid., 484–485.
48 In its own way this image of the dead, violated body of an ascetic, spiritually elevated person recalls the Holbein painting of the dead Christ in Dostoevsky's *Idiot*.
49 Kristeva, *Powers of Horror*, 15.
50 Ibid., 70.

CHAPTER 14

The thinking oyster
Turgenev's "drama of dying" as the decay of Russian realism
Ilya Vinitsky

The pearl is the illness of the oyster, and style, maybe, the flowing out
of a pain more profound.
— Gustave Flaubert, in a letter to Louise Colet[1]

And we need neither Kant, nor Herodotus
To know that an oyster goes not in the nose, but in the mouth.
— From the comic poems of Turgenev[2]

The theme of this chapter is the interpretation of the agony and death
of one of the founders of Russian realism, Ivan Turgenev (1818–1883), in
Russian culture of the late realist and early modernist periods. In the
first four sections, I will consider the writer's "drama of dying,"[3] which was
striking to his contemporaries from a dual point of view: through the prism
of his work — the focus of this analysis will be an existential "ante-mortem
metaphor" that the writer often used in reference to his grave condition —
and the ontology of nineteenth-century Russian realism. In the last sections,
I will turn to the idiosyncratic interpretation of Turgenev's demise offered
by a leading symbolist poet and critic, Innokentiy Annensky (1855–1909).
I conclude that in the eyes of a new, modernist generation, Turgenev's
illness and death metonymically expressed the fate of the movement that
the writer founded — its inevitable disillusionment, disintegration, and
eventual transformation into a new aesthetics, promoted by the Russian
symbolists and their descendants.

The rhetoric of resistance

"Death," wrote Turgenev's biographer L. S. Utevsky, "is one of the problems [the writer] studied throughout the course of his whole life; he feared
death and never forgot about it."[4] It is one of the main themes that runs
through the entire extent of his work. In literary martyrology of the writer,
"[t]here is the death of the fighter and the death of the victim, the death of

the unlucky and the death of the gambler who fearlessly stakes his life on a card for a moment's pleasure."[5] The theme of human consciousness in the face of death and the "seemingly inescapable indifference" of nature to human sufferings[6] occupies a central place in Turgenev's works. Paraphrasing Pascal, Turgenev wrote that "if the universe crushed a man, he would be much greater than the universe because he would know that the universe is crushing him, and it would not know this."[7] Hence the greatness of human identity lies in its moral, intellectual, and spiritual opposition to non-being. In contrast to his contemporaries Tolstoy and Leskov, who were just as captivated by the mystery of death, Turgenev depicts the "drama of dying" not as a gradual revelation, a transition to a new state or liberation from the pangs of earthly existence, but as the final test of a proud, rational mind – the "feat" of Bazarov in D. I. Pisarev's interpretation – or as the revelation of the inner strength and beauty of a humble soul in the vision of the paralyzed peasant Lukeria in "The Living Relic."[8] The metaphysical tragedy of the thinking person, according to Turgenev, is the inability to solve the riddle of his existence in the world.[9]

Turgenev's contemporaries understood his suffering through the prism of the tragic ethics expressed in his works.[10] *Meditsinskii vestnik* printed the chronicle of Turgenev's terminal illness in 1882–1883, as well as the last letter to his doctor, L. B. Bertenson.[11] The short biography included in the first "posthumous" volume of his collected works in 1883 provided the details of the "superhuman suffering" he endured in the last year of his life. The same year, the celebrated doctor S. P. Botkin gave a lecture at the Russian Society of Doctors on "The Progression of Turgenev's Illness."[12]

In some sense, the writer's agony became as much a public event and cultural fact for Russian society starting in the 1880s as would Tolstoy's withdrawal and death in 1910. Descriptions of Turgenev's physical suffering and death entered the hagiographical canon and became the object of philosophical and psychological speculation on the heroic demise of the knight of Russian realism. "Only a champion of thought could suffer so and die," wrote I. Ivanov, Turgenev's biographer, in 1896.[13] "It's amazing how hard he fought!" exclaimed Boris Zaitsev, another Turgenev biographer, a half-century later. "He did not want to give up literature at all."[14] "Confined to his bed, he became the 'living relic' that he so touchingly described in his short story."[15] Contemporaries perceived Turgenev's broken-off deathbed letter to Tolstoy calling the latter back to artistic work as the writer's bequest of literary ministry over the nation to his compatriot and successor. Finally, Turgenev's critics and biographers correlated his "truly holy end"[16] not only with his own heroes' "literary" deaths, but also with the intelligentsia's hagiographic tradition of recording the torturous ends of other precedent-makers of the "realist" trend such as V. G. Belinsky, once described by Turgenev himself, and N. A. Nekrasov in F. M. Dostoevsky's description.

One image, which aided Turgenev in defining his tragic state in the fall of 1882, drew the attention of critics and biographers. "At this time, Turgenev found one quite fitting expression for his personal life," wrote Ivanov. "Exactly one year before his death, he equated himself to the oyster, clinging to the rock, and then he constantly returns to this comparison."[17] "For life, women, and for love, he was already 'an oyster clinging to the rock,'" continued Boris Zaitsev, "but not for literature."[18] "Completely alone, unable to walk, stand, or ride, precisely 'an oyster or mollusk' in uninterrupted, terrible agony," Turgenev, in the words of his ecstatic biographer, "sends his last precept to humanity from the brink of his grave: 'Live and love others, as I have always loved them.'"[19]

In what follows, I will try to reconstruct the literary genealogy and philosophical implications of Turgenev's "ante-mortem metaphor," considering it against the ontological background of Russian realism: the original conflict between and indivisibility of the material and spiritual bases; the initial striving to rid oneself of romantic phantoms and illusions; and the resulting recognition of the illusoriness of one's own being. In my view, Turgenev's "drama of dying" as mirrored in the image of the mollusk, adhering to the cliff, prefigures the fin-de-siècle fascination with death and creativity, although the latter presents a very different – sober and tragic – perspective.

The history of the oyster

It is of note that the image of the oyster is one of the oldest in the European cultural tradition.[20] The mollusk's "fleeting" freshness, exquisite taste, isolation, self-sufficiency, immobility, total dependence on its surrounding environment, dualism of mollusk and shell, the birth of the pearl, as well as tremendous vitality[21] related to its symbolization.

The "philosophical" oyster is located on the cusp of spirit and matter, organic and inorganic life, consciousness and unconsciousness, being and non-being. The liminality of the oyster's existence attracted the attention of philosophers, religious mystics, and writers. The oyster is represented varyingly as the ideal of a harmonious existence, a symbol of a man whose soul is languishing in the shell of his body, the absolute realization of the principle of hedonistic pleasure,[22] and as a metaphor for creative imagination, painful in its nature. In positivistic discourse of the second half of the nineteenth century, the oyster symbolizes the lowest degree of the organic ladder, the apex of which is man.[23] Finally, in realist eidology, the oyster clinging to the rock serves as a metaphor for social determinism – in this case, the indissoluble link between man and the social environment, in the sense that this metaphor is used in Balzac's *Père Goriot*. Turgenev's oyster distinguishes itself in that it is not a metaphor for some such abstract principle or method, but the image of the author himself, his tragic *Verwandlung* (metamorphosis). According to Turgenev, in this physical *reductio ad ostream* – the forced descent of a person with all his hopes, plans, and wishes down to the lowest rung of organic life – is the realization of the irony of human existence.[24]

The formula of the oyster

It is difficult to say exactly when the oyster image acquired its existential significance for the writer, a great lover of the seafood delicacy. I propose that the literary impulse toward the anthropomorphization of the mollusk could be a poem by his friend, Yakov Polonsky. In a letter to Polonsky dated January 6, 1875, Turgenev acknowledges the character (worldview) of the author in his poetry, but the obtrusive use of the word "mollusk... returning in the last line of every stanza... grates"[25] on him. According to the commentators of the writer's collected letters, here Turgenev refers to Polonsky's poem "A Night Thought" ("Nochnaia duma"), in which the writer's fate in this world is compared to the lot of a worm, lying on the ocean floor:

> Dlia sebia ia dukh, stremlenii polnyi
> Dlia drugikh ia cherv' na dne morskom
> ... Mezhdu mnoi i tseloiu vselennoi
> Noch', kak more temnoe, krugom
> I uzh esli Bog menia ne slyshit
> V etu noch' ia cherv' na dne morskom.[26]

> (For myself I am a spirit, of aspirations full / For others,
> I am a worm on the ocean floor / ... Between me and
> the whole universe / Is night around, like the dark sea, /
> And it is as if God no longer listens to me / In this
> night, I am a worm on the ocean floor.)

Clearly, Polonsky borrows the image of the human-worm from Derzhavin's famous poetic aphorism in the ode "God" (1784), found in the epigraph to the poem: "I am a worm – I am God." It is interesting that Turgenev replaces the Slavic "worm" (*cherv'*) with the French "mollusk"[27] in his letter, thus translating Polonsky's anthropomorphic metaphor into a different literary tradition, namely, the Balzacian tradition that offended Turgenev's philosophical pretenses and often likened a person to a powerless mollusk. For example, the hero of *Père Goriot* is called "an anthropomorphic mollusk to be classified with the *Casquettifères*."

Precisely this tradition leads to the image of the oyster clinging to the rock that obsessively haunted Turgenev when he was dying of spinal cancer. As I show in a 1997 article, the writer had adapted this image directly from Balzac's *La Peau de chagrin* (1831).[28] In the well-known finale of the novel's third part, "Agony," Raphaël de Valentin, his life rapidly dwindling, runs away from his beloved Pauline to Auvergne. He instinctively feels a need to commune with nature, with these authentic impressions, to this vegetative life to which people happily surrender amidst the fields. From the Pic de Sancy, a wonderful, peaceful, and harmonious world of nature reveals itself to him, which he dreams of joining:

> It was a dying man's fancy. For him the prime model, after which the customary existence of the individual should be shaped, the real formula for the life of a human being, the only true and possible life, the life-ideal, was to become one of the oysters adhering to this rock, to save his shell a day or two longer by paralyzing the power of death. One profoundly selfish thought took possession of him, and the whole universe was swallowed up and lost in it. For him the universe existed no longer; the whole world had come to be within himself. For the sick, the world begins at their pillow and ends at the foot of the bed; and this countryside was Raphaël's sick bed.[29]

The hero decides to stay forever in this beautiful place and soon it begins to seem to him that he has already fused with the life of the rock upon which he is sitting. Thanks to this "mysterious illuminism" (*mystérieux illuminisme*) and imagined recovery, he relives the joy of a "second childhood" in Auvergne. But this fusing with nature proves impossible: his time is running out. Raphaël returns to Paris and dies in Pauline's arms.

The central image of this episode – the oyster clinging to the rock – is the symbol of "vegetative" life that voluntarily releases the human being from thought, memory, and desire. This "ideal human existence" is a direct echo of the Rousseauian utopia driven to, it seems, its biological limit. In the pessimistic philosophy of Schopenhauer, a significant influence on Turgenev, the unconscious existence of mollusk is more enviable than the life of a human or an animal, although not as enviable as that of a plant or a stone.[30] Meanwhile, in the context of Balzac's novel, the hero's dream of turning into an oyster is presented mainly as the illusion of dying, his naïve attempt at playing hide and seek with death, the last outburst of egoism in the face of non-being.

Existential realism

The thought of Balzac preoccupied the dying Turgenev. In a letter to P. I. Weinberg on November 3, 1882, he spoke harshly of the writer: "I can never read more than ten pages in a row before he becomes disgusting and alien to me."[31] It is well known that he never liked Balzac,[32] but the severity of this assessment relates, it seems, not only to an aesthetic aversion to his work but also to the painful recognition of his own position in the novel as a disliked, "pompous," and "artificial" author. In fact, Turgenev's situation was similar to that of Raphaël de Valentin. His life, like that of Balzac's hero, was nearing its end. Turgenev understandably reacted as Balzac's hero did to the people surrounding him: with hate, fear, rudeness, and irritation caused by consolatory talk about future recovery as Turgenev's visitors reported of his outbursts of anger and capriciousness.[33] Even the names of the two female companions coincide: Raphaël's Pauline and Turgenev's Pauline Viardot. Turgenev, like the hero of the novel, left Paris and installed himself in a picturesque spot on the banks of a river, in a small house-chalet in Swiss style. Similar to Raphaël, here he ate pure, natural foods as the doctors prescribed him a milk cure, and tried to forget about his pain with the help of narcotics. Finally, the striking metaphor of Balzac's hero – "to become an oyster, clinging to the rock" – seemed to be realized in Turgenev's case: almost completely immobile, the limits of the whole world enclosed within the "headboard" and "foot" of the bed.[34]

It is possible that the recognition of his miserable plight in the lush mirror of the "opulent" French novel explains Turgenev's psychological and ideological rejection of the Balzacian image. Turgenev demonstratively depicts his suffering as if from outside of it; he ironizes his own weakness. This cruel self-irony recalls the expression of his own nihilist hero: "But now the whole problem of the giant is how to die decently, although that makes no difference to anyone either . . . It doesn't matter: I will not wriggle out of this."[35] Turgenev's oyster is definitively a weak but thoughtful creature or, rather, soberly conscious of his plight. In a sense, this is a realistic variant of the famous philosopheme that played an important role in Turgenev's life: Blaise Pascal's "thinking reed."[36] Inside of a languishing shell, the human spirit unwillingly is forced to come to terms with bodily weakness.[37]

By bestowing consciousness upon the oyster, the writer seamlessly translates Balzac's symbol onto another interpretational plan, which is associated with Plato in the Western tradition. In *Phaedrus*, Socrates likens the human soul suffering inside the body's prison to the oyster inside its shell.[38] However, in contrast to Plato's spiritualism and the naïve belief of the paralyzed peasant, Lukeria, in Turgenev's short story "A Living Relic," the writer did not believe in the soul's liberation in the afterlife. The dying person consciously banishes any thought of the future altogether. It is noteworthy that the Russian spiritualists' journal, *Rebus*, having printed materials about Turgenev's illness, to the very last moment hoped that the writer would develop a belief in the afterlife.[39]

Key for Turgenev appears to be the search for a temporary compromise with the material: to attempt, for as long as possible, to hold on to one's thinking and creative "I" within the decomposing body-shell. In other words, Turgenev's "thinking oyster" is not only an apt metaphor for his immobile position, but also an existential symbol expressing the tragic conflict between consciousness and the doom of a man, between "spiritual" and "material." A conflict, as already stated, deeply rooted in Turgenev's worldview. In this context, one might call the oyster a sister image to Tropmann's straitjacket, aptly defined by Lieber in the present volume as an icon of Turgenev's behavioral ethic, represented in the extreme.

Significantly, this theme develops the "liminal existence" of the thinking oyster in the writer's last letters. It seems that Turgenev first compared himself with "an oyster, clinging to the spot, which cannot even be eaten" in a letter to Yakov Polonsky, the author of the poem about the godforsaken "mollusk" that irritated the still healthy Turgenev, from July 17, 1882.[40] Evidently, in the beginning of his illness, Turgenev was most tormented by the meaninglessness and uselessness of his own life.[41] Gradually, he learns to content himself with little. "The main amusement for me," he writes to Zh. A. Polonskaia (the poet's wife) on August 4, "is a nightly game of whist; sometimes a little bit of music. This is the best regime for the oyster I have become."[42] "I still imagine myself as an immobile 'something,'" he writes to L. Pich, "le patriarche des mollusques."[43] In a letter to writer M. E. Saltykov-Shchedrin on August 23, 1882, Turgenev described his state: "I sleep well, drink only milk – but cannot stand, walk, or ride in a carriage – not without arousing the most unpleasant pain in the chest, shoulders, etc. The result: sit, lie down, my dear – and don't think about anything! – And how long this will continue . . . is also not your concern. I understand the position of the oyster in full, clinging to the rock. But oysters have experienced nothing else – and wish for nothing else."[44]

From his real circumstances, Turgenev derives his principal rules of life: "One should reflect on the past, meet the demands of the present, and never think about the future."[45] The absence of a future is a fact that must be tolerated. In a letter to Polonskaia from October 17, 1882, Turgenev says:

> Imagine yourself as a person who is completely healthy . . . only cannot sit, walk, or ride – without the immediate appearance of a sharp pain in the left shoulder, like a tooth. What should one tell him to do? To sit, to lie down, sit again – and to know that one cannot escape from under these conditions, neither in Russia, nor in Paris . . . However, my state of mind is very calm. I have made peace with this thought and even find that nothingness is not bad for the oyster. And then, it is even possible to work. I could go blind, my legs could be taken away, et cetera. Only private life, of course, has ceased. And even then just to say: as of a few days ago, I am sixty-four years old.[46]

"And now I can work, namely since I have given up all thoughts of the future," he writes on December 22, 1882 to Dr. Bertenson. "I have turned into an oyster. Thus, I conduct myself like an oyster."[47] A letter to Polonsky on October 25, 1882 reflects Turgenev's final reconciliation to his position: "I sit or lie down for a whole twenty-four hours in a row – and that's that! A real mollusk! They live, sometimes for many years, and feel no desire to move."[48] On the same day, Turgenev writes the last entry on his "Feuille d'observation," a journal of his illness: "My infirmness is determined forever. Sometimes a little bit better, sometimes a little bit worse . . . but to recover is unthinkable . . . And my position will never change. For the rest of my life, I will not be in condition to stand or walk. I've gotten used to milk and, for other foods, I have no appetite. I will continue on milk, as it is still useful for the stomach and kidneys. And that will do!"[49]

The last hope of the dying man relies on his physical pain being unable to suppress his mind, will, and imagination. But creative consciousness inevitably deforms under the effects of illness. In summer and fall of 1882, he writes the mystical short story "Klara Milich: After Death," considered his swan song, as well as several new "prose poems" about suffering and death such as "Partridges," "Nessun maggior dolore," "Fallen Under the Wheels," "Wah . . . wah!" and "My Woods." Notably, in Turgenev's short stories, poems, and conversations of this time, the theme of dream-hallucination plays a significant role, in which the infirm finds a temporary physical and spiritual respite. This "escape" to dream and morbid vision (under the influence of morphine) that oscillates between mysticism and prosaic life is the last refuge of human consciousness – the "lyrical retreat" of Turgenev's realism.[50]

Turgenev's mystically oriented contemporary, writer N. S. Leskov, admired his last fantastical short story.[51] Certainly, he saw "Klara Milich" as resonant with his own work and religious expectations of theme: ghostly visions, spiritual strength, the suffering soul's liberation from the prison of the decaying world, blissful unification with the departed. These same themes have elicited sharp condemnation on the part of realist critics who immediately accused Turgenev of an infatuation with spiritualism.[52] Meanwhile Turgenev's "strange" spiritualism fundamentally distinguishes itself from positivistic concepts of the afterlife's benefit of "champions of thought" as lighting the way for humanity,[53] but also from the mystical worldview of Leskov and the convictions of writer-spiritualists of the *Rebus* circle.[54] At the same time, the narrator's rational viewpoint does not allow the hero's imagination to go out of control for a moment: as befits a realist, Turgenev reconstructs the social and biological "genealogy" of the consciousness of his hero-visionary; realistic interpretation constantly colors mystical revelations until the very last moment, the story's denouement.[55] In fact, the blissful smile on the face of the dying Aratov does not denote the soul's liberation from the material world, the typical ending of Leskov's "spiritualistic plot,"[56] or "awakening from a dream of life," which, according to Tolstoy, Prince Andrei experiences. It indicates only that the hero dies happy, but this happiness might be a mere delusion,[57] a consequence of mental illness, a parody of the human "possession" of the "eternal, unquestionable truth."[58] However, what happens next, after his death, does not interest the author.

In other words, Turgenev tries to remain in a realistic frame of consciousness and analytical method to the very end, although he takes it to its outer limits. The artistic world of his later works such as "Klara Milich" and the poems in prose is a sort of "border zone" inhabited by shadows, the fate of which can in no way be decided. The spiritualist prototype of balancing on the cusp of the living world is ancient Cimmeria, the edge of the world and the land of perpetual dream, not the Leskovian kingdom of "sublime" spirits, the toilsome Dostoevskian world of spiritual existence, or the gnostic "lost world" created by Saltykov-Shchedrin in *The Golovlev Family*.[59]

The agony of realism

In mid-January 1883, Turgenev's health sharply declined; his suffering became unbearable, and the image of the oyster clinging to the rock disappeared from his letters altogether. It can be said that the story of the "thinking oyster" in the writer's letters is none other than the story of the loss of the final illusion, which incidentally alludes also to Balzac and, in the philosophical context, to Schopenhauer's pessimistic philosophy.

This last illusion of the realist, the hope for a dream, above all interested the symbolist Innokentiy Annensky, in whose poetry the problem of art and pain occupies a central place. In the 1906 essay "The Dying Turgenev. Klara Milich," Annensky debunks the Russian intelligentsia's myth that Turgenev's physical sufferings and death are a heroic act of the writer's faithfulness to his realist and rationalist convictions; he harshly, if not cruelly, assesses Turgenev's last short story as a miserable "drama of dying."

The essay begins with the author's memories of Turgenev's funeral: contrived, meaningless, boring, a monotonous procession, the intelligentsia's empty speeches, the unsuccessful attempts to cover the reality of death as the "champion's" corpse lies "with ichor upon the satin pillow of the grave."[60] This intonation's gospel allusion is obvious: the dead bury their own dead or, in historical-cultural "voicing," a dead culture stretches behind the body of its deceased idol.

These memories of the funeral procession of the "champion" and "Bard" serve as a prologue to Annensky's discussion of Turgenev's "Klara Milich," written in the fall of 1882: "That fall was his last story: grey, then pink, still careful-precise and in soft *but already frozen contours*."[61] Of this last short story the critic claims: "In the music of Turgenev's work, there entered a new note, not for long – a new and somehow resounding note" – "the note of physical suffering."[62] According to Annensky:

> The old, sick Turgenev is positioned like Aratov; he instinctively fears the fluctuations of life; he fears that life will not call him to motion, to its sun and din; the patient who decided neither to love nor hope for anything – if only he could work. The last strength of Aratov-Turgenev left upon the ruining of the illusion that existence became more grey, less noticeable, and most importantly, passed more slowly.[63]

Symptomatically, Annensky depicts Turgenev's "drama of dying" in a completely Balzacian key and its likeness to the literary prototype of Raphaël de Valentin is notable. In a novel like *La Peau de chagrin*, Balzac's hero fears every new reduction in the skin of the wild ass to the point of his desires being paralyzed; he fears movement, hope, an inundation of life, illusions, and tries to slow down his existence to cheat death. From this he derives his aspiration to become an oyster, clinging to the rock – "unbeknownst" to him, his own desires inevitably shorten his life.

In his article, Annensky cites the extract from Turgenev's letters in which the dying man, trying to console himself and his friends "with the humor of patient old age," says that he happily accepts the oyster's immobile existence: "a little bit longer and I will not wish to leave this state of stillness, which prevents me not from working or sleeping"; "It's time";

"Then, I can work"; etc. In this context, Annensky conceptualized "Klara Milich" as "new for Turgenev, the realistic dream" that is "no longer a reality that resembles a dream as it was previously – but the dream that breaks with reality" (63). Terminal illness, the most persuasive of realities, penetrates into the last refuge of human thought and hope, the dream which is, in Annensky's interpretation, poetry. The "shell" of art can no longer save and the dying writer begins to feel and recognize the reality of death.

"The circumstances surrounding the bitter taste of illness in Turgenev's mouth," concludes Annensky, "this is his weary mind that does not wish to placate itself with romanticism[64] because through this theatrical mantle, one cannot see the body and the animal anguish of its doomed decomposing."[65] Annensky symbolically interprets Turgenev's agony as a drama of the dying realist, grasping for the despised "romanticism"[66] (in all likelihood, a hidden allusion to Bazarov's dilemma) as the last straw – in other words, as the last mutation and disintegration of realism in the second half of the nineteenth century.[67] In Annensky's symbolic language, Turgenev's realism is extinguished, abandoned by beauty and associated with the mysterious heroine of the story: "And once again, Beauty departs from [people], unembodied and unloved." However, realism does not die for nothing, since it provides us with a spiritual lesson:

> When it [Beauty] departs, a subtle aroma remains in the air, the chest expands and one wants to say: yes, it is worth it to live and even suffer, if it purchases the possibility of thinking of Klara Milich.[68]

Conclusion

In Annensky's vision, the "death of realism," unable to hold on to beauty, signifies the birth of a new literary school. If, in his 1906 article, the poet drew attention to the "frightening realism" and "animal torment" that ruined the fake mantle-shell of realist art, then his subsequent attitude to the illusion of the "oyster" changes or, to be more exact, adjusts itself to his own modernist program. In particular the synopsis of Annensky's lecture on the "poetic forms of contemporary modernist sensibility" read by the poet on October 13, 1909, a month and a half before his death, evinces this.

In his last speech, Annensky spoke to his young listeners about the importance of "humility of thought," "wise perplexity," and "incompleteness, puzzlement, the irrepressible naïve desire to become one with the boundless" as vital sources of poetry: "Do not rush to explain or give answers – think, think – for God's sake, think. Forget about poet-tsars, prophets. A conversation with the ailing Turgenev. Be this mollusk in a shell that envisions dreams and is not ashamed that he knows nothing about his lying in the ocean."[69]

In other words, Annensky, in his literary last will and testament, seems to return to the "ideal" of Raphaël de Valentin, but transfers it into the sphere of art. Turgenev's works did not contain a metaphor of the oyster sleeping on the ocean floor – Yakov Polonsky's poem built this image and it irritated Turgenev – but Annensky "synthesized" the image from Turgenev's motifs connected with artistic creation and death: dream, oyster, sea.[70] Moreover, Annensky extols the oyster's naïve ignorance of the ocean pressing down upon it, as opposed to the tragic sense of the poet's abandonment as expressed by Polonsky and the Turgenevian idea of a person's heroic awareness of his impending doom.[71] Clearly, Annensky's interpretation breaks with Turgenev's sense of the importance of the balance between a sober outlook on life and suffering, searching but not finding satisfaction or release. The "dream of the mollusk," pure art, here is presented as a metaphor of the artistic departure from the material world for the otherworldly kingdom of beauty.[72]

Annensky's last speech, in the words of R. D. Timenchik, became a poetic program for his most talented students. Thus, the scholar believes, the "fresh and sharp" (*svezho i ostro*) oysters smelling of the sea in Akhmatova's well-known poem refer the dedicated reader to Turgenev and Annensky, as if voicing their pain.[73] Turgenev's oyster is therefore brought to a completely different context, at once relevant for the romantic worldview as well as the decadent one that succeeded it:

> Or is poetry perhaps a disease of humanity as the pearl is the morbid matter of the deceased oyster?[74]

In this tradition, beauty springs from suffering; artistic creation is this "grand illness"; the pearl is the result of the oyster's physical suffering. The pitiful, powerless mollusk, characteristic of Turgenev's pessimistic worldview, becomes the lofty mystical symbol of an artist's life and creativity, akin to Mikhail Vrubel's magnificent painting *The Pearl* (1904), one of the major artistic manifestoes of Russian modernism.[75] Needless to say that such an aesthetic utopia, championed by Russian decadents and symbolists, is impossible for the sober realist, who knows that the opening of the shell means the death of the mollusk itself.

TRANSLATED BY AMANDA ALLAN

NOTES

This chapter reworks and expands my notes dedicated to the "oyster theme" in nineteenth-century Russian literature, published in *Elementa: A Journal of Slavic Studies and Comparative Cultural Semiotics* 3:4 (1997): 325–337. The impulse to write those notes came from R. D. Timenchik's brilliant essay "Ustritsy Akhmatovoi i Annenskogo," which researches the literary genesis of the famous "oysters on ice" (*ustritsy v l'du*) from Akhmatova's poem "In the Evening." V. V. Ivanov develops this theme in the "postscriptum" to my notes; see "Postscript to Ilya Vinitsky's Article 'Formula of an Oyster'" in *Elementa* 3:4 (1997) as well as Vadim Besprozvannyi's "'Literaturnye ustritsy' ili eshche raz o teme ustrits," *Toronto Slavic Quarterly* 36 (2011): 21–51.

1 "La perle est une maladie de l'huître et le style, peut-être, l'écoulement d'une douleur plus profonde." *La Correspondance de Flaubert, étude et répertoire critique*, edited by Charles Carlut (Columbus: Ohio State University Press, 1968), 797.

2 "I chto ne nuzhen nam ne Kant, ne Gerodot,/Chtob znat' chto ustritsu kladut ne v nos, a v rot." Turgenev, *Polnoe sobranie sochinenii i pisem v dvadtsati vos'mi tomakh* (Moscow: Nauka, 1960–1968), xx:246. Hereafter referred to as *PSSP*.

3 Annensky's expression.

4 L. S. Utevskii, *Smert' Turgeneva 1883–1923* (St. Petersburg: Atenei, 1923), 7.

5 Iurii Mann, *Dialektika khudozhestvennogo obraza* (Moscow: Sovietskii pisatel', 1987), 121.

6 Elizabeth Cheresh Allen, "Introduction," in *The Essential Turgenev* (Evanston, IL: Northwestern University Press, 1994), xv.

7 *PSSP* xvi:117.

8 For Turgenev's "sexual politics" in this story – as Emma Lieber puts it, "a gentleman watching the body of a peasant woman disintegrate" – see her contribution to the present volume.

9 For the characteristics of Tolstoy's metaphysics in the context of the pessimistic philosophy of Schopenhauer, see Marina Ledkovsky, *The Other Turgenev: From Romanticism to Symbolism* (Würzburg: Jal-Verlag, 1973), 24–26.

10 Over the course of forty years after the writer's death, the theme of his struggles with a serious ailment attracted critics' and biographers' attention, from A. A. Meshcherskii's article, "Predsmertnye chasy I. S. Turgeneva," in *Novoe vremia*, September 3–15, 1883, to L. S. Utevskii's *Smert' Turgeneva* (1923).

11 Utevskii, *Smert' Turgeneva*, 25.

12 "Mnenie S. P. Botkina o khode bolezni I. S. Turgeneva," *Novosti* 209, October 29, 1883.

13 I. Ivanov, *Ivan Sergeevich Turgenev. Zhizn', lichnost', tvorchestvo* (St. Petersburg: Tipografiia I. N. Skorokhodova, 1896), 384.

14 Boris Zaitsev, *Zhizn' Turgeneva* (Paris: YMCA Press, 1949), 256.

15 Aleksandr Evlakhov, "I. S. Turgenev – poet mirovoi skorbi," *Russkoe bogatstvo* 6 (1904): 39.

16 Ivan Smirnov, *Zastupniki narodnye: I. S. Turgenev, N. A. Nekrasov* (Moscow: Tipo-litografiia T-va I. N. Kushnerev i ko, 1908), 27.

17 Ivanov, *Ivan Sergeevich Turgenev*, 384.

18 Zaitsev, *Zhizn' Turgeneva*, 256.

19 Smirnov, *Zastupniki narodnye*, 27.

20 See Ad de Vries, *Dictionary of Symbols and Imagery*, 1st edn. (Amsterdam: North-Holland, 1974), s.v. "Oyster," 426. About oysters in literature from ancient Rome to the present, see Tomas Bolitho, *The Glorious Oyster, its history in Rome and Britain; what various writers and poets have said in its praise* (New York: Horizon Press, 1961). The book's appendix gives a short anthology of works related to the topic of oysters from Chaucer to Thackeray. In an article about the "oyster thematic" in Russian literature, Timenchik recalls Viazemsky's poem, "V lagunakh, kak frutti di mare..." Severianin's exotic mollusks, Akhmatova's oysters that smell of the sea, the "merry mollusks" of Arkady Averchenko, Chekhov's short story, and so forth. B. Katz adds Pushkin's oysters from "Excerpts from the Travels of Evgenii Onegin" to this list. "Philosophical" oysters are mentioned in one of Kiukhel'beker's "gnomes" (1829): "like oysters are inspiration." Stiva Oblonsky consumes "slurping Flensburg oysters" with pleasure, stripping their mother-of-pearl shells with a silver seafood fork while his dining companion, Levin, would have preferred a slice of white bread with cheese. Mayakovsky equated the oyster with the petit-bourgeois, gazing at the world from the "shell of possessions." Mandelstam placed oysters among the signs of the alien, old, and dangerous (for him) world: "With the world of the state, I was only childishly connected, / Feared oysters and looked at guardsmen furtively" (1931). For the history and typology of oysters in Russian literature, see Besprozvannyi, "'Literaturnye ustritsy.'"

21 Mystic Karl von Eckartshausen, when arguing for the biological possibility of the resurrection of the flesh, cited the example of oysters: if the oysters are transformed "into salt" and laid in sea sand, in time one can see the mollusk's "countless multitude of young emerging there." Karl Ekkartsgauzen, *Kliuch k tainstvam natury* (St. Petersburg, 1804), III:84.

22 For the erotic subtext of the oyster theme, see Besprozvannyi, "'Literaturnye ustritsy,'" 28–43.

23 Compare to the "Oyster for an Alderman" problem in Charles Darwin's work. See Robert Mackenzie Beverley, *The Darwinian Theory of the Transmutation of Species Examined by a Graduate of the University of Cambridge* (London: James Nisbet & Company, 1867), 340. As Terry Eagleton notes, "the theory of evolution has blurred the distinction between man and mollusk. So there is something inherently democratic and liberal-minded about literary realism. It involves a loving fidelity to the ordinary." *The English Novel: An Introduction* (Oxford: Wiley Blackwell, 2013), 168.

24 It is tempting to compare this regressive vision of man's plight with the one presented in Osip Mandelstam's poem "Lamarck" (1932).

25 Ivan Turgenev, *Pis'ma v vosemnadtsati tomakh* (Moscow: Nauka, 2002), XIII:489.

26 Ia. P. Polonskii, *Stikhotvoreniia* (Leningrad: Sovetskii pisatel', 1957), 272.

27 It is possible, though unlikely, that this word appeared in an earlier draft of Polonsky's poem.

28 Vinitsky, "Formula of an Oyster," 325–337.

29 Honoré de Balzac, *Oeuvres complètes* (Paris: Calmann Lévy, 1882), xv:229. English translation: *The Magic Skin, The Quest of the Absolute, and Other Stories*, translated by Ellen Marriage (Philadelphia: Avil Publishing House, 1901), 257.

30 Arthur Schopenhauer, *The Two Fundamental Problems of Ethics* (Oxford University Press, 2010), 39.

31 *PSSP* xiii:76.

32 Ledkovsky, *The Other Turgenev*, 92–93. In 1868 Turgenev wrote, "Great talent can exist next to a misunderstanding of artistic truth in the same person, such as in the striking example of Balzac. All of his characters smack of his typicality, developed and exquisitely finished down to the tiniest detail – and not one of them ever lived or could live; not one of them is even a shadow... of the truth." Ivan Turgenev, *Polnoe sobranie sochinenii i pisem. Sochineniia v dvenadtsati tomakh* (Moscow: Nauka, 1978–1986), x:347. The revulsion Turgenev felt toward Balzac as the founding father of the French realist school is suggested in his January 8, 1857 letter to S. T. Aksakov. Regarding this curiosity, P. D. Boborykin is not inclined to believe Turgenev's anti-Balzacian declarations: "there might be hidden influence. Not long before his death, Turgenev wrote P. I. Weinberg that he never liked Balzac and had practically not read him at all. But this did not prevent him from being a realist writer, to move in the direction of the novel that Balzac had been developing since the 1830s." Boborykin, *Vospominaniia v dvukh chastiakh* (Moscow: Khudozhestvennaia literatura, 1965), 1:319.

33 "The physical torment," wrote Turgenev's attending physician, Girtz, "is accompanied by a psychological disorder, marked by vague ideas of persecution and impassioned hostility toward all who surround him, a systematic distrust of his most loyal friends. From time to time, the patient has thoughts of suicide or homicide." Botkin, "Mnenie S. P. Botkina."

34 It is possible that Turgenev remembered not only the "Valentinian" oyster, but also the terrible agony of Balzac himself and his ante-mortem self-description in a letter to Théophile Gautier: "I... am a mummy, deprived of speech and movement." Mary F. Sandars, *Honoré de Balzac, His Life and Writings* (London: Kennikat Press, 1970), 367.

35 *PSSP* viii:396.

36 "L'homme n'est qu'un roseau, le plus faible de la nature; mais c'est un Roseau pensant." Blaise Pascal, *Pascal, Pensées*, edited by Ch. M. des Granges (Paris: Garnier, 1964), no. 347, 162. On the role of Pascal in Turgenev's work, see B. N. Tarasov, *"Mysliashchii trostnik": Zhizn' i tvorchestvo Paskalia v vospriiatii russkikh filosofov i pisatelei* (Moscow: Iazyki slavianskoi kul'tury, 2004), 467–474.

37 In contrast with Raphaël de Valentin, who sought a complete denial of movement and thought in order to preserve his life.

38 *Phaedrus* 250c, in vol. ix of *Plato in Twelve Volumes*, translated by Harold N.
    Fowler (Cambridge, MA: Harvard University Press, 1925).

39 "Kakuiu rol' igraet spiritualizm v poslednikh proizvedeniiakh I. S. Turgeneva,"
    Rebus 14 (1883); Viktor Ostrogorskii, *Pamiati Ivana Sergeevicha Turgeneva*
    (St. Petersburg: Rebus, 1883).

40 Ivan Turgenev, *Polnoe sobranie pisem* (St. Petersburg, 1885), 457.

41 Compare to what is written in the same June prose poem "Nessun maggior
    dolore": "Blue sky, light as a feather clouds, the scent of flowers, the sweet
    sounds of young voices, the radiant beauty of great works of art, the smile of
    happiness on an exquisite woman's face and these enchanting eyes . . . for what?
    What is all of this? The foul spoon of useless medication every two hours –
    that, that is what is needed!" *PSSP* xiii:215.

42 Quoted in Utevskii, *Smert' Turgeneva*, 24.

43 Quoted in A. G. Ostrovskii, *Turgenev v zapisiakh sovremennikov* (Leningrad,
    1929), 293.

44 Turgenev, *Polnoe sobranie pisem*, 475.

45 Ibid., 489.

46 Ibid., 502–503.

47 Ibid., 534.

48 Ibid., 506.

49 *PSSP* xiii:313.

50 Under the influence of opium, Balzac's hero drifts into dreaming, but unlike
    Turgenev's artistic dreams, Raphaël's visions are erratic and meaningless. In
    general, "Klara Milich," imbued with Schopenhauerian spiritualism, can be
    read as the ideological antithesis of *La Peau de chagrin*: Aratov's "integrity"
    versus Raphaël's depravity; Turgenev's will to death versus Balzac's characters'
    fear of death; Aratov's victorious cry in the finale and Raphaël's despairing
    cry at the moment of death; Aratov's soul "passing into the possession" of his
    beloved's ghost and Raphaël's corpse in Pauline's arms: "He is mine; I killed
    him; did I really not foresee this?" Balzac called his novel "the formula of
    human life" (*la formule de la vie humaine*). Turgenev's "Klara Milich" can be
    called "the formula of death."

51 Leskov, according to his son's memoirs, over the course of two or three months
    "allowed no one to pass by without talking to them about Turgenev's short
    story." Quoted in *PSSP* xiii:582.

52 *Sovremennoe obozrenie* 2 (1883), 33.

53 In his speech at Turgenev's funeral, Beketov, the rector of Petersburg University
    and grandfather of Alexander Blok, likened the deceased to a star whose shin-
    ing path illuminates the way to progress. The writer's end, in the professor's
    words, should prompt his compatriots to "turn to the sciences with renewed
    vigor," which Turgenev revered, and to the arts, which he "served with such
    selflessness." See A. F. Koni, ed., *Turgenevskii sbornik* (St. Petersburg, 1921), 63.

54 For spiritualist conflict in Russian culture of the second half of the nineteenth
    century in detail, see Vinitsky, *Ghostly Paradoxes*.

55 See L. V. Pumpianskii, "Gruppa 'tainstvennykh povestei,'" in Ivan Turgenev, *Sochineniia* (Moscow and Leningrad: Gosizdat, 1929), VIII:v–xx.

56 Compare to, for example, the death of Akhila in Leskov's novel *Cathedral Folk* (1872) or the death of the protagonist in the novella *The Rabbit Warren* (1894).

57 This doubt provides the principal contrast between Turgenev's version of realism and the materialistic realism of Saltykov-Shchedrin. Compare to the biting satirical critique of the flight from reality into dream presented in Saltykov-Shchedrin's *The Golovlev Family* (1875–1880).

58 In this regard, see the prose poem "Istina i pravda" (June 1882) in which belief in the immortality of the soul (*istina*) contrasts with earthly things, human Truth (*Pravda*): "All of life is built upon the knowledge of Truth (*Istina*), but how to 'possess it'? Yes, and more, to find bliss in it?" *PSSP* XIII:214.

59 It is of note that in M. E. Malyshev's illustration accompanying Turgenev's obituary, the writer is depicted sailing on Charon's boat in the underworld kingdom of sorrow. Seeing him, Diogenes says: "Oh, thank Jupiter, now it seems I can relax and put out my lantern. The man has been found, recognized . . . and sent to the other world." *Turgenevskii sbornik*, 331.

60 I. F. Annenskii, *Kniga otrazhenii* (St. Petersburg, 1906), 62. Annensky's essay can be read as the poet's singular response to the numerous panegyrics written for Turgenev over twenty years. In particular, the object of the poet's critique is the dead language of these panegyrics, testifying to the deep anachronism of the realist intellectual tradition that produced them.

61 Ibid., 63, italics mine.

62 Ibid. Annensky's interest in Turgenev's illness was symptomatic. The poet, in addition to heart disease, suffered from pain in the tongue, possibly caused by a cancerous tumor, and severe back pain. Vsevolod Setchkarev, *Studies in the Life and Work of Innokentij Annenskij* (The Hague: Mouton, 1963), 43.

63 Annenskii, *Kniga otrazhenii*, 67. Note that this description is polemically directed against the heroic descriptions of Turgenev's death by his contemporaries.

64 This rejection of cowardly "romanticism," by all appearances, is a motif inspired by the description of Balzac's death in Victor Hugo's "Mort de Balzac." The translation of this letter by D. V. Averkiev appeared in his introduction to *La Peau de chagrin* (St. Petersburg, 1901). The description of Turgenev's death evidently was written by Annensky under the influence of Tolstoy's description of the death of Ivan Ilych.

65 Annenskii, *Kniga otrazhenii*, 39.

66 "Yakov Aratov himself [that is, in Annensky's interpretation, Turgenev – I. V.] was ashamed of his ghosts all the more, it seems, and occupied himself with the most prosaic thing in the world – painting for photographic purposes" (65). It is of note that Annensky compares Turgenev's hero to Hippolytus without Antigone, Romeo poisoned by Juliet's kiss, Faust "having forgotten to take on the semblance of youth" and frightening the devil (68). The common denominator of all of these comparisons is the hero's "tired soul."

67 As per the observation of Lea Pil'd, the "illness" of the writer here "in addition to referring to an objective fact of Turgenev's biography, refers to the metaphorical language of the last third of the nineteenth century," which characterized the state of contemporary Russian and Western European culture ("twilight," "illness," "powerlessness," etc.). Lea Pil'd, *Turgenev v vospriiatii russkikh simvolistov, 1890–1900-e gody* (Tartu: Ülikooli Kirjastus, 1999), 37. It is worth adding that in Annensky's historical-cultural concepts these epithets characterize the still dominant but already long obsolete realist tradition.

68 Annenskii, *Kniga otrazhenii*, 73.

69 Cited in R. D. Timenchik, "The Oysters of Akhmatova and Annenskii," *Elementa: A Journal of Slavic Studies and Comparative Cultural Semiotics* 2:3–4 (1996): 313. In this quietist tirade, the repetition of negative particles and prefixes is noteworthy.

70 Compare to one of Turgenev's last "visions": "I was at the bottom of the ocean and saw monsters and the coupling of organisms which no one has ever described because no one has been resurrected after such a spectacle." On the symbols of sleep and the sea in Turgenev's works, see V. N. Toporov, *Strannyi Turgenev (chetyre glavy)* (Moscow: Russian State University for the Humanities, 1998), 104–129.

71 In Annensky's appeal, Timenchik sees a polemic with the scathing critique of decadence by Max Nordau, which likened symbolist poetry's tendency toward a syncreticism of feelings to the Pholas dactylus mollusk that "sees, hears, smells with one part of the body." Timenchik, "The Oysters of Akhmatova and Annenskii," 315.

72 It should be underscored that no matter how much Turgenev admired Schopenhauer, this idea of art as a transcendental force could hardly satisfy his sober realist consciousness.

73 Timenchik, "The Oysters of Akhmatova and Annenskii," 315. In his article on the history of the oyster in Russian literature, "'Literaturnye ustritsy' ili eshche raz o teme ustrits," Vadim Besprozvannyi disputes this genealogy of Akhmatova's image.

74 Heinrich Heine, *The Romantic School*, translated by L. Fleishman (New York: Henry Holt and Company, 1882), 133. See "Die romantische Schule," in Heinrich Heine, *Die romantische Schule* (Hamburg: Bey Hoffmann und Campe, 1836), 194.

75 John E. Bowlt observes that, in this evocative painting, "Vrubel's escape to a world of fantasy ... reached its creative culmination." "The Pearl," Bowlt writes, "provided a further stimulus to the younger artists of Moscow to seek inspiration in the mystical and the symbolic." Bowlt, *Russian Art, 1875–1975: A Collection of Essays* (New York: MSS Information Corporation, 1976), 66.

On the potential of ends

Caryl Emerson

Can there be a muse of Ends? The question hangs in the air throughout this volume with tantalizing hopelessness. Holding the fin de siècle strictly to the letter of its rhetoric, everything can only get worse until it's over. And yet the writer continues to write, often with inspiration – for an audience that perhaps will not exist, about characters incompetent to shape their own futures or even to seek a dignified exit from their desiccated present. In their Introduction, Ani Kokobobo and Katherine Bowers emphasize the era's exhaustion, impotence, boredom, decay, longing for the end. But they go further, encouraging us to look beyond familiar literary periodization, with its place-holding label "transition out of realism," to grasp this distinctive mood as a "fluid mentality outside of temporal framing." That it was. They note Max Nordau's observation, in his 1892 bestseller *Degeneration*, that the greatest Russian writers were precocious in thinking outside the positivist box: beginning in the 1850s, early works of Turgenev and Tolstoy already breathed eschatological despair. Robin Feuer Miller, in her chapter on the horror of Russia's destitute and dying street children, adds the early and late Dostoevsky. Responsible for this existentially dark worldview, the editors observe, is the fact that realist prose in the Russian Empire never developed into a comfortable, smug, middle-class genre. So when the End celebrated by European symbolism and decadence arrived in earnest in the 1890s, Russians had no self-satisfied bourgeois novel to disrupt or estrange. There was no veil to raise, no illusion to dispel. They could take the mood further, darker, deeper, gloomier.

In making Russian literature exemplary of pan-European decline, Nordau was not disinterested. He had a thesis to defend. But with the Great War and its catastrophic aftermath, some eminent Russian thinkers came around to Nordau's judgment on their greatest writers. The origin of moral and physical contamination would be pushed back to even earlier eras. One who did so was the Russian religious philosopher who provides the epigraph to the Introduction, Nikolai Berdiaev (1874–1948), soon to be expelled on Lenin's order from the young Bolshevik state. In a series of lectures delivered in Moscow in 1919–1920, he castigated the classics of Russian literature for his country's crisis in humanism, made all the quicker and more terrible because Russia began her decline without having passed through a genuine Renaissance.[1] In 1919 Berdiaev published a grim essay titled "Specters of the Russian Revolution."[2] In his view, beginning with Gogol's monstrous caricatures, the human image had been steadily repressed in Russia. A quest for Truth and a mania for justice were indeed present – but in so extremist and maximalist a form (Tolstoy erring in one direction, Dostoevsky in another) that no hope was held out for reasonable human flourishing, nor for an affirmative creativity respectful of transitional states. If the Frenchman is either a dogmatist or a skeptic, and the German either a mystic or a critic, then a Russian, Berdiaev assured his readers, "*is either an apocalypticist or a nihilist.*"[3] The first pole is at times positive, the second is always negative, but the options are equally degenerate.

Neither Berdiaev nor Nordau would have been satisfied by the consolatory, merely psychological explanation for end-hunger that Frank Kermode provides in his *Sense of an Ending*.[4] They sought in literary works some objective clinical evidence for the pathological exhaustion and millennial impatience of the Russian nineteenth century. As the essays in this volume demonstrate, an ample body of such depleted texts exists. This Afterword, however, picks up on another and minor strand in the Introduction: not the fascination with degeneration or horror at decay (such curiosity and awe before biophysical processes is a constant in all eras), but the fact that the era's dead-ended themes – nurtured, deified, essentialized – produced so many energized, inspired literary masterpieces. The source of the energy was precisely a sense of unavoidable crisis and doom. At several points, the Introduction hints at this sharpened genius, which verges on creative affirmation. Alongside Satanism and burning cities, "foreboding about the end" fostered optimism and a utopian search for meaning; alongside obligatory tracts by Schopenhauer, the fin-de-siècle mood "served also as a catalyst for realism's never-ending artistic creativity and literary experimentation."

The idea that doom can facilitate the life-force is not new. Philosophers of happiness speak of "posttraumatic growth."[5] In the biological sciences, theorists of creativity have long observed that a wounded but still living organism, if not pushed below the minimal threshold necessary to sustain fundamental life-functions, exhibits a phenomenal drive to create new wholes from shattered or maimed parts.[6] The Russian semiotician and cultural critic Yuri Lotman (1922–1993), in his final two books *Culture and Explosion* (1992) and *The Unpredictable Workings of Culture* (posthumously published in 2013), suggests something similar on the aesthetic plane: that a peaceful, productive sequence ending in sudden explosion or crisis might appear to destroy a great deal, but in fact reveals "the possibility of unexpected semantic recombinatory structures, which were perhaps impossible or forbidden at a preceding stage."[7] For the fin-de-siècle mood throughout Europe was not solely one of rot and degeneration. The paths out of nineteenth-century realism were diverse. Although paradigms of disintegration and grinding to a halt attracted many strong minds, the era was also marked (in the words of one historian of interwar France) by "a newfound capacity for synthesis," which integrated materialism with eternalism and traditional religious thought with "spiritual naturalism."[8] This is not a trivial matter. For a writer might at times create out of a void, as Leo Shestov claimed Chekhov had done, but no artist can create *into* one. Through mastery of their given medium, artists generate viable worlds. A durable work of art, whatever its themes, demands an uncanny degree of integrity and harmony. Most of the works discussed in this volume achieve that high degree of integration. And while we might dispute placing an Artsybashev, Korolenko, Andreev, even Saltykov-Shchedrin in this masterpiece class, we cannot question Gogol, Dostoevsky, Turgenev, Tolstoy, Chekhov.

Several of the essays here read differently when we focus not on their trajectory of disintegration – empirically real as that is – but on their attention to moments of creative synthesis and symbiosis. Such moments, however confused or tentative, add to the work's complexity and provide the impetus to go on. At times, these moments can govern the tone. Always they interrupt expectations, provoke an inner reconciliation (marked by a laugh or a smile), and point to a way out, physically or conceptually. If Frank Kermode's *Sense of an Ending* was basically backward-looking and tragic in its shape – the world begins Golden, degenerates, and ends with everyone dead – then a symbiotic or synthesizing lens on the shape of a story produces something akin to comedy. It has been argued, most recently by the philosopher Dmitri Nikulin, that creativity is always comedic, in that it looks forward and presumes the survival of unforeseen relationships (between ideas, lovers, hopes, plot options).[9] Serious comedy is rarely start-to-finish *happy*. But, Nikulin observes, it is always ingenious, fertile, pragmatic, devoted to an optimal degree of communal wellbeing – and thus difficult to carry off. One cannot slide toward the denouement of a comedy the way one slides toward the Apocalypse. To bring about a benevolent ending takes cleverness, sobriety, cooperation (that is, symbiosis and reciprocity), and hard work. For this reason are its heroes so often the workers: servants, slaves, fools, illegitimates without legacy and misfits without rank.

Comedy can, but need not, endorse the metaphysical or otherworldly realm.[10] Featured in the present book are dark discussions of secular as well as faith-based texts that contain a pivotal comedic moment. One is Yuri Corrigan's probe of *The Adolescent*, with its association of transfigurative light with laughter in an "illumined corner" of the confused hero's soul; another, more profane, is Connor Doak's "hysterical, effeminate, and ineffectual" Stepan Trofimovich from Dostoevsky's *Demons*, a man available for redemption largely because he has been for so long a comic buffoon. Chekhov called two of his plays comedies, including *The Seagull*, which ends on a suicide. In her discussion of Nina Zarechnaia, the play's romantic lead, Jenny Kaminer remarks on the boldness of the image: a Russian woman failed, betrayed, publicly disgraced, probably of mediocre talent, but undeterred in her devotion to the stage. Here is black comedy that allows dying for love – but insists on living for creative art. "Nina *endures* in a purposeful way and without a 'fear of life,'" Kaminer writes. What matters at the end (as at the end of *Uncle Vanya*) is endurance and survival after a collapse of one's ideals – which is to say, acceptance of that middle space of indeterminate duration that apocalypse would drain of all meaning. Comedy means tolerating the growth options of the present. Or to take a cue from Newlin's discussion of *Uncle Vanya* (and its early variant, the comedy *The Wood Demon*), it means, at the very least, a conscientious *mapping* of options in the present. Alongside the ravaged emptied-out areas on Dr. Astrov's regional chorographs, patches of new growth testify to his (and Chekhov's) planting of new trees.

The play text, written in expectation of embodiment, is more malleable than a piece of prose. Nina's final confession to Konstantin, like Sonya's closing monologue to her uncle Vanya, can be performed in an ironic, embittered, hysterically melodramatic key. The play permits that interpretation, as it permits those hilarious Moscow Art Theater productions of the late Soviet period that featured Chekhov's protagonists perpetually drunk. Any one intonation is incomplete. But to follow the lead of critic James Wood in his work on laughter and the novel, the purest comedic instincts are probably embodied not in a comedy of correction (didactic, doctrinaire, satiric) but in a comedy of forgiveness.[11] And at some level, all works of art are comedic offerings – if only because they contain fantastically well-crafted, well-organized energy that cannot insist on immediate reciprocity.

This energy is caught in artistic structures and suspended there. Authored works are gifts at the open end of a relationship, not at the contractual, tragic, score-keeping end.

Such a capacious view of comedy does not apply to all subject matter discussed in this book. But to a surprising extent Russian writers during this period, even those dazzled by the most extravagant nihilism, default to one marker for comedy: after the catastrophe, a glimpse of the ambivalent, spiritually fertile, and open-ended end. That a void opens up beneath one's feet, none would deny. In the process of actively creating art in response to that perceived void, however, the writer generates a new energy field with its own unprecedented economy. The need for such new fields, if sufficiently intense, signals the end of an era. As realism (with its positivist and empiricist bias) tipped toward a less confident twilight in the 1880s, anxieties mounted. Novelistic heroes became less classically "heroic," that is, less elite, select, ambitious, tied to their deed. Unlike the earlier aristocratic dandies and melancholics, these new subjects were less in control of their bodies, psyches, or chosen masks. As Thomas Pavel writes in his history of the novel, by mid-century the genre was bringing forth "another, more ordinary kind of solitary being," the unglamorous and vulnerable loner who would people a "wave of pessimistic novels" during the last third of the century.[12]

Alone and of poor cheer: however ecstatic the symbiosis achieved during its prime, the individual subject faces eventual dissolution. When body and spirit both fail before their time – the fin-de-siècle mood – it is natural to seek more sustaining relations between the material world, now seen as brutally punitive, and some potentially immaterial supra-personal realm.[13] In retrospect we recognize this tension-filled shift as the beginning stir of symbolism, mystic decadence, and, in Russia, the Third or religious Renaissance. But note that neither faith nor energy is a prerequisite for this quest. Ennui, apathy, and spiritual exhaustion might even spur it on, lowering the human creature's resistance and furthering its receptivity to unexpected syntheses. In the final tally, art probably does not command the means to express total despair or total ends. Both these absolutes are too shallow. The deeper the negative polarity, the more it enters into tension with those redemptive or open-ended dimensions that I have called comedic: reconciliation, relief, laughter, a tolerance for the unknown, or creativity. How do the chapters in this volume (three on Dostoevsky, two each on Tolstoy, Turgenev, and Chekhov, one on Gogol, and four on lesser-known writers) fare with this idea of a lifeline, or "loophole," out of the end?

It must be said that some essays resolutely decline to explore this possibility, and with good reason. Their subject matter, conceptual framework, and tough-minded commitment to an ideology of non-transcendence preclude any exit. Emma Lieber takes two masterpieces by Turgenev, the sentimental "A Living Relic" and the perversely cruel *First Love*, and by concentrating not on the loving bodies that carry the plot but on the voyeuristic narrator (carefree hunter, helpless rival son) who relates the plot, implicates teller and reader alike in unpardonable violence. Katherine Bowers, a scholar of the gothic, chronicles the special awfulness of the "fall of a house" in the Russian context, where isolation, backwardness, and the barbaric habits of feudalism intensify the dire effects of any disruption to an estate system dependent upon stable farming. Ani Kokobobo too sees no viable way out of her chosen subsistence economy, which is grotesque realism: its bodies – monstrous because violated, non-transcendent because realistic – can estrange reality only by dehumanizing it. (Although her bodies know of no way out, Kokobobo provides keen insight into her authors at the fin de siècle: Tolstoy's death-like "darkening" of the canon with his *On Life*, and the scandalous Artsybashev – for whom sexuality was healthier, more straightforward, less polluting than it was for the bard of Yasnaya Polyana – insisting that he disapproved of decadent symbolism and sided with Dostoevsky and Tolstoy.)

Muireann Maguire and Edith Clowes also take on authors who are loophole-resistant. Maguire juxtaposes the predecessor Gogol and antecedent Krzhizhanovsky as two "fantastic realists" bookending the fin de siècle. In so doing she enriches the topography of escape routes out of an unacceptable present – but very differently than Newlin with his ecological maps. Gogol's Akaky and Krzhizhanovsky's Sutulin are each "little men" who break frame. There is liberation in this illicit breaking out, which is transformative for them before it is annihilating. But where the nineteenth-century romantic writer draws on devices of the grotesque, the twentieth-century modernists Sologub and Krzhizhanovsky experiment with Einstein's fourth dimension, and with a Swiftian play with scale taken to ghastly extreme. Their "little men" literally get littler and littler without respite, or else get stuck in expanding space. In parables like these, matter must speak for itself until it disappears. Clowes is less metaphysical, and unusual in this volume for her attention to readerships and the market. Andreev, the period's most popular middlebrow writer, created in his horror stories an accessible "abject realism" that satisfied the popular appetite for radical despair through close-ups of abused bodies and vivid hallucinations of death. But even Andreev gives us a glimpse of Musia, the doomed revolutionary of "Seven People Hanged," whose body glows with strength and ascetic purity as she prepares it for death. Abjectness is a state of the irreversible flesh but also a state of the attuned mind.

Then there is Saltykov-Shchedrin. This great Russian satirist is discussed in two essays, by Bowers in the context of the extinction of a family, and by Kate Holland as the prototypical Russian text of atavistic degeneration, biological determinism, and the Russian response to Émile Zola. James Wood (who gave us the comedy of correction and forgiveness) praises this "strange, raucous book whose characters aspire to the condition of nothingness."[14] He is especially taken by the pious figure of Porfiry, Bloodsucker and Judas, a hypocrite beyond what the enlightened Molière could ever have imagined on stage. For Wood, there is no morality in sight anywhere on the estate of Golovlevo, no ethical marker from which a soul might fall away. Holland, in her chapter, acknowledges that the craze for scientific documentation of inherited "moral and physiological stigmata" held Russian readers mesmerized by French naturalism for the better part of a decade. But her history of Saltykov-Shchedrin's slow "assembling" of his novel out of more rudimentary journalistic parts is instructive. A collection of satirical sketches could resemble Zola; so, even, could a chronicle. When the work became a full-fledged novel, however, it developed a morally inflected narrator – and, in the tradition of Russian novels, offered a way up and out. Porfiry's guilt is revealed to him toward the end of Holy Week. "Up and out" does not mean some rosy utopia or pie-in-the-sky otherworldliness. It is too late to change the plot of this disintegrated family. But it is never too late to prod open the Russian reader, who need not be limited to the "surgeon's scalpel." The Fall of Zola in Russia by 1881 reaffirmed the survival, in that astonishingly fecund culture, of the committed human face.

In his final entry Vinitsky performs a huge service by analyzing Turgenev's long, immobilized dying as the capstone of a "tragic ethos" that is materialist, earth-bound, realist. No comedic transcendent moment here. Thus the metonym of the oyster: clinging to the rock, categorically unwilling to entertain an afterlife or an immaterial realm, Turgenev remains "in a realistic frame of consciousness . . . to the very end." For all that doctors delivered public lectures on the progress of the famous writer's bodily decay, we are never privy to a precise diagnosis of Turgenev's illness. His dying became emblematic of animal torment that was neither transition nor liberation but a principled test for the "proud, rational mind." This was a test honestly undertaken. For it is only after the mollusk dies that any possible pearl might be harvested. Vinitsky cites the eloquent symbolist poet Innokentiy Annensky on the lesson of the oyster: away with realism's rush to answers and to purposeful activity. Be not ashamed that something precious might be growing in you of which you know nothing.

Thus the loophole – positing a hypothetical way out of the disasters we now know – is not a reality that all our twilight-of-realism writers in good conscience can accept. One of the essays, Jane Costlow's on Vladimir Korolenko, almost apologizes for entertaining it. Here it has arrived, Costlow admits, the fin de siècle, and my chosen subject "seems like a bizarrely robust outlier, encountering rural Russia with humor, generosity, and probing intelligence." Working with the genre of the *ocherk* or "sketch from life," Costlow develops a "phenomenological realism" that resists depression and decay because it resists generalization, discredits the false glance of a solitary voyeur on a speeding train, and insists that the writer get up, get out, walk, and make eye contact. This motif of wandering extends to the *ocherk*'s lack of resolution, its habit of "leaving questions unanswered." Open-endedness leads to open-heartedness. But darkness is by no means absent: Korolenko describes eclipses, famines, failed miracle cures on the far side of an icon with its "dark blotch" of the Mother of God. To the eyewitness ethnographer, however, catastrophe on the ground rarely looks the way it does when it is written up. Tragic moments are "pauses" in relentless forward movement. In assigning these sketches of rural Russia to more than mere journalism (calling them a "complicated map of fiction, non-fiction, and memoir"), Costlow anticipates the "in-between genres" created by that survivor of a time incomparably more awful than anything the fin-de-siècle writers ever knew: Lidiia Ginzburg's quasi-fictive eyewitness stories of the Leningrad Blockade.

Korolenko's ethnographic realism is shared by many of Russia's great novelists, who also "loophole" it. Dostoevsky is an obvious case, for a symbiotic leap out of failed or compromised matter is highly characteristic of his vision. In Chapter 2, Yuri Corrigan provides three consecutive theories for coherent selfhood devised by Arkady, the half-grown, illegitimate, comedic misfit in search of his "non-material indwelling identity," to help him process his rudderless adolescence. First the deeply secretive autonomous self, with its precious "idea," is posited and sorely tested. The second theory, "a relational self anchored in others," is the canonical Bakhtinian solution to personality in Dostoevsky; in the context of father-worship, however, such a self-image supplies only a "whirlwind anthropology," gusting anxiously around a possible void. The third theory, through which the hero has a chance to grow up, is incarnational (a synthesis of body and psyche) and robust enough to enable Arkady to survive that "blank piece of paper," the "placeholder soul" on which he had pinned all his needy hopes. Something of the same dynamic, played out in even more helpless children, is detected in Robin Feuer Miller's reading of "A Boy at Christ's Christmas Party" in Chapter 3. She notes the steady darkening of childhood in the post-exile Dostoevsky, the shift away from Dickens's sentimental endings that snatch the afflicted back from the brink of death and toward a more ascetic resolution – if resolution it be – on the transcendent plane. To the confused freezing child on the streets, clarification comes only as its soul is being whisked away to heaven, a thoroughly comedic, communal place of reunions and holiday gifts. Miller writes that "the human spark – the capacity for wonder, for imagination – remained with him until the end." In this wonder she finds the perfect focus for a fin-de-siècle Dostoevskian hybrid between Christmas tale, Andersen-style naturalism, and Russian fairy tale (the last permitting the marvelous without "the hesitation of the fantastic"). Whether or not we grown-up readers can accept at face value Dostoevsky's second variant of the story ("They met in God's heaven"), the martyred child surely could. For a young child lives – and we must presume, dies – on a continuum with wonder and imagination, the raw material for art.

As regards comedic loopholes, Tolstoy is a more difficult case, for all the harsh reasons that Berdiaev supplied in 1919. Alexander Burry and S. Ceilidh Orr's analysis of apocalyptic motifs in *Anna Karenina* begins with a refreshingly revisionist look at that amoral life-force, that exemplary symbiotic body-and-psyche, Stiva Oblonsky, sexual philanderer and social lubricant. Is he a loophole out of degeneration into the light? There is no easy answer. Like Count Ilya Rostov in *War and Peace* (arguably a more precise model for "Slavophilism" among Tolstoy's characters), Stiva functions as a generous, tolerant, inclusive Russian type, his charm distinguishing him from the later more brittle and aggressive Pan-Slavic hero. The authors suggest a parallel between Stiva's unreflective celebration of the present and the peasant Karataev, prisoner of the French, in *War and Peace*. Without a doubt, the naturally rejoicing human organism delighted Tolstoy, who is one of the very few world-class writers able to portray intense happiness at length, in depth, and without a false note. But Stiva's moral pragmatism, roundness, fertility, and instinctive democracy dry up with appalling abruptness in the final part of *Anna Karenina*. The Oblonsky siblings, Stiva and Anna, both feel life sensitively, sensually – and by means of selective forgetting, wish to have it all. Their comedic utopianism tying them to the present tense of their appetites is ultimately revealed as a doomed one-way railroad journey. By the end of the 1870s, Tolstoy was seeing everywhere in the animal principle only decay and degradation, most acutely in himself.

* * *

In the deep cold winter of 1978–1979, six years before his death, the *enfant terrible* of Russian formalism and its longest-living survivor, Victor Shklovsky (1893–1984), granted a series of interviews with the Italian Slavist Serena Vitale.[15] There was no glimmer yet of glasnost; during the second week of her visit, Vitale was run down on the street by the KGB thugs assigned to trail her, leaving her badly bruised and with two cracked ribs. Shklovsky urged her to return promptly to Italy with her precious tapes; over seventy years in literary harness, he had learned how to bend so as not to break. On December 23, the eighty-six-year-old writer had discoursed on the nature of artistic ends. Of course Russia's greatest writers are famous for avoiding formal conclusions, he remarked. But more generally, "talking about a beginning, middle, and end has nothing to do with art . . . And I myself, with all the love I have for novels, I prefer to doze off before the denouement." Shklovsky did just that, dying a year or two before the end of the Soviet era, a collapse he could not have foreseen. When Vitale pressed this venerable formalist, on the third day of her interviewing, on the interaction of historical reality with artistic creativity, Shklovsky recalled Pushkin's comment in 1825 that he would probably never complete his *Eugene Onegin.* "Art always echoes with the screech of icebergs scraping against the ship, keeping it from moving forward." The fin de siècle sensed that iceberg heading for the ship. If a muse of Ends exists, however, most likely her eye is fixed on the survivors teeming on the far shore.

NOTES

1 For a compact discussion of the young Berdiaev in the context of Nordau (and the rising Marxists who agreed with Nordau: let depravity proceed, let the artists degenerate, they argued; it clears the way for wholesome culture), see Galina S. Rylkova, "A Silver Lining to the Russian Clouds: Remembering the Silver Age in the 1920s and 1930s," *Kritika: Explorations in Russian and Eurasian History* 1:3 (2000): 481–500, especially 485–489.

2 Nikolai Berdiaev, "Specters of the Russian Revolution" (*Dukhi Russkoi revoliutsii*), in *Out of the Depths (De Profundis): A Collection of Articles on the Russian Revolution,* edited and translated by William F. Woehrlin (Irvine, CA: Charles Schlacks, 1986), 33–64. *Iz glubiny* (*Out of the Depths*) was the final volume in a trilogy of anthologies by eminent Russian religious and idealist philosophers

against the materialist, positivist, utilitarian ideology of the Russian radical intelligentsia (the first was *Problems of Idealism*, 1902, the second and most famous, *Landmarks* [*Vekhi*], 1909).

3 Ibid., 41, italics in original. Berdiaev's case against Dostoevsky (that he popularized the image of revolutionary as Antichrist and the Russian people's messianic task) is not as savage as his case against Tolstoy. A thinker with no sense of historical dynamism, Tolstoy was a paradoxical mix: the extreme individualist who, in the name of a universal ideal, preached the destruction of everything that possessed its own qualities, history, and personal face. Because a nation's culture was the cumulative product of individual creativity, Tolstoy would abolish the entire cultural stratum (59). And thus "in the holiness toward which he strove, there was a terrible gracelessness, an abandonment of God." In the legacy of Tolstoy, concludes the personalist Berdiaev, Russian moralism fused with Russian nihilism (57), transforming the great writer into a "poisoner of the wells of life" (60).

4 According to Kermode, both transitoriness and the idea of eternity are intolerable, even unimaginable. Thus do structures of literature appeal to us, for they allow us to draw boundaries and manipulate time. Among the most satisfying of these manipulations is the positing of a Golden Age before our era and a purged eschatological moment (usually full of terrors) after it. The present, meanwhile, is consigned to a "decadent middle," usually in decline, which yearns toward its own extinction. Kermode suggests that we not only sense endings, but also crave them. In his new Epilogue to a turn-of-the-century reprinting of his famous book after thirty-five years, Kermode – in the spirit of the present volume – notes that the mid-1960s had indeed seemed to him a "terminally bad time. All of which at least goes to show that the apocalypse can flourish on its own, quite independent of millennia." See Kermode, *The Sense of an Ending*, 182.

5 See the section so subtitled in Chapter 7, "The Uses of Adversity," in Jonathan Haidt, *The Happiness Hypothesis: Finding Modern Truth in Ancient Wisdom* (New York: Basic Books, 2006), 135–154.

6 See, for example, Edmund W. Sinott, "The Creativeness of Life," in *Creativity and Its Cultivation: Addresses Presented at the Interdisciplinary Symposia on Creativity, Michigan State University, East Lansing*, edited by Harold H. Anderson (New York: Harper & Brothers Publishers, 1959), 17. In that same volume, Erich Fromm, in his essay "The Creative Attitude," notes that the ability of an organism to be confused, puzzled, and yet still curious under conditions of conflict and tension is directly related to its creative survival (51–52). "The willingness to be born – and this means the willingness to let go of all 'certainties' and illusions – requires courage and faith" (53).

7 Yuri M. Lotman, "The Pseudo-New and the New," in *The Unpredictable Workings of Culture*, translated by Brian James Baer and edited by Igor Pilshchikov and Silvi Salupere (Tallinn University Press, 2013), 190. Lotman suggests that such explosion mimics revelation: "These structures have the capacity to shock

with an unexpected artistic language, with an unexpected meaning. The spasmodic shift to a new level of complexity is experienced by an audience as an instantaneous insight, an explosion of thought."

8 For this "synthetic mentality" as it affected Catholic France, 1890 to 1920, see Stephen Schloesser, "Prologue: Realism, Eternalism, Spiritual Naturalism," in his superb monograph *Jazz Age Catholicism: Mystic Modernism in Postwar Paris, 1919–1933* (University of Toronto Press, 2005), 18–19. Although wider in timespan than the Russian fin-de-siècle malaise, Schloesser's Chapters 1 ("Cultural Manicheanism: Apocalyptic Melodrama") and 2 ("Trauma and Memorial: Repatriating the Repressed") provide a valuable French counterpoint to the present volume. For many symbolist and decadent artists in these two closely linked cultural elites, *le Renouveau catholique* filled the role of the Russian Third (religious) Renaissance.

9 Dmitri Nikulin, *Comedy, Seriously: A Philosophical Study* (New York: Palgrave Macmillan, 2014). Nikulin argues for the vigor, humanity, and hard work of "New Comedy" (the Greek Menander and the later Romans Plautus and Terence) in opposition to the "Old Comedy" (the satires of Aristophanes). This vision of comedy resembles Bakhtin's carnival in that it deals with people as vulgar and base. But unlike carnival, its success requires not only the lower bodily stratum but also intelligence and wit (thus is the dynamic of all philosophy "comedic"). Nikulin argues that the modern subject of European romanticism found tragedy more congenial than comedy; under the spell of the autonomous Cartesian model and its solipsistic rationalism, this subject "always confronts its own end and, consequently, is oriented toward death" (vii). The nineteenth century, Nikulin argues in his Chapter 2, lost the legacy and worldview of New Comedy. Nikulin's thesis supplies a provocative "theatrical" prehistory to the rise of naturalism – both Zola's hardcore practice and the tentative, eventually skeptical Russian response to it.

10 There is comedy of the divine sort, like Dante's, where Final Ends are suffused with grace. But there is also Chekhov's droll, dry designation of "comedy" for his *Seagull*. The comedic cue comes in Act Four, when Doctor Dorn answers Sorin's remark about the animal fear of dying: "It only makes sense to fear death if you believe in immortality and are scared because you've sinned."

11 James Wood, *The Irresponsible Self: On Laughter and the Novel* (New York: Farrar, Straus and Giroux, 2004), 6–8. Wood notes that comedies of correction, with their origins in Aristotle, are more stable; "there is the stability of didacticism . . . [and] of allegory or fable" (8–9), to which he opposes a more Shakespearean, "irresponsible" (that is, unreliable, flexible, responsive, unpredictable) "subset of the comedy of forgiveness." He includes in this group both Tolstoy and Chekhov.

12 Thomas G. Pavel, *The Lives of the Novel: A History* (Princeton University Press, 2014), 268. Earlier in his discussion, Pavel notes that the production of mainstream European novels in the second half of the nineteenth century was concentrated in France and England; the boldest experimentation and

syntheses occurred in the European periphery (Germany, Russia, and Spain) (226).

13 This shift might be considered in terms of two binary pairs, each of which has the potential of a symbiotic or mutually enhancing relationship between its two terms. The first binary consists of the creaturely body and the creaturely psyche; the second, of the natural or material cosmos and some supra-natural or transcendent cosmos. When the symbiosis possible within the first pair ages or exhausts itself, the second pair is conjectured and thrust outward. For this to happen, the creature need not possess a clear definition of this immaterial realm, and certainly need not feel threatened, frightened, or for that matter reverent in the face of it. But actualization of the potentials in both pairs is nowhere guaranteed. They must be created, after which new syntheses are possible between resultant binary pairs. This conceptual framework is indebted to discussions about this volume in the summer of 2014 with my father, David Geppert, who at ninety-three remains my most astute consultant on matters of creative survival, and to refinements suggested by my colleague Yuri Corrigan.

14 "Saltykov-Shchedrin's Subversion of Hypocrisy," in Wood, *The Irresponsible Self*, 95.

15 Serena Vitale, *Shklovsky, Witness to an Era: Interviews by Serena Vitale*, translated by Jamie Richards (Champaign, IL: Dalkey Archive Press, 2012 [Italian orig. 1979]). Quotes successively on 54, 55, 57, 92.

Bibliography

Afanas'ev, A. N. "Tsarevna-liagushka," in *Narodnye russkie skazki A. N. Afanas'eva*. Moscow: Nauka, 1985.

Aksakov, S. T. *Sobranie sochinenii v piati tomakh*. Moscow: Pravda, 1966.

Allaby, Michael, ed. *A Dictionary of Ecology*, 2nd edn., s.v. "Ecology." Oxford University Press, 1998.

Allen, Elizabeth Cheresh. *Beyond Realism: Turgenev's Poetics of Secular Salvation*. Stanford University Press, 1992.

Andersen, Hans Christian. *The Stories of Hans Christian Andersen: A New Translation from the Danish*, translated by Diana Crone Frank and Jeffrey Frank. Durham, NC: Duke University Press, 2005.

Andreev, Leonid. *Sobranie sochinenii v shesti tomakh*. Moscow: Khudozhestvennaia literatura, 1990.

  Sobranie sochinenii v shesti tomakh. Moscow: Knigovek, 2012.

Andrievskii, Ivan, ed. *Brokgaus-Efron Entsiklopedicheskii slovar'*, s.v. "Ekologiia," vol. XL/LXXIX. St. Petersburg, 1904.

Annenskii, I. F. *Kniga otrazhenii*. St. Petersburg, 1906.

Arsen'ev, K. K. *Saltykov-Shchedrin (Literaturno-obshchestvennaia kharakteristika)*. St. Petersburg: Tipografiia "Obshchestvennaia Pol'za," 1906.

Artsybashev, Mikhail. "Introduction," in *The Millionaire* by Michael Artzibashef, translated by Percy Pinkerton, 5–10. New York: B. W. Huebsch, 1915.

  Sanin. St. Petersburg: Zhizn', 1908.

  Sanin, translated by Michael Katz. Ithaca, NY: Cornell University Press, 2001.

Avramenko, Richard and Jingcai Ying. "Dostoevsky's Heroines: Or, on the Compassion of the Russian Woman," in *Dostoevsky's Political Thought*, edited by Richard Avramenko and Lee Trepanier, 73–90. Lanham, MD: Lexington Books, 2013.

Badcock, Sarah. "Autocracy in Crisis: Nicholas the Last," in *Late Imperial Russia: Problems and Prospects*, edited by Robert McKean and Ian Thatcher, 9–27. New York: Manchester University Press, 2005.

Bakhtin, Mikhail. "Author and Hero in Aesthetic Activity," translated by Vadim Liapunov and Kenneth Brostrom, in *Art and Answerability: Early Philosophical Essays by M. M. Bakhtin*, edited by Michael Holquist and Vadim Liapunov, 4–256. Austin: University of Texas Press Slavic Series, 1990.

Problems of Dostoevsky's Poetics, edited and translated by Caryl Emerson. Minneapolis: University of Minnesota Press, 1984.

Rabelais and His World, translated by Helene Iswolsky. Bloomington: Indiana University Press, 1984.

Balasubramanian, Radha. *The Poetics of Korolenko's Fiction*. New York: Peter Lang, 1997.

Balukhatyi, S. "Biblioteka Chekhova," in *Chekhov i ego sreda*, edited by N. F. Bel'chikov, 335. Leningrad: Akademiia, 1930.

Balzac, Honoré de. *Oeuvres completes*, vol. xv. Paris: Calmann Lévy, 1882.

The Magic Skin, The Quest of the Absolute, and Other Stories, translated by Ellen Marriage. Philadelphia: Avil Publishing House, 1901.

Barsht, Konstantin. "Defining the Face: Observations on Dostoevskii's Creative Process," in *Russian Literature, Modernism and the Visual Arts*, edited by Catriona Kelly and Stephen Lovell, 23–57. Cambridge University Press, 2000.

Baudelaire, Charles. "Notes nouvelles sur Edgar Poe," in *Selected Critical Studies of Baudelaire*, edited by D. Parmée, 50–69. Cambridge University Press, 1949.

Bayley, John. *Tolstoy and the Novel*. London: Chatto & Windus, 1966.

Beer, Daniel. *Renovating Russia: The Human Sciences and the Fate of Liberal Modernity, 1880–1930*. Ithaca, NY: Cornell University Press, 2008.

Belknap, Robert L. "The Didactic Plot: The Lesson about Suffering in *Poor Folk*," in *Actualité de Dostoevskij*, edited by Nina Kauchtschischwili, 67–69. Genoa: La Quercia Edizioni, 1982.

Belyi, Andrei. "Gogol'," in *Kritika, estetika, teoriia simvolizma*, vol. 1, 302–318. Moscow: Iskusstvo, 1994.

Berdiaev, Nikolai. *Mirosozertsanie Dostoevskogo*. Prague: YMCA Press, 1923.

The Origin of Russian Communism, translated by R. M. French. Ann Arbor: University of Michigan Press, 1960.

"Specters of the Russian Revolution," in *Out of the Depths (De Profundis): A Collection of Articles on the Russian Revolution*, edited and translated by William F. Woehrlin, 33–64. Irvine, CA: Charles Schlacks, 1986.

Besprozvannyi, Vadim. "'Literaturnye ustritsy' ili eshche raz o teme ustrits," *Toronto Slavic Quarterly* 36 (2011): 21–51.

Bethea, David. *The Shape of the Apocalypse in Russian Fiction*. Princeton University Press, 1989.

Beverley, Robert Mackenzie. *The Darwinian Theory of the Transmutation of Species Examined by a Graduate of the University of Cambridge*. London: James Nisbet & Company, 1867.

Bezzubov, Valerii Ivanovich. *Leonid Andreev i traditsii russkogo realizma*. Tallinn: Eesti Raamat, 1984.

Bialyi, G. A. *Russkii realism ot Turgeneva k Chekhovu*. Leningrad: Sovetskii pisatel', 1990.

V. G. Korolenko. Moscow and Leningrad: Khudozhestvennaia literatura, 1949.

Blagosvetlov, Grigorii E. "Kritik bez kriticheskoi merki," *Delo* 2:2 (1878): 327–345.

Boborykin, P. D. *Vospominaniia v dvukh chastiakh*, vol. 1. Moscow: Khudozhestvennaia literatura, 1965.

Boele, Otto. *Erotic Nihilism in Late Imperial Russia: The Case of Mikhail Artsyba-shev's Sanin.* Madison: University of Wisconsin Press, 2009.

Bolitho, Tomas. *The Glorious Oyster, its history in Rome and Britain; what various writers and poets have said in its praise.* New York: Horizon Press, 1961.

Botkin, S. P. "Mnenie S. P. Botkina o khode bolezni I. S. Turgeneva," *Novosti* 209, October 29, 1883.

Botting, Fred. *Gothic.* London: Routledge, 1996.

Bowlt, John E. *Russian Art, 1875–1975: A Collection of Essays.* New York: MSS Information Corporation, 1976.

Brauer, Fae. "The Stigmata of Abjection: Degenerate Limbs, Hysterical Skin and the Tattooed Body," in *A History of Visual Culture: Western Civilization from the 18th to the 21st Century,* edited by Jane Kromm and Susan Benforado Bakewell, 169–184. Oxford: Berg, 2010.

Brooks, Jeffrey. *When Russia Learned to Read: Literacy and Popular Literature, 1861–1917.* Princeton University Press, 1985.

Brooks, Peter. *Realist Vision.* New Haven, CT: Yale University Press, 2005.

Buell, Lawrence. "Environmental Apocalypticism," in *The Environmental Imag-ination: Thoreau, Nature Writing, and the Formation of American Culture,* 280–308. Cambridge, MA: Harvard University Press, 1996.

Bulgakov, Mikhail. *Sobach'e serdtse,* in *Sobranie sochinenii,* edited by V. I. Losev, vol. III, 217–332. St. Petersburg: Azbuka-Klassika, 2002.

Bulgakov, Sergei. "Heroism and Asceticism," in *Vekhi: Landmarks: A Collection of Articles about the Russian Intelligentsia,* translated by Marshall S. Shatz and Judith E. Zimmerman. New York: M. E. Sharpe, 1994.

Bunin, I. A. *Dry Valley,* in *Ivan Bunin: Collected Stories,* translated by Graham Hettlinger. Chicago: Ivan R. Dee, 2007.

  Sukhodol, in *Sobranie sochinenii v piati tomakh,* vol. II. Moscow: Pravda, 1956.

Busch, R. L. "Turgenev's *Ottsy i deti* and Dostoevskii's *Besy,*" *Canadian Slavonic Papers* 16:1 (1984): 1–9.

Bushmin, A. S. *Khudozhestvennyi mir Saltykova-Shchedrina.* Leningrad: Nauka, 1987.

Casey, Edward S. "Cartography and Chorography," in *Representing Place: Land-scape Painting and Maps,* 154–170. Minneapolis: University of Minnesota Press, 2002.

Chances, Ellen. *Conformity's Children: An Approach to the Superfluous Man in Russian Literature.* Columbus, OH: Slavica, 1978.

Chekhov, A. P. *Anton Chekhov's Life and Thought: Selected Letters and Commentary,* translated by Michael Heim and edited by Simon Karlinsky. Evanston, IL: Northwestern University Press, 1973.

  Anton Chekhov's Selected Plays, translated by Laurence Senelick. New York: W. W. Norton, 2005.

  Chekhov's Uncle Vanya *and* The Wood Demon, translated by Donald Rayfield. London: Bloomsbury, 1995.

  The Complete Plays, edited and translated by Laurence Senelick. New York: W. W. Norton, 2006.

Polnoe sobranie sochinenii i pisem, edited by N. F. Bel'chikov et al. Moscow: Nauka, 1974–1983.

Selected Stories, translated by Richard Pevear and Larissa Volokhonsky. New York: Random House, 2000.

"Son reportera," *Budil'nik* 7 (1884): 86–87.

Chekhov, M. P. *Vokrug Chekhova: vstrechi i vpechatleniia*. Moscow: Moskovskii Rabochii, 1980.

Chiuko, Vladimir. "Vtoraia Imperiia v romane Emilia Zola. Les Rougon Macquart, histoire naturelle et sociale d'une famille sous le second Empire, par Émile Zola. Tome premier: La fortune des Rougon. Paris, 1871. Stat'ia pervaia," *Vestnik Evropy* 7 (1872): 112–168.

"Vtoraia Imperiia v romane Emilia Zola. Les Rougon Macquart, histoire naturelle et sociale d'une famille sous le second Empire, par Émile Zola. Tome deuxième. La curée. Paris, 1871. Stat'ia vtoraia," *Vestnik Evropy* 8 (1872): 549–663.

Christoff, Peter. *An Introduction to Nineteenth-Century Russian Slavophilism: K. S. Aksakov*. The Hague: Mouton, 1982.

K. S. Aksakov, A Study in Ideas. Princeton University Press, 1982.

Chulkov, G. I., ed. *Pis'ma Leonida Andreeva*. Letchworth, Eng.: Prideaux Press, 1977.

Clayton, J. Douglas. "Diagnosis and Balagan: The Poetics of Chekhov's Drama," in *Adapting Chekhov, The Text and Its Mutations*, edited by J. Douglas Clayton and Yana Meerzon, 17–31. New York: Routledge, 2013.

Clowes, Edith W. "From Populist to Popular Art: Superman and the Myth of Self-Determination," in *The Revolution of Moral Consciousness: Nietzsche in Russian Literature, 1890–1914*, 83–113. DeKalb: Northern Illinois University Press, 1988.

Clyman, Toby. "Čexov's Victimized Women," *Russian Language Journal* 28 (1974): 26–31.

Conrad, Joseph. *Notes on Life and Letters*. Cambridge University Press, 2004.

Constable, Liz, Dennis Denisoff, and Matthew Potolsky, eds. *Perennial Decay: On the Aesthetics and Politics of Decadence*. Philadelphia: University of Pennsylvania Press, 1999.

Costlow, Jane. *Heart-Pine Russia: Walking and Writing the Nineteenth-Century Forest*. Ithaca, NY: Cornell University Press, 2013.

"Imaginations of Destruction: The 'Forest Question' in Nineteenth-Century Russian Culture," *The Russian Review* 62 (2003): 91–118.

Worlds within Worlds. Princeton University Press, 1990.

Cox, Gary. *Tyrant and Victim in Dostoevsky*. Bloomington, IN: Slavica, 1984.

Danilevskii, Nikolai. *Rossiia i Evropa*. Moscow: Kniga, 1991.

Davie, Donald. "Mandelstam's Classicism," in *Slavic Excursions: Essays on Russian and Polish Literature*, 287–289. University of Chicago Press, 1990.

Davison, Ray. *Camus: The Challenge of Dostoevsky*. University of Exeter Press, 1997.

Debreczeny, Paul. "Nikolay Gogol and his Contemporary Critics," *Transactions of the American Philosophical Society* 56 (1966): 1–68.

Delektorskaia, I. B. "Gogolevskie motivy v tvorchestve Sigizmunda Krzhizhanovskogo," in *Gogol' i mirovaia kul'tura*, edited by V. P. Vikulova, 122–128. Moscow: Universitet, 2003.

de Maegd-Soëp, Carolina. *Chekhov and Women: Women in the Life and Work of Chekhov*. Bloomington, IN: Slavica, 1987.

de Vogüé, Eugène-Melchior. *The Russian Novel*. New York: Knopf, 1916.

de Vries, Ad. *Dictionary of Symbols and Imagery*, 1st edn., s.v. "Oyster." Amsterdam: North-Holland, 1974.

Dickens, Charles. *The Life of our Lord: Written for His Children during the Years 1846–1849*. New York: Simon & Schuster, 1934.

Dijkstra, Bram. *Idols of Perversity: Fantasies of Feminine Evil in Fin-de-Siècle Culture*. New York: Oxford University Press, 1986.

Dobroliubov, Nikolai. "Luch sveta v temnom tsarstve," in *A. N. Ostrovskii, Teatr i zhizn': Izbrannye p'esy*, 465–518. Moscow: Shkola-Press, 1995.

Dostoevskii, F. M. *Biografiia, pis'ma i zametki iz zapisnoi knizhki F. M. Dostoevskogo*. St. Petersburg: Tipografiia A. S. Suvorina, 1883.

The Notebooks for The Possessed, edited by Edward Wasiolek and translated by Victor Terras. University of Chicago Press, 1968.

Polnoe sobranie sochinenii i pisem v tridtsati tomakh. Leningrad: Nauka, 1972–1990.

Poor Folk and Other Stories, translated by David McDuff. London: Penguin Books, 1988.

A Writer's Diary, translated by Kenneth Lantz. Evanston, IL: Northwestern University Press, 2009.

Duncan, Philip A. "Echoes of Zola's Experimental Novel in Russia," *Slavic and East European Journal* 18:1 (1974): 11–19.

"The Fortunes of Zola's *Parizskie pis'ma* in Russia," *Slavic and East European Journal* 3:2 (1959): 107–121.

Dunham, Vera S. "The Strong Woman Motif," in *The Transformation of Russian Society*, edited by Cyril E. Black, 459–483. Cambridge, MA: Harvard University Press, 1960.

Durkin, Andrew. *Sergei Aksakov and Russian Pastoral*. New Brunswick, NJ: Rutgers University Press, 1983.

Eagleton, Terry. *The English Novel: An Introduction*. Oxford: Wiley Blackwell, 2013.

Egdorf, Brian. "Fyodor Dostoevsky's *The Adolescent* and the Architectonics of Author and Hero," *The Dostoevsky Journal: An Independent Review* 12–13 (2011–2012): 15–36.

Ehre, Milton. "A Classic of Russian Realism: Form and Meaning in *The Golovlyovs*," *Studies in the Novel* 9:1 (1977): 3–16.

Eikhenbaum, Boris. *Tolstoi in the Seventies*, translated by Albert Kaspin. Ann Arbor, MI: Ardis, 1982.

Ekkartsgauzen, Karl. *Kliuch k tainstvam natury*, vol. III. St. Petersburg, 1804.

Eliot, T. S. "Turgenev," *The Egoist* 4:10 (1917): 167.

Ellis, Kate Ferguson. *The Contested Castle: Gothic Novels and the Subversion of Domestic Ideology.* Urbana: University of Illinois Press, 1989.

Eltis, Sos. "The Fallen Woman on Stage: Maidens, Magdalens, and the Emancipated Female," in *The Cambridge Companion to Victorian and Edwardian Theatre*, edited by Kerry Powell, 222–236. Cambridge University Press, 2004.

Ely, Christopher. *This Meager Nature: Landscape and National Identity in Imperial Russia.* DeKalb: Northern Illinois University Press, 2002.

Emerson, Caryl. *The First Hundred Years of Mikhail Bakhtin.* Princeton University Press, 2000.

Engelstein, Laura. *The Keys to Happiness: Sex and the Search for Modernity in Fin-de-Siècle Russia.* Ithaca, NY: Cornell University Press, 1992.

Engelstein, Laura and Stephanie Sandler, eds. *Self and Story in Russian History.* Ithaca, NY: Cornell University Press, 2000.

Evdokimova, Svetlana. "The Anatomy of the Modern Self in *The Little Tragedies*," in *Alexander Pushkin's Little Tragedies: The Poetics of Brevity*, edited by Svetlana Evdokimova, 106–143. Madison: University of Wisconsin Press, 2003.

Evlakhov, Aleksandr. "I. S. Turgenev – poet mirovoi skorbi," *Russkoe bogatstvo* 6 (1904): 1–44.

Evtuhov, Catherine. *Portrait of a Russian Province: Economy, Society, and Civilization in Nineteenth-Century Nizhnii Novgorod.* University of Pittsburgh Press, 2011.

Fanger, Donald. *Dostoevsky and Romantic Realism: A Study of Dostoevsky in Relation to Balzac, Dickens and Gogol.* University of Chicago Press, 1965.

Feuer, Kathryn. "Stiva," in *Russian Literature and American Critics*, edited by Kenneth N. Brostrom. Ann Arbor: University of Michigan Press, 1984.

Finke, Michael. "Heal Thyself, Hide Thyself: Why Did Chekhov Ignore His TB?," in *Chekhov the Immigrant: Translating a Cultural Icon*, edited by Michael C. Finke and Julie de Sherbinin, 285–297. Bloomington, IN: Slavica, 2007.

  Seeing Chekhov. Ithaca, NY: Cornell University Press, 2005.

Finney, Gail. *Women in Modern Drama: Freud, Feminism, and European Theater at the Turn of the Century.* Ithaca, NY: Cornell University Press, 1989.

Flath, Carol Apollonio. *Dostoevsky's Secrets: Reading Against the Grain.* Evanston, IL: Northwestern University Press, 2009.

Flaubert, Gustave. *La Correspondance de Flaubert, étude et répertoire critique*, edited by Charles Carlut. Columbus: Ohio State University Press, 1968.

Florensky, Pavel. "Spiritual Sobriety and the Iconic Face," in *Iconostasis*, translated by Donald Sheehan and Olga Andrejev, 52–56. Crestwood, NY: St. Vladimir's Seminary Press, 1996.

Frank, Joseph. *Dostoevsky: The Mantle of the Prophet, 1871–1881.* Princeton University Press, 2003.

  Dostoevsky: The Miraculous Years: 1865–1871. Princeton University Press, 1995.

Freud, Sigmund. *Five Lectures on Psychoanalysis.* New York: W. W. Norton, 1990.

Fridlender, G. M. *Realizm Dostoevskogo.* Moscow and Leningrad, 1964.

Frieden, Nancy Mandelker. *Russian Physicians in the Era of Reform and Revolution.* Princeton University Press, 1981.

Fromm, Erich. "The Creative Attitude," in *Creativity and Its Cultivation: Addresses Presented at the Interdisciplinary Symposia on Creativity, Michigan State University, East Lansing,* edited by Harold H. Anderson, 44–54. New York: Harper & Brothers Publishers, 1959.

Furneaux, Holly. "Childhood," in *Dickens in Context,* edited by Sally Ledger and Holly Furneaux, 186–193. Cambridge University Press, 2011.

Fusso, Susanne. *Discovering Sexuality in Dostoevsky.* Evanston, IL: Northwestern University Press, 2006.

"The Weight of Human Tears: *The Covetous Knight* and *A Raw Youth,*" in *Alexander Pushkin's Little Tragedies: The Poetics of Brevity,* edited by Svetlana Evdokimova, 229–242. Madison: University of Wisconsin Press, 2003.

Gauthier, E. Paul. "Zola's Reputation in Russia prior to 'L'Assommoir,'" *The French Review* 33:1 (1959): 37–44.

Gessen, L. A. and A. G. Ostrovskii, eds. *Russkie pisateli ob izorazitel'nom iskusstve.* Leningrad: Khudozhnik RSFSR, 1976.

Gheith, Jehanne. "The Superfluous Man and the Necessary Woman: A 'Re-Vision,'" *The Russian Review* 55:2 (1996): 226–244.

Gilman, Sander L. *The Case of Sigmund Freud: Medicine and Identity at the Fin de Siècle.* Baltimore: Johns Hopkins University Press, 1994.

Gogol', Nikolai. *Arabesques,* edited by Carl Proffer and translated by Alexander Tulloch. Ann Arbor, MI: Ardis, 1982.

Dead Souls, translated by Christopher English. Oxford University Press, 2009.

"The Greatcoat," translated by Robert Chandler, in *Russian Short Stories from Pushkin to Buida,* edited by Robert Chandler, 38–66. London: Penguin, 2005.

Mertvye dushi, in *Polnoe sobranie sochinenii v chetyrnadtsati tomakh,* vol. IV. Moscow: Pushkinskii Dom, 1951.

Sobranie sochinenii v shesti tomakh. Moscow: Khudozhestvennaia literatura, 1952–1953.

Gor'kii, Maksim. "A. P. Chekhov," in *A. P. Chekhov v vospominaniiakh sovremennikov,* edited by N. I. Gitovich, 453. Moscow: Khudozhestvennaia literatura, 1986.

Goscilo-Kostin, Helena. "Tolstoyan Fare: Credo à la Carte," *Slavic and East European Review* 62:4 (1984): 481–495.

Gould, Stephen Jay. *Time's Arrow, Time's Cycle.* Cambridge, MA: Harvard University Press, 1987.

Graffy, Julian. *Gogol's "The Overcoat."* London: Bristol Classical Press, 2000.

Greenslade, William. *Degeneration, Culture and the Novel, 1880–1940.* Cambridge University Press, 1994.

Gregg, Richard. "The Decline of a Dynast: From Power to Love in Aksakov's Family Chronicle," *The Russian Review* 50:1 (1991): 35–47.

Grossman, Joan Delaney. *Edgar Allan Poe in Russia: A Study in Legend and Literary Influence.* Würzburg: Jal-Verlag, 1973.

Gukovskii, G. A. *Realizm Gogolia*. Moscow and Leningrad: Khudozhestvennaia literatura, 1959.

Gustafson, Richard. *Leo Tolstoy: Resident and Stranger*. Princeton University Press, 1986.

Haidt, Jonathan. "The Uses of Adversity," in *The Happiness Hypothesis: Finding Modern Truth in Ancient Wisdom*, 135–154. New York: Basic Books, 2006.

Hall, Donald, ed. *Muscular Christianity: Embodying the Victorian Age*. Cambridge University Press, 1994.

Harpham, Geoffrey. *On the Grotesque: Strategies of Contradiction in Art and Literature*. Princeton University Press, 1982.

Harris, Jane Gary. "Image Criticism Revisited: Chekhov's Reception in the Early 20th Century Russian Women's Periodical Press," *Essays in Poetics* 31 (2006): 234–257.

Heine, Heinrich. *The Romantic School*, translated by L. Fleishman. New York: Henry Holt and Company, 1882.

Die romantische Schule. Hamburg: Bey Hoffmann und Campe, 1836.

Helbling, Robert. *The Power of "Negative" Thinking: The Grotesque in the Modern World*. Salt Lake City: Fredrick William Reynolds Association, 1982.

Heldt, Barbara. *Terrible Perfection: Women and Russian Literature*. Indianapolis: Indiana University Press, 1987.

Hemmings, F. W. J. *The Russian Novel in France*. Oxford University Press, 1950.

Hepburn, Allan. *Troubled Legacies: Narrative and Inheritance*. University of Toronto Press, 2007.

Higonnet, Margaret. "Speaking Silences: Women's Suicide," in *The Female Body in Western Culture*, edited by Susan Rubin Suleiman, 68–83. Cambridge, MA: Harvard University Press, 1986.

Hingley, Ronald. *The Undiscovered Dostoevsky*. London: Hamish Hamilton, 1962.

Hughes, Michael. "The Russian Nobility and the Russian Countryside: Ambivalences and Orientations," *Journal of European Studies* 36:2 (2006): 115–137.

Hugo, Victor. "Preface to *Cromwell*," in *The Harvard Classics*, edited by Charles W. Eliot, vol. xxxix, 336–387. New York: P. F. Collier & Son, 1910.

Hurley, Kelly. *The Gothic Body: Sexuality, Materialism, and Degeneration at the Fin de Siècle*. Cambridge University Press, 2004.

Hutchings, Stephen. *A Semiotic Analysis of the Short Stories of Leonid Andreev, 1900–1909*. London: Modern Humanities Research Association, 1990.

Ivanov, I. *Ivan Sergeevich Turgenev. Zhizn', lichnost', tvorchestvo*. St. Petersburg: Tipografiia I. N. Skorokhodova, 1896.

Ivanov, S. I. *Botanicheskii atlas N. P. Zivotovskii*. Moscow: Belyi Gorod, 2013.

Ivanov, V. V. "Postscript to Ilya Vinitsky's Article 'Formula of an Oyster,'" *Elementa* 3:4 (1997): 339.

Jackson, Robert Louis. "On the Ambivalent Beginning of *Anna Karenina*," in *Semantic Analysis of Literary Texts*, edited by Eric de Haard, Thomas Langerak, and Willem G. Weststeijn, 345–352. Amsterdam: Elsevier, 1990.

The Art of Dostoevsky: Deliriums and Nocturnes. Princeton University Press, 1981.

"The Root and the Flower: Dostoevsky and Turgenev: A Comparative Esthetic," *Yale Review* (Winter 1974): 228–250.

"The Turgenev Question," *Sewanee Review* 93 (1985): 300–309.

Jackson, Rosemary. *Fantasy: The Literature of Subversion*. London: Methuen, 1981.

Jakobson, Roman. "On Realism in Art," in *Readings in Russian Poetics: Formalist and Structuralist Views*, edited by Ladislav Matejka and Krystyna Pomorska, 38–46. Cambridge, MA: MIT Press, 1971.

"Two Aspects of Language and Two Types of Aphasic Disturbances," in *On Language: Roman Jakobson*, edited by Linda Waugh and Monique Monville-Burston, 115–133. Cambridge, MA: Harvard University Press, 1990.

Jones, Malcolm V. *Dostoyevsky After Bakhtin: Readings in Dostoyevsky's Fantastic Realism*. Cambridge University Press, 1990.

Justman, Stewart. "Stiva's Idiotic Grin," *Philosophy and Literature* 33 (2009): 432–433.

Kaminer, Jenny. "A Mother's Land: Arina Petrovna Golovlyova and the Economic Restructuring of the Golovlyov Family," *Slavic and East European Journal* 53:4 (2009): 545–565.

Karlinsky, Simon. "Huntsmen, Birds, Forests, and Three Sisters," in *Chekhov's Great Plays: A Critical Anthology*, edited by Jean-Pierre Barricelli, 144–160. New York University Press, 1981.

Kasatkina, Tatiana. "Dostoevsky's *Raw Youth*: The 'Idea' of the Hero and the Idea of the Author," translated by Liv Bliss. *Russian Studies in Literature* 40:4 (2004): 38–68.

Kayser, Wolfgang. *The Grotesque in Art and Literature*. New York: McGraw Hill, 1966.

Kermode, Frank. *The Sense of an Ending: Studies in the Theory of Fiction with a New Epilogue*. Oxford University Press, 2000.

Kern, Gary and Christopher Collins, eds. *The Serapion Brothers: A Critical Anthology*. Ann Arbor, MI: Ardis, 1975.

Khomiakov, Alexey. "The Church is One," in *On Spiritual Unity: A Slavophile Reader*, edited by Boris Jakim and Robert Bird, 31–54. Hudson, NY: Lindisfarne Books, 1998.

"Letter to the Editor of *L'Union Chrétienne*, on the Occasion of a Discourse by Father Gagarin, Jesuit," in *On Spiritual Unity: A Slavophile Reader*, edited by Boris Jakim and Robert Bird, 135–140. Hudson, NY: Lindisfarne Books, 1998.

Kivelson, Valerie. *Cartographies of Tsardom: The Land and Its Meanings in Seventeenth-Century Russia*. Ithaca, NY: Cornell University Press, 2006.

Kleman, M. K. "Iz perepiski E. Zolia s russkimi korrespondentami," *Literaturnoe nasledstvo* 31–32 (1937): 943–980.

Knapp, Liza. *The Annihilation of Inertia: Dostoevsky and Metaphysics*. Evanston, IL: Northwestern University Press, 1996.

Knowles, A. V. "Russian Views of Anna Karenina, 1875–1878," *Slavic and East European Journal* 22:3 (1978): 301–312.

Kokobobo, Ani. *Freakish Others and Monsters Within: Russian Realism and the Grotesque, 1869–1899*, forthcoming.

Kolstø, Pål. "Power as Burden: The Slavophile Concept of the State and Lev Tolstoy," *The Russian Review* 64 (2005): 559–574.

Koni, A. F., ed. *Turgenevskii sbornik.* St. Petersburg, 1921.

Korolenko, S. V. *Desiat' let v provintsii.* Izhevsk: Udmurtia, 1966.

Korolenko, Vladimir. "O naznachenii literatury," in *Vospominaniia. Stati'i. Pis'ma.* Moscow: Sovetskaia Rossiia, 1988.

   Sobranie sochinenii v desiati tomakh. Moscow: Khudozhestvennaia literatura, 1953–1956.

   "Svetloyar," translated by Jane Costlow, in *The Russia Reader: History, Culture, Politics*, edited by Adele Barker and Bruce Grant, 222–236. Durham, NC: Duke University Press, 2010.

   Zapisnye knizhki (1880–1900). Moscow: Khudozhestvennaia literatura, 1935.

Kostyleva, T. A. and S. R. Nemtseva. "Programma elektivnogo kursa 'Ocherk v russkoi literature: zhanrovaia spetsifika, istoriia razvitiia,'" *Literatura* 14 (2011). http://festival.1september.ru/articles/419022/ (accessed July 27, 2014).

Krafft-Ebing, Richard. *Psychopathia Sexualis*, translated by F. J. Rebman. New York: Rebman Company, 1894.

Kramer, Karl. "Satiric Form in Saltykov's *Gospoda Golovlyovy*," *Slavic and East European Journal* 14:4 (1970): 453–464.

Krinitsyn, Aleksandr. "Problema 'vyrozhdeniia' u Chekhova i Maksa Nordau," in *Chekhov v Germanii*, edited by V. B. Kataev and R.-D. Kluge, 165–170. Moscow: Universitet, 1996.

Kristeva, Julia. *Powers of Horror: An Essay in Abjection.* New York: Columbia University Press, 1982.

Kroeker, P. Travis and Bruce K. Ward, eds. *Remembering the End: Dostoevsky as Prophet to Modernity.* Boulder, CO: Westview Press, 2001.

Krzhizhanovsky, Sigizmund. *Autobiography of a Corpse*, translated by Joanne Turnbull with Introduction by Adam Thirlwell. New York Review Books, 2013.

   "Quadraturin," translated by Joanne Turnbull, in *Russian Short Stories from Pushkin to Buida*, edited by Robert Chandler, 208–216. London: Penguin, 2005.

   Sobranie sochinenii v piati tomakh. St. Petersburg: Symposium, 2001–2010.

Kurkin, Petr. *Detskaia smertnost' v Moskovskoi gubernii i ee uezdakh v 1883–1897 gg.* Moscow, 1902.

   Statistika boleznenosti naseleniia v Moskovskoi gubernii za period 1883–1902 gg. Moscow, 1907.

Kuzmic, Tatiana. "'Serbia: Vronskii's Last Love': Reading *Anna Karenina* in the Context of Empire," *Toronto Slavic Quarterly* 43 (2013): 40–66.

Lalo, Alexei. *Libertinage in Russian Culture and Literature.* Leiden: Brill, 2011.

Laqueur, Walter. *Fin de Siècle and Other Essays on America and Europe.* New Brunswick, NJ: Transaction Publishers, 1997.

Laursen, Eric. "Transformation as Revelation: Sologub, Schopenhauer, and the Little Man," *Slavic and East European Journal* 39:4 (1995): 552–567.

LeBlanc, Ronald. "Saninism Versus Tolstoyism: The Anti-Tolstoy Subtext in Mikhail Artsybashev's *Sanin*," *Tolstoy Studies Journal* 18 (2006): 16–31.

Ledkovsky, Marina. *The Other Turgenev: From Romanticism to Symbolism.* Würzburg: Jal-Verlag, 1973.

Lehan, Richard. *Realism and Naturalism: The Novel in an Age of Transition.* Madison: University of Wisconsin Press, 2005.

Leiderman, N. L. "The Intellectual Worlds of Sigizmund Krzhizhanovsky," *Slavic and East European Journal* 56:4 (2012): 507–535.

Lemke, M. K., ed. *M. M. Stasiulevich i ego sovremenniki v ikh perepiske*, 5 vols. St. Petersburg, 1912.

Levin, Iu. I. "Zametki k stat'e Mandel'shtama o Chekhove," *Russian Literature* 5:2 (1977): 174–175.

Lieber, Emma. "'Pardon, Monsieur': Civilization and Civility in Turgenev's 'The Execution of Tropmann,'" *Slavic Review* 66:4 (2007): 667–682.

Lodge, Kirsten, "Introduction," in *The Dedalus Book of Russian Decadence*, edited by Kirsten Lodge, 1–18. Sawtry, Eng.: Dedalus, 2007.

Lönnqvist, Barbara. "Geroi romana Anna Karenina v zerkale slavianskogo voprosa," in *Severnyi sbornik: Proceedings of the NorFA Network in Russian Literature 1995–2000*, edited by Peter Jensen and Ingunn Lunde. Stockholm: Almqvist & Wiksell International, 2000.

Lotman, Yuri M. *The Unpredictable Workings of Culture*, translated by Brian James Baer and edited by Igor Pilshchikov and Silvi Salupere. Tallinn University Press, 2013.

Lunacharskii, A. V., ed. *Literaturnaia entsiklopediia*, s.v. "Ocherk," vol. VIII, 381–388. Moscow: Sovetskaia entsiklopediia, 1929–1939.

MacMaster, Robert. *Danilevsky: A Russian Totalitarian Philosopher.* Cambridge, MA: Harvard University Press, 1967.

Maguire, Muireann. *Stalin's Ghosts: Gothic Themes in Early Soviet Literature.* Oxford: Peter Lang, 2012.

Maguire, Robert. *Exploring Gogol.* Stanford University Press, 1994.

    ed. and trans. *Gogol from the Twentieth Century: Eleven Essays.* Princeton University Press, 1974.

Maiorova, Olga. *From the Shadow of Empire: Defining the Russian Nation through Cultural Mythology, 1855–1870.* Madison: University of Wisconsin Press, 2010.

Makarova, Veronica. "Stylistic Features in the Novella 'Darkness' by Leonid Andreev," *Russian Literature* 68:3–4 (2010): 327–344.

Malikova, Mariia. "'Sketch po koshmaru Chestertona' i kul'turnaia situatsiia NEPa," *Novoe literaturnoe obozrenie* 78 (2006). http://magazines.russ.ru/nlo/2006/78/mm2.html (accessed March 13, 2013).

Mandel'shtam, Osip. "A Conversation about Dante," in *The Complete Critical Letters and Prose*, edited by Jane Gary Harris, 397–442. Ann Arbor, MI: Ardis, 1979.

"O p'ese A. Chekhova 'Diadia Vania' (Nabrosok)," in *Collected Works/Sobranie sochinenii*, edited by Gleb Struve, Nikita Struve, and Boris Filipoff, vol. IV, 107–109. Paris: YMCA Press, 1981.

Mann, Iurii. *Dialektika khudozhestvennogo obraza*. Moscow: Sovietskii pisatel', 1987.

Mantzaridis, Georgios. *The Deification of Man: St. Gregory Palamas and the Orthodox Tradition*, translated by L. Sherrard. Crestwood, NY: St. Vladimir's Seminary Press, 1984.

Marsh, Cynthia. "The Stage Representation of Chekhov's Women," in *The Cambridge Companion to Chekhov*, edited by Vera Gottlieb and Paul Allain, 216–227. Cambridge University Press, 2000.

Marshall, Gail, ed. *The Cambridge Companion to the Fin de Siècle*. Cambridge University Press, 2007.

Marx, Karl. "Economic and Philosophic Manuscripts of 1844," in *Collected Works*, vol. III, 228–346. New York: International Publishers, 1975.

Marx, Karl and Friedrich Engels. *Manifesto of the Communist Party and Selected Essays*. Rockville, MD: Arc Manor, 2008.

Matich, Olga. *Erotic Utopia: The Decadent Imagination in Russia's Fin de Siècle*. Madison: University of Wisconsin Press, 2005.

"A Typology of Fallen Women in Nineteenth Century Russian Literature," in *American Contributions to the Ninth International Congress of Slavists*, vol. II, 325–343. Bloomington, IN: Slavica, 1983.

Matley, Ian M. "Chekhov and Geography," *The Russian Review* 31:4 (1972): 376–382.

McKellor Reid, John. "Ivanov: The Perils of Typicality," *Modern Drama* 49:1 (2006): 76–97.

McKibben, Bill. *The End of Nature*. New York: Anchor, 1989.

McNair, John A. "V ob'ezianykh lapakh (O Leonide Andreeve)," in *V tikhom omute*. Moscow: Sovetskii pisatel', 1991. http://philology.ruslibrary.ru/default.asp?trID=233&artID=316 (accessed July 4, 2013).

"Zolaizm in Russia," *Modern Language Review* 95:2 (2000): 450–462.

Meshcherskii, A. A. "Predsmertnye chasy I. S. Turgeneva," *Novoe vremia*, September 3–15, 1883.

Miller, D. A. *The Novel and the Police*. Berkeley: University of California Press, 1988.

Miller, Robin Feuer. "Dostoevsky's *Poor People*: Reading 'as if for Life,'" in *Reading in Russia: Literary Communication and Practices of Reading, 1760–1930*, edited by Raffaella Vassena and Damiano Rebecchini. University of Milan Press, 2014.

Dostoevsky's Unfinished Journey. New Haven, CT: Yale University Press, 2007.

Mirsky, D. S. *Contemporary Russian Literature, 1881–1925*. New York: Knopf, 1926.

A History of Russian Literature from its Beginnings to 1900. New York: Knopf, 1927.

"Turgenev's Prose," in *Critical Essays on Ivan Turgenev*, edited by David A. Lowe, 35–42. Boston: G. K. Hall, 1989.

Mochulsky, Konstantin. *Dostoevsky: His Life and Work*, translated by M. A. Minihan. Princeton University Press, 1967.

Møller, Peter Ulf. *Postlude to* The Kreutzer Sonata: *Tolstoj and the Debate on Sexuality in Russian Literature in the 1890s.* Leiden: E. J. Brill, 1988.

Moon, David. "The Debate over Climate Change in the Steppe Region in Nineteenth-Century Russia," *The Russian Review* 69 (2010): 251–275.

The Plough That Broke the Steppes: Agriculture and Environment on Russia's Grasslands, 1700–1914. Oxford University Press, 2013.

Moravčevich, Nicholas. "Women in Chekhov's Plays," in *Chekhov's Great Plays: A Critical Anthology*, edited by Jean-Pierre Barricelli, 201–217. New York University Press, 1981.

Morel, B. A. *Traité des dégénérescences physiques, intellectuelles et morales de l'espèce humaine et des causes qui produisent ces variétés maladives.* Paris: J. B. Baillière, 1857.

Morrissey, Susan K. *Suicide and the Body Politic in Imperial Russia.* Cambridge University Press, 2006.

Morson, Gary Saul. *"Anna Karenina" in Our Time: Seeing More Wisely.* New Haven, CT: Yale University Press, 2007.

The Boundaries of Genre: Dostoevsky's Diary of a Writer *and the Traditions of Literary Utopia.* Evanston, IL: Northwestern University Press, 1981.

"Uncle Vanya as Prosaic Metadrama," in *Reading Chekhov's Text*, edited by Robert Louis Jackson, 214–227. Evanston, IL: Northwestern University Press, 1993.

Murav, Harriet. *Holy Foolishness: Dostoevsky's Novels and the Poetics of Cultural Critique.* Stanford University Press, 1992.

"Maslova's Exorbitant Body," *Tolstoy Studies Journal* 14 (2002): 35–46.

Russia's Legal Fictions. Ann Arbor: University of Michigan Press, 1998.

Nabokov, Vladimir. *Lectures in Russian Literature.* London: Weidenfeld & Nicolson, 1981.

Naiman, Eric. *Sex in Public: The Incarnation of Early Soviet Ideology.* Princeton University Press, 1997.

Newlin, Thomas. "At the Bottom of the River: Forms of Ecological Consciousness in Mid-Nineteenth-Century Russian Literature," *Russian Studies in Literature* 39:2 (2003): 71–90.

The Voice in the Garden: Andrei Bolotov and the Anxieties of the Russian Pastoral, 1738–1833. Evanston, IL: Northwestern University Press, 2001.

Nicolosi, Riccardo. *Degeneration erzählen. Wissenschaft und Literatur im Russland der 1880er und 1890er Jahre.* Munich: Wilhelm Fink, 2015.

"Degeneraty gospoda Golovlevy. Saltykov-ščedrin i diskurs vyroždenija 19-ogo veka," in *Telo, duch i duša v russkoj literature i kul'ture*, edited by J. van Baak and S. Brouwer, *Wiener Slawistischer Almanach* 54 (2004): 337–350.

"Vyrozhdenie sem'i, vyrozhdenie teksta. 'Gospoda Golovlevy': frantsuzskii naturalizm i diskurs degeneratsii xix veka," in *Russkaia literatura i meditsina. Telo, predpisania, sotsialnaia praktika*, edited by K. Bogdanov, J. Murašov, and R. Nicolosi, 170–193. Moscow: Novoe izdatel'stvo, 2006.

Nietzsche, Friedrich. *On the Genealogy of Morality*, edited by Keith Ansell-Pearson and translated by Carol Diethe. Cambridge University Press, 1994.

Nikulin, Dmitri. *Comedy, Seriously: A Philosophical Study*. New York: Palgrave Macmillan, 2014.

Nordau, Max. *Degeneration*. Lincoln: University of Nebraska Press, 1993.

Nye, Robert A. *Masculinity and Male Codes of Honor in Modern France*. Oxford University Press, 1993.

Orwin, Donna. "Strakhov's *World as a Whole*: A Missing Link between Dostoevsky and Tolstoy," in *Poetics. Self. Place. Essays in Honor of Anna Lisa Crone*, edited by Catherine O'Neill, Nicole Boudreau, and Sarah Krive, 473–493. Bloomington, IN: Slavica, 2007.

Ostrogorskii, Viktor. *Pamiati Ivana Sergeevicha Turgeneva*. St. Petersburg: Rebus, 1883.

Ostrovskii, A. G. *Turgenev v zapisiakh sovremennikov*. Leningrad, 1929.

Ostrovskii, A. N. *Groza*, in *A. N. Ostrovskii, Teatr i zhizn: Izbrannye P'esy*. Moscow: Shkola-Press, 1995.

Pascal, Blaise. *Pascal, Pensées*, edited by Ch. M. des Granges, no. 347. Paris: Garnier, 1964.

Pavel, Thomas G. *The Lives of the Novel: A History*. Princeton University Press, 2014.

Peace, Richard. *Dostoevsky: An Examination of the Major Novels*. Cambridge University Press, 1971.

The Enigma of Gogol: An Examination of the Writings of N. V. Gogol and their Place in the Russian Literary Tradition. Cambridge University Press, 1981.

"Gogol and Psychological Realism: *Shinel'*," in *Russian and Slavic Literature*, edited by Richard Freeborn, R. Milner-Gulland, and Charles A. Ward, 63–91. Cambridge, MA: Slavica, 1976.

Perel'muter, Vadim. "Posle katastrofy," in Sigizmund Krzhizhanovskii, *Sobranie sochinenii v piati tomakh*, vol. 1, 5–70. St. Petersburg: Symposium, 2001–2010.

Peterson, Dale. "Russian Gothic: The Deathless Paradoxes of Bunin's *Dry Valley*," *Slavic and East European Journal* 31:1 (1987): 36–49.

Pevear, Richard. "Introduction," in *War and Peace* by Leo Tolstoy, translated by Richard Pevear and Larissa Volokhonsky. New York: Vintage Classics, 2008.

Pick, Daniel. *Faces of Degeneration: A European Disorder, c. 1848–c. 1918*. Cambridge University Press, 1993.

Pil'd, Lea. "Tipy narodnogo soznaniia v proze V. G. Korolenko 1880-x – nach. 1890-x gg," *Trudy po russkoi i slavianskoi filologii* (1994): 146–155. http://www.ruthenia.ru/reprint/trudy_i/pild.pdf (accessed July 7, 2014).

Turgenev v vospriiatii russkikh simvolistov, 1890–1900-e gody. Tartu: Ülikooli Kirjastus, 1999.

Pirog, Gerald. "Bakhtin and Freud on the Ego," in *Russian Literature and Psychoanalysis*, edited by Daniel Rancour-Laferriere, 401–415. Philadelphia: John Benjamins Publishing Company, 1989.

Pisarev, D. I. "Motivy russkoi dramy," in *A. N. Ostrovskii, Teatr i zhizn': Izbrannye p'esy*, 519–527. Moscow: Shkola-Press, 1995.

Plato. *Phaedrus* 250c, in *Plato in Twelve Volumes*, translated by Harold N. Fowler, vol. ix. Cambridge, MA: Harvard University Press, 1925.

Poggioli, R. "Realism in Russia," *Comparative Literature* 3:3 (1951): 253–267.

Polonskii, Ia. P. *Stikhotvoreniia*. Leningrad: Sovetskii pisatel', 1957.

Pomper, Philip. *Sergei Nechaev*. New Brunswick, NJ: Rutgers University Press, 1979.

Popkin, Cathy. "Chekhov as Ethnographer: Epistemological Crisis on Sakhalin Island," *Slavic Review* 51:1 (1992): 36–51.

Praz, Mario. *The Romantic Agony*. Oxford University Press, 1978.

Presner, Todd Samuel. *Muscular Judaism: The Jewish Body and the Politics of Regeneration*. New York: Routledge, 2007.

Pumpianskii, L. V. "Gruppa 'tainstvennykh povestei,'" in Ivan Turgenev, *Sochineniia*, vol. viii, v–xx. Moscow and Leningrad: Gosizdat, 1929.

Punter, David. *The Literature of Terror: The Modern Gothic*. London: Longman, 1996.

Pyman, Avril. *A History of Russian Symbolism*. Cambridge University Press, 1994.

Rabinowitz, Stanley. "Fedor Sologub and his Nineteenth-Century Russian Antecedents," *Slavic and East European Journal* 22:3 (1978): 324–335.

Rabow-Edling, Susanna. *Slavophile Thought and the Politics of Cultural Nationalism*. Albany: State University of New York Press, 2007.

Rancour-Laferriere, Daniel. *The Slave Soul of Russia: Moral Masochism and the Cult of Suffering*. New York University Press, 1995.

Rayfield, Donald. *Understanding Chekhov: A Critical Study of Chekhov's Prose and Drama*. London: Bristol Classical Press, 1999.

Reynolds, Kimberley. *Children's Literature in the 1890s and the 1990s*. Plymouth, Eng.: Northcote House, 1994.

Rosen, Nathan. "Breaking Out of the Underground: The 'Failure' of 'A Raw Youth,'" *Modern Fiction Studies* 4:3 (1958): 225–239.

Rosenflanz, Karen Link. *Hunter of Themes: The Interplay of Word and Thing in the Works of Sigizmund Krzhizhanovskij*. New York: Peter Lang, 2005.

"Overturned Verticals and Extinguished Suns: Facets of Krzhizhanovsky's Fourth Dimension," *Slavic and East European Journal* 56:4 (2012): 536–552.

Rosenshield, Gary. *Western Law, Russian Justice: Dostoevsky, the Jury Trial and the Law*. Madison: University of Wisconsin Press, 2005.

Rozanov, Vasilii. "Pushkin i Gogol'," in *O Gogole*, 5–17. Letchworth, Eng.: Prideaux Press, 1970.

Rylkova, Galina S. "A Silver Lining to the Russian Clouds: Remembering the Silver Age in the 1920s and 1930s," *Kritika: Explorations in Russian and Eurasian History* 1:3 (2000): 481–500.

Rzhevsky, Nicholas. "*The Adolescent*: Structure and Ideology," *Slavic and East European Journal* 26:1 (1982): 27–42.

Saltykov-Shchedrin, M. E. *The Golovlyov Family*, translated by Natalie Duddington. New York Review Books, 2001.

Sobranie sochinenii v dvadtsati tomakh. Moscow: Khudozhestvennaia literatura, 1965–1976.

Sandars, Mary F. *Honoré de Balzac, His Life and Writings.* London: Kennikat Press, 1970.

Sattaur, Jennifer. *Perceptions of Childhood in the Victorian Fin de Siècle.* Cambridge Scholars Publishing, 2011.

Schloesser, Stephen. "Prologue: Realism, Eternalism, Spiritual Naturalism," in *Jazz Age Catholicism: Mystic Modernism in Postwar Paris, 1919–1933,* 18–45. University of Toronto Press, 2005.

Schopenhauer, Arthur. *The Two Fundamental Problems of Ethics.* Oxford University Press, 2010.

Seifrid, Thomas. *Andrei Platonov: Uncertainties of Spirit.* Cambridge University Press, 1992.

Seigel, Jerold. *The Idea of the Self: Thought and Experience in Western Europe since the Seventeenth Century.* Cambridge University Press, 2005.

Setchkarev, Vsevolod. *Studies in the Life and Work of Innokentij Annenskij.* The Hague: Mouton, 1963.

Shane, Alex M. "Remizov's *Prud*: From Symbolism to Neo-Realism," *California Slavic Studies* 6 (1971): 71–82.

Shaposhnikova, L. A. *Izobrazhenie lesa na kartakh.* Moscow: Akademiia nauk, 1957.

Shepard, Elizabeth. "Pavlov's 'Demon' and Gogol's 'Overcoat,'" *Slavic Review* 33 (1974): 288–301.

Shevchenko, Mila B. "Melodramatic Scenarios and Modes of Marginality: The Poetics of Anton Chekhov's Early Drama and of Fin-de-Siècle Russian Popular Drama," PhD diss., University of Michigan, 2008.

Showalter, Elaine. *Sexual Anarchy: Gender and Culture at the Fin de Siècle.* New York: Viking, 1990.

Singleton, Amy. *No Place Like Home: The Literary Artist and Russia's Search for Cultural Identity.* Albany: State University of New York Press, 1997.

Sinott, Edmund W. "The Creativeness of Life," in *Creativity and Its Cultivation: Addresses Presented at the Interdisciplinary Symposia on Creativity, Michigan State University, East Lansing,* edited by Harold H. Anderson, 12–29. New York: Harper & Brothers Publishers, 1959.

Smirnov, Ivan. *Zastupniki narodnye: I. S. Turgenev, N. A. Nekrasov.* Moscow: Tipo-litografiia T-va I. N. Kushnerev i ko, 1908.

Smith, Andrew. *Victorian Demons: Medicine, Masculinity, and the Gothic at the Fin-de-Siècle.* Manchester University Press, 2004.

Smith, Barbara Herrnstein. *Poetic Closure: A Study of How Poems End.* University of Chicago Press, 2007.

Sologub, Fedor. *Sobranie sochinenii v shesti tomakh.* Moscow: Intelvak, 2000.

Solov'ev, Vladimir. *Chteniia o bogochelovechestve.* St. Petersburg: Khudozhestvennaia literatura, 1994.

Solzhenitsyn, Aleksandr. *Nobelevskaia lektsiia po literature 1970 goda.* Munich: Deutsch Taschenbuch Verlag, 1972.

Steinberg, Mark. *Petersburg Fin de Siècle*. New Haven, CT: Yale University Press, 2011.

Steiner, Lina. *For Humanity's Sake: The Bildungsroman in Russian Culture*. University of Toronto Press, 2011.

Stenli, Genri M. *Kak ia nashel Livingstona*, Parts 1–2. St. Petersburg, 1873.

V debriakh Afriki, Parts 1–2. St. Petersburg, 1892.

Stites, Richard. *The Women's Liberation Movement in Russia, 1860–1930: Feminism, Nihilism, Bolshevism*. Princeton University Press, 1978.

Straus, Nina Pelikan. *Dostoevsky and the Woman Question: Rereadings at the End of the Century*. New York: St. Martin's Press, 1994.

Sychevskii, S. I. "Zhurnalnye ocherki," *Odesskii vestnik* 3 (1877): 465–466.

Tait, Peta. *Performing Emotions: Gender, Bodies, Spaces, in Chekhov's Drama and Stanislavski's Theatre*. Aldershot, Eng.: Ashgate, 2002.

Tarasov, B. N. *"Mysliashchii trostnik": Zhizn' i tvorchestvo Paskalia v vospriiatii russkikh filosofov i pisatelei*. Moscow: Iazyki slavianskoi kul'tury, 2004.

Tatar, Maria. *The Classic Fairy Tales*. New York: W. W. Norton, 1999.

Off With Their Heads! Fairy Tales and the Culture of Childhood. Princeton University Press, 1992.

Tikhomirov, Boris Nikolaevich. "Dostoevsky on Children in the New Testament," in *Dostoevsky on the Threshold of Other Worlds: Essays in Honour of Malcolm V. Jones*, edited by Sarah Young and Leslie Milne, 189–206. Ilkeston, Eng.: Bramcote Press, 2006.

Timenchik, R. D. "The Oysters of Akhmatova and Annenskii," *Elementa: A Journal of Slavic Studies and Comparative Cultural Semiotics* 2:3–4 (1996): 311–317.

Tkachev, P. N. "Rol' psikhicheskoi nasledstvennosti," in *Petr Nikitich Tkachev: Sochineniia v dvukh tomakh*, vol. 1. Moscow: Mysl', 1976.

"Tkachov Attacks Tolstoy's Aristocraticism: 1875," in *Tolstoy, the Critical Heritage*, edited by A. V. Knowles, 250–261. London: Routledge and Kegan Paul, 1978.

Todd, William Mills, III. "The Anti-Hero with a Thousand Faces: Saltykov-Shchedrin's Porfirii Golovlev," *Studies in the Literary Imagination* 9:1 (1976): 87–105.

"The Ruse of the Russian Novel," in *The Novel*, vol. 1: *History, Geography, and Culture*, edited by Franco Moretti, 401–427. Princeton University Press, 2006.

Todorov, Tzvetan. *The Fantastic: A Structural Approach to a Literary Genre*, translated by Richard Howard. Ithaca, NY: Cornell University Press, 1975.

Tolstoi, Lev. *Anna Karenina*, translated by Richard Pevear and Larissa Volokhonsky. New York: Penguin Books, 2000.

Polnoe sobranie sochinenii v 90 tomakh, akademicheskoe iubileinoe izdanie. Moscow: Khudozhestvennaia literatura, 1928–1958.

Tolstoy's Letters, edited and translated by R. F. Christian. London: Athlone Press, 1978.

War and Peace, translated by Ann Dunnigan. New York: Signet, 1968.

Toporov, V. N. "'Minus'-prostranstvo Sigizmunda Krzhizhanovskogo," in *Mif, ritual, simvol, obraz: issledovaniia v oblasti mifopoeticheskogo*, 476–574. Moscow: Kul'tura, 1995.

Strannyi Turgenev (chetyre glavy). Moscow: Russian State University for the Humanities, 1998.

Tsvetkov, M. A. "Cartographic Results of the General Survey of Russia 1766–1861," in *Essays on the History of Russian Cartography, 16th to 19th Centuries*, edited and translated by James R. Gibson, Supplement No. 1 to *Canadian Cartographer*, vol. XII. University of Toronto Press, 1975.

Tulloch, John. *Chekhov: A Structuralist Study*. London: Macmillan, 1980.

Turgenev, Ivan. *First Love*, in *First Love and Other Stories*, translated by Richard Freeborn, 144–202. Oxford University Press, 1989.

Pis'ma v vosemnadtsati tomakh. Moscow: Nauka, 2002.

Polnoe sobranie pisem. St. Petersburg, 1885.

Polnoe sobranie sochinenii i pisem v dvadtsati vos'mi tomakh. Moscow: Nauka, 1960–1968.

Polnoe sobranie sochinenii i pisem. Sochineniia v dvenadtsati tomakh. Moscow: Nauka, 1978–1986.

"Zhivye moshchi," in *Zapiski okhotnika*. Chicago: Bradda Books, 1965.

Tverdokhlebov, I. Iu., ed. *Letopis' zhizni i tvorchestva A. P. Chekhova*, vol. II. Moscow: Nasledie IMLI, 2004.

Utevskii, L. S. *Smert' Turgeneva. 1883–1923*. St. Petersburg: Atenei, 1923.

Valenčius, Conevery Bolton. "Chekhov's *Sakhalin Island* as a Medical Geography," in *Chekhov the Immigrant: Translating a Cultural Icon*, edited by Michael C. Finke and Julie de Sherbinin, 299–314. Bloomington, IN: Slavica, 2007.

van Baak, Joost. *The House in Russian Literature: A Mythopoeic Exploration*. Amsterdam: Rodopi, 2009.

Vinitsky, Ilya. "Formula of an Oyster: Turgenev in a Mirror of Balzac," *Elementa: A Journal of Slavic Studies and Comparative Cultural Semiotics* 3:4 (1997): 325–337.

Ghostly Paradoxes: Modern Spiritualism and Russian Culture in the Age of Realism. University of Toronto Press, 2009.

Vinogradova, K. M. *Chekhov v Melikhove*. Moscow: Moskovskii Rabochii, 1959.

Vitale, Serena. *Shklovsky, Witness to an Era: Interviews by Serena Vitale*, translated by Jamie Richards. Champaign, IL: Dalkey Archive Press, 2012. (Originally published in Italian, 1979.)

W., "Roman i kritika vo Frantsii," *Russkii mir* 37:9 (Feb. 21, 1877): 37–39.

W., V. "Nravy i literatura vo Frantsii," *Russkii vestnik* 11 (1873): 239.

Walicki, Andrzej. *The Slavophile Controversy: History of a Conservative Utopia in Nineteenth-Century Russian Thought*, translated by Hilda Andrews-Rusiecka. Oxford: Clarendon Press, 1975.

Wasiolek, Edward. *Tolstoy's Major Fiction*. University of Chicago Press, 1978.

Watt, Ian. *The Rise of the Novel: Studies in Defoe, Richardson, and Fielding*. Berkeley: University of California Press, 2001.

Weber, Eugen. *France: Fin de Siècle*. Cambridge, MA: Harvard University Press, 1986.

Weikart, Richard. "Marx, Engels, and the Abolition of the Family," *History of European Ideas* 18:5 (1994): 657–672.

Weisman, Alan. *The World Without Us*. New York: St. Martin's Press, 2007.

Wilde, Oscar. *The Major Works*. Oxford University Press, 1989.

Williams, Anne. *Art of Darkness: A Poetics of Gothic*. University of Chicago Press, 1995.

Williams, John S. "Stavrogin's Motivation: Love and Suicide," *Psychoanalytic Review* 69:2 (1982): 249–265.

Williams, Rowan. *Dostoevsky: Language, Faith and Fiction*. London: Continuum, 2008.

Wood, James. *The Irresponsible Self: On Laughter and the Novel*. New York: Farrar, Straus and Giroux, 2004.

"Saltykov-Shchedrin's Subversion of Hypocrisy," in *The Irresponsible Self: On Laughter and the Novel*, 87–95. New York: Farrar, Straus and Giroux, 2004.

Woodward, James B. "Devices of Emphasis and Amplification in the Style of Leonid Andreev," *Slavic and East European Journal* 9:3 (1965): 247–256.

Leonid Andreev: A Study. Oxford University Press, 1969.

Worster, Donald. *Nature's Economy: A History of Ecological Ideas*. Cambridge University Press, 1985.

Z., Z. (K. K. Arsen'ev). "Sovremennyi roman i ego predstaviteliakh. 4. Viktor Giugo," *Vestnik Evropy* 1 (1880): 286–329.

Zaitsev, Boris. *Zhizn' Turgeneva*. Paris: YMCA Press, 1949.

Zamiatin, Evgenii. *Sochineniia*. Moscow: Kniga, 1988.

Ziolkowski, Theodore. "The Mine: The Image of the Soul," in *German Romanticism and its Institutions*, 18–63. Princeton University Press, 1990.

Zohrab, Irene. "Mann-Mannliche Love in Dostoevsky's Fiction (An Approach to *The Possessed*): With Some Attributions of Editorial Notes in *The Citizen*. First Installment," *The Dostoevsky Journal: An Independent Review* 3–4 (2002–2003): 113–226.

Zola, Émile. *Les Rougon-Macquart, Histoire naturelle et sociale d'une famille sous le second Empire*. Paris: Gallimard, 1960–1967.

"Prostupok abbata Mure," *Vestnik Evropy* (1875) 1:253–329; 2:694–774; 3:271–364.

Index